Diane McSweeney
Houston TX
July 1996

MORTAL WOUNDS

by
Anthony West

McGraw-Hill Book Company
New York
St. Louis   San Francisco
Toronto

Grateful acknowledgment is made to the following for permission to quote from the works of Marcel Proust: Editions Gallimard, for lines from *Les Plaisirs et Les Jours,* © Editions Gallimard 1924; Random House, Inc., for lines from *Remembrance of Things Past: Swann's Way,* translated by C. K. Scott-Moncrieff, copyright 1928 and renewed 1956 by Random House, Inc., *The Past Recaptured,* translated by Andreas Mayor, copyright © 1970 by Chatto and Windus; Chatto and Windus, Editions Gallimard and George Borchardt, Inc., for lines from *By Way of Sainte-Beuve,* translated by Sylvia Townsend Warner.

Similar acknowledgment is made to Atlantic–Little, Brown for permission to quote from George Painter: *Proust: The Early Years* and *Proust: The Later Years.*

123456789BPBP79876543

Library of Congress Cataloging in Publication Data

West, Anthony, date
  Mortal wounds.

    1. Staël-Holstein, Anne Louise Germaine (Necker), baronne de, 1766–1817.
2. Charrière, Isabella Agnéta (van Tuyll) de, d. 1805. 3. Sand, George, pseud.
of Mme. Dudevant, 1804–1876. I. Title.
PQ149.W4   840'.9 [B]   72-10469
ISBN 0-07-069475-3

Foreword

This book, the body of which consists of behavioral studies of three women writers, had its origin in a change of opinion. I would many years ago have agreed with Proust's contention that "a book is the product of a different self from the one we manifest in our habits in society, and in our vices," and have refused to go along with Sainte-Beuve in arguing that an author's writing must be inseparable from the rest of him. I was an uncritical admirer of Blake in those days, and, having difficulty squaring my conviction that I was about to become a major artist with my knowledge that I was making a very considerable mess of my own affairs, found an irresistible attraction in the conception of the spectre, the false self which did the artists day-to-day living for him, and whose thoughts and actions were things quite apart from his real life as a creator.

I passed by a natural progression from an uncritical admiration of Blake to a passionate devotion to D. H. Lawrence and his works. This led me to plunge into the extensive literature produced by the host of claimants and interpreters who offer one their several true and only Lawrences. The net effect of this disconcerting cloud of witness was to make the theory of the binary structure of the artist's persona an absolute necessity. It does not seem to me to be possible to read the accounts of Lawrence that have been written by those who knew him at various stages in his life without being overwhelmed by a sense of the pettiness of the man's spirit and the mediocrity of his associations: with the possible exception of Baudelaire, there is no writer who combines so great a claim to one's attention with so complete a lack of personal distinction. In both cases one is compelled either to ignore what one knows of the quality of the artist's life or to proceed to a very drastic revaluation of

his work. While I was in the first flush of my enthusiasm for
Lawrence, Mr. Geoffrey Grigson gave me a sufficiently clear
warning that there was an organic connection between the
man and the artist that would become apparent to me if I
succeeded in growing up, and that in that event my view of
this writer would undergo a major change. I have to admit
that I was not ready for this warning when it was given me,
and my enthusiasm for Lawrence's work was still undimin-
ished when Mr. Herbert van Tahl was kind enough to invite
me to write a short biography and critical introduction to
Lawrence's work for a series of short monographs on the
English novelists that he was then preparing to produce. I
undertook this task with pleasure, but presently found,
after reading and thinking about everything that Lawrence
had ever, to my knowledge, written, and fitting each of his
works into its proper place in the context of his history,
that it was altogether impossible to maintain a distinction
between the artist and the man. His work was so immediately responsive to his day-to-day experience, and was so
clearly shaped in a decisive way by just those imperatives
that governed his personal behavior, that it was soon out of
the question to think of the one as anything but an aspect of
the other. And it was not long before it also became evident
to me that there were grounds for supposing that Lawrence's
decision to become a writer was a matter of the adoption of
a strategy for dealing with those imperatives. This in its
turn suggested that his individual works might have to be
considered in the light of performances required to sustain
the role that he had adopted. It has since come to seem more
and more likely to me that what appears to be true of
Lawrence will prove to be true of writers as a class, and that
the source of the creative impulse where fiction is concerned
will be found to lie in this region. The three women I have
taken as my subjects in this book have been chosen—it
might more aptly be said that they presented themselves for
the purpose—because their writing can be seen to rise so
directly from the necessities of their conveniently documented psychological situations. They all had a common
compulsion to claim to be more than ordinarily important

people, and they all resorted to the novel to justify and reinforce their claims. I have tried to show, by an analysis of their patterns of behavior, the probable sources of their compulsion in the large demands of love denied in early life; and I have tried to show the very direct way in which the content of their work was determined by the forces that dictated their behavior. It is my considered view, for what it may be worth, that these three persons are typical as writers, and that over the long haul there is more to be learned about writing from such behavioral studies of writers as are here proposed than from the painstaking analysis of their works to which literary criticism is so largely limited at the present time.

This view is not currently well received in either literary or critical circles, and it is probably in the nature of professional suicide to espouse it as I here do. I am compelled to say, however, that in spite of the inherent attractions of the binary theory of the personality of the artist (for anyone who wants to write on one plane and live on another) and the obvious economic inducements for accepting it, I have never been able to find any grounds in the domains of either logic or experience for giving it serious attention, much less for accepting it. All the evidence seems to point in the other direction, and I am confident that insofar as literary criticism has a future it is as a form of applied psychiatry.

I do not believe in the autonomous work of art, or in the uniqueness of the artist: he is a human being like any other who has responded to special stresses in a specific way as have the people who have become clergymen, bankers, lawyers, dentists, acrobats, or prison guards. These people have adopted roles consistent with the programming inflicted upon them in infancy and childhood, and their performances in their roles have been crystallized by their subsequent experiences as role players. The rationale for their day-to-day behavior and understanding of it is to be found in an analysis of the circumstances in which the original programming took place, and of the subsequent modifying experience. In the case of the writer of fiction the explanation of what he says, why he says it, the particular way in which he says it, and the meaning of what he says will all be found in the same region. Writing is what he *does:* it is part of his characteristic pattern of behavior, and of a piece with it. What accounts for the one will be found to account for the other.

In this book it has been my intention to show that the literary performances of my three subjects were called for by the roles they had adopted in order to carry out the behavioral policies they had been programmed to execute: that they were, in short, moves in the games that they played in order to sustain their roles, and in order to secure to themselves the psychological benefits or advantages that were to be obtained from sustaining them. I may add that I first became interested in Madame de Staël when it occurred to me that Proust might have borrowed from her something of her genius for self-delusion, of her amazing talent for making scenes, and of her knowledgeableness about the arts and complete insensitivity to them, when converting his friend Madeleine Lemaire into Madame Verdurin. Madame de Charrière comes logically into the book as a footnote to the story of Madame de Staël's entanglement with Benjamin Constant, but my personal interest in her was aroused long ago by the inexplicable hostility with which she is treated by the principle biographers of James Boswell and Constant. The determination with which she sought out frustration and unhappiness and the resolution with which she walked out of her winning position into the most dismal of losing ones place her among the classics of compulsion. It seems strange to me that she has so often been discussed, without pity or sympathy, as a monster of arrogance and pride, when she was so clearly dying slowly of a hidden wound close to her heart.

It should not be necessary to explain my interest in George Sand. Anyone who has seen the line and wash drawing by Delacroix which shows her face as it was in her early womanhood, and who has seen the photographs that were taken of her in her old age, must feel a desire to know by what process the one human became the other. But she was not only a fascinating human being; she was also a writer who did more than almost any other to break down the boundaries between her inventions and the realities of her existence. It has come to light in recent years that from middle age onwards she devoted a quite extraordinary amount of her time and her energy to the task of eliminating whatever she didn't like from the documentary evidence relating to her own past, and to revising her autobiography in her own favor. She gave almost as much of herself to falsifying the record of her own behavior as she did to the more immediately rewarding work of destroying her wretched husband's reputation and happiness. But my account of her proceedings will, I hope, speak for itself. I will only ask those who read it to dismiss the notion that I have written about her because she was a monster: I have done so only because it is so clear by what process she became a writer. She was, when she was a small child, repeatedly given convincing reasons for entertaining the supposition that she could very easily improve on the realities with which she was confronted. She was not a born writer—there is not such a thing—but she was made one at a very tender age by the pressure of an experience that must have made it as necessary for her to take refuge in fantasy as it was for her to breathe if she was to survive.

Some of the language used in the body of the text may require explanation. Transactions are the normal units of social intercourse, when both parties or all involved are acting in good faith. Games are sequences of transactions in which one or more of the parties has an undeclared, ulterior motive for proceeding with the exchanges. Scripts are life plans, generally shaped by the first six years of the individual's experience, which determine what games he or she will play. Roles are patterns of behavior facilitating the playing of the games called for by the script. Performances are the adaptations of given roles to the exigencies of particular games, or particular sets in a continuing game. "Soft" games are played for internal or external advantage by parties with a common interest in structuring their time while waiting for death, and may be called pastimes. "Hard" games involve the complete disintegration of the ego structure of at least one player and are played with lethal intent by psychotic players. Rituals involve the reconstruction of the formal situations on which scripts are based in order to provide psychic justification for the initiation of sets of hard games. Programming is the process by which an individual is committed to given responses to given situations, generally those which in some sort duplicate elements in a primal situation.

A fuller explanation of the theory of games, and of the relationships between games and scripts, will be found in Dr. Eric Berne's book *Transactional Analysis in Psychotherapy*, and in his popularization of one of its chapters, the light-hearted but illuminating little book called *Games People Play*.

Contents

Madame de Staël

The case of Madame de Staël is an outstanding illustration of the general truth of the proposition that one way of obtaining a good reputation is to have the right enemies. Her good fortune in this respect has been made all the greater by the fact that her great enemy, Napoleon, appears at first sight to have been the political ancestor of a succession of increasingly wicked and evil men which begins with Napoleon III and ends with Stalin, Mussolini, and Hitler. It is almost impossible for members of the generations who were confronted with these last three figures either to arrive at an objective assessment of the balance of the first Napoleon's virtues and defects or to deny a large measure of respect and admiration to his opponents. The current assumption is that he was for tyranny, the expedient, and the arbitrary; and that anyone who was against him must have been for the essential freedoms, for principle, and for equity, due process, and the rule of law. That Madame de Staël was personally disliked by Napoleon, that he ordered the suppression and confiscation of her books, and that he had her expelled from France and spied upon when she was in exile in Switzerland, consequently gives her the standing of a liberal heroine in the struggle for freedom and justice which has been the theme of Western history since the outbreak of the French Revolution.

That she was a woman and that Napoleon was a man is also a matter that has done her no harm. Generations of women conscious of their disabilities as women have included her in the list of those who by their record of achievement made an outstanding contribution to the course of what used to be called feminism, but which is now known as Women's Liberation. Napoleon's hostility to her, and his conviction that she was self-seeking, foolish, irresponsible, and a dangerous meddler in affairs that she did not understand are consequently rather generally attributed to reactionary male prejudice by her female admirers and taken as creditable to her. The possibility that Napoleon was a man of quite unusual intelligence and perception, and that he may have been right about a woman who at once enjoyed the privileges that go with enormous wealth and the handicaps that go with being the spoiled child of ill-assorted parents, is less often considered.

A recent biography of Madame de Staël begins by saying that she was the daughter of Jacques Necker, and that "this was the salient fact of her life." It seems rather more important, from the psychologist's point of view, that she was the only child of parents who did not care very much for each other, and that her mother was a very odd human being indeed.

As Suzanne Churchod, the daughter of a Protestant clergyman with a country living in the Swiss canton of Vaud, Madame Necker undoubtedly went through some set of experiences that initiated the process that ultimately turned her into a species of snow queen with the ability to freeze everything she touched; but what these were there is no way of knowing. All that can be said is that by the time she emerged from the schoolroom as a notably attractive and unusually well-educated young woman she had developed an advanced technique for drawing young men toward her and holding them at armslength with a stream of words calculated to keep them interested while cooling them off. When she reached marriageable age she managed to escape the village manse in which she had learned this dubious art and moved into the monied society of Lausanne to look for a husband under the sponsorship of some well-to-do relatives. For some years she practiced her arts without success, the rules of Lausanne society being iron bound on the matter of principle that money should marry money, and in the end she came to recognize that her one hope was to marry an outsider. She accordingly set her cap at a young Englishman called Edward Gibbon, who had been sent to Lausanne to live in the custody of a reliably Protestant tutor-jailor until he could tell his father that he had out-grown an adolescent flirtation with the Roman Catholic Church; and she got him. But when, having proved that he was no longer under Roman influences in the matter of religion, Gibbon returned to England and told his father that he was planning to marry a foreign woman without a penny to her name, he was forcibly made to understand that his project would not do—or not at any rate if he wished to be his father's heir. Gibbon saw reason and jilted Suzanne Churchod.

Six years went by before Gibbon returned to Lausanne, and in them Suzanne Churchod's situation and prospects steadily deteriorated. Her father died at the end of two years, and her mother three years after that, leaving her penniless and without prospects, other than those open to a governess on the brink of passing what was then considered to be the marriageable age for a young girl without a dowry. When Gibbon returned to Lausanne he did not communicate with her, but she allowed herself to build one last flicker of hope on the event, and wrote a desperate and pathetic letter to him.

> *Sir—I blush at the step I am taking. I would like to hide it from you. I would like to hide it from myself.—I beg you on my knees to release my crazed heart from its doubts. Sign the complete admission of your indiffer-ence, and my soul will become reconciled to its fate. Certainly it will give me the repose for which I long....*

Like most neurotic persons Suzanne Churchod sought disaster as eagerly as she claimed to seek happiness, and she proceeded from this point to add threats to her supplications in a manner calculated to turn Gibbon's indifference into loathing:

> *You would be the most contemptible of men if you re-fused me this act of frankness, and the God who can look into my heart, and who loves me no doubt, al-though he makes me pass through the most painful*

> *ordeals—this God, I say, will punish you despite my*
> *prayers if there is the least dissimulation in your*
> *answer, or if by silence you toy with my peace....*

Gibbon replied with the offer of his friendship and good-will and a very clear indication that marriage was out of the question. The Genevan clergyman who was employing Suzanne as governess for his children and who was a friend of Jean-Jacques Rousseau then told the philosopher of her hopes and fears, and asked him to do a little arm-twisting on her behalf if the occasion should arise, while she wrote a softer letter accepting Gibbon's offer of friendship with a good grace and offering him in return an introduction to Jean-Jacques.... He left her letter unanswered for three weeks, and then wrote breaking off the correspondence.

This should have been the end of their transactions, but chance brought them together shortly after this false conclusion at a party at Voltaire's house at Ferney. Gibbon teased her with the contrast between the cheerful and flirtatious performance she was able to put on for this theatrical fête and the account she had given him in her letters of her desperate emotional state. She was not pleased and, after six weeks of angry consideration of what he had said, wrote to him breaking off their relationship all over again.

> *... I shall therefore no longer threaten you with celes-*
> *tial punishment—an expression that once escaped me*
> *on the impulse of the moment—but I can assure you*
> *now, without having a gift for prophecy, that you will*
> *some day regret your irreparable loss in discarding*
> *forever the too loving and too open heart of... S.C.*

The rest of this communication is very bad, and if it does not altogether justify Gibbon's statement that it revealed her to be a dangerous woman, it does confirm his belief that she was a disingenuous one, and that she had never had a spark of real feeling for him, or the capability of it. This somewhat dark view of her is further supported by the fact that while she was making this last desperate play for Gibbon she was

also working a stand-by or back-up suitor, a lawyer from
Yverdon called Correvon, with whom she was negotiating
a rather unusual marriage treaty, by which she was to have
it, and in writing, that she would not be required to cohabit
with her husband for more than four months of any given
year. She dragged this preposterous negotiation out interminably because she was determined to marry *someone*,
and when the worst had been said of Correvon he was at
least *that*.... Meanwhile, she did not care to close with him
because she could not, even at twenty-seven and without
a penny, believe that she could not do better.

Before time ran out on her with Monsieur Correvon her
luck changed. A young, beautiful, and wealthy widow
called Madame de Vermenoux who was, among other
things, in search of a governess came to Lausanne. Her late
husband had been a partner in Thélusson's Bank, a Swiss
banking house of major importance, and he had left her a
fortune, large enough to allow her to live the life of a
woman of fashion in Paris and to maintain a country house.
Although Madame de Vermenoux was only offering four
hundred francs a year, the job promised an abundance of
rich living and of those worldly and fashionable contacts
to which Suzanne had grown accustomed—and the probable loss of which made the prospect of life in Yverdon so
repugnant to her. She accordingly took the position, in June
of 1764, and in December of that year she was safely home
and dry—married, and to an authentic millionaire.

Jacques Necker had entered the employment of a Swiss
bank with a Paris branch at the age of fifteen, and had been
transferred to its office in the French capital three years
later. As the rules of the medieval Roman Catholic Church
prohibiting usury, the making of money by lending money
at interest, were still in force in France, there were no French
banks in this line of business, and foreign Protestants with
venture capital to lend were in an extremely advantageous
position in that country throughout the eighteenth century.
Under conditions of permanent credit shortage those with
cash on hand found eager buyers of loans at rates of twenty

and even thirty percent. In this situation Necker began by making large sums of money for his employers and was presently making larger sums for himself, no small part of his success being attributable to his shrewdness in establishing a clandestine relationship with an official in the French bureaucracy who in exchange for a pension fed him inside information likely to effect the money market. A series of coups based on this information gave Necker such good standing with his bank that when his original employer died, and Vernet's bank became Thélusson's, the new head of the firm offered him a partnership and twenty-five percent of the action. Three years later Thélusson moved out to become director of the bank's London branch, and Necker became effective head of the firm, seventeen years after entering its service as a clerk.

At this point in his career it became apparent to Monsieur Necker that he would have to have a wife if he were to occupy a social position commensurate with his business success, and he set out to acquire a suitable woman much as he would have set out to acquire any other useful piece of property. He mentioned his intentions to his partner Thélusson who immediately recommended Madame de Vermenoux to him. She had brought a substantial sum of money into the family when she married into it, and now that she had been widowed there was a strong possibility that she would marry again and take her fortune and a good part of her late husband's out of it. If she married Necker the fortune would at least be going no further than into the family bank, even if it were to go technically out of the family. Following Thélusson's recommendation of this "good thing," Necker went after Madame de Vermenoux. He bored her. When she discovered this she rapidly developed a self-protective technique of getting him involved with her admittedly gifted but nonetheless hideously boring governess, and slipping away as soon as they got to talking.

Necker, who had a background very like Suzanne Churchod's, and was descended from a line of Protestant clergymen who had led austerely provincial lives in Germany, liked the twenty-seven-year-old virgin well enough, and may possibly have thought that she would make him a much less troublesome wife than some willful woman with a knowledge of the great world and with the expensive tastes that go with the possession of wealth. He was not, however, the man to enter into any sort of binding contract without finding out what he was letting himself in for and before he committed himself he went off to Switzerland to make the necessary inquiries about her previous conduct and reputation. He did not want to acquire an unsound property. She knew what was going on and could hardly believe her luck. But she was not going to allow herself to be upset, even if Monsieur Necker should disappear. "If our castle in the air should tumble down," she wrote to her former employer in Geneva, "I shall marry Correvon next summer." The statement says all that needs to be said about the depth of her feelings for Monsieur Necker. He was quite simply one man she would rather marry than another, because he was better off.

The pleasures of sex have often enough turned such loveless marriages into workable arrangements, and when they have not proved to be the answer many women have found it possible to take refuge from the unsatisfactory primary relationship behind a wall of children. But sex proved to have few attractions for Madame Necker, and her first experience of childbirth was so little to her liking that she was careful to make it her last. The child born to the couple at the end of April 1766, and christened Anne Louise Germaine Necker, was destined not to have any brothers or sisters and had to bear the brunt of her mother's peculiarities and her father's indifference alone.

The word indifference may seem a rather odd one to apply in view of the legendary intensity of the relationship between Jacques Necker and his daughter. But in the years following Germaine Necker's birth her father, who was only more interested in power than in money, was occupied, to the exclusion of almost everything else, with building up the position that was to enable him to embark on a second career as a statesman in the service of the French crown. The year after Germaine was born he moved to

Paris to take up an official post as Ambassador for the Republic of Geneva at the Court of Versailles, and when she was four he moved into the center of French financial affairs by assuming the directorship of the Compagnie des Indes. By the time she was ten he was ready to succeed Turgot as the head of the Controller General's Office with the special title of Director General of Finance. Under the *ancien régime* the Controller General of France exercised the combined functions of a Minister of Finance and a Minister of the Interior, and the man who held it was the most powerful man in the royal administration. Since Necker, as a Swiss national and as a Protestant, was barred from taking a seat in the King's Council of Ministers, it was necessary to give him this special title and to allow him direct access to the King, a faculty that in practice added a great deal to the power inherent in his office. At each successive step in his rise toward this dizzy height the load of Necker's work and responsibility increased, and he had correspondingly less time for his personal life. He was extremely affable and charming to his daughter when he was with her, but that was less and less often until, when Germaine was fifteen, he was dismissed from his post for committing the tactical error of lifting the veil of secrecy that had until then surrounded the national finances. This he did by drawing up and publishing what was in effect the first French budget report, the famous *Compte rendu au roi* that inadvertently revealed the imminence of the Crown's bankruptcy to discerning readers. It was only when Necker had withdrawn from Versailles to his country house at Saint-Ouen on the northern outskirts of Paris after his first fall from power that the intimacy with his daughter that was to become a by-word developed. And that was two years after Germaine's relationship with her mother had brought her to the point of nervous breakdown.

Suzanne Necker having bitterly resented the experiences she had to undergo in childbed, hated the business of breast-feeding even more. She had, however, endured it for more than four months, and had only given up what was for her an unpleasant form of torture when she was advised by her medical men that her child was starving to death. A wet nurse was then found to take her place, but while this solved the physical problem it created another by making Madame Necker passionately jealous of the woman who was feeding her child and arousing a possessiveness that presently became a mania. Germaine Necker appears to have reached the age of twelve without ever having been allowed either to go anywhere without her mother or to have a friend or playmate her own age. She was not only brought up in complete isolation from the world of childhood, she was also educated on a system devised by her mother. This denied her all exercise and play and concentrated on forcing her intellectual development to follow the lines of Madame Necker's mature interests—those of an intellectually sophisticated Protestant bigot with a taste for theoretical arguments about such matters as ethics, morals, and Christian duty. Germaine Necker could maintain discussions of such subjects with adult interlocutors from the time she was ten years old, but while she had been brilliantly trained as a performer in this region she was to remain profoundly ignorant of everything that lay outside it.

But while Madame Necker was training her child to be an isolated intellectual freak she was also teaching her a more sinister art by power of example. Madame Necker had developed a technique of assaulting her husband and breaking down the barrier of indifference that he liked to put between them by staging attacks of nervous and physical prostration that suggested that she was hovering on the margin between life and death and might die at any moment. By the time Germaine was beginning to take notice of these things her mother had become a formidable artist in the realm of emotional blackmail with something like a genius for nourishing the sense of guilt in those around her with her tears. On top of all this she was constitutionally incapable of responding to warmth with warmth, and although she gave an enormous amount of time to her daughter's miseducation she was never seen to be either naturally affectionate or even humanly playful with her.

When, in the normal course of her development, Germaine outgrew her infantile emotional dependence on her mother and turned toward her father for affection and support in the prepubertal phase of her sexuality, she found that there was, in effect, nobody at home there either. The world at large misunderstood the encounter and saw the father delighting in the daughter. What they did not discern was that he delighted in her as a drawing-room performer and as the monster of precocity and pretentiousness that her mother had made her, not as his daughter.

That Necker was being called on to supply a missing element in the life of a vulnerable and desperate child was a thing that he was either too busy or too obtuse to realize. Their famous nonphysical love affair was fabricated when she was fifteen, after a nervous breakdown in her fourteenth year, in which she underwent an almost complete mental and physical collapse. Soon after she had turned thirteen she began to show signs of a serious disorder, with alternating periods of apathy and wild excitement. The Dr. Trochin who was put in charge of the case prescribed a regime so foreign to anything that Madame Necker could approve, with no more cramming and no more restraints, as to move her to bow out of her daughter's upbringing altogether and to hand her over to the care of Madame Huber, a Swiss friend of her own childhood days who had a daughter the same age as Germaine and who could be her playmate. The new governess and the two girls were packed off to the country house at Saint-Ouen, where Germaine's father presently discovered her as a relatively liberated being, rather than an extension of his wife's personality. He was delighted with the change in her, and according to Catherine Huber, the daughter of her governess, who wrote an account of her convalescence, began to pay his daughter a great deal of attention at this time. But it was already too late to repair the damage done by his failure to function as a father in the vital years of her childhood. The extravagant hyperboles that Germaine used in her accounts of the affair testify to its unreality. In the famous diary for 1785 in which Germaine wrote such things of her father as "of

all the men in the world it is he whom I would have wished
for a lover," she recorded a characteristic and revelatory
incident. In the course of a ball at his house Jacques Necker
cut in on Germaine as she was dancing with the man she
was by then engaged to, Eric Magnus Staël von Holstein,
the Baron de Staël. "Now, sir," he said as he took her over,
"I'll show you how one dances with a girl when one is in
love with her."

In the world of vulgarizations of Freudian doctrines
this would be no more than a commonplace piece of middle-
brow badinage, and it could be written off as meaningless.
But the context of the small joke was worldliness of another
kind. The Baron de Staël was a courtier from an exceedingly
sinister court, that of Gustavus the Third of Sweden, a
monarch whose two great passions in life were handsome
young men and wizards who could speak with the dead.
The Baron had come to Paris as a protégé of Gustavus, who
had himself played a leading part in persuading the Neckers
to accept this sexually ambiguous young man as a son-in-
law. There could be only one explanation of his interest in
the matter.

In the light of his almost certain knowledge of this aspect
of the Baron's life Necker's remark can be seen to have been
a truly atrocious one. And although there are good reasons
to believe that Germaine was inexperienced sexually at the
time, something about the difference between the dancing
styles of her entirely masculine father and her ambiguous
fiancé led her to tear herself out of her father's arms and to
escape from the ballroom to a private place where she could
cry her eyes out. It speaks eloquently of the real nature of
the relationship between this father and his daughter that
he did not lift a finger to save her from the disagreeable
experience of being handed over, in a state of innocence,
to a man who was notoriously an *homme-femme*.

The Baron de Staël had come to Paris in 1776 as a well-
connected young man without a fortune, and had been
living there by flying the kite ever since. That is to say,
he had, on the strength of the entrée to court circles which
made it seem plausible that he would sooner or later find

some heiress or woman of property to marry him, lived by borrowing new money to pay off his previous loans, increasing the amount borrowed each time in order to meet his current expenses. The heiress he picked on as his target in 1778 was Germaine, who was then twelve years old. De Staël had a bad scare in 1783, when Madame Necker decided that her daughter should marry England's William Pitt. But as Pitt had not been consulted about this plan, it fell through, and de Staël was given a second chance at the girl. When she was seventeen he began negotiating in earnest and achieved some astonishing feats in pursuit of his aim. He persuaded his friend Count Fersen, who was Marie Antoinette's lover, to get the Queen to ask for his appointment to the vacant post of Ambassador to France. Gustavus agreed to make the appointment if de Staël could persuade the French Crown to cede an island in the West Indies, preferably Tobago, to him. Tobago (large) was not available, but Saint Barthélemy (small) fortunately was. The King of Sweden expressed himself satisfied, and with the Ambassadorship safe in his pocket, the baron then made his approach to the Neckers through the aging Madame de Boufflers, a former mistress of King Gustavus. The Neckers replied that they would be delighted to let the Baron have their daughter if:

• the King of Sweden were to make his appointment to the Ambassadorship permanent;

• the King of Sweden were to guarantee him a pension of twenty thousand livres a year in the event that his Ambassadorship should, for whatever reason, be terminated;

• the King of Sweden should elevate the Baron to the rank of Count;

• the King of Sweden should make the Baron a member of the Order of the Polar Star;

• Marie Antoinette, Queen of France and daughter of the Emperor of Austria, should approve and sign the marriage contract.

And the Baron de Staël should give an undertaking that his wife would in no circumstances whatever be required to become resident in Sweden.

The Baron was not able to get the title of Count of the Order of the Polar Star, but he was able to obtain all the rest, and rather more. When the marriage contract was signed it was witnessed by the King and Queen of France and by all the princes of the Blood Royal.

It was all very magnificent, but it was not only that the Baron de Staël was the Baron de Staël, weak, vicious, mercenary, and dubiously honest; Germaine de Staël was also Germaine de Staël. Madame de Boufflers did not believe that they had winning chances:

> There is no doubt that she has absolutely no idea of social behavior and conventions, or that she is so spoiled by admiration for her wit that it will be hard to make her realize her shortcomings. She is imperious and strong willed to excess, and she has self-assurance that I have never seen matched in any person of her age, no matter of what rank.

The marriage was further doomed by the skill and care that Jacques Necker had put into the business of giving Germaine control over her money and making it impossible for the Baron to get hold of it. His one hope would be that he would be able to dominate her by delighting her sexually. But in this field he was negligible, and he proved unable either to arouse her interest or to satisfy her appetites. For a few months she was off balance, surprised by the mechanical aspects of love-making and disconcerted to find herself in a physical relationship with a man who could not please her and who seemed to fulfill no role whatever in her life but that of an unwanted, and compulsively extravagant, dependent.

At the bottom of her depression, during the winter of 1786–87, Madame de Staël picked up her pen and cleared her mind of her discontents by exteriorizing them as fiction. *Sophie, or, The Secret Sentiments* is a three-act play which abolishes her unwanted marriage and restores her to her family. In a sense it is a last fling with her compensatory fantasy about her love affair with her father. He appears in the play as the Comte de Sainville, she as his seventeen-year-old adopted daughter, Sophie Mortimer. When a suitor appears to ask Sophie's hand in marriage she refuses him for reasons that she fails to understand. But the Comtesse de Sainville, a character who is clearly modeled on Madame Necker, has no difficulty in penetrating her secret. The poor girl is in love with the Comte without knowing it. No sooner has Sophie learned this awful truth from her foster mother than she finds herself faced with another. By accident she discovers the secret of a mysterious closed pavilion which is a disturbing feature of the Sainvilles' grounds. It contains a bust of herself which the Comte is in the habit of decking with flowers. He is in love with her! He cannot deny the charge when she faces him with it. Yes, indeed, he does nourish a guilty passion for her.... The Countess joins them by chance. She sees how things are! She faints dead away! When she has been brought round everything is sorted out with extreme rapidity and simple-minded reasonableness. The suitor is packed off. Who needs him? And when he is gone the Comte, the Comtesse, and Sophie agree to settle down to live a life of sexless bliss as the best of passionate friends.

It is characteristic of Madame de Staël that having written this she should find no embarrassment in reading it aloud to her mother and father. Madame Necker was horrified beyond measure, but her father's view of the thing has gone unrecorded. Perhaps he felt that it showed that she was incorrigible and would never grow up. But if he did take that view of this outpouring of an infantile fantasy he was wrong. When she had finished *Sophie* she was through with her childhood, and its dreams, and she would not indulge in such regressions again. She would go on to the point at which she could write of her parents with the clarity of insight that is to be seen in a letter that she addressed to Louis de Narbonne in November 1792. She mentions their son:

*Auguste is really a charming child... my parents like
him a great deal. My mother would like to demonstrate
through him that she would have been able to love me,
and that but for the vicious character which, etc. My
father, who treated me as if I was a doll for so long, is
delighted to have this replacement. The feeling that is
so much of a necessity for all species alike means nothing to him, and the generality of humankind or children, as such, suits him more than friends. That's the
way he's made....*

The route she had to follow to reach this degree of detachment and perception was an arduous one. In 1785, the
year before her marriage, her father had begun his campaign to regain his position as the King's first minister by
ousting Calonne from that office. In February of 1787 his
maneuvers, as elaborate, painstaking, and byzantine in
their character as those he had resorted to in his earlier attack on Turgot, were beginning to make Calonne uncertain
of his position and he struck back at Necker with an analysis of the now famous *Compte rendu* of 1781 which raised a
storm of controversy about Necker's competence on the one
hand, and the financial stability of the regime on the other.
The King was infuriated to find that his minister had initiated a public discussion of what he considered to be state
secrets and eased his aggravation by dismissing Calonne
and ordering Necker to leave Paris and the court and to con-
fine himself within the limits of the park of his country
house at Marolles. The King was, in a sense, right to be
angry with the two men, since the debate provoked by Calonne's attack on his rival had destroyed what little faith
the nation at large still had in the Government's solvency. It
made it clear to everyone with the ability to balance an account that the bankruptcy which had been immiment in
1781 had now arrived.

The situation was sufficiently alarming in itself, but behind the immediate threat of social paralysis that would be
produced by the collapse of the Crown's ability to carry out
its governmental functions there lay the two unanswerable

questions: How does a national government go into liquidation? And, when it does, what procedures corresponding to reorganization should be followed, and how? There was no precedent for a national backruptcy, and all that could be seen clearly was that if it occurred the state power would be up for grabs and that a violent contest for control of the legislative and administrative machinery would ensue. More than the commonplace dread of an untoward or disagreeable event was involved, the impending social collapse threatened the whole system of social identifications based on money and property rights.

In all this Necker was outstanding as the man of unshaken confidence who knew that France was fundamentally sound, and that a social upheaval could easily be averted if the Crown would reorganize the tax structure, limit government expenditures, and give the socially responsible element in the middle and professional classes a voice in the national councils. He radiated confidence as he told the nation's property owners and the court party surrounding Marie Antoinette just what they most wished to hear. He was recalled to office at the beginning of the autumn of 1788 supremely confident of his ability to handle the situation, and wholly unaware of the extent to which the situation was already beyond control.

If the problems with which France was faced had been soluble by balancing the accounts and providing for the retirement of outstanding debt in an orderly fashion Necker would no doubt have been able to do it. And during the winter of 1788–89 he appeared, momentarily, to those who looked no further than the accounts, to be doing it. But while he was brilliantly, from a banking point of view, negotiating a series of new loans that solved for the time being the problems created by the administration's cash shortage, the 1788 harvest was failing, and the hardest winter in nearly a century was setting in. When spring came, and the financial corner seemed to have been turned, food stocks in a number of provincial centers were running low and famine was threatening.

When the States-General—the long-disused French parliament which had been summoned by Brienne just before Necker took office—finally assembled in May of 1789, everyone present, with the apparent exception of the King's first minister, knew that the country was faced with what was potentially a revolutionary situation. They listened with astonishment and dismay while the infatuated banker read them a lecture on the sound funding of public debt which led up to an assurance that the state of French economy was such as to make it possible to solve all the problems with which the Crown was faced without levying any new taxes.

This address, uninspiringly delivered, unsuitable to the occasion, and irrelevant to the historical situation, brought about one of those public disappearances (such as that of General MacArthur at the Chicago convention) that make political failure absolute. From that moment on, until he left for Switzerland in September 1790, Necker was merely an inept ghost haunting the center of the stage.

While it has been said that power corrupts and absolute power corrupts absolutely, the destructive effects of public failure, so evident in the after-lives of defeated Presidential candidates, are less often acknowledged. Necker's abysmal performance at the opening session of the States-General was as nothing to his final official act. Although the whole family, Germaine de Staël, her mother, and her father, had been present on the occasion when the mob broke into the Royal apartments at Versailles in October 1789 in order to fetch the King and Queen away to Paris, and had been eyewitnesses to the death of all possibility of further evasion of the fact of revolution that then occurred, Jacques Necker continued to fight his meaningless battle of the accounts. Although he was staving off the national backruptcy from day to day throughout the spring and early summer of 1790, by raising thirty-day loans in ludicrously small amounts and at fantastic rates of interest, he finally produced an account of the financial state of the nation for the National Assembly in July that showed everything in order, with a surplus of income over expenditures of ninety-nine million francs.

This feat of creative accounting was so ridiculous as to

blunt the edge of its scandalous aspects, and people pitied its author more than they despised him. He had, in a sense, exorcised himself, and there was nothing left for him to do but vanish from the scene. He was to be a wealthy nonentity for the remainder of his life.

The impression made upon Madame de Staël by her father's spectacular failure must have been very powerful, and made all the more striking by the altered condition of her own affairs. The naïve and extremely unworldly young person who had written *Sophie,* and who had been as dismayed by her first experience with the mechanical aspects of sex as by finding herself committed to a sexual relationship with a man she didn't care for, perished rather rapidly. With the facility of the inexperienced she moved from the extreme of naïveté to that of sophistication. She discovered, practically overnight, the degree of sexual freedom that went with the status of a married woman at the court, and she discovered the use that could be made of it by a woman who had effective control of her own income and who had the social leverage of the wife of an Ambassador and the daughter of the man thought most likely to succeed Calonne. Germaine found herself being courted by ambitious men who wanted to be at the center of things, and as she was sophisticated and not worldly she assumed that she was being sought after because she was powerful rather than because she might, if she could be seduced, be made into a useful tool.

The first of the series of cold-hearted and calculating men who moved in on her was Hippolyte de Guibert, a forty-four-year-old military theoretician who had a plan for the structural reorganization of the French army, and the revision of its tactical concepts. Mr. Christopher Herold writes patronizingly of him in his biography of Madame de Staël, and alleges that when he met her he was posing as a misunderstood and persecuted genius. This is less than just since the Comte de Guibert was indeed misunderstood by all the soldiers of his day, with one notable exception, and was persecuted in the sense that he was deliberately frus-

trated, ignored, and blocked off in his professional career
by the senior officers of a military establishment committed
to the Roman simplicities of Frederick the Great. And if he
was not recognizable as a genius by virtue of his own
achievements as a field commander he was certainly one
by proxy since the notable exception among the serving
officers of his day who did take his ideas seriously was no
less a person than Napoleon Bonaparte, whose mind was
set on fire by the book in which Guibert not only described
the organization and the tactical principles to be adopted
by his ideal army, but also suggested that the current of
history was running in a direction that would make it possible for a successful soldier with such a weapon at his
command to become another Julius Caesar.

Since all Napoleon's campaigns, up to the time of his
disastrous reversion to the doctrines of military brutalism at
the Battle of Wagram, are text-book exercises in the practical application of Guibert's theoretical ideas, it can be said
that Madame de Staël began her experiments in infidelity by going to bed with one of the most immediately in-
fluential men of her day, for however obscure Guibert may
have been in his own right there is no doubt that he provided Napoleon with the ideas that were the foundation of
his success. In view of Madame de Staël's later love–hate
relationship with Napoleon, and his curiously obsessive
interest in her, it is ironic that her first lover should have
been the man who both provided the spark that lit the flame
of his ambition and provided him with the means for its
realization.

It is even more ironic that Madame de Staël should have
lived through the Napoleonic era from start to finish without ever knowing this, and that she should have gone to her
death valuing him only for his skill as an amorist and the
grace and charm of his manner. His greatest kindness to her
was that he convinced her of her attractiveness. He wrote a
pen portrait of her, as she was at twenty, under the fancy
name of *Zulmé* which makes it clear why, having been the
lover of such a woman as Julie de Lespinasse in his younger

days, he should still have wanted her, and it is as clear that she was grateful for the reassurance that his flattering attentions gave her.

It may be felt that such reassurance was the last thing that the subject of Madame de Boufflers's acidulous report would be in need of, but the element of the extravagant in Madame de Staël's behavior, her eccentricities of dress, her exhibitionist habit of displaying her physical charms, her noisy whoopings, and her fidgetings and attention-getting maneuvers, are all classic indications of self-doubt. Guibert, whatever else he may have been after, made her feel that she could be wanted for her own sake. A little while after his death, when she wrote a novel as a vehicle for her passionate declaration that "love is above the laws, above the opinion of men; it is the truth, the flame, the pure element, the primary idea of the moral world"; she showed what store she set by Guibert's vision of her by calling it *Zulma*.

Be that as it may, however, Guibert vanished from her life when Calonne was dismissed and her father was packed off to Marolles by *lettre de cachet*. Germaine regretted him while she was idling away a lost summer at that pleasant house waiting for her first child. This unlucky creature, a girl who was born ailing, and who did not live to complete her second year, may just as well have been Guibert's as the ambiguous de Staël's, but its birth seems to have come between them, and the liaison was not renewed when Necker was recalled to power and his family returned with him to Versailles.

When Guibert died, in 1790, Madame de Staël was involved with two other men who were to be as prominent historically as he was fated to be obscure, the first of them Monsieur de Talleyrand, the most improbable of all bishops, and the second Louis de Narbonne, the illegitimate child of Louis XV of France by the Comtesse de Narbonne-Lara. Talleyrand, who possessed one of the most acute political intelligences of the day and a charm of manner that made him irresistible to women in spite of his physical deformities, enchanted Madame de Staël, made her his

mistress, took large sums of money from her, found her a
bore and something of a fool, and passed her on to Narbonne. He did not do this merely to get rid of her, but rather
to help a man who seemed to have a brilliant opportunity in
front of him out of a frustrating difficulty.

There was nothing secret or underhand about Narbonne's
connection with Louis XV. He had been christened in the
chapel at Versailles in the presence of the King's legitimate
children, and he had been brought up as a Prince of the
Blood of France. In his youth he had shown unusual intelligence and capacity for administration, and in the first
stages of the collapse of the absolute monarchy, when it
seemed possible that revolution could be averted by the
adoption of a constitution and some form of representative
government under the Crown, he emerged as a possible
bridge figure, a man who would be acceptable to both the
Crown and the moderates as the King's first minister during
the period of adjustment. Unfortunately, in addition to his
real gifts (they were later to be recognized by Napoleon),
he had a remarkable talent for squandering money, and
when his opportunity arrived he had, although he was only
thirty-three, already run through fortunes provided for him
by his half-sister Madame Adelaide, by his mother, and by
his wife, and he was strapped. Madame de Staël raised a
hundred thousand livres to pay off his most pressing debts,
and made her house in the Rue du Bac a political salon
where the moderate royalists and the moderates in the National Assembly could foregather and work out a constitutionalist strategy. With her help Narbonne rose rapidly
from regimental commander, to head of the National
Guard, to the Ministry of War. For two years after her father had vanished into the limbo of absolute failure Madame de Staël was at the center of things as the mistress,
and on occasion the policy maker, of the coming man, cher-
ishing the illusion that she was making history by helping
him along the road to power.

She was in fact making one fantastic blunder after
another. In addition to her work for Narbonne she was
throughout this period writing the report, on the developing

political situation in France, that it was her husband's duty to submit to King Gustavus at regular intervals. Without bothering to inquire what view of the questions at issue the King was likely to take, she made her reports straight propaganda for the constitutionalist cause without even a hint of objectivity about them. They infuriated the King, who was passionately hostile to the concept of any invasion or limitation of royal power in any circumstances, and who lived in terror that there might be something contagious about what was occurring in France. As Madame de Staël went on telling him what wonderful things were happening, or were about to happen, he was busily organizing a species of union of crowned heads whose members were to supply an international army of intervention which was to march on Paris, to liberate Louis XVI, and to restore his powers as they had been before the calling of the States-General. When it was pointed out to him that the Paris mob would probably kill the King and Queen and any of their legitimate heirs that they could lay their hands on as soon as the army of intervention crossed the frontier, Gustavus proceeded to Aachen in the Rhineland and organized the famous flight to Varennes that sealed the doom of the French monarchy. When this Swedish operation failed Gustavus first instructed his Ambassador to break off all formal relations with the French government, and then, in January 1792, ordered him to return home. He arrived in Sweden in March, crossing a letter from the King telling him to stay away, just in time to be a participant in the fantastic sequence of events that were to provide the foundation for the plot of Verdi's *Un Ballo in Maschera*, and which culminated in Gustavus' assassination at a masked ball. When the King finally died of his wounds two weeks later his successor immediately restored diplomatic relations with the French government and reinstated de Staël in his Ambassadorship, but by that time the whole social and political framework in which his wife's schemes had some claim to relevance had disintegrated.

Before it did so, however, Madame de Staël had effectively cooked Narbonne's goose. She began her work shortly after

France had declared war on the antirevolutionary confederation of northern monarchs by pushing her lover into a secret negotiation with Marie-Antoinette in which he offered to sell out his left-of-center Girondist support in exchange for his nomination as the King's first minister.

When this offer was not taken up Madame de Staël wrote a letter to the Minister for Foreign Affairs, de Lessart, suggesting that he should resign his post to Narbonne in view of the latter's manifestly superior qualifications for the job. De Lessart read this disarming piece of impudence to the Conseil des Ministres. Its members were amused, but Narbonne's credit was not enhanced.

Narbonne was next persuaded to submit a memorandum to the King which embodied Madame de Staël's recommendation that the Crown should abandon its aristocratic supporters in order to make an alliance with the reformers and moderates of the center parties on the ground that only they could command the support of the bourgeoisie and prevent the revolution from going to extremes. After their experiences with the mob on the occasions of the invasion of their apartments at Versailles, and of their return from Varennes, the King and Queen had good reason to doubt the ability of the center to control anything, and this memorandum had the sole effect of further increasing their mistrust of Narbonne.

As his memorandum had been ignored, Narbonne then proceeded to attempt to force a crisis intended to bring him to power. He first served the King with an ultimatum saying that he could no longer work with the Minister of Marine—either one or other of them would have to resign. As soon as he had made this move he received letters of support from the three commanders of the principal military districts in metropolitan France, Lafayette, Rochambeau, and Luckner, telling him that they would resign their commands if Narbonne ceased to be Minister of War. Madame de Staël, who had apparently drafted the letters, then leaked them to a Paris newspaper. The King thereupon fired Narbonne as the script required him to do. The expected sequel, an uproar in the National Assembly and disorders in the streets that would have forced Narbonne on the King as his first minister, did not take place. What happened in fact was that the Girondists exploited the situation created by Narbonne's resignation in such a way that they were able to ditch him and set up their own ministry.

Between March and September of 1792 the avalanche of the revolution swept the whole world of upper-class drawing-room conspiracy, in which Madame de Staël had been able to cherish the illusion that she was a power, into the discard. For a time she fought against the realities of the situation by immersing herself in a ridiculous and theatrical plot to save the Royal family in which Narbonne was to have had the role of a coachman, and then, as the Terror began, she started with greater realism to use the privileges that went with her standing as the wife of a foreign diplomat to get as many of her friends who were threatened with proscription and the guillotine out of the country as she could. When a warrant was issued for the arrest of Narbonne she hid him for a time in the Swedish Embassy, but after a narrow escape in which he had been forced to take refuge under the altar of its chapel while Madame de Staël lectured a search party on the subject of extraterritorial rights, it became necessary to smuggle him across the Channel and into England. Ten days later at the beginning of September she was within a hair's breadth of being caught in an attempt to get the Abbé de Montesquiou out of Paris and into Switzerland. She found herself being dragged before a revolutionary tribunal by a hooting crowd, and her sense of invulnerability abruptly deserted her. Her diplomatic status saved her from imprisonment and perhaps death, but without any credible margin. She knew that another time she might not reach a tribunal where her claims to be an exception to all the rules would be given a hearing. She might simply be torn to pieces on the street. And she was not only afraid for herself. She had already borne Narbonne a son, Auguste, in 1790, and she was now between six and seven months gone with her second child by him. She left Paris for Switzerland the day after her encounter with the mob and the tribunal, within a few days of the second anniversary of her father's flight into obscurity. She sat in silence as her carriage rumbled out of the city. For the first, and possibly the only, time in her life, she had nothing to say.

The family reunion was not a happy affair. Madame Necker had become a hysterical neurasthenic who had adopted as her Christian duty the task of making those about her as miserable as possible. Her opportunities in the present situation were all that she could ask for. The revolution in France had been an inspiration to all those in Switzerland who had to endure the hardships created by the many anomalies and archaisms in its social structure and members of its privileged elite lived in hourly dread of a Jacobin rising that would lead to the confiscation of their property if not to the loss of their lives. Monsieur Necker shared the anxieties of his wealthy Swiss neighbors and friends on this account, and had worries of his own into the bargain. With his reputation and position gone all that he could look for was the recovery of the immense fortune that he had at hazard in France. One large part of this consisted of real estate, his town house in Paris, and his properties at Saint-Ouen and Marolles; and the other of a credit with the French government of two million francs.

This credit had been established in the hungry winter of 1788–89 when Monsieur Necker advanced the sum as a personal loan for the purchase of wheat that was said to be available in the Netherlands. The deal had not gone through, and the sum had remained on deposit with the Treasury. In the confused situation prevailing at the time of his fall and flight from France Monsieur Necker had not been able to withdraw the money, and there it still was. A large proportion of his waking hours was spent on concocting plans for keeping his claim on "the deposit," as it was always referred to in the family, alive no matter what social changes might take place in France, and in these his connection with the Baron de Staël as his son-in-law and the Swedish Ambassador played no small part, since the French

Government, no matter what its complexion, would be more likely to deal considerately with a friend of Sweden than with a Swiss individual.

It was thus distinctly unnerving for Monsieur Necker to have his daughter emerge from the murk of the Terror in a state of almost suicidal despair at being parted from Monsieur de Narbonne, proclaiming her intention of divorcing Monsieur de Staël as soon as it could be arranged and of joining her lover in England. This not only threatened him with the loss of his Swedish identification, but also with a positive connection with a proscribed émigré that would probably lead to instant confiscation of both the real estate and the deposit. While her father brought pressure on her to abandon her project for rejoining her lover for prudential reasons, her mother moralized at her. She had been warned when she was first married that Monsieur de Narbonne was one of those libertines without honor or conscience that she was never to receive in her home, and here she was, abandoned by him with one child, and another on the way. It was her Christian duty to reconcile herself with her husband and to forget her lover.

Madame de Staël doubted that it could be either her duty as a normally constituted woman or as a Christian to reconcile herself with a husband who publicly flaunted a relationship with the Baron Reuterholm, whose sexual ambiguity was as notorious as his own, and who was even more deeply involved in black magic and the other Witch of Endor–like proceedings then popular in Sweden than de Staël himself was. Madame Necker grudgingly conceded the point after nearly two months of recrimination and argument, and late in October her daughter was able to write to Narbonne to tell him:

> I've just had a talk with my mother that makes me much happier. She give her consent to my divorce with Monsieur de Staël—that's how she puts it—if I give up seeing you; and if I can arrange things with him without a scandal, she will be agreeable to my not leaving you. Given time I'll possibly come to what I want. But

can you understand this thing they call religion? She makes deals with herself, of the oddest possible kind. People like us who only follow the rules of common decency are a lot easier to make sense of....

Monsieur Necker also modified his attitude in the face of his daughter's evident unhappiness and imminent delivery, and she had perhaps begun to hope that there might be a way out of her difficulties when she bore Narbonne a second son on November the twentieth. But the language of the note that she wrote to him to inform him of the fact was strained and uncertain:

...the day before yesterday...I gave life to a fine brown boy, who will exist as his mother does to love you and to be one more link between our two inseparable destinies. I'm suffering a great deal at the moment from nervous tension, but there's not the least likelihood that I'll die of it. To make me better I think that here I am free at last to go to rejoin you, and that by looking after myself I hasten the day... oh, not having been able to call on your name! If they'd allowed me to do that I know that I would have suffered less. Goodbye. Write to me. My life is all I am asking from you. They don't want me to write any more. When my third day fever goes down I'll write again. Good-bye...

Her nagging fear was not that her parents might keep them apart, but that Monsieur de Narbonne might not feel that their destinies were as inseparable as all that. He might not wish her to come to him in England.

Monsieur de Narbonne was indeed in a somewhat difficult position there as a Constitutionalist among the émigrés. While he believed that everything that the Constitutionalists had done from 1788 onwards was part of an effort to stave off the revolution while preserving the monarchy and what was worth retaining of the old order, the view of the hard-line aristocrats of the King's party was that they were reckless triflers who had made the revolution possible by undermining the established order. Many Englishmen took the same view, and looked on noblemen such as Monsieur de Narbonne who had been with the *Constituants Revolutionaires* as traitors to their class and plain and simple revolutionary enemies of ordered society. William Pitt was believed to be thinking of deporting them, and as the date set for the trial of Louis XVI approached, upper- and middle-class English opinion hardened against them.

Monsieur de Narbonne was affected by the climate of opinion surrounding him and began not only to question the wisdom of what he had done under Madame de Staël's influence, but also to consider changing his political alliances and going over to the counterrevolutionary King's party. Knowing the extent of the aristocratic prejudice against him, both as a Constitutionalist and as Madame de Staël's collaborator, he considered it necessary to go to extreme lengths to prove his bona fides, and hit on the idea of going to Paris to appear as a voluntary witness for the defense at the King's trial as the perfect means of doing so. He gave Madame de Staël a hint of his intention, though without explaining his motives, in a letter that reached her at the end of November. She replied instantly: "You end up with a phrase that can't mean anything: that you're returning to France without me. I beg you to have the decency to kill me yourself before you dream of doing such a thing— it would be much kinder."

Presumably she had only considered the risk he would be running when she wrote in that strain. But two days later it had dawned on her that she was being repudiated, and she began to fight: "The moment you set foot in France I'll blow my brains out...," one note of December began, and another, written on the same day, began, "You have given me my death blow, Monsieur de Narbonne. I thought that my life was worth more in your eyes than the maddest, most useless, and, most dangerous of demonstrations, whether for the King or for you...." This note ends wildly: "If there is a spark of human feeling left in you, you won't carry out this insane project and my ruin. Oh God above! Can you wish *him* to be the one, can you want *him* to do this...*adieu*..." Later in the day she wrote to Monsieur de Narbonne yet a third time, on a more personal and more anguished level: "...what have I done to you that you should make my life a continuous torment...what man has the right to pluck the heart out of the person who loves him whenever he feels like it, to inflict on her time and time again the pains and agonies of death..."

On December the third, after what must have been a sleepless night, the bombardment was resumed:

> I've already told you that you've given me my death blow.... I don't think I've much time left. Give me these last days. Let me go down into the grave you've dug for me in peace. What an idiotic proposal! You know very well that it's a wildly silly step for you—and useless as a service to the King. You know that you're the most hated of all Frenchmen among the Jacobins, and that if they give you time to say a word before they kill you it will only be to find yet another reason for killing him in what you say. You know it, but you have such a need to make a sensation that these three months in which you've not been able to get yourself talked about have seemed like centuries to you....

She then gave him a realistic account of the precise dangers that he would be running, and told him that the only thing he could reasonably do would be to send the court a written statement. If he were to do more than that he would be merely making himself ridiculous by showing his complete lack of commonsense.

After Madame de Staël had written her lover this rocket she heard that the National Assembly, which was now calling itself the Convention, had declined even to listen to a reading of his offer to appeal at the trial, and that the whole question had thus been made academic.

A partial reconciliation followed, and in January, in spite of the plaintive protests of both her mother and father, Madame de Staël went to join Monsieur de Narbonne in England and was with him at Juniper Hall in Surrey, to the great scandal of the neighborhood, until the end of May, when she returned to Switzerland.

The visit had the results foreseen by Monsieur Necker. While his daughter was en route to his home, his name was inscribed on the list of those deemed to be political émigrés by the authorities in Paris, and all his properties in France were placed in escrow. And Narbonne didn't write to her.

> Almost a month without hearing anything of you— that's a new one on me. This month is an abyss. Why did I leave? I needn't tell you that as soon as I got here I learned that all my father's French assets had been seized and made state property, and the seals put on the houses in Paris and Saint-Ouen. This would have been terrible news at any other time, but you do me the service of making me indifferent to everything. I've already written in an attempt to obtain justice for my father. I don't know if it will be necessary for me to go to Paris for a week or so. I don't think so. In any case I'm in no shape for it—I've never been so unhappy in my life....

A few days later, there still being no letter from Monsieur de Narbonne, she tried another line:

> An inflammatory fever leaves me in an awful state. The sore throat, the fainting fits, last, I suppose, for the rest of one's life. Monsieur de Staël is taking wonderful care of me, but he doesn't seem able to understand why all his lemonade-pouring doesn't put him in the niche you occupy in my heart. On the day that [Dr.] Butini said that he'd never seen such a raging fever my mother decided that it was nothing, but nonetheless begged my father to protect himself from the contagion of a malignant fever....

The health theme built on this foundation developed until she broke into the middle of a letter early in July to say that "I had to put this letter aside because I was feeling so awful. I'm not going to get my health back until I see you—and I die when you don't write...."

That line also having proved unproductive by the end of the month, she then tried another:

*There's a Count Ribbing here now under an assumed
name, the famous accomplice of Anckarstrom [in the
matter of the assassination of Gustavus the Third]. We
don't receive him. But under two different pretexts
he's found ways of speaking to us when we've been
out walking. He has a magnificent face, for women
who like what are called good looks, but for a conspirator he's too much like Comte Etienne, too plump
and too foppish. And his talk is more teasing than
forceful. For the rest he has a great fancy to be in love
with me, but as Monsieur de Staël is here the ambas-
sadorial dignity attaching to me doesn't allow me to
see him. Seriously, is there a man in the world who
would dare to love your mistress....*

A year of increasingly despairing, and increasingly
bullying, letters lies between this reference to Ribbing and
its explanation:

*You'll remember what I said on the subject of M.
Ribbing. I went further twenty times. I was ready to
give myself to him. I was wrong enough to let him
love me madly, so that I could pick up from the excess
of the despair in this strong soul a sort of excitement
that would relieve for a moment the terrible weight
that was pressing on my heart. If I thought that his
inconceivable beauty could move me, and that by
giving myself to him I could enjoy five minutes of
intoxication, I'd do it tonight.*

But, she went on, experience had taught her that it
couldn't be done:

*I told him, "All right. I love you. I think I can do it."
He threw himself at my feet. He wanted to take me in
his arms, but the chill of death swept over me and I
had to tell him that you alone, of all the men in the
world, have the rights to my heart. After one of these
scenes he was left unconscious for half an hour....
I was forced to send him away, at least for a time. He's
too good, too kind, for me to allow him to attach himself by hope to my sad life....*

There is an almost appealing transparency about these lines, recalling those bogus confessions offered by Proust's Albertine to his Marcel which revealed even more than they were intended to conceal. But the question of why Ribbing should have been brought into Madame de Staël's correspondence with Monsieur de Narbonne at all is not altogether simple. She begun sleeping with him soon after she first met him—the indications are that by this time she was thinking of sexual intercourse as little more than the logical sequel to an interesting or intellectually challenging conversation with a likable man—and it seems extraordinary that she should bring his name up in a fashion calculated to raise Monsieur de Narbonne's suspicions of what was going on when trying to persuade him to join her in Switzerland and to resume their relationship.

But the more thought that is given to this correspondence, the less it seems straightforward in the realm of motivations and intentions. In its later stages Madame de Staël was clearly bent on being unpleasant to her lover and on establishing conditions that would make it impossible for them to get together again—unless he had some pressing need to be made to live a dog's life. When she had gone to join him in England in January of 1793, Monsieur de Narbonne was sick with misery brought on by the recent execution of Louis XVI and the horrors of the Terror in general. The only tolerable future that he could imagine for himself was based on a script in which he maintained his position as an important public figure in order to take part in the restoration of stability, order, and some kind of limited monarchy when the wave of revolution had passed its peak and begun to recede. It was essential to the execution of this game plan that he should reappear on the postrevolutionary scene so far as possible uncompromised by connections with those responsible for the prerevolutionary debacle.

When Madame de Staël left England in May she had bulldozed him into giving her his word that he would join her in Switzerland within four months. As his execution of this program would have established him as her creature—and as a pensioner of her father, who was then looked upon by most aristocrats as the primary architect of the Revolution—she had in fact persuaded him to promise her to commit political suicide. Since the promise was one that could not be kept by a man in his right mind, it seems legitimate to assume that she was driven by some psychological necessity to put herself in the position of his moral creditor. From the time that she parted from him at Dover in May 1793 until the correspondence finally came to an end a year later, she bore down on him with all the affectionate warmth of a finance company's collection agent. Each time he presented her with some fresh pretext for postponing his self-immolation she pounced on him, tearing his arguments apart with the contemporary equivalent of a triumphant "now I've got you, you son-of-a-bitch." Toward the end of November 1793, she produced the following:

> You tell Mathieu in a letter of the 27th of October that you're coming here, and then in another to Monsieur Lock of the 7th and to de Ricé of the 12th, you deny that you've any such plan. What wretched trickery! But let's leave expressions of feeling out of it. Nothing can move you, and you demean yourself by your extraordinary ingratitude, just as you lose both the respect of your friends and the love of a woman whose life or death will teach you to regret her, by your incredible blindness. Are you still left with the capacity to do anything straightforward, and would your staggering hypocrisy allow you to try a day of truthfulness? I'm coming round to my original project of coming to England. It suits me personally, and, further, I've things to talk to you about—not about a feeling for you that has been destroyed, along with the respect that inspired it, but about my situation, which could be made a good deal less unpleasant by a few gestures on your part. The fate of my children, and my peace of mind, are in your hands.... I'm still supposing that you won't decline to lend yourself to what would perhaps prevent the ruin of my children's lives and

fortunes. That apart, there's very little that I wouldn't put past you, and if it wasn't for the children's sake I wouldn't ever want to see you again. Answer me only if you will be in England in six weeks or two months time, but tell me the truth. You've been wallowing in lies to such an extent for six months now that a moment of simplicity and candor would give you a nice rest. I've the cold scorn for you of a soul above yours...and I foresee an end to my long sufferings with calm, with that detachment from life which has to be born in a heart that understood you too late, and which lost in a painful moment the illusion it had cherished. The spectacle of what goes on in France encourages, there's no possibility of doubting it, every kind of crime and indecency. Indecency, yes, the word is the right one for the ungrateful man who, the minute that he realizes that he has no further need for you, abandons you to despair. You're as far from being what I thought you as Danton is from Tancredi. I've lost Monsieur de Narbonne. The father of my children must still look out for their interests, but my friend is dead and I wish to follow him. The man I loved is dead, the specter who has taken his name dishonors it, and it's in the grave that I'll find him again.

This delightful love letter, dated November 23, crossed another, rather more restrained, communication from Monsieur de Narbonne saying that he was about to leave England for Switzerland. Not altogether surprisingly he canceled this plan when he received the letter above and felt relieved of the necessity of replying to it. Since Madame de Staël was a games player, it did not occur to her that she could have offended him by writing as she had done, just as it would not occur to a tennis player that an opponent could resent being served an ace. When he failed to appear she consequently assumed that he had carried out his plan and that he had run into some kind of trouble en route. When she still had heard nothing of him by December 12 she asked her husband to use his position as a diplomat to try to find out if anything untoward could have happened to him. On the following day she had a letter from the missing man letting her know that he had never left England. When she realized that she had been worrying over nothing she immediately snatched up her pen to take vengeance:

> *You can't be expecting anything from me, sir, but an expression of the profound contempt with which your letter has filled me. You tell me on the fifteenth that you are leaving, and ten days later a new pretext holds you back. And you dare to speak to me thus, and you dare to use the language of understanding to me after this exhibition of the brashest and vilest ingratitude. I'm staying in Switzerland. I'm not leaving. And let me assure you that I'll die there in despair at having known and loved you, the least of men. If it's possible for you to have any feeling of pity for me after the way you've been playing with me you will come to accept the treasure that I wish to entrust to you. You are detestable, but perhaps it will be too much even for you to refuse to accept your son from the hands of the mother you've managed to kill....*

Madame de Staël kept up this fantastic bombardment through January and February and in March 1794 wrote an eight-page diatribe (with a two-sheet appendix written on the following day) that reached a new level of intensity and absurdity.

> *I don't know what this letter means. Perhaps it's crazy—perhaps it is self-defeating—it could turn you against me. For the last six months I haven't been able to open a book or to write a single line of my own. All I can do when I'm alone is cry or move about in the agitation of madness. When I'd written this letter I spent a day coughing up blood, a consequence of the convulsions that racked me when I'd finished it; poor Monsieur de Ribbing...thought I was going to die, and in spite of his own feelings for me, prayed for your arrival as the only thing that might save me....*

Soon after this Madame Necker began to die, and this new element in the situation was rapidly turned to account.

> I must write you once again to tell you what hap-
> pened to me this morning. My mother almost died
> during the night of a horrifying attack of suffocation.
> She sent for me. She said to me: "My child, I'm dying
> of grief brought on by your guilty and public attach-
> ment. You are being punished for it by the way its
> object is treating you: he is breaking off what my
> prayers couldn't persuade you to give up. The care you
> take of your father will win you my forgiveness in
> heaven. Don't answer me. Leave me. I haven't the
> strength to argue with you now....

This might have been more effective had it not been immediately recognizable as a paraphrase of the remarks addressed to the Princesse de Clèves by Madame de Chartres when she was dying in the pages of the famous novel, and if it had not been linked to a discussion of the possibility of Monsieur de Narbonne's chances of recovering his—or rather his wife's—colonial properties before some radical change in the French internal situation should occur. Madame de Staël argued vehemently, as she had often done before, that this possibility did not exist, either in the short term or the long, and insisted that he had much more to gain financially by sticking to her than by pinning his hopes on a dramatic change in his wife's fortunes. The coarseness of her efforts to buy him, and the rapidity with which she switches from emotional to purely mercenary appeals are among the more repulsive aspects of the correspondence, but they seem to be comparatively innocuous in the general context of her sustained and determined effort to make the man she was pretending to be in love with think ill of himself and concede that his only role in life was to be her creature.

The steam ran out of the exchange after Madame de Staël's mother died, but, more significantly, after Monsieur de Narbonne decided that he could no longer stay on as a refugee in a country that was at war with France and that he would, after all, join his importunate mistress in Switzerland. This decision, coming when it did, finally convinced her that he would never wholly subordinate his interests to hers and that he was determined that their relationship should never be the dominant element in his life: like most active and ambitious men he believed that his personal affairs should be fitted to his career rather than that they should shape it. As she began to recognize that there was something obdurate in him that she wasn't going to be able to overcome she eased the pain of her defeat by writing him out of her system. During the early summer of 1794 she revised an essay that she had been working on for the past three years, entitled *On the Influence of the Passions on the Happiness of Individuals and of Nations* so as to make room for a description of him as the archetype of the ungrateful man and to omit the more flattering account of him that she had put into it when she was under the impression that she had him where she wanted him. She also settled down to write the novel called *Zulma*, which has the central theme of the sufferings endured by a warm-hearted, generous, and noble-spirited woman who made the mistake of loving and doing tremendous things for an ungrateful and unworthy man. As soon as that was finished she plunged into a second novel, *Mirza*, in which another female paragon made sacrifice after sacrifice for another undeserving monster of male egotism.

While working on these almost entirely meritless productions Madame de Staël went to call, in the capacity of a professional colleague, on one of the most intellectually distinguished women writers of the day, Madame de Charrière, whose *Caliste* she was striving to imitate. The two women had encountered each other in a literary, though not a physical, sense six years earlier when Madame de Staël had first broken into print with her *Letters on the Work and Character of Jean-Jacques Rousseau*. This contained a gratuitous libel on Thérèse Levasseur, the servant who had been Rousseau's mistress until he tired of her and who had thereafter stayed on with him for several years, to nurse him devotedly through his last illness. For reasons best

known to herself Madame de Staël chose to tell the world
that Rousseau had been driven to desperation by Thérèse's
infidelities to him and had committed suicide. The poor
woman suddenly found herself with the reputation of a
murderess and was soon in deep trouble. Subjected to a
boycott by her neighbors in her native village, she could
neither get work nor buy anything in the local shops. She
was illiterate and without the means she would require
to clear her name in the courts. A friend of Rousseau's who
knew the facts brought Madame de Charrière's attention
to the case, and in order to put the record straight she wrote
Madame de Staël an open letter over Thérèse's signature and
distributed it to a number of newspapers for publication.
As it was written in a beautifully simple and direct style,
and effortlessly convicted Madame de Staël of having been
unkind, unjust, and irresponsible, it attracted a great deal
of attention and did not please her at all. She did what
she could to suppress the letter by buying up all the unsold
copies of the journals in which it had appeared, and had
elaborate inquiries made in order to find out who had
written it. When she learned who had been responsible
she affected to have known all along—"Who else could
have written it but Madame de Charrière?"

There was thus a certain tension in the air on the day
in the summer of 1794 when Madame de Staël's enormous
yellow coach pulled by six horses deposited her at Madame
de Charrière's doorstep at Colombier. Madame de Charrière's baptismal name was Agnes Isabella Elisabeth van
Tuyll van Serooskerken van Zuylen, and she was a member
of one of the most aristocratic and austerely virtuous
families in Holland. She received Madame de Staël in a
dress of gray homespun. Madame de Staël was in mourning
for her mother and wearing a grotesque outfit that involved
yards and yards of black tulle and inordinate quantities
of dyed plumage from birds-of-paradise. Madame de Charrière thought Madame de Staël an extravagant vulgarian,
and Madame de Staël thought *her* a frump who had let
herself go disgracefully.

The two women exchanged civil incivilities for what re-

mained of a long Sunday afternoon, and when the visitor
had gone Madame de Charrière sat down to put her impressions on paper for the benefit of the young man, twenty-
seven years her junior, who had been her passionate friend
and the center of her life for nearly eight years. They had
often talked about Madame de Staël, her goings-on, her pretensions, and the awfulness of her style—particularly in her
grotesquely inflated appeal to the women of the world to
rally to the rescue of Marie-Antoinette ("Women of all
countries, of all classes, listen and be moved, as I am..."),
and they had agreed that she must be a horror. But now
Madame de Charrière had to admit that there was something to be said for her.

The first impression admittedly was bad. Madame de
Charrière did not care for the large red face, the badly arranged hair, the indecent (as she thought) display of cleav-
age, the way the woman continually fidgeted and twiddled
a twig between her fingers as she talked, or for her extrava-
gances of gesture and expression; but if her ideas were mediocre, they were fluent, and they had color and glow:

> I think that if I were a queen I would keep her at
> court to talk to me, for she talks amazingly well. She
> has a beautiful voice and her diction is perfect—how
> rare to find so many things together. Yes—I must con-
> cede that this young woman has so much charm that
> she makes you believe that she is beautiful.... We have
> been less than just to her, I think. But I am still of your
> opinion, Madame de Staël's brilliance is false, and her
> sentiments are all glitter. But you must hear her talk.
> I'm impatient to know what you think of her.

This inflamed the young man's curiosity, and when he
next passed Monsieur Necker's house at Coppet he called
and left his card. He was told that Madame de Staël had
just left for the rented house at Mézéry where she had been
living since her mother's death in May. He overtook her
huge coach at Nyon, where its six horses were being wa-
tered at a roadside fountain, and introduced himself. Madame de Staël asked him to join her on the next stage of

her journey to Lausanne, and when he had handed his horse to a groom he stepped into the famous yellow vehicle.

Madame de Staël was returning to her home after attending the bizarre funeral that her mother had demanded: it had called for her to be laid to rest in a glass-topped stone tank filled with alcohol in which she hoped to be preserved like a medical specimen. She was not upset by that, however, but by an article attacking her which had appeared in a newspaper that morning, accusing her of harboring dangerous revolutionists and constitutionalists in her house at Mézéry. She railed at the author of the article and told the young man how she intended to make things hot for him. The young man argued the point: if she was, as she declared, truly a liberal, she was bound to stand up for the freedom of the press, even when the press attacked her family and her friends, and she could not with a good conscience bring sanctions to bear on the offending journalist...

Madame de Staël enjoyed the argument, and four days later the young man wrote to tell Madame de Charrière that he had ridden with her to Mézéry, and that he had supped, breakfasted, and supped again with her. When Monsieur de Charrière went into Lausanne on business a couple of weeks later he found that everyone was talking about Madame de Staël's conquest of the young man who had been his wife's protégé for the past eight years. When he returned to Colombier he let her know of it, and she wrote the young man a letter of rebuke in the form of a rhymed fable about a faithful old hound who didn't like being abandoned by its master when he fell for a sleek young mongrel bitch with a lot of smart tricks. He replied, crushingly:

> *Far from feeling it an effort to find praise to throw to Madame de Staël, it is with difficulty that I refrain from extolling her extravagantly. I have seldom seen such a combination of amazing and attractive qualities, so much brilliance coupled with so much good sense, such expansive, positive kindness, such im-*

mense generosity, such gentle and sustained polite-
ness in society, and such absence of all restraint in
intimacy. She is the second woman I have known who
could be all the world to me, who could become to me
a world in herself, you know who was the first.... In
short she is a being apart, a superior being, such as is
found perhaps once in a century, and those who have
access to her, and who know her and are her friends,
must ask no other happiness.

Madame de Charrière was appalled and gave up on him instantly. If *that* was what he wanted! "Love her! Become an Enthusiast! You have the right—just as I have the right to send you no more letters...."

The second of Madame de Charrière's ironic recommendations is easy to misunderstand since the sting has gone out of the words "Enthusiast" and "Enthusiasm." Most people nowadays would assume that it was better to be an enthusiast than not, and that enthusiasm was a good thing in itself, as evidence of a positive rather than a negative frame of mind. For an eighteenth-century rationalist, such as Madame de Charrière was, the words meant something specific and pejorative. To her an Enthusiast was a sloppy, undisciplined thinker who avoided the difficulties of difficult problems by using a wordy rhetoric composed of ill-defined terms; and Enthusiasm was self-serving posturing designed to inflate the Enthusiast's sense of his own importance. Madame de Staël was later, in her book on Germany and German culture, *De l'Allemagne*, to define Enthusiasm in terms that confirm Madame de Charrière's view of the matter:

Many people are prejudiced against Enthusiasm: they
confuse it with fanaticism, and that's a big mistake.
Fanaticism is an exclusive passion which has an opin-
ion as its object. Enthusiasm rallies to the idea of
universal harmony: it's the love of the fine, the eleva-
tion of the soul, the sweetness of dedication, englobed
in a single feeling which possesses grandeur and calm.

The meaning that the word held for the Greeks is its
noblest definition: for them Enthusiasm meant God
within us. Indeed when a human being lives his life
to the full there is something of the divine in it....

As a woman of the rationalist enlightenment, Madame
de Charrière was in effect telling the young man to go to
the Romantic hell of his own choosing in a less kindly way
than her words might at first suggest. The young man so
dismissed was Benjamin Constant, and for thirteen years
he was to fill the place in Madame de Staël's life that she
had designed originally for Monsieur de Narbonne.

From the time his mother died when he was just two
weeks old onward, everything conspired to make Benjamin
Constant the perfect match for Madame de Staël. His
father, a professional soldier named Juste de Constant de
Rebecque, who was Colonel commanding the Swiss regiment in the Dutch army, viewed his son with that nice
balance of affection and loathing often found when the
birth of the child has cost the mother her life. Constant
himself felt that shyness accounted for the fact that his
father could not bear to show him any signs of affection
when they met, and could not endure his company for more
than an hour at a stretch; but his account of their relationship makes it sound much more likely that his father's am-
bivalence had its source in feelings of guilt roused by the
mother's death.

But however that may have been, Juste de Constant's eccentricities of judgment and lack of plain commonsense
were such that there were no circumstances in which it
would have been easy to be his son. When he was on leave
in the summer of 1761, before his marriage to Benjamin's
mother, he visited his sister who was living in the neighborhood of Lausanne and learned from her that a nine-
year-old girl in a nearby village, called Jeanne Suzanne
Magnin, was attracting a good deal of interest and attention by virtue of her unusual intelligence. Juste remarked
that it would be a wonderful thing for a man to get hold of

such a child in order to raise it up to be his ideal woman. Nobody attached any importance to his indulgence in this Pygmalion fantasy at the time, but at the end of his leave Juste de Constant took his post-chaise to the child's village, found her, bundled her into it, and drove off with her to Holland. And there, in spite of violent protests from the girl's parents and most of the members of his own family, he kept her until she had turned twenty and he had made her his mistress. He then brought her back to Switzerland and, to the accompaniment of another storm of protest from his female relatives, put her in charge of the five-year-old Benjamin. Though the arrangement lasted for only two years, and he claimed not to have realized the nature of his father's relationship with the girl (now known as Marianne) until nearly twenty-eight years later, he clearly divined something of what was going on, for he conceived an obsessive hatred of her which lasted for the rest of his life.

After Marianne, Constant had a succession of tutors, each less wisely chosen than the last: a German sadist who whipped him furiously and then smothered him with kisses, a maddish Frenchman who took the boy to live with him in a brothel, a Belgian music master who simply turned him loose to read what he liked in a lending library specializing in pornography, a French lawyer who had been forced to leave Paris after being involved in some kind of scandal and who turned out to be as disreputable as he was ignorant, an unfrocked priest called Duplessis, an Englishman called Mr. May, and an immensely slow and unintelligent Mr. Brudel.

When these impossible tutors had done their worst with the boy, his father placed him at the University of Erlangen for a year before transferring him to Edinburgh University. At Erlangen Constant, who was then fourteen years of age, became a sort of pet monster of the Dowager Margravine of Anspach-Bayreuth who taught him how to gamble. He ran heavily into debt, and had to be bailed out by his father. In his eighteen months at Edinburgh he gambled even more recklessly, lost such large sums that he doubted his father's ability or willingness to pay up, and absconded leaving his debts unpaid. Juste de Constant then sent him to Paris to be a private pupil of a distinguished man of letters, Jean Baptiste Suard, but Benjamin ignored his new tutor-custodian in favor of a young English rake who took him the rounds of the Parisian brothels and gaming houses and got him into more trouble. At the end of that episode Juste de Constant put Benjamin in the charge of a moral guardian, recommended for the job by the chaplain of the Dutch Embassy, who proved in the event to be even more dissolute and irresponsible than the young Englishman—and just as fond of brothels and high play.

It is not altogether surprising that with this upbringing behind him Constant should have spent the early years of his manhood sponging on a series of older women and bored wives from whom he "borrowed" the money he needed to spend on prostitutes and to lose at cards. But the full strength of his basic compulsion to seek out losing situations for himself only became apparent when he embarked on his first marriage. In the winter of 1787 there was trouble in Juste de Constant's regiment which led to a strike of its officers, all of whom refused to serve under his command for any further period. A court of inquiry was convened, and a verdict in favor of the officers, reprimanding Juste de Constant and suspending him from duty, was about to be handed down in August 1788 when he disappeared. Benjamin, who was then an official at the Court of Brunswick, was notified and made his way to Amsterdam to find out what had happened. He learned that his father was not only in trouble in the matter of his career, he was also enormously in debt.

Constant became convinced that his father had committed suicide and spent several altogether fruitless and unhappy days trying to find out what had happened to the body. He then returned to Brunswick, where he learned that his father had simply run away and hidden himself in Switzerland, a move that complicated his situation by making him technically a deserter. What would happen to him was not clear, but what was obvious was that he was a ruined man whose debts, and the legal costs of extricating him from his present difficulties, would eat up the greater part of his estate, if not all of it.

Constant, who had until then lived as a rich man's son with the expectation of a substantial inheritance to look forward to, now realized that he was, in effect, ruined too. His reaction was to seek out a means of compounding his ill fortune. In November 1788 he was attending a court ball in Brunswick in his line of duty as a court chamberlain when he noticed a young woman sitting weeping in one of the anterooms. He asked her what the matter was, and she told him that nobody loved her or wanted her and that she was consequently feeling as miserable as could be. He immediately proposed to her and was accepted.

Wilhelmina von Cramm was plain, she had no money, she was nine years older than Constant, she did not love him, he didn't love her, and they had few tastes in common. The marriage was patently one of those arrangements in which misery can be seen to be seeking out misery in search of further affliction, and which may be said to be made to block off even the possibility of anything else. It had, significantly, been ended by divorce in January of the year in which Constant met Madame de Staël for the first time. When he got up into her coach at Nyon that day in September he was for the moment free of any entanglement that he could rely on as a source of humiliation and distress.

The year that saw the end of Madame de Staël's relationship with Monsieur de Narbonne and the beginning of her involvement with Benjamin Constant was a turning point in the development of the Revolution in France. The Terror reached its peak of horror in the late spring and early summer, and the enormous numbers of manifestly unnecessary arrests and executions brought on an anti-Jacobin reaction, leading to the arrest and execution of Robespierre at the end of July. During the winter that followed his fall the Revolutionary Tribunal, the Committees of Public Safety, and all the other improvised organs that had been the engines of the Jacobin tyranny were either done away with altogether or brought under the restraint of formal legal procedures. In the following March the surviving Girondists were amnestied and invited to return from exile, and in April a Committee of Eleven charged with the task of drafting a constitution was empaneled by the Convention. At the end of the month Monsieur de Staël, who had been declared *persona non grata* when the Jacobins were in power, was given a vote of confidence by that body, and asked to reopen the sealed Swedish Embassy in the Rue du Bac.

Encouraged by these signs that the wave of revolutionary violence and extremism was spent, and by the restoration of the diplomatic immunity that she enjoyed as an Ambassador's wife, Madame de Staël found a safe harbor in the territory of the Bishop of Basle for the little nest of Constitutionalist refugees, Monsieur de Narbonne included, that she had been maintaining at Mézéry, and she left for Paris with Constant in May. Monsieur Necker saw them go with a good deal of apprehension and sent his daughter a note of caution just before she set out:

> *Do not forget, my dearest Minette, all the troubles and vexations that you let yourself in for last time. And may I implore Monsieur de Constant not to encourage you, but to give you counsel of prudence and patience....*

Madame de Staël paid him no heed and soon had a political salon established in the Embassy's drawing-rooms. She issued a pamphlet, *Reflections on Peace, Addressed to Mr. Pitt and to the French,* calling for a negotiated end to the war of intervention by the allied monarchies which she had previously supported as the one hope of crushing the revolution, and she gathered round her a group of middle-of-the-road Republicans who favored the introduction of representative government on the English plan, with the vote restricted to the property-owning classes, at the earliest possible date.

Whatever might be said in favor of the English system in theory, the situation in France at that time made the program reckless in the extreme. It was quite clear that the property owners in the country would, if given the chance, elect a legislature with a mandate to take vengeance on the members of the Convention who had either supported or failed to resist the Terror. This hypothetical question became a vital issue when the Committee of Eleven reported to the Convention in June with the recommendations that universal suffrage be abolished, and that the vote should be restricted to owners of property above a stated annual value who should elect property owners over the age of thirty to a bicameral legislature. When it became obvious to the Convention that the mood of the country was such as to make it impossible for them to reject the Committee of Eleven's draft constitution out of hand, its members fell into something of a panic in which they came up with the Baudin Amendment. This provided that two-thirds of the membership of the two chambers should consist of former members of the Convention, who would not be required to stand for election.

Soon after the terms of the proposed amendment had been published Benjamin Constant published three anonymous articles in the magazine *Les Nouvelles politiques* attacking it as being unsound in principle and manifestly unjust. The articles were eagerly received by the reactionaries and the Royalist counterrevolutionaries who were hoping to legislate a new Terror of the right, and Constant was approached by a leader of the Girondists who, not knowing who had written them, insisted that they urgently required an answer and that he was the man for the job.

As Constant had given no serious thought to the practical aspects of the question up to that point, the Girondin's arguments struck him with considerable force, and he spent most of the succeeding forty-eight hours writing a brilliant refutation of his own articles which proved that the passage of Baudin's amendment was essential if the Republic were to survive. This was the first of the long series of wild plunges followed by self-reversals that were to make Benjamin himself and the Constant–Madame de Staël team notorious for lack of principle and opportunism.

The Baudin Amendment was passed and became law in

August, and at the beginning of October, a month before
the two-chamber system was to replace the Convention,
the Royalists called the Paris mob into the streets to protest
against the installation of this unelected legislature. The
protest turned, as its promoters had hoped, into something
like an insurrection, but just as it seemed to reach the
brink of success Paul Barras called on the young General
Buonaparte to come to the aid of the civil power. He broke
the back of the rising in a matter of hours by bringing massive forces into Paris and using artillery to clear the streets.

In the face of this display of firmness the Royalist threat
disappeared instantly, and the new bicameral legislature
under control of former members of the Convention was
installed in November, though not precisely as planned.
Between the "whiff of grapeshot" of October 4 and the
changeover on November 3 Barras had invented a new body,
to which the reformed legislature was subordinate, the
five-man Directory. Its members consisted of three non-
entities, La Revellière-Lépeaux, Rewbell, and Letourner;
a used-up man, Carnot; and Barras, who was in effective
control. Madame de Staël was shrewd enough to recognize
that much, but not to see that Barras, who had organized
the destruction of Robespierre, could not have reached his
position as head of the Directory if he had been a fool. She
accordingly made the mistake of approaching him, on Constant's behalf, in a manner that aroused his indignation
and contempt:

> She advanced toward me, holding Benjamin Constant
> by the hand. "Here," she said, "is a young man of
> astonishing intelligence who is with us; he is devoted
> to the good cause, he is entirely ours." Madame
> de Staël's protégé was a tall, affected, and foolish-
> looking youth, with fiery red hair, and small eyes
> which one would have supposed also to be red had
> they not been hidden by green spectacles. A delicate,
> ironical mouth—seeming to make fun of everything,
> even of its owner—such was Benjamin Constant.
> I thanked Madame de Staël, and waited for the young
> neophyte to say something in his turn. Twisting his

body into all sorts of contortions, he stammered out:
"Citizen Director, it would make me very happy if
you would accept this short treatise which I now
have the honor to offer you." This sentence was spoken
with...an effeminate stutter, in which the letter "s"
was pronounced as if it were "z"....

Unaware of the impression she was making, and of the
folly of her proceedings, Madame de Staël moved in on the
lower house of the new legislature and attempted to operate
as a species of floor leader for the group of deputies who
attended her salon from the seat in the diplomatic gallery
in which she was entitled to sit as the Swedish Ambassador's wife. Her lordly way of summoning the ushers as
if they were her personal servants whenever she wished
to send a note to one of the deputies on the floor soon attracted the attention of those who were not of her party
and gave rise to hostile comment—but it did not occur to
her that there was anything odd or objectionable about what
she was doing. Monsieur de Staël was made almost frantic
with anxiety as the volume and the bitterness of the criticism of his wife's behavior grew, and he was reduced to
dropping hints to the authorities that he would be greatly
obliged if they would deport his wife before she got him
into serious trouble with his government. His pathetic
maneuvers were forestalled when a deputy in the lower
house named Legendre rose to denounce Madame de Staël
as a Swiss meddler in French affairs who should be sent
back where she came from without delay. She was, as a result, ignominiously expelled from France in December,
after a stay of eight months.

When Madame de Staël returned to Switzerland to stay
with her father at Coppet she was smarting from more than
a political defeat; her amatory life had also taken a turn
that she did not like when a man she set out to capture
had turned her down flat. The story of this reverse, when
it is placed in the context of her developing relationship
with Constant, is full of a sinister interest. At the beginning
of 1795, in January, Madame de Staël had entered into a

compact with Constant which was given written form and signed by both parties:

> *We promise to dedicate our lives to each other; we declare that we regard ourselves as indissolubly bound to each other; that our future destiny shall be in every sense a common destiny; that we shall never, either of us, contract any other connection; and that, the moment we are in a position to do so, we shall render even closer the bonds which now unite us.*

This idealistic bond was presently reinforced by the financial one that Madame de Staël had constructed with both Talleyrand and Monsieur de Narbonne. French currency was exceedingly soft at the time and Swiss francs were hard. Anyone who had Swiss money could therefore buy French francs at an enormous discount. In ordinary circumstances there is little point in exchanging soft for hard currency, but in this instance there was a plausible reason for doing so. The French government was selling off the real estate confiscated during the Revolution from the church, the proscribed aristocrats, and the émigrés, and was accepting its own depreciated currency at its face value in payment. Anyone able to obtain cheap francs was thus in a position to make a killing. Madame de Staël apprised Constant of the opportunities open to him in this field, and when he told her what his financial position was approached her father on his behalf in order to raise a loan. Monsieur Necker agreed to make Constant a loan equal to any amount that he could raise himself. This neat standoff failed of its purpose as Juste de Constant, the prodigal father, had taken elaborate steps to save the properties that had come to him as part of his first wife's dowry from the shipwreck of his fortunes and had deeded them to her son. Constant had thus become the owner of a charming country house known as La Chablière which had been the home of his crippled cousin Rosalie for the greater part of her life.

Rosalie de Constant had been horribly injured by a fall

in her childhood, and had armed herself against the long years of spinsterhood to which she appeared to be doomed by training herself as a botanical draftsman and undertaking an index of the flora of the Swiss mountains. This field had not then been covered, and her collection of three thousand exquisite drawings with their attached descriptions was a work of real value to botanists. Madame de Staël, however, cared nothing for Rosalie or work, and pointed out that if Constant were to sell La Chablière the sum he would then have, with the matching loan from her father, would be an interesting one, in the French sense. Constant initially resisted this infamous proposal, but he was borne down, with the result that Rosalie presently described in a letter to Madame de Charrière:

> ...one day Madame de Staël burst into my room with Benjamin. I was working on my paintings of Alpine flowers. She brushed them aside rudely. "What a silly occupation!" she said. She meant no harm, she is just imperious, careless of the feelings of others. She came to tell me that La Chablière must be sold. It was she, of course, who pushed Benjamin to decide upon this. Madame de Staël, who seems so enchanting, at first, is a person it is not safe to know, except at a distance....

She was in due course evicted from La Chablière, but what did that matter, when Constant had his seventy thousand Swiss francs to gamble on the French real estate market and was to that extent under an obligation to his captor? What is curious and revealing is that her immediate reaction to her success in getting Constant into her debt was to embark on a campaign to subjugate another man. This was François de Pange, a young aristocrat and a member of Monsieur de Narbonne's circle of Constitutionalists, who was very much in love with a Madame de Sérilly, a young widow who had narrowly escaped sharing her husband's fate as a victim of the guillotine, and who was in love with him. He had no interest in becoming Madame de Staël's lover and told her so politely but firmly from the outset, but she nonetheless kept up her efforts to break up his engagement and to force herself on him throughout the year. There is no record of what they said to each other when they met, but a fascinating correspondence survives in which an altogether adult de Pange refuses again and again to be drawn into the destructive game that Madame de Staël was proposing to him. De Pange knew Constant well (they were arrested together by a suspicious patrol as they were walking home from a gambling den on the night of the whiff of grapeshot), and it may well have been that he realized that his function as her lover would have been primarily to complicate her relationship with his friend and to be the necessary third in a game of "Let's you and him fight." All she could manage in that line, however, as a result of de Pange's cool determination to retain control of his situation and his options, was to throw a tremendous scene, with attempts at self-strangulation with a scarf and much noisy screaming, for Constant's benefit when the news that de Pange was married reached Coppet in January of 1796.

For the greater part of the next two years Madame de Staël and Constant paid the price for their ill-advised meddling in the crisis that gave birth to the Directory. When they were permitted to return to France toward the end of the year, they were not allowed to go to Paris or to come within approximately twenty miles of it. Madame de Staël thus exchanged boredom at Coppet (the worst aspect of which was the necessity of listening to her father's conversation) for boredom at Hérivaux, Constant's newly acquired country estate in the neighborhood of Chantilly to the north of Paris.

In their last days at Coppet Madame de Staël became pregnant, and this had more than the obvious effect on their life at Hérivaux since the property that Constant had acquired had been an Abbey before its confiscation. The people of the neighborhood did not care to see an unmarried Protestant couple taking the place of the monks, and when Madame de Staël's pregnancy became evident they were even less pleased. She may or may not have been aware that the servants at Coppet always referred to her as "the monster," but at least the surrounding countryside had a proper respect for her father's fortune. At Hérivaux, however, she was simply an immoral foreigner, and for the first time in her life she had to face an openly contemptuous neighborhood. She was happy to get away when she received permission to go into Paris for her *accouchement* in June.

Constant's daughter Albertine was born to her on June 9, and in July she was already involved in the deepening crisis in French affairs created by the victory of the Right in the May elections. The now deeply discredited Directory was faced with the problem of governing in conflict with a hostile Legislature that it had no legal means of dissolving, and was in serious trouble. Madame de Staël, presuming on her earlier acquaintance with Barras, the strong man in the Directory, made her way to him and persuaded him that a first step toward a solution of his difficulties would be to strengthen his cabinet by appointing Talleyrand, lately back from exile in the United States, to be Minister for Foreign Affairs. All the available evidence suggests that she didn't understand the gravity of the situation and that she believed Talleyrand to be a Constitutionalist—as he had been, back when. She also appears to have believed that the former Bishop of Autun was capable of gratitude and would pay the new debt he owed her by making her Benjamin Secretary General of the Foreign Office.

Talleyrand, however, seems not only to have thought very little of Constant's abilities, but also to have come to the conclusion that the ideas of the Constitutionalists had been made irrelevant by developments that made some sort of *coup d'état* a necessity. As soon as he was a Minister he became a partner in Barras's conspiracy to solve the problem of the right-wing legislature by military action.

The general Barras turned to was, again, Bonaparte; but he was in the thick of his second Italian campaign and for the moment too busy to leave the front. He sent his lieutenant, General Angereau, to Paris to take the necessary action in his place. The military moved in on the legislature on

September 4, after taking possession of all the key points in the city, and compelled it to pass a bill which annulled the elections of May, unseated the two hundred deputies forming the backbone of the counterrevolutionary right, and gave the Directory power to send any persons conspiring against the Republic to the penal colony of Cayenne.

Madame de Staël and Constant were, as liberals and Constitutionalists, oddly employed on the night of the coup. They were dining with Barras in his apartment in the Luxembourg Palace. The experience of being once again at the very center of things was exhilarating, and in the intoxication of the moment they both endorsed the coup, and went on record as hailing September 4 as "this immortal day."

Soon after this stirring event had taken place Madame de Staël learned from either Barras or Talleyrand that the real man behind the coup was not General Angereau but Bonaparte, and that the future lay with him. Her reaction was to concoct a fantasy in which she took the place of Joséphine and became a partner in his destiny. She began her campaign to realize this dream by bombarding the general with letters addressed to his headquarters in the field in Italy, one of which contained the striking thought that it was grotesque that so great a man should be married to "an insignificant creole, altogether incapable of understanding or appreciating his heroic qualities."

When Bonaparte reached Paris with the radiance of his Italian success about him in December he was aware that Madame de Staël was after him, but he was utterly unprepared for the vulgar silliness and folly with which she would carry on her public and private campaign to get him. This not only revolted him in the way that men and women are apt to be revolted by persistent sexual overtures from the totally unsympathetic and physically repellent, but also outraged him as a public man with a lively sense of what could make him ridiculous. The Royalist press had been caricaturing Madame de Staël viciously ever since her plunge into Republican politics when the Baudin Amendment was the issue of the day, and the reckless way in which she had carried on her affairs with Constant and her other

lovers under her husband's nose had given them a powerful lever to use against her. The phrase that she herself
had used as a description of her husband in the early days
of her marriage, the *homme-femme*, was now being freely
applied to her in pointed lampoons and scandal sheets
distributed by the Royalists. In them she was depicted as
a sexually ambiguous lecher running a string of "wives,"
who were in turn held up to contempt as having more interest in Monsieur Necker's millions than in their own
pride. When those feminists and Napoleonophobes who
find Madame de Staël admirable speak of Bonaparte as
having been overcome by panic when faced with her, because his antifeminist attitude made him fearful of a truly
liberated woman, they ignore the fact that even the appearance of involvement with her would have made it possible
for his Royalist opponents to ridicule him as a member of
a grotesque sexual circus. He avoided and repulsed her for
the sake of his immediate and future political health, and
with good reason. His negative determination to have nothing to do with her changed to active hostility after a ridiculous incident in which his butler had to use force to prevent
her from breaking in on him when he was stark naked in
his bathtub in his house in the Rue Chantereine. Infuriated by this episode, Bonaparte insisted that she be expelled
from France, so she found herself once again in exile at
Coppet in January 1798. Her complete lack of any ability
to come to terms with political realities had once again
cost her the position near the center of things that she
craved more than anything.

Almost two years later, in October of 1799, she was given
another chance when Talleyrand summoned her back to
Paris for reasons that are unfathomable—unless he was
motivated by sheer kindness toward a friend with an insatiable appetite for a ringside seat at great events.

When Barras had purged the legislature with the help
of Angereau and Bonaparte, he had also eliminated two
right-wing members of the Directory, Carnot and Barthélemy, and had replaced them with Ducos and the Abbé
Sieyès, the one human being alive who was more cynical

and unscrupulous than Talleyrand himself, though lacking his extraordinary charm and verbal grace. Within
months Talleyrand, Sieyès, and Lucien Bonaparte were
plotting the overthrow of the Directory, and in October
1799, when their plans were complete, Madame de Staël
was informed by her former lover that something exceedingly interesting was about to take place.

When she reached Paris with Constant on November 9
they found that General Bonaparte had been put in command of all the troops in and around the city and had been
given a free hand to suppress a Jacobin plot for the seizure
of power; that three of the Directors had resigned; that two
were under arrest; and that the Legislature was to convene
on the following day, not as was usual in the Tuileries,
but at Saint Cloud, in the Orangerie attached to the palace.
They rose the next morning in a city electrified by the tensions of an uncompleted coup, and Constant was sent off
to Saint Cloud to observe events and to keep Madame de
Staël informed of them as they occurred. At intervals
throughout the day a series of messages was brought to her
in the Rue de Grenelle by the grooms who had gone with
Constant to serve as runners.

When Madame de Staël learned that Bonaparte had
fluffed his first entry into the Orangerie and had been
howled down by the Jacobins, she gave her servants orders
to start packing for flight, but soon after she had done so
another message, saying that Constant had just seen the
deputies jumping out of the Orangerie windows as Bonaparte's troops cleared the chamber, caused her to counter-
mand them. Later on she was to say that she wept for liberty when she heard that the deputies were running away;
but at the time she was a Bonapartist, and she was as delighted by the coup as Constant was. They both expressed
their delight with its success, and hurried to ingratiate
themselves with the new regime.

It was at this point that Constant made another of those
blunders which were, in the long run, to be fatal to his
reputation and to his claims to be taken seriously as a man
of principle. It is easy to see how he argued himself into

his mistake. It was still not clear who had been using whom when he made it: there was the possibility that Bonaparte was using Sieyès, and there was just as great a possibility that Sieyès was using the General. All that was clear was that a regime that had come to power on the bayonets of an infantry regiment would be tempted to use force again as soon as it ran into trouble, and that it might easily drift into becoming a tyranny.

Constant was sure that he was under an obligation to speak out for the rule of law in these circumstances, and felt that it was his duty to find a platform from which he might do so. Under the constitution of the new regime power was to be in the hands of three Consuls who were to be assisted, nominally at least, by four consultative and advisory bodies, a Senate, a Legislature, a Council of State, and a Tribunate, the last of which was to have a purely critical function and was to discuss pending legislation from a purely legal point of view. It was to have a hundred members who were to receive a substantial salary. It was to the last of these bodies that Constant aspired to belong. In order to make the aspiration a reality Madame de Staël approached a friend who was a member of the committee which was drafting the regime's new constitution and asked him to set up an interview at which Constant might press his claims to a seat on the Tribunate upon Bonaparte.

The meeting was arranged, and Chabaud-Latour escorted Constant into the presence of the First Consul. They talked for a while, and at last Constant came to the point. "I wish to assure you, Citizen Consul, that I am your man. I am not one of those merchants of ideas who believe that everything can be done by theories. What I admire is action at the level of the practical; if you nominate me you can count on my support."

The pair then left the First Consul, and as they came out into the street Chabaud-Latour announced that he was about to go to Sieyès. Constant asked if he could come along too, and a few minutes later Chabaud-Latour was astonished to hear him telling the Abbé that he abominated the use of force. "I am not on the side of the sword; what I

look to are principles, justice, ideas. If you give me your
support you can count on me. I am wholehearted in my
hostility to Buonaparte."

After this remarkable exhibition of duplicity in the pursuit of office, Constant proceeded to infuriate the First
Consul by a display of what the latter took to be treachery
and ingratitude—which he attributed to the malignant
influence of Madame de Staël. Five days after the first meeting of the Tribunate in January 1800 Constant rose to
address that body in opposition to a government motion
imposing a limit on the time that it might allot to the criticism of any given measure. In his speech Constant went
beyond the merit of the motion to make a personal attack
on Bonaparte, in which he criticized him for his impatience
and his evident contempt for parliamentary protocol.
Shortly after this he delivered a solemn rebuke to a relative
who had reacted unfavorably to his suggestion that the
slanders of malicious enemies had turned the First Consul
against him by advising him to use his common sense, and
either accommodate himself to the realities of the situation
he had put himself into by taking a salaried post from the
General or get out. "No human consideration," Constant
replied, "would induce me to sacrifice what I consider to
be right, or worthy, or honorable." Having thus put the
issue on the highest moral plane, he went on drawing his
salary and biting the hand that fed him.

Being moralized at by her agent did nothing to increase
the First Consul's respect or liking for Madame de Staël.
In March, having discovered that the poor useless Baron de
Staël was living in squalid poverty after being stripped of
everything he possessed by a seventy-year-old harpy,
Mademoiselle Clairon, who had once been a beautiful
actress, he addressed a characteristic memorandum to his
brother Joeseph:

> To the Citizen Joseph Buonaparte,
> 17 Ventôse, Year VIII
> Mr. de Staël is in the greatest poverty and his wife is
> giving dinners and balls. If you are still seeing her,

would it not be a good idea to persuade this woman to make her husband an allowance of a thousand or two thousand francs a month? Or have we already reached the stage where not only morals but even more sacred duties than those between fathers and children can be trodden under foot without honorable people thinking it wrong? By all means let us judge Madame de Staël's morals as though she were a man; but a man who inherited the fortune of Monsieur de Necker, who had long enjoyed the privileges of a distinguished name, and yet who left his wife in misery while he lived in abundance, would that be a man with whom one could keep company?

His evident ill will was further exacerbated when he learned that Madame de Staël was talking up a nebulous plot to have him replaced by General Bernadotte in the name of moderation. His irritation with both Constant and Madame de Staël stemmed in large measure from the precariousness of his situation and that of France. It was taking sixty thousand government troops to contain the Royalist guerillas who had gained control of large parts of the departments of Ille-et-Vilaine, Loire-Inférieure, Côtes-du-Nord, and Morbihan; the allied armies of intervention, fighting to restore France's absolute monarchy, were scoring success after success in their campaigns on the Rhine and in Italy; and Royalists all over the country were eagerly awaiting the opportunity for taking a bloody and appalling vengeance for the Terror that a counterrevolutionary success would give them. Rightly or wrongly, the First Consul felt that in these circumstances a parliamentary reverse, of the kind that Constant and Madame de Staël were trying to inflict upon him—was the most likely event, after his defeat in battle, to throw France back into the stage of confusion and disorder from which he had rescued it.

When the First Consul returned from Italy in June, after fighting the successful campaign to reestablish the French position south of the Alps that culminated in the touch and go victory at Marengo, he was not pleased to learn, from the

reports of the spies his Minister of Police had placed about
her, that Madame de Staël had been noisily praying for
his defeat. He was still further aggravated later in the year
when Constant used his position as a Tribune to oppose
the passage of a law setting up special courts to handle
political crimes and crimes against the public order. As
this piece of legislation had been inspired by two elabo-
rately planned (and in once case bloodily executed) attempts
to assasinate him, Constant's opposition struck the First
Consul as a piece of reckless legalistic trifling in the face of
necessities. By the end of the year his patience had been
exhausted, and Constant found that he was no longer a
Tribune. In twelve months he had finished himself off
politically for the lifetime of the regime, a period that was
to cover the next thirteen years.

It was at this point that the First Consul's relationship
with Madame de Staël underwent a fundamental change.
Marengo had been followed by Hohenlinden and by a
series of military events which had knocked Austria out of
England's counterrevolutionary coalition. A treaty of peace
was signed at Luneville, and in the belief that it would
last the First Consul turned his mind to the problem of
consolidating his position in France itself, first of all by
clamping down on dissidents and subversives. "As I am
now free to devote more of my time to police matters," he
wrote to his Minister of Police, "I wish to be informed of
everything, in the greatest detail, and intend to work with
you for at least an hour...every day."

Until he began these daily sessions with Fouché, the
First Consul had been only intermittently aware of Madame
de Staël as a person and largely unconscious of the extent,
persistence, and almost total irresponsibility of her mis-
chief-making. He was now faced with a mosaic composed
of reports from the police, from officials, from informers
in society, from tradesmen and craftsmen she patronized,
and from servants in her own household and the house-
holds she frequented, which gave him an astonishingly
complete picture of her daily life, her activities, and her
contacts. Since she was always talking, since she invariably

said whatever came into her head, whether she had anything to base it on or no, since she was as incapable of moderation as she was of discretion, and since she had an obsessive interest in the First Consul and his affairs, these
reports confirmed his darkest suspicions of her as an irresponsible and malignant meddler. Her admirers say that
he came to hate her at this time because he recognized her
as an unconquerable spirit and a threat to his ambitions,
but his recorded remarks are more expressive of irritation
than hatred or even real anger, and his feelings can more
correctly be compared to those of a dedicated chess player
who has to deal with a child who cannot bear to see a board
set up for a game without overturning it.

Much has been made of his persecution of Madame de
Staël, but in view of what he could do to those opponents
who had to be taken seriously, it cannot be said that he
treated her harshly. In spite of her determined efforts to
make the worst possible kind of trouble for him—and, as
he saw it, for France—he never did more to her than an
indulgent father does to a naughty child. He scolded her,
or had her scolded by one of his agents, and gave her a
punishment equivalent to being sent out of the room, ordering her to remove herself from Paris and to take up residence
more than a specified distance from it. She responded at
the same level, with the kind of outrageous provocativeness
that is produced in naughty children by the knowledge that
their indulgent fathers won't, in any circumstances, do
anything *really* nasty to them. She would sneak back into
Paris for flying visits when it had been forbidden to her,
and she specialized in minor violations of the orders affect-
ing the distance that she was to keep between herself and
the city. The essentially infantile character of her gestures
of "resistance" and their lack of seriousness are exemplified
by the fact that she assumed, and assumed correctly, that
they would not imperil her father's claim to the two million
francs owed him by the French state and that the First
Consul never thought of disputing the validity of the claim,
either during his Consulate or later when he had become
Emperor and Madame de Staël had inherited the claim as

part of Monsieur Necker's estate. It should be added that although her capacity to take the role of an opposition leader was a simple function of her wealth, her great enemy never resorted to economic sanctions of any kind in order to bring her to heel. In the context of the historical situation, and in view of her habitual extravagance of expression, she was treated with an astonishing mildness.

Any lingering possibility that the First Consul might at length have realized that Madame de Staël's political pretensions were ludicrous and become reconciled to her irritating but harmless presence in France was destroyed by three publications which appeared between 1800 and 1802, two of them under her own name and the third under her father's. The first to be published was an essay, *On Literature Considered in Its Relation to Social Institutions*, a production which can be described as the ill-advised inflation of a work by her dead friend Francois de Pange, his *Essay on the Causes and the Effects of the Progress and Decadence of Literature*. In her version Madame de Staël loads the structure of the none-too-impressive original with virtually all the fashionable clichés from the field of general ideas that were in circulation at the moment and with a large number of *obiter dicta* on matters, such as Arabic and Italian literature, that she very clearly knew nothing about. It would have been an entirely harmless work from the First Consul's point of view if it had not included a section in which she argued that the Revolution had coarsened the texture of France's national life by creating conditions in which it had been possible for self-seeking, vulgarly ambitious, and mercenary men to come to the top. The necessities of the day that gave them their chances had now passed away, and it was time for intellectuals and all cultivated persons motivated by moral and ethical considerations to combine in order to remove them from the social position they had usurped and to restore the tone of the national life to its former elevation. Misled by the *succès de scandale* that greeted the book and by the rapid exhaustion of its first edition, Madame de Staël assumed that she was building a position of strength for herself that would soon force the First Consul to come to terms, and she inserted a preface to the second printing in which she made it clear that she was calling on intellectuals as a class to rally to the opposition.

This earned Madame de Staël no more than an official rebuke in the government newspaper and a measure of social ostracism that led to her exclusion from some of the balls and receptions she would have liked to go to—and she complained of this to the Minister of Police, who advised her to leave Paris until the whole thing blew over. She went first to her father's country house at Saint-Ouen and then left for her usual May-to-November sojourn under her father's roof at Coppet.

When she returned to Paris for the winter of 1800–1 she found that Fouché had been right: her essay had been forgotten. She was invited everywhere and warmly received by such committed adherents to the regime as the First Consul's brother, Joseph Bonaparte, and his eternally faithful right-hand man General Berthier. It was in the house of the latter that she had the face-to-face encounter with her enemy that she had been longing for, in the certainty that if she could only talk to him everything in their relationship would be changed and they would become friends, allies, collaborators, and heaven alone knew what more. She was primed with brilliant and beguiling arguments that she had rehearsed for the occasion, and she knew that she could simply overwhelm him by the sheer force of her intellect if she were given the chance. He approached, accompanied by his brother Lucien. They were before her. She looked speechlessly at the First Consul as he gazed with apparent fascination into the depths of her décolletage. "I've no doubt you nursed your children yourself?" he said. She remained speechless. "There you are," he said to his brother. "She won't say yes, and she won't say no." They passed on.

It was their last innocent transaction. When Madame de Staël came back to Paris the following winter the First Consul knew too much about her activities from the police reports to be able to take her meddling lightly. Futile though her efforts had been, she had done her best to sabotage the

negotiations for the Concordat, the treaty which had healed
the breach between the Vatican and the French State opened
by the Revolution. She had been, if only marginally, involved in the conspiracy of the twelve generals which had
his replacement as its object. And wherever she went, and
whoever she talked to, she left behind her a record of extravagantly derogatory remarks about his intellectual powers,
his motives, and his intentions. Like all active and ambitious men who have a clear idea of what they wish to do and
how it should be done, he tended to interpret criticism as
simple negativism, the product of a desire to frustrate or
postpone action, and he found the persistence of Madame
de Staël's destructive nagging exasperating. That she was in
essence purely destructive was a matter on which he had no
doubts—look at what she had done to the Baron de Staël!

That story had come to its end in the spring of 1802, just
over a year after the First Consul had written his memorandum to his brother Joseph suggesting that in her position
Madame de Staël could well afford to allow the Baron two
thousand francs a month. She had not risen to this, but had
agreed to give him three thousand six hundred a year (a
little more than her mother had been paid, over and above
her room and board, when she was working as a governess).
This did him little good, as that elderly harpy Mademoiselle
Clairon, having stripped him of all she could get by being
nice to him, threw him out and sued him for what he had
left. When he lost the case he was sold up to satisfy the
judgment, and in his distress and dismay he was knocked
down by a stroke which left him paralyzed, helpless, and
unable to speak coherently. Madame de Staël ignored the
reports saying that he was living in squalor and misery for
nearly a year and only decided to accept financial responsibility for his care then when she realized that his situation
was becoming the subject of a scandal. In the spring of 1802
she decided to take the living corpse to Coppet and to leave
it there with her father. He suggested that she would do
better to leave it in the care of her servants in her establishment in the Rue de Grenelle, so that if the First Consul
should think of ordering her to leave Paris she would be able

to reply that she could not leave her dying husband. Madame de Staël was not convinced, and adhered to her project. The strain of the journey finally killed him, and he died of exhaustion in an inn at Poligny, half way between Dijon and Geneva, early in May.

The date of the Baron de Staël's death, May 8, was the same day that the Corps Législatif voted to extend the First Consul's term of office for ten years. The Prussian Minister noted how things were going in a dispatch to his government. "Everything around the First Consul and his wife is resuming the general character and etiquette of Versailles.... He is developing some liking for the chase, and the forests where the Kings of France and the Princes of the Blood once hunted are now being reserved for him and the officers of his suite." These and many other indications that the regime was moving in the direction of a monarchy were confirmed in August when a national plebiscite approved the proposition that the First Consul should hold office for life and have power to nominate his successor. This event was celebrated by a huge reception at the Tuileries followed by a *Te Deum* at Notre Dame to which Napoleon rode in regal state in a carriage drawn by eight horses. It was evident to all who saw or read accounts of these occasions that the First Consul was embarking on an attempt to found a dynasty.

It was at this moment that Jacques Necker chose to publish the work he had written in collaboration with his daughter, *Last Views on Politics and Finance,* and to send a copy to the First Consul. In its text Bonaparte found himself referred to as *"l'homme nécessaire"* in a way that seemed to imply that what was meant was that he was a necessary evil, and that the necessity was one that would pass. From this the book went on to argue that if the First Consul were to attempt to found a dynasty he would fail, and that the best thing for him to do was to prepare to hand his powers over to a seven-man directory when he had replaced the Constitution of 1799 (which was the charter of the Consulate) with something more liberal. After making this helpful suggestion the book goes on to put forward three specimen

constitutions as working models of the sort of thing that
the First Consul should espouse as an improvement on his
own defective instrument. These inept suggestions angered
Bonaparte less for what they were than as part of an attempt
on the part of Madame de Staël to use her father's name,
and such prestige as might still be attached to it, in an
effort to damage him.

The First Consul's irritation was much increased when
Madame de Staël's novel *Delphine* appeared in December.
In the interval she had somehow managed to persuade herself that the barrack-room language in which the First
Consul had expressed his dislike of the book bearing her
father's name indicated that he was afraid of her political
influence, and that the time had come for her to make some
public gesture of defiance. She had accordingly added a
preface to the novel saying that she did not expect it to be
liked by those who were in charge of the destinies of the
French people, but that this did not matter, as it was addressed to the silent majority of enlightened French men and
women who were unrepresented in the government.

The work so introduced is a vivid illustration of the in-
correctness of Madame de Staël's belief that the novel is the
easiest of all forms of fiction to produce and that anyone
who has had interesting experiences is in a position to sit
down to write one. It was written in imitation of the novels
of Madame de Charrière, but what Madame de Staël had
chosen to imitate was not the economy and precision of
language which gives them their considerable merit, but
their formal structure, which is amateurish and clumsy,
and the ruthlessness of approach which allowed for the
inclusion of clearly recognizable portraits of living people
without regard for their feelings or reputations. The First
Consul would probably not have cared about any of these
things had not two of Madame de Staël's victims been
Monsieur de Narbonne and Talleyrand. Monsieur de
Narbonne had become an adherent to the regime in the
course of 1800, and the First Consul placed a special value
on his support, both on account of his considerable diplomatic talents and for the fact of his being a son of the royal

house of France. His anger at finding that *Delphine* contained vicious caricatures of this valued supporter of his cause and of his Minister for Foreign Affairs does not seem to require much explanation. He made his feelings plain, and within a few weeks of the publication of the book Madame de Staël was given unmistakable indications that she had at last gone too far, and that it was in the last degree unlikely that she would be allowed to live in Paris or in France again while the First Consul was in power.

The winter of 1802–1803 was not a happy one for Madame de Staël. As it went on she alternated between periods of exhilaration, in which she was able to see herself as a heroine in the forefront of the resistance to the First Consul, and periods of intense and agitated depression in which she fought against facing the fact that she was powerless and had been brushed aside. Her anxieties gave her sleepless nights, and in order to calm herself and to get some rest she began to use opium more and more frequently, thus establishing a habit that was to remain with her for the rest of her life. When she was not under the tranquilizing influence of the drug, she found relief from her nervous tensions in tormenting her father and Benjamin Constant by overloading their capacities for emotional response with her inordinate demands. Her game with both men was to ask more and more of them in the way of attention and commitment until they were brought to the threshold beyond which lay the complete subordination of their lives to hers. Then, when they at last made a stand to resist her remorselessly increasing pressures, she would turn on them with abuse, with tears, with screams of rage, with threats of suicide, and with denunciations in which they were accused of failing her and betraying her. All through 1800 and 1801 she had been trying to persuade her seventy-year-old father to move from Coppet to a house in Paris, on the ground that the First Consul would find it impossible to use the sanction of expulsion against her if that would entail parting her from so venerable and distinguished a parent. Monsieur Necker had declined to be used in this way and had insisted that Coppet was his home and the only place in which he felt inclined

to live. He was now made to pay a heavy price for this refusal: his daughter impressed upon him, in scene after
scene, that it was all his fault that she was not in Paris and
that she was being bored to death in a provincial backwater.
She in the end forced him to make an appeal to the Consul
Lebrun begging him to ask the First Consul to lift the ban
that had been placed upon her. The reply was a cutting one,
calculated to remind the old man that the day when he
could ask for favors had gone by, that he had become an ir-
relevance, and that his daughter was a trivial nuisance.

The structure of the game that Madame de Staël was playing with Constant at this time was of another kind and almost identical with that in which Monsieur de Narbonne
had been her partner. There was, naturally enough, a Ribbing in the script. A pamphleteer called Camille Jordan who
had attacked the First Consul was invited to fill the role at
the beginning of the winter, with the promise of a trip to
Italy, all expenses paid, thrown in as an inducement for him
to accept. When he declined the handsome offer a young
Irish visitor to Geneva called O'Brien was offered the part,
but as he was too shy and timid to avail himself of his opportunity and further troubled by religious scruples, he was
soon dropped in favor of a Dr. Robertson, the personal phy-
sician of Lord John Campbell, the heir to the Duke of Argyll.

Dr. Robertson's success displeased another Scot, a man
named MacCulloch who felt that the prize should rightfully
have gone to him. When he heard that his expectations had
been disappointed and that Dr. Robertson and Lord John,
having passed several days at Coppet, had then set out (with
Madame de Staël acting as cicerone) on a tour round the
shores of the Lac de Neuchâtel, he decided to pursue them.
He took with him a Swiss friend called Ferdinand Christin
who was to act as his second in the duel which he intended
to fight with his rival. Although Swiss, Christin was a
member of the Russian foreign service. For this reason he
was—as was Madame de Staël—an object of interest in the
eyes of the French military authorities who were then in occupation of the region. When the spies watching them both
reported their convergence, in the company of a member of

the English House of Lords, on the small town of Yverdon, they became extremely interested. The Peace of Amiens of the year before had turned out to be no more than a brief truce, and the counterrevolutionary war to which the British Tories had dedicated their country was about to break out once more. In the context of an imminent resumption of hostilities this meeting in an out-of-the-way spot was highly suspicious. It thus happened that as soon as Madame de Staël had succeeded in talking the bloodthirsty MacCulloch out of his projected fight with Dr. Robertson in the inn at Yverdon the parties to the event were warned that they were all in danger of arrest if they didn't clear out immediately. Madame de Staël bolted for Coppet; Lord John made it over the Austrian border disguised as a woman; and Dr. Robertson, MacCulloch, and Christin went to Geneva to face the music. The three of them were arrested there, but while MacCulloch and the doctor were let go almost at once, Christin was arrested, discharged, rearrested, and in the end taken to Paris where he had to endure sixteen months in solitary confinement.

While this episode is on the one hand nicely illustrative of the way in which troubles were apt to shower down on those who became even marginally involved with Madame de Staël, it is on the other demonstrative of the way in which her double standard operated. While Madame de Staël was making her attempt on the virtue of young O'Brien, Constant's relatives had been making a match for him with Amélie Fabri, a well-born young woman with good connections, money, a house of her own, and a great deal of charm. Constant saw that the marriage would be a good one from a purely mercenary point of view, but he was not much interested in the girl. Nonetheless he considered binding himself to her quite seriously as a means of freeing himself from "a Germaine always more anxious, more unstable, and more demanding." Madame de Staël became aware that he was thinking of marriage with Amélie at the beginning of February, and a series of scenes began that lasted into April. They were at their peak in mid-March. On the eighth of that month Constant made an entry in his journal:

Scene upon scene, and torments upon torments. For three days now Germaine has been in a fury, and bothers me so much with abuse, with tears, and with reproaches, that I find myself moving alternately from indifference to fury, and from fury to indifference... there is no more horrible relationship than that of a man who no longer loves and a woman who doesn't want to stop being loved. In the necessary clarifications there is either such harshness, or else something so superficial and so vague, that one is either ashamed not to be more responsive to the pain one is causing, or of doing what one is doing while seeming to understand nothing of what it means. As always, the idea of losing me makes Germaine value me more. A long-established habit of running my entire life makes her feel that it is my duty to come back to her. A single ambiguous word misleads her in this respect, and since I still truly love her the pain she experiences when she doesn't get the response she needs from me is extremely upsetting. On the other hand her unfairness revolts me....

The crisis came on the fourteenth:

Germaine has succeeded in making me lose my self-control, in making me say many violent things, in making me admit my liking for Amélie, in a word in making me mad. With everyone else I've regained the mastery of my character. With them I'm wise and good natured and sure of not saying more than I want to say. But in her case the memory of my old feelings for her, the perpetual agitation in which she has forced me to live, the complaints she has showered on me, the unfairness of her accusations, the insistence of her demands, and above all the horror that fills me at the thought of living under her yoke, make me be beside myself....

But by the tenth of April he had capitulated:

It's been ten days since I last saw Amélie. There's no more than a hazy idea of her left in my memory....

I've spent eight days tête à tête with Germaine....
What spirit!

He had not, however, given up his longings for a quieter
life:

I'm sticking to my plan. I want to go on being Ger-
maine's friend, to serve her, and to contribute to her
happiness, but always to appear with her, or at least at
her bidding, no longer suits me. I have to make a peace-
ful and orderly life for myself. I'm going to pull myself
together again at my country place....

The inner meaning of this last expression of intent is that
he had just received a guarded communication from Fouché
telling him that although the First Consul didn't want him
back in Paris, it would—provided that he was willing to
behave with discretion—be in order for him to return to Les
Herbages, the modest country house that he had acquired in
place of Herivaux after the collapse of his political ambitions. With this snug harbor to make for, Constant felt able
to run away from Madame de Staël as soon as he had given
up Amèlie for her sake. Her plunge into the affair with Dr.
Robertson was her riposte to his disappearance, a parallel to
his habitual resort to the consolations of the brothel when
he was especially exasperated by her behavior.

Madame de Staël's secondary response to Constant's flight
to Les Herbages was of a more elaborate and consequential
character. Between April and August 1803 she managed to
convince herself that the First Consul must have intended
the relaxation of his ban on Constant's approach to Paris as
a hint that she, too, might come back into France to live
where she pleased. Once she had formed this idea in her
mind it was an easy step for her to turn the wish into reality
by asserting that she had received "private assurances" that
all would be well if she ignored the First Consul's repeated
warnings that he would have her sent back to Geneva with
a police escort if she came anywhere near Paris while he was
in office. Monsieur Necker begged her not to do anything so
foolish as to act on these assumptions without first obtain-

ing an official clearance, but she was not accessible to rational arguments and made her move in the middle of September.

Before Madame de Staël left Coppet she wrote poor Monsieur Necker one of those letters in which she displayed her special gift for making the objects of her interest and affection aware of the thorns with which her roses were so plentifully armed. She told him in it that he was to take great care of his health while she was gone—not because she wished to see him alive again, still less because it might be nice for him to go on living, but because *she* would die in the convulsions of despair into which she would be thrown by news of his death. Having warmed his seventy-two-year-old heart with this generous sentiment, she went on to beg his forgiveness for having abused him so cruelly for not making his home in Paris to suit her. "Forgive me," she wrote, "if I applied absurd expressions to you in my insane spasms. God knows that I love and adore you and that I don't even feel any bitterness about your refusal to go to France." Having thus turned the knife of her resentment in that wound once more, she made the necessary arrangements for a trauma-free parting. To avoid the possibility of anything painful (and also of any occasion for displaying a genuine emotion), they would pretend that the day set for her departure was a day like any other. Monsieur Necker was to retire to his study after breakfast to read the journals and deal with his correspondence as usual, and while he was so engaged the carriage would come to the door for her and she would slip away. There were thus no farewells or fond embraces on what was to be the last occasion on which they were to see each other alive.

Madame de Staël's destination was a small house at Maffliers, a village eleven miles to the northwest of Paris in the general direction of Pontoise and a mile or two from Les Herbages, which she had rented from her legal representative in Paris. She loathed the house and the place as soon as she saw them, but she had never had the intention of remaining in either for very long. On the day of her arrival she sat down and wrote a letter to the First Consul assuring him that he had changed his mind. She was convinced, she told him, that her exile had lasted long enough in his eyes, and that he was "willing to take into consideration certain family reasons" that made her return to Paris "an absolute necessity." The day after that she wrote to Coppet to tell her father that she would be moving into Paris within a couple of weeks "on the pretext of my daughter being ill." She then took up the lease of a house in the Rue de Lille in Paris itself.

To Madame de Staël's enormous surprise this naive strategy did not succeed, and she was thunderstruck when she received, on October 4, official notification that if she was still at Maffliers on October 7 she would be taken back to Geneva by four police officers. She tried to evade the consequences of this order by going underground on the seventh. She moved from the house of one friend or acquaintance to another's for the next five days, apparently under the illusion that a letter she had written to the First Consul would persuade him to reverse his decision. A passage from it describing her situation shows the extent of her extraordinary capacity for transforming her fantasies into what she believed to be objective realities: "I was living peacefully at Maffliers," she wrote, "*relying on* the assurances you had kindly conveyed to me that I could stay there." She followed up this bold lie with an attempt to bargain: if the First Consul wanted her to leave France, he might at least let her have a week in Paris so that she could raise the money for a trip to Germany and take her ailing daughter to see her doctor....

When this last thought had been put onto her sheet of writing paper another immediately wafted into her head. Her daughter wasn't the only one who needed medical attention, exhausted as she had been by the journey from Geneva. Her son Auguste, too, was far from well. The season was late. It would be only reasonable to allow the whole family to move into her father's house at Saint-Ouen for the remainder of the winter. "I shall leave in the spring, when the season will make it possible for my children to travel safely."

The bland impertinence of this proposal does not become fully apparent until it is realized that Saint-Ouen lies, like Maffliers, to the northwest of Paris but at a point six miles closer in toward its center.

The First Consul's response took the form of an order, dated October 13, requiring Madame de Staël to remove herself to some place further than a hundred and ten miles from Paris within twenty-four hours of her notification of its issue. A specially chosen "literary" police lieutenant, discreetly dressed in civilian clothing of some elegance, caught up with her and served her with a copy of the order on October 15, but its terms were immediately varied for her convenience. She was initially allowed three days in Paris to put her affairs in order, but she managed by one device and another to extend this period of grace until October 24. On that day she at last left the city, but only to travel for just over six miles before stopping for the night at Bondy. She waited at that place until noon on the following day, hoping against hope for a reprieve. But no word came, and soon after one o'clock she started out for Germany in a state of tearful hysteria....Constant, who had rallied to her side as soon as he heard that she had been ordered to leave Maffliers, was traveling with her and did his best to comfort her. That was some consolation for her. However much of a failure her campaign for the reconquest of Paris might have been, she had at least recovered him.

Madame de Staël's celebration of that compensatory victory was typical of the relationship. Two days after it left the coaching inn at Bondy her carriage rolled to a halt in the courtyard of the Hôtel de Pont-a-Mousson at Metz where Charles de Villers was waiting for her arrival. He was a French émigré who had been living in Germany since the Revolution and who had become an enthusiast for things German. He had made a special study of the latest developments in German literature and philosophy, and what little Madame de Staël had been able to say on those topics in her essay De la Littérature had been freely pirated from articles upon them that he had contributed to an émigré review published in Hamburg. De Villers had been flattered rather than angered by the theft of his material and had entered into a correspondence with her which, while largely devoted to an exploration of the ideas of Immanuel Kant, had also assumed the character of a flirtation. Madame de Staël had heard, shortly after October 15, that he would be passing through Metz on his way to Paris toward the end of the month, and she had arranged to meet him there. After a week at the Hôtel de Pont-à-Mousson picking de Villers's brains about what was going on in Germany and quarreling with him about France, whose art and culture he had come to despise, Madame de Staël was giving serious thought to a program for detaching him from the German mistress he was traveling with and ditching Constant in his favor. She had got as far as writing to tell her father that she was beginning to discover all manner of deficiencies in Constant's character when the German woman, Frau Senator von Rodde, put her foot down.

When de Villers had been hustled off along the road to Paris, Constant's status as one of Madame de Staël's necessities of life was immediately restored. De Villers had assured her that her name was well known in Germany and that an enthusiastic reception was waiting for her there should she press on. But while Constant read and spoke German like a native, she did not speak it at all and could only pick her way through a written text in that language with very great effort. She correctly foresaw that, welcome or not, she would run into practical difficulties of the most tiresome sort if she crossed the Rhine without him. Her daughter Albertine put the matter in a nutshell when she wrote to Monsieur Necker after they had been on the further shore of that river for several days: "Without Benjamin, who plays with me, neither of us, Maman and I, would know what to do in the middle of these Germans."

Constant's usefulness increased rather rapidly, since Madame de Staël, who had begun to make generalizations about German life and the German character after spending her first night in a German hotel, had decided, at sometime between the beginning of November, when she crossed the Rhine, and the last week in December when she reached

Weimar, that she was going to write a book explaining the
German people and their culture to the French. Her method
of disposing of the principal difficulty standing in the way
of her accomplishing this aim is made plain by her famous
reply to the Englishman who tentatively suggested that she
might not, perhaps, be getting all that she should from the
works of Goethe and from her meetings with the great man
himself. "Sir," she answered, in the manner of the great Dr.
Johnson, "I understand everything which deserves to be
understood. What I do not understand is nothing."

Madame de Staël meant by it that if anything had value
the basis of that value could be explained to her, and that if
it had meaning that, too, could be explained to her. She
would then understand the thing's value and significance
and be in a position to hand on her knowledge. For her ideas
were what counted, and, since writing was communication,
a digest or condensation containing the message was just as
good as the original text in her eyes. On top of that it was information rather than ideas themselves that interested her;
she did not so much want to know as to know about. As
Schiller (who found conversation with her an exquisite
form of torment) put it: "She wants to explain everything, to
take hold of everything, to measure everything. Wherever
her torch cannot throw its light, nothing exists further."

Her approach to the very deep waters into which she was
plunging is typified by the accounts of her brush with Jo-
hann Gottlieb Fichte, the most abstruse metaphysician of
the day. Introduced to him at a purely social gathering
Madame de Staël immediately asked him to explain his
concept of the Ultimate Self, one of the most complex of his
exceedingly elaborate verbal constructions, "as briefly as
possible, in, say, a quarter of an hour." She then cut him off
after a moment or two with a vulgar witticism that she had
clearly prepared in advance on the basis of a misunder-
standing of someone else's explanation of Fichte's name for
the rather dubious entity he was attempting to define, the
Ich-Ich. "Oh, that's quite enough," she said, and having recalled the episode from the Tales of the Baron Munchausen
in which he swings himself across a river by grabbing his

left sleeve with his right hand and throwing himself across, she went on to tell "Monsieur Fisht" as she called him, that this was exactly what he was doing in formulating his concept of the "I" within the Self. Her remarks on this occasion created an appalled and embarrassed silence. Why had she asked the question if she did not want the answer? And why had she wished to be so rude to Fichte?

The melancholy catalogue of such encounters and such misunderstandings which constitutes the record of Madame de Staël's contacts with the elite of intellectual Germany led Rachel Levin, one of the most intelligent and acute of the younger generation of Berlin's women, to say of her visit that "she has seen nothing, heard nothing, and understood nothing." This was true enough, but it involves an underestimate of Madame de Staël and her intelligence. She herself, though she would have been willing to die rather than admit it, recognized the inadequacy both of her German experiences and of her comprehension of the subjects that she was talking about so glibly when she had her arguments with German philosophers and literary men. Goethe succeeded in reaching her on a vital issue. She believed, as a convinced utilitarian, that all works of art were, or should be, *for* something, and that they should be either morally elevating or capable of in some way contributing to the betterment of the individual and society in general. She was consequently very much put out to find that Goethe was committed to the view that a work of art was an autonomous identity requiring no justification in terms of function or utility. It existed as itself, and was to be valued, like any other aspect of reality, for its own sake. Madame de Staël tried hard to convince him that he was wrong about this, and he experienced a perverse delight in disconcerting her with extreme arguments against the assumptions on which her system of beliefs was founded. Although the idea that the discussion of serious topics was a form of social amusement was initially abhorrent to him (so much so that he refused to have anything to do with her when she arrived on the scene in Weimar), he came in the end to enjoy his intellectual Indian wrestling with her, much as Lord Byron

did later on in her career. Somewhere along the line Goethe
made a breach in her confidence that, between her quick
intuitions and the explanations of what she had seen and
heard that she was pumping out of Constant, she was getting the essences of German thought. She consequently decided to acquire a portable German literary and philosophical intelligence that she would be able to take home with
her for use as a source and an explanatory mechanism.
Whether Goethe was fully aware of the nature of the transaction she had in mind or not is a matter of doubt, but when
she left Weimar for Berlin in March 1804 she was armed
with his letter of introduction to exactly what she was looking for, an extremely well-informed literary journalist
called August Wilhelm Schlegel who had been functioning
for several years as an intermediary between the German
book-buying and -lending library publics and the intellectuals of the avant-garde. He was a skillful simplifier and
encapsulator, and he had made something of a name for
himself with his smooth and easily digestible German
translations of Shakespeare's plays; but he had not, at thirty-
six, satisfied his ambition for financial success. He had, on
the other hand, achieved social success and had developed
expensive tastes. He was thus for sale, and Madame de Staël
was able to buy him. She offered him a salary of twelve
thousand francs a year, free room and board at Coppet, an
annuity if he were to stay with her for more than a certain
number of years, and a guarantee that he would have the
position of a member of the family and not that of an em-
ployee. It was also proposed to him that he would be able to
look on himself as her collaborator on the book that she was
to write on Germany. Either by accident or design all this
was put to him in such a way that he assumed that something warmer and more intimate than a mere literary collaboration was in Madame de Staël's mind; the one objection
to it all was that his official title in her household was to be
that of tutor to Albert de Staël. Tutors in great houses at that
time were a very low form of life indeed, and Schlegel hesitated to demean himself to that extent even in order to become Madame de Staël's lover.

Schlegel's hesitations on this rather special "point of honor" were resolved abruptly by an exterior event. On April 18, 1804, the news was brought to Madame de Staël, while she was visiting at the house of the Princess Radziwill in Berlin, that her father was gravely ill and was asking for her. Although she immediately assumed, and quite correctly, that Monsieur Necker was dead, she went straight home to pack and sent a note round to Schlegel telling him that she would be leaving for Coppet in the morning and that there would be a place for him in her carriage if he wished to come. Persuaded by the fact of her thinking of him at such a moment that she must be a little in love with him, very much enthralled by her, and suspecting that if he let this opportunity of attaching himself to her slip away from him it might not come again, Schlegel decided to go. On the following morning he committed himself to a servitude even more complete than that in which Constant had been bound ever since he had climbed up into Madame de Staël's carriage by the roadside fountain at Nyon ten years earlier. He was not to be released until she was dead.

Madame de Staël's takeover of Schlegel had been facilitated by Constant's absence. In their last days together at Weimar he had been becoming increasingly restless and desperate, and when she moved on to Berlin he had turned back for Lausanne with the intention of visiting his cousins before returning to Les Herbages and his neglected work. He learned about Monsieur Necker's illness when he reached his destination on April 8 and found him dead when he rode out to Coppet to ask for him on the following day. After considering the situation for the best part of a week he set out for Weimar again, in the hope of intercepting Madame de Staël on her way back from Berlin and of being able to break the news to her as gently as possible.

Constant reached Weimar after seven days hard going on April 21, the day before the arrival of Madame de Staël and her unexpected companion. The two men disliked each other on sight, but they had for the moment little chance to develop their feelings of hostility. Madame de Staël did not take the news well in spite of her premonitions of what had happened. She fell to the ground, according to Schlegel, with a piercing scream as soon as she had taken in what she was being told. She then began to thrash about so violently that the bystanders felt it necessary to put her under physical restraint to prevent her doing herself an injury. She continued to scream as if she had lost her reason, and kept her performance going for four-and-a-half hours. Schlegel's report of the event is an interesting one, and, although he attributes her reactions to grief and to her sense of remorse at having left her father to die alone, his description reads much more like an account of a child's attention-getting tantrum than of a display of feeling for the dead man.

It was nine days befor Madame de Staël felt able to travel on from Weimar toward Coppet. The journey, which could be done, as Constant had just demonstrated, in a week, began on the last day of April and stretched out interminably until May 19. Scenes of jealousy between Madame de Staël and Constant on the subject of the addition of Schlegel to her entourage had begun even before the party left Weimar, and Constant and Schlegel bickered jealously with each other at various points en route. The days of tension in the coach were followed by nights at inns along the way in which Madame de Staël indulged herself in hysterical displays of anguish. She put on a particularly appalling exhibition, with much screaming and simulated convulsions, when the coach at last pulled up in the forecourt at Coppet. When it was over she was carried, apparently unconscious, into the house. But once inside she revived and resumed the performance which continued without a let-up for several hours.

In the days of relative calm that followed Madame de Staël absorbed herself in a reading of her father's private papers and literary remains. This was the first step toward the preparation of her adulatory essay *On Monsieur Necker's Character and Private Life,* a work which was intended to transform the coldly selfish man who had neglected her as a child, and who had driven her out of her mind with exasperation and boredom as a young woman, into the ideal of a loving and understanding father. She was frustrated in this, however, by the surfacing of resentments that were evidently beyond her control.

> *I counted upon him to annul the effects of my mistakes. Nothing seemed beyond remedy as long as he lived: it is only since his death that I have come to know what real terror is, only since then have I lost the confidence of youth which relies on its own strength to attain all its desires. In his strength I found my strength; in his support my confidence. Where is he now, my protecting genius?*

The question has an obvious answer. He is gone, stolen away, departed. He will not come back. She asks other questions, the answers to which are just as obvious in the light of universal experience if not in that of faith:

> *Will he guide my steps? Will he spread his wings over my children, whom he blessed with his dying voice? And can I gather up enough of him in my heart to consult him still and listen to his voice?*

He will not, and she will not. She has been finally abandoned, and the debt of love, affection, and support owing to her has become uncollectable forever. It is this truth, and her knowledge that the debtor had never wished or intended to meet his obligation, that fights its way to the surface through the conventional mourning and rhetoric.

What is perhaps more indicative of the real nature of the relationship between the father and daughter is the revolution that took place within the walls of Coppet while Madame de Staël was working on her tribute to her father. He had established an orderly private universe in his house, modeled to some extent on the routines of Versailles as he had known them in his days of greatness. His household rose, ate, and retired at set hours, and one rigidly structured social day followed the next, predictably and inevitably. The whole smoothly running apparatus testified to the dignity and importance of Monsieur Necker, whose movements from bed to table and from table back to bed appeared to

regulate its operation. In the course of a few weeks Madame
de Staël tore it all apart, and turned the place into a nightmare of shapeless disorder. Her father's respect for the privacy of his guests and the members of his household had
been absolute; but Madame de Staël considered it no more
than her natural right to enter any room in the house whenever she felt like it and to impose herself on whoever might
be there, regardless of what they might be doing. Once she
had taken possession there was to be no more privacy for
anyone at Coppet, unless she happened to be away. She
would appear, even in the bedrooms, at any hour of the day
or night, with her fidgeting-sprig of laurel between the
fingers of one hand and her green morocco leather writing
case pressed to her stomach. She would plump herself down
anywhere she felt inclined and begin a conversation that
might run on from whatever hour of the day or night in
which it began until three or four in the morning. Breakfast was taken at an hour that reflected this custom, between ten o'clock and noon, lunch was eaten around five
in the afternoon, and dinner was served between eleven
and midnight. There was no way of knowing how many
people would be sitting down to a given meal, and huge
quantities of food prepared by the fifteen people who worked
in the kitchens were sent back untouched and later given
away. It was a hideous pattern of existence, and its principal
justification, the claim that it was an elastic system made
necessary by the intense intellectual life that was being
lived by the mistress of the house, appears to be without
foundation. Madame de Staël wrote a certain amount, it is
true, while she was mistress of Coppet; but her rule there
lasted for thirteen years, and her output spread over that
length of time is unimpressive. The Comtesse de Boigne,
an impartial observer with no ax to grind, records that
whenever she was in the house its owner gave her the impression of being as "idle as she was inconsequent," and
she added that in her experience Madame de Staël worked
at her writing only when she had nothing better to do and
that, when it came to making a choice between working
and playing, "the most trivial social amusement always had

priority." It was this aspect of her regime at Coppet that was the most appalling. She professed a great respect for the things of the mind, and she insisted on keeping intellectuals about her; but while they were with her she made it virtually impossible for them to make use of their gifts.

It is arguable that the member of her little clan who was most regular in his attendance at Coppet, the facetious and dubiously masculine Charles Victor de Bonstetten, would never have made very much of his minor talents in any case; and that fate had already determined that Schlegel would one day dwindle into a tiresome pedant before his meeting with Madame de Staël. The fact remains, however, that the least was made of their virtues and the most was made of their defects when they were under her governance at Coppet. The species of suicide note written on the occasion of Schlegel's final surrender of his integrity and independence, at the end of the first year and a half of his servitude, has survived:

You wanted a written promise, adorable friend. You thought I would hesitate. Here it is.

I declare that you have every right over me and that I have none over you. Dispose of my person and of my life—tell me to do this, forbid me to do that—I shall do what you wish in all things. All I ask in the way of happiness is to accept what you see fit to give me. I don't want to own anything—I want to owe everything to your generosity. It is not in the least difficult for me to agree to give up all thoughts of fame and to devote all my knowledge and talents to your personal use. I am proud to be your property.

Schlegel went on to tell her that he doubted if it could be right for one human being to make so complete a surrender to another, and ended by signing himself "your slave." Constant watched the process of his German rival's subjugation with fascination and horror, partly because he could recognize in Schlegel an exaggerated caricature of his own failings and weaknesses. As it was approaching its climactic point he dashed off a biting analysis of Schlegel's character for his own benefit in the pages of his journal:

> *Constant preoccupation with himself and excessive cowardice. This does not greatly surprise me, in spite of his pretensions to virility, horsemanship, and courage. He is a man who is consumed by self-love and who derives from his devotion to himself all his good and bad qualities—his enthusiasm, his irritability, his gentleness; when he falls out of love with himself—it happens whenever he feels threatened—all that remains is a typical man of letters who has been weakened in body and soul by a life of study.*

Had Bonaparte felt called upon to produce an analysis of Constant's character he would in all probability have written something very much the same. Constant was, naturally enough, kinder to himself and possibly even unaware of the nature of his own failures of courage, which were of an emotional rather than a physical character. In January 1805 he went to dinner with Madame du Tertre, a woman who had been in love with him for twelve years, and who had at that moment come back out of his past life to challenge him to break off his infantile games-playing relationship with Madame de Staël and to enter into an adult one with her. His initial reaction to her challenge was recorded in his journal:

> *A ridiculous dinner with Madame du Tertre. A husband present, who begins to show signs of jealousy, and other people who had nothing to talk of but the gossip of the provincial towns they hailed from. And I am shy in the middle of all this—how foolish of me to feel this sense of inferiority when among such inferior people. That is the worst of shyness—it robs one of all sense of one's own value.*

Soon after that dinner party had taken place, Madame du Tertre managed to slip away from the jealous husband and to join Constant for a platonic idyll at Les Herbages that lasted for several days. He was so upset at finding himself in the company of a woman who had no destructive intentions toward him, and who offered him a devotion and understanding that could only build his sense of his own value, that he failed to exploit the opportunity she had given him, left her physically untouched, and hastened back to Coppet to take up his game with Madame de Staël where it had been left off. There was only one improvement in his behavior on this occasion over that which he had indulged in twelve years before when he had run away from the twenty-four-year-old Baroness von Marenholtz, as she had then been, rather than face the menace of her love. He had then taken refuge with Madame de Charrière and had said many cruel and malicious things about her to his friend. He did not say anything at all about her to Madame de Staël.

The member of the inner circle of regulars at Coppet with whom Constant felt most at ease was Sismondi, the young historian and social theorist who was being transformed into a second-rate literary critic by the demoralizing influence of their patroness. It was, appropriately enough, a failure of literary judgment that had drawn Sismondi and Madame de Staël together in the first place.

When her essay *De la Littérature* had appeared in 1800 its critics had been derisive about her attribution of importance to the works of Ossian, a poet she felt able to describe as "the father of English literature," in spite of the fact that all the works to which his name was attached had been shown to be fabrications produced by a contemporary Scotchman called Macpherson. Sismondi was one of the many who were responsive to the souped-up Celticism of the spurious poems and he persisted, in spite of the abundant evidence of their lack of authenticity, in believeing in Ossian and disbelieving in Macpherson as their creator. He was excited by the attacks on Madame de Staël's credulity in this matter because they reflected on his own, and he was inspired to write to her to provide her with a variety of specious arguments with which she might defend her position. This warmed her heart and led her to take him up.

When he joined the Coppet household in 1802 he was rather splendidly called Jean-Charles Léonard Simonde de Sismondi, but he had originated as the son of a Protestant pastor in Geneva who had been a simple Gédéon Simonde. When Jean-Charles was twenty his father had moved into Tuscany, where, in the course of his researches into the history of the Italian Republics, he had learned of the existence of the Sismondis of Pisa, a family which had achieved power and distinction in medieval times. When he returned to Geneva at the age of twenty-seven he had become a Sismondi. He was an ugly, clumsy, naïve, sweet-natured, playful, and genuinely brilliant young man; and Constant could afford to sympathize with him and enjoy his company because he was in no sense a threat or a challenge, and above all because he could not endure Schlegel and thought him a madman. It was also in his favor, so far as Constant was concerned, that Schlegel couldn't endure *him* and was exasperated at having to treat this self-taught former bookkeeper (Sismondi had never been to a university and had briefly worked in a Swiss bank before his father moved into Italy) as his intellectual and social equal. It was a source of more serious aggravation to poor Schlegel that Sismondi's relationship with Madame de Staël was so much purer and more genuine than his own. Schlegel never fully recovered from the shock of recognition that had blasted him when he first met Constant at Weimar and realized that he was not going to have exclusive possession of his owner and mistress, and he experienced a renewal of the initial blow every time that he was called upon to face the fact that she had taken another lover, suffering all the torments of jealousy until the episode was over. It was quite otherwise with Sismondi, who loved Madame de Staël generously and without jealousy; he could actually feel fond of those luckier men than himself who were loved by her. The crown of Schlegel's sufferings vis à vis Sismondi was, however, a matter of ideology. Sismondi, who invariably argued the classical case against Schlegel's Romantic idealism in debate with him or with Madame de Staël, was the embodiment of all the Romantic virtues. He was direct, uncalculating, candid, sincere, and absolute in his commitments to his friends and loves. Poor Schlegel tried to be all these things, but, for the reasons so precisely identified by Constant, he was doomed to be a calculating schemer who hedged every bet and who was incapable of spontaneity. He found it unbearable to see Sismondi living effortlessly on a plane that he could not even aspire to reach.

This little group, having crystalized round the grieving Madame de Staël at Coppet during the summer of 1805, disbanded temporarily in the late autumn. Madame de Staël then went off to Italy accompanied by Schlegel and Sismondi; the impish Bonstetten remained in Geneva; and Constant went off to Dole to see his father before going on to Paris and Les Herbages. Sismondi kept Bonstetten up to date on Schlegel's sufferings in Italy in a series of immensely readable letters. The unlucky German could not understand that paintings, statues, and architecture were of no interest to Madame de Staël because they were complete in themselves, and could not be intruded upon by her in the role of an executant or an interpreter. He accordingly attempted to educate her into an appreciation of these things, with the result that she became very short with him. "One," wrote Sismondi, referring in this way to his patroness, "has become much harder on poor Schlegel. One allows him four paradoxes a day at the outside, but if he ventures on a fifth the rumblings of a thunderstorm on the way can be heard...."

Schlegel's sufferings became still more acute when the party reached Rome and Madame de Staël had an extraordinary social success. It culminated in her election to an honorary membership of the Accademia dell'Arcadia, and her introduction to a young Portuguese nobleman, Dom Pedro de Souza e Holstein. She was thirty-nine, and he was twenty-four and as handsome as he was talented. Schlegel was beside himself with dismay when he realized that they had become lovers, and was barely able to console himself with the thought that the affair could not last. Sismondi,

characteristically, was delighted to see Madame de Staël
happy, and was more than willing to accept the situation.
He found Dom Pedro an agreeable and interesting fellow....

In the event the liaison lasted through April and a visit
to Naples, and into May, when the lovers returned to Rome
and parted. Madame de Staël wrote the young man a letter,
full of gratitude and tenderness, when she reached Florence
on the first stage of her homeward journey. In it she assured
him that her father had, in heaven, forgiven her for the episode, and she told him that she had made notes of some of
the best things he had said to her while they were together
for use in a novel she was planning to write. "You will find
yourself in it," she wrote, "exactly as you are." To this in-
timation that he was to become one of her characters, she
coupled the suggestion that the affair should be renewed on
an educational basis, with curious postgraduate possibilities.
She undertook, if he were to join her at Coppet for a season,
to liberate him and to teach him to know himself—he
was more gifted than he supposed, and capable of finer
things than he imagined, and nothing could be better for
him than prolonged association with a superior woman.
When he had achieved self-knowledge, and had "become
even worthier of love than you are now, you will leave, and
I will dream that you may, it could be, marry my daughter
some day."

The confusion of sexual attitudes and functional roles
envisaged in this proposition is remarkable. At one point
Madame de Staël even speaks of herself as a rescuing knight,
a male character whose traditional duty is that of coming
to the aid of maidens in distress, and the general tone is that
of an experienced man proposing to do a young girl the
kindness of awakening her.

Dom Pedro made no immediate response to the proposition that had been made to him, and Madame de Staël
heard nothing from him as she made her way home by way
of Venice, Milan, and Turin. He did not make his appearance at Coppet until the whole summer and a large part
of the autumn had gone by, and when he did arrive he
found that Madame de Staël had plunged into another

affair. Her new lover was the same age as Dom Pedro. He
was Prosper de Barante, and he was the son of the official
in charge of the French effort to assimilate the neighborhood
of Geneva and Lausanne under the title of Préfet of the
Department of Léman. He was himself a junior official in
the French Ministry of the Interior, but he was on leave
on medical grounds and was for the moment free to dance
attendance upon his fascinating mistress. Prosper's father,
Claude-Ignace de Barante, was horrified when he discovered
that what he had assumed would be no more than a flirtatious acquaintanceship, or at most a *passade,* had become a
serious matter, and found that his son was talking in terms
of lifelong devotion and marriage. He reasoned with
Prosper, putting it to him that it was unlikely that a man
of his age would find lasting happiness or even contentment
in marriage with a woman of forty who was not only a
great deal richer than he could ever hope to be but who was
also notoriously at odds with the regime on whose future
they were both dependent. Prosper de Barante would have
none of this, and harsh words were said by both men in a
scene that ended with the delivery of an ultimatum: the
younger man was to break with his aging mistress or to be
cut out of his father's life. This was so much catnip to
Madame de Staël, who was able to come to the older de
Barante in the role of a suppliant and to weep at him until
he agreed to allow the affair to go on for a month, at least.
It was when this month was nearly over that Dom Pedro
reappeared.

Prosper de Barante seems to have found this confrontation
enlightening. Until then he had been blind to the nature of
the entourage which had reassembled round his mistress
as the summer ended, and unaware of the humiliating
servitude that she had in her Circe-like way imposed upon
Constant, Schlegel, and Sismondi. A further stage in his
enlightenment came when Madame de Staël moved from
Coppet into an apartment in Geneva for the worst of the
winter. She had developed a passion for amateur theatricals
at this stage in her career, and she now offered the society
of Geneva a theater season extending from December into

March. The last play she put into production as her season
ended was *Phèdre*, in which she herself played the title
role, and in which Prosper de Barante figured, at her
request, and to the great delight of the gossips, as Hippolyte.
That she should so recklessly expose herself, and him, to
the derision of an unsympathetic and covertly hostile
audience finally convinced him that his father was right
and that the connection was an impossible one to maintain.
He left for Paris a few days after his appearance as Hippolyte, in order to take up a new post in the Government
service that his father had obtained for him. But it was not
that easy, as Benjamin Constant could have warned him,
to break off a relationship with Madame de Staël once it
had been established.

The years 1804 and 1805 were especially galling for Constant, just as the years 1792 and 1793 had been especially
hard for Monsieur de Narbonne to endure, and for the same
reason. He had burned his political boats on Madame de
Staël's instructions, and he had come to realize that he had
made a tremendous blunder. The regime showed no signs
of being transitory, and in May 1804 the Tribunate and the
Senate had proclaimed that "Napoleon Bonaparte, at present First Consul of the Republic, is Emperor of the French."
This provocative act failed to stir its opponents into any
show of opposition. The new development was given overwhelming popular support when it was made the subject
of a national plebiscite the following November. The great
administrative and legislative reforms that were the Emperor's most impressive and most lasting achievements
were well under way, and the shower of honors that was to
make Marat a king and Talleyrand Prince of Benevento—
and which in the end was to produce 31 dukes, 452 counts,
1,500 barons, and 1,474 chevaliers—was beginning to fall.
A world of dazzling opportunities and rich rewards, enormously attractive to so ambitious a man as Constant, could
be seen to be coming into being, and solidifying. The Pope
himself, Pius VII, had come to Paris to confirm the reality
of the coronation of the Emperor. He had given the new
monarch his blessing in Notre Dame: *"In hoc solio con-*

firmare vos Deus, et in regno aeterno secum regnare faciat Christus" ("May God confirm you upon this throne, and may Christ cause you to reign with Him in his eternal kingdom"). With this said the Pope had kissed the Emperor on the cheek and repeated the words that had last been said by a Pope when Leo III had crowned Charlemagne in Rome: *"Vivat Imperator in aeternum"* ("May the Emperor live forever"). And if the beginning of the following year had been shadowed by the threat of war, and its summer darkened by the catastrophic destruction of the French fleet at Trafalgar, the autumn and winter were made radiant by the brilliantly successful campaigns of Ulm and Austerlitz which broke the power of the house of Hapsburg and ended the thousand-year history of the Holy Roman Empire. It looked more and more like the beginning of a French century. And while Talleyrand, and Monsieur de Narbonne, who had been in Madame de Stael's net and had escaped in time, could be seen close to the glittering center of it all, Constant was in limbo, and doing nothing....

In his desperation and unhappiness Constant began to behave with a foolishness and inconsequence that led Sismondi to rebuke him for his frivolity, and with a lack of discretion that led his father to write a stinging letter to him in which he said, among other things as wounding, that it was all wrong for him to accept the position of a kept man. That was, indeed, the nub of the thing. He owed her money, he lived off her for months at a time, and every time that he appeared with her, or interceded with the Imperial authorities on her behalf, he added a little more weight to the burden of ill repute that he had to carry as her dependent. Before Madame de Staël went off on her Italian excursion he expressed himself with more than the usual bitterness in his journal:

> *Conversation with Biondetta [Madame de Staël]. Little by little, the storm blew up. Horrible scene, going on until three in the morning—about how I'm lacking in sensibility, about how I don't inspire trust, about how my feelings don't correspond with my ac-*

tions, and so on. Alas, I'd like to do without monoto-
nous lamentations that aren't about real miseries but
protests against the laws of nature, against growing
old. As a man, I don't want to have to put up with the
spite of a woman whose youth is going. I don't want
to be asked for love, after ten years of being lovers,
when we're both nearly forty, and when I've said two
hundred times in ten years that it's not like that any
more—a declaration that I've never gone back on ex-
cept when I've been trying to moderate her convul-
sions of unhappiness and rage, which frighten me as
if they were physical injuries.

He went on to say that he could not go on with her as
things were, and that he would have to break with her if
he were to survive. It was at this precise moment that Madame du Tertre reappeared to give him a transient glimpse
of what his life might be like if he were sharing it with
someone who loved him.

Madame du Tertre was a German woman who had been
born Charlotte von Hardenberg. She was as kind as she was
generous, and she was softly pretty. While she was still a
girl her parents had arranged a conventionally "good" marriage for her with a wealthy man who was a great deal older
than herself. She had lived with him dutifully for several
years, and had borne him a son, when she met Constant
and fell in love with him. Her husband, the Baron von
Marenholtz, had realized by then that he was not destined
to make her happy, and he accepted the situation with
good grace, giving her freedom and a handsome allowance
so that she could do as she pleased with Constant or anyone
else she fancied. All might have gone easily and well had
not Charlotte's father, the Graf von Hardenberg, learned
what was going on and raised violent objection. He insisted
that his daughter should return to her family, that she
should agree to have nothing more to do with Constant.
Since she was reluctant to give him any such undertaking,
he shut her up for a while in the ancient and partially dis-
mantled castle of Hardenberg near Göttingen from which
the family derived its name, and ordered her relations not

to speak to her until she gave in. While she was in this grim situation and looking to Constant for support he was being overwhelmed by the difficulties that were being created for him by the vindictive Minna von Cramm, and the even greater difficulties arising from the shipwreck of Juste de Constant's military career. He consequently failed the loving captive, and taking to his heels ran off to take refuge at Colombier with Madame de Charrière. It was the Baron von Marenholtz who made peace between her and her father, and who, sure that her happiness required it, divorced her without bitterness and made a lavish settlement on her that made her independently wealthy. The Hardenberg–von Marenholtz divorce went through early in 1794, at just about the same time that the Cramm-Constant marriage was dissolved, but by then, having spent a good deal of time running the Baroness von Marenholtz down to Madame de Charrière, Constant had discovered that he was in love with his freedom. Charlotte wrote to him several times in an effort to convince him that she would respect his independence if they were to marry, but it was no use. He had escaped from her, and he wasn't coming back. A silence fell between them that lasted for a year. At the end of that time she made a visit to Switzerland and wrote a note to him from Constance:

> Thinking that M. de Constant must still remember a person who will always think of him with a special concern, and that he will be the man to put himself out a little for her sake, Madame de Hardenberg wishes him to know that she would be very pleased to see him again. She has been in Switzerland for nearly three weeks, and here for the last few days.
>
> my address: at the Aigle Noir.

Less than two weeks after he had received this note, to which he made no reply, Constant met Madame de Staël on the road to Nyon. Charlotte did not try to communicate with her love again for seven years, though she occasionally had news of him from third parties, as he did of her. In

1802 she was at a dinner party in Paris when from down the table she heard the voice of a Monsieur de Sanne telling his neighbors that "that poor fellow Constant is in a terrible state!" Her first thought was that this must mean that he was in bad health, and she was reassured when she learned from Monsieur de Sanne after the meal that the trouble was economic: Constant was ruined, and was being forced to clear fell the timber on his country property. She was relieved; that she could do something about. When she got home she wrote to him to let him know that half her fortune was available to him if he should need it. He did not reply to this generous offer, and she heard nothing from him, on that or any other subject, for three more years. He only then decided to write to her after a year's internal debate, set off by the recollection of several days of happiness he had once shared with her there, that came back to him when he passed through Göttingen with the lamenting Madame de Staël as he was taking her from Weimar to Coppet after her father's death. Then, at long last, in January 1805, he managed to bring himself to write to her, and a meeting took place at which she did her best to explain, and to explain away, her marriage to the émigré General du Tertre. The dinner at which Constant was tormented by what he called shyness followed, and then, after the interlude at Les Herbages, his second flight—but this time he came back and talked of marriage.

Madame du Tertre was delighted and immediately started to fight her way through the tremendous tangle of difficulties standing in the way of getting a valid divorce from her French Catholic husband. But while she attended to practical matters Constant agonized over such questions as whether it would look well if he married a woman who had twice been divorced; whether it would be fair and honorable for him to take her from du Tertre; and whether he had the right to abandon Madame de Staël, to whose side he was constantly returning, between interludes with common prostitutes, and with Anna Lindsay, the beautiful Irish tart who was being kept by Auguste de Lamoignon, and who longed to marry him.

When he was at the height of his distress and confusion, and successfully enfuriating Madame de Staël, while making Madame du Tertre and Anna Lindsay exceedingly miserable by promising them a great deal and then failing them, he had one of those experiences that change a man's life. His old friend Julie Talma died in his presence. She was one of those heroic beings who attempt to stand up to outface death in their last moments, and he saw her die with a look of combative fury on her once-gentle face. The transformation of the lucid, fully conscious human being of one moment into the unfeeling carcass of the next made a very powerful impression upon him, and it is significant that the style in which he kept his journal underwent a complete change on the day after her funeral: on that date its lengthy self-dramatizations gave way to laconic notes, partly expressed in a numbered code. This may only mean that Constant was afraid of what might happen if Madame de Staël got hold of the journal and found it full of entries recording his steadily increasing determination to break with her in order to settle down with Charlotte, but it might, and possibly did, mean that he had been shocked out of his adolescent habit of posturing, and was beginning to grow up.

What is perhaps more significant is that in October of this critical year in his life he was at last able to enter into the physical relationship with Madame du Tertre that she had wanted so badly and for so long. He attempted to maintain a coldly cynical attitude and to denigrate the importance of the event after he had first possessed her: "God, how this thing attaches a woman to a man!" But after his fifth night with her he was finding that something was happening to him:

> Unbelievable blend of pleasure and pain. Most delicious night in my life...nobody has loved me as she loves me. It must be she, cost what it may. There's no more doubt about it—it's a sacred duty."

Being who and what he was, Constant parted from Madame du Tertre on the following day and returned to Ma-

dame de Staël. She was holding court at Rouen, on the rim
of the forbidden zone a hundred and ten miles wide that
she was still forced to keep between herself and Paris. The
demon of fiction was already stirring within him, and two
days after he had enjoyed Charlotte and left her, he noted
that he had "begun a novel which will be our story. No
other work seems possible to me." On the next day he was
saying that he had taken his novel a great deal further, and
on November first he remarked that he was having no
trouble in painting the portrait of an angel. By the thirteenth the work was finished and Constant was able to give
his first public reading of it—to Madame de Staël and her
little clan. There are those who have imagined that the work
in question must have been a first draft of Constant's best-
known novel, *Adolphe,* but this cannot be so, as Madame
de Staël listened happily and subsequently wrote to Bonstetten, approving of what she had heard: "Benjamin has just
written a novel, the most original and touching thing I've
ever read."

The subject is wrapped in mystery, since Constant's descendants have not, so far, allowed anyone to see the manuscript, which is preserved in the library of Lausanne under
restrictions enabling them to withhold it from publication
and inspection. It is further confused by the fact that a few
days before the reading, on November 7, Constant had
brought Madame du Tertre into his game with Madame de
Staël and initiated its three-handed phase. Madame de
Staël had come into the room in which Constant was sitting
writing a letter, and he had tried to hide it. As she had long
since made it one of the conditions of their association that
she should be allowed to read all his incoming and outgoing letters if she wished, this was a certain way of drawing
attention to what he was doing. She responded, entirely
correctly from a games player's point of view, by asking
in an imperious manner to see what he had been writing.
He then formally announced that some kind of big deal
was in the works by refusing and burning the letter in her
presence. She again made the formally correct response by
pressing him for an explanation, and he then told her all

about Madame du Tertre without naming her. This produced the explosion that he had been working for, and
scene followed scene for what remained of the day and
for most of the night.

Madame de Staël had an insatiable appetite for this sort
of transactional situation, guaranteed to produce exchanges
of a high level of emotional intensity but of an entirely
infantile character, enabling the parties to them to postpone their entry into the world of adult and responsible
emotional relationships indefinitely. She was simultaneously deeply into another three-handed game with
Prosper de Barante and the exceedingly sinister Madame
Récamier. As the young and beautiful wife of an elderly
banker, Madame Récamier was ideal material for incorpora-
tion into games of a high order of destructiveness. She was
an exhibitionist who enjoyed displaying her physical
attractions, and she was a flirt who enjoyed exciting men.
But her marriage was never consummated, and she never
went to bed with any of her innumerable "lovers." While
Constant was involving himself with Madame du Tertre,
Madame de Staël, using every device that she could to bring
pressure on de Barante, was drawing Madame Récamier
into their game. De Barante was in Paris, declining to come
to Madame de Staël at Rouen; and she persuaded Madame
Récamier to see him in order to try to talk him into a
resumption of their affair, with the inevitable result that
Madame Récamier had got up a flirtation with him. Madame de Staël was then able to relieve herself of some of
her tensions by abusing them both for adding to her sufferings. By the summer of 1806 she had broken de Barante
into the games routine almost as thoroughly as Constant,
and he was coming regularly to take his rations of torment
and abuse, at Coppet, or Rouen, or Auxerre, or wherever
it might be that she was for the moment encamped, under
threat that she would commit suicide with opium, or some
other spectacular folly. He would submit for a few days
or a few weeks in which she treated him just as she treated
Constant, ordering him to make love to her, ordering him
to love her, abusing him for wishing to live his own life

on his own terms, and threatening him with her death if
he should ever abandon her. By November 1806 the patterns
of the games she was playing with the two men had become
so nearly identical that they were writing interchangeable
entries in their private diaries, each man expressing the
same distaste for the whole grueling business, the same
longing to be free of her and her demands, the same desire
to be married to someone kind and reasonable, and to have
some peace and order in their lives.

In between the active periods of their various games
Madame de Staël and Constant were both busy with their
pens. Madame de Staël had reconstructed the novel she had
begun to celebrate her Italian fling with Dom Pedro (who
had since married a sixteen-year-old girl) and had converted
it into an assault upon de Barante, whose heartless and
selfish desertion of the talented and passionate Corinne
proves to be fatal to her at its conclusion. Constant, for
his part, was adding several new chapters to the novel
describing his relationship with Madame du Tertre. These
extra chapters began, apparently, as an account of Constant's subsidiary affair with Anna Lindsay, and became
an analysis of his games-playing relationship with Madame
de Staël without his being fully aware of what he had done.
He was enlightened on that score on December 28 when he
read the new chapters aloud to her and the little clan at
the Château d'Acosta in Meulan, to which she had moved
from Rouen in November. She exploded with fury. The
scene of the night of the reading was followed by a fight
of two hours on the following day, a tempest that lasted
until four in the morning on the thirtieth and by two hours
of screaming and convulsions on New Year's Eve.

Constant reeled away from this ordeal to tell his journal
all over again that his position was intolerable, that Madame de Staël was the most selfish, demented, ungrateful,
empty, and vindictive of women, that she was odious and
unendurable to him, and that he might die if he didn't end
it. He then reexamined the new chapters that had caused
so much uproar, and realized suddenly that they could be
made into an autonomous novel which would contain the

whole story of their complicated, destructive, and guilt-ridden relationship. He spent most of January 1807 giving them their independent life.

Adolphe, as he named the novel, is as fascinating a document as it ever was, and it may even have gained in interest since the development of psychiatry has thrown so much light upon the mechanical processes that it intuitively explored. It is now clearer than it was that Constant was not indulging himself in romantic exaggerations but was describing clinical entities in such passages as the following:

> *I recall the hopes of my youth, the confidence with which I once imagined that I could determine my own future, the praise accorded to my early endeavors, a reputation that dawned so brightly, and then faded. I repeat to myself the names of friends of my school days I was once able to patronize and who have now left me far behind on the road to fame, fortune and esteem. When I tell myself these things I am filled with rage against her, and, curiously enough, my rage in no way lessons my fear of causing her anguish.*

It is a classic description of the way in which resentments are accumulated to justify the release of feelings of hostility and aggression, which must then be paid for by displays of self-abasement and guilt. The book also contains a classic description of the rewards and satisfactions that games players obtain from their confrontations and which bring them back together to perform their grisly rituals again and again.

> *My pride was stung by her jeers; she abused my character, she told me that I was such a miserable weakling that I had to turn my anger against her rather than against myself. A storm of rage took possession of us—all restraint was forgotten, all delicacy cast aside. We hurled every insult at each other that the most implacable hatred could have inspired, and there we were—the only two beings on earth who truly*

understood each other, who could do each other justice,
who could give each other real comfort and under-
standing—there we were, together, in the semblance
of two irreconciliable enemies intent on tearing each
other limb from limb.

In another passage he puts his finger on the compulsive
haracter of the association and the way in which the ill-
assorted pair have become addicted to their sufferings:

In moments of calm we decide upon escape; we tell
ourselves that we can't wait for the moment when
we shall be free; but when the moment comes it fills
us with fear...it becomes excruciatingly painful for
us to leave the person whose company gives us no
satisfaction.

Madame de Staël's reception of the first draft of the novel
is easy enough to understand. It is obvious to anyone who
reads the book that a player who has received such profound
insight into the structure and function of the game situations that he has been setting up must be on the brink of
either moving on to some other kind of game or giving
up games-playing altogether in favor of more creative and
genuinely rewarding activities. It is also easy to understand
de Barante's reaction to the three volumes of *Corinne*,
which came out in April 1807; it was a work of illusion and
self-deception rather than of insight, but for him it was
simply a repetition of the offense of the production of *Phèdre*
in which he had taken part:

I told you some time ago what a mess my life was
in as a consequence of my knowing you and of having
ignored my forebodings: you can use that too as mate-
rial for a book...Oh! don't speak to me of applause
and success—when you've lived on it, and have stopped
at nothing to get it, and haven't been afraid of making
literature out of the most private experiences of the
heart, of things so personal that a kind of shame

should make it impossible for anyone to use them as
means for making a splash.

This letter, whatever its effect upon Madame de Staël, almost certainly entertained the Emperor. Although neither Madame de Staël, nor Constant, nor de Barante, nor any other members of the little clan were aware of it, all her ingoing and outgoing correspondence was being intercepted at this time by the military secret service under Savary which was independent of Fouché's control. The intercepted letters were copied and resealed before being sent on in the ordinary way, and copies of all the interesting communications that came to light were passed on to the Emperor. He read them for recreation, and with attention, and he was never more than a couple of weeks behind the latest developments in her circle, even when he was over twelve hundred miles from Paris, in the remotest corner of northeastern Prussia. He was always especially pleased when Constant was living apart from Madame de Staël, since he then had the pleasure of reading the diatribes that she showered upon him. He was still able to recall them with relish when his great adventure was over and he was a prisoner on St. Helena. It was ignorance of this close surveillance by the Emperor himself that accounted for her move from Rouen to the Château d'Acosta, a mere twenty-nine miles from Paris, at the end of 1806. When she had been living there for several weeks without being ordered back to the 110-mile line, and Napoleon had moved on from the battlefields of Jena to those of Friedland, still further to the east, she concluded that she was getting clear away with her campaign to sidle back into Paris, and she entered into negotiations for a property at Cernay, a hamlet near Enghien and Montmorency to the north of the city and some nineteen miles closer in.

The winter of 1806-7 was one of intense strain for the Emperor, who had seriously underestimated the difficulties of fighting through the cold weather in East Prussia. His men died like flies of the hardships that they were called

upon to endure between battles, and the losses suffered by
his formations in their stubbornly contested conflicts with
the Russians were appalling. Between the time of Eylau,
when the Russian and French armies fought each other to
exhaustion in a February snowstorm, and the decisive
victory at Friedland in June, the Emperor was continuously
on the brink of his first major disaster. He was irritated
when he heard of Madame de Staël's projected move to
Cernay in March, and enfuriated when he heard from
Savary's special agents that she had fooled Fouché's regular
spies and had slipped into Paris itself in the middle of April,
when the Police Minister's daily reports were claiming
that she was on her way to Geneva in obedience to an expulsion order, giving her twenty days notice to leave, that had
been served to her at the Château d'Acosta in March. It
was his conclusion that Madame de Staël's evident determination to get into the city at a time when his fortunes
were at hazard in a distant theater of war must indicate
that she was in touch with some group of conspirators
making preparations for a seizure of power as soon as word
of his death in battle, or his defeat, should reach them. The
consequences might have been serious for her but for the
publication of *Corinne*. An advance copy of the novel
reached him when he was at the height of his anger, and
he spent much of an April night in a bivouac at Osterode
skimming through it. He then sent for Talleyrand, who
was with the army in readiness for instant peace negotiations as soon as a victory had been secured. The Prince
of Benevento, who had been roused out of his sleep, came
yawning and blinking into the candlelit tent and was con-
siderably surprised to have the novel thrown to him: "You
stick up for the woman—let's see you find a word of commonsense in all this stuff—read it to me." When Talleyrand had dutifully embarked on what looked like a promising passage, the Emperor almost immediately broke in
upon him to denounce it as a hodgepodge of nonsense:
"It's always the way," he said, "whenever a writer brings
himself into the picture as one of his own characters the

book's no good—it's a waste of time, reading that stuff."
And he sent the sleepy Talleyrand back to bed.

Blissfully unaware of the impression that her book had
made upon the Emperor, Madame de Staël was, as usual,
overestimating the political significance of a literary *succès
de scandale.* She allowed herself to think that because
Corinne was being talked about in Paris she could enter
into negotiations with the Emperor as an equal power, or,
at least, as one genius to another. In May when she was
at the height of this postpublication euphoria she sent him
a lengthy letter in her most inflated style telling him that
she had bought the property in the neighborhood of Montmorency and therefore considered herself entitled to live
in Paris. He did not reply to her but sent Fouché a harshly
worded letter telling him to disabuse her of her illusions
without further delay. "I tell you once again, that to allow
that woman to cherish any such hope is to torture her
pointlessly." He went on to order the rigorous enforcement
of the original order of expulsion against her.

Fouché did not find it necessary to act on this instruction.
Madame de Staël had already gone back to Coppet. Constant
had been so struck by the extravagance of her behavior in
the latter part of April, when she had made her clandestine
visit to Paris, that he had begun to wonder if she might
not, in fact this time, be going out of her mind. He had
persuaded her to go back to Geneva as soon as *Corinne* had
been published, and she left the vicinity of her beloved
city before the end of the month.

How long her belief in the success of *Corinne* lasted it
would be difficult to say. It was a success of a peculiar kind,
in that the book's interest has to depend on the reader's
interest in Madame de Staël and on his being to some extent
familiar with her circumstances. Readers who knew who
she was, and with whom she had been connected, could
take pleasure in comparing what they were reading with
what they had heard of her and her friends, and in discuss-
ing the possibility that such and such a character might
be intended for a portrait of this person or that. In a char-

acteristic passage in the book the heroine—who has made herself an international reputation by improvising prose poems while strumming on a lyre—discusses a paper that the hero, with the subtly off-the-target name of Oswald, Lord Nelvil, has found among his late father's literary remains: its topic is an indictment of children in general for the indifference and impatience with which they respond to expressions of their parents' hopes and fears for them and their future well-being. Oswald asks her to read this complaint, and when she has done asks her if she can believe that it was aimed at him. "No, no!" cries Corinne. "You know that he loved you and that he did not doubt your love!" And so on. The father's complaint is quoted in full, and a footnote points out that it is taken verbatim from Monsieur Necker's essay on the subject of religious morality.

There can be no objecting to what Madame de Staël is doing here. It is the artist's privilege to make direct use of his experience if he wishes to do so, and it is the strength of Constant's *Adolphe* that nothing in it is invented and that everything in it has been experienced. But whereas Constant is being ruthless with himself, and does his best to disclose the precise truth about himself and his experience, so far as he knows it, Madame de Staël's *Corinne*, like her *Delphine*, her *Zulma*, and her *Mirza*, is a rectification of objective reality in her interest. She deals with the truth of any given situation inadvertently, if she deals with it at all. In the case of *Corinne* the most revealing things in the book are descriptions of the heroine's art. Corinne improvises on themes given to her by members of her audiences—someone gives her a theme, she plucks her lyre for a while, and she then delivers a softly structured flow of rhetoric vaguely related to the subject that is to be accepted as poetry because it is, in the vulgar sense, "poetic," that is to say, gaseous and unprecise. The circumstances in which her improvisations are produced are as revealing as their nature: Corinne performs at fêtes and festivals given in her honor, her performances are solo performances, and her hushed and reverent audiences

always take whatever she elects to hand out, even when
she has nothing more to offer than a string of complaints
about how painful it is for her, as a genius and a superior
person, to associate with ordinary people such as themselves. Corinne's triumphs not only represent the child's
dream of glory; of being accepted without challenge at
one's own valuation; they also embody a child's conception
of the creative process as a simple matter of the uninhibited
disclosure of strongly felt emotions. As *Corinne* moves
on from its original subject, Madame de Staël's happy
discovery of Naples and the charm of things Italian in the
company of Dom Pedro, and closes with its main concern,
Prosper de Barante's failure to do his duty by her, the short-
comings of this conception become increasingly obvious.
When Corinne, driving through the streets of Rome in a
chariot drawn by four white horses, is cheered by enthusiastic crowds shouting "Long live Genius! Long live
Beauty!" it is fairly clear that one is dealing with a rather
low grade of wish-fulfillment. It is downhill all the way
to the point at which the dying Corinne comforts herself
by thinking of the sufferings that the wicked Oswald will
have to undergo when he realizes that his heartlessness
has killed "the woman who could feel and think more
deeply than any other of her time." At this point the level
of fantasy can only be described as infantile. It is argued
in favor of the book that Corinne is intended to represent
an ideal balance between instinct and intellect, and that
the wicked Oswald typifies the kind of modern man whose
instinctive self has been atrophied by his dangerous habit
of thinking about abstractions; but if that is the case these
intentions are not realized within the book. What *Corinne*
does deliver, on the other hand, is a very clear picture of
the compensatory daydreams and the resentments of a very
vain and very wealthy woman who cannot understand why
life is not giving her exactly what she wants. Madame de
Staël may not have realized this while she was writing
her novel, but she almost certainly became aware that she
had in some way prejudiced her reputation in intellectual
circles from the many ambiguities surrounding its recep-

tion. It created a sensation, and from the commercial point of view it was an enormous success, but it established her as a personality—in the modern sense—without adding anything to her claims to be taken seriously as a thinker. It may even have been borne in upon her that it had diminished them. Stendhal, naturally hostile to her as a convinced supporter of the regime, had been bowled over by the qualities of the first volume of *Delphine;* but was unconvinced by the second, and contemptuous of the third. He found *Corinne* an absurdity from first to last, and he was not alone in thinking so. But whether this aspect of her life was troublesome to her or not, her behavior within a few weeks of the publication of the book showed signs that she was going through something like a breakdown. The scenes at Charenton, and elsewhere, that had made Constant fear that she was going out of her mind in April were no more than pale shadows of the extravaganzas that were to come.

In May 1807 Madame du Tertre learned that her prolonged negotiations with her husband and her lawyers were moving, and that if she were to spend the summer in Germany she might actually obtain the long-awaited divorce. At the same time Constant, who was for the time being unable to enter Germany because of passport difficulties, began to have serious trouble with his eyes. His doctor told him that a weakening of the optic nerve, which could lead to blindness, was involved, and advised a course of painful bleedings spread over a month followed by a complete rest, preferably in the country. The couple consequently made appropriate plans for this situation. Constant would undergo his bloodlettings, and then leave Paris with Madame du Tertre. They would travel together as far as Chalons and then part, Madame du Tertre going on into Germany via Verdun, and Constant turning off to the southwest on the road to Dole and his father's home at Brévans. It was all cut and dried, but when the time set for their departure came round Constant was nowhere to be found. He was missing for two days, and when he reappeared he was in an appalling state of physical exhaustion

and mental anguish. When he was able to explain himself
he told Madame du Tertre that Madame du Staël had been
bombarding him with increasingly insulting and acrimoni-
ous letters ever since she had left Paris for Coppet, and
that the last of these, peculiarly violent and insulting in
tone, having been brought to him while one of his horribly
painful eye treatments was in progress, had stung him
into sending her a point-blank refusal either to return to
Coppet or to have anything more to do with her. Madame
de Staël's answer to this had been to send her Figaro-like
major domo, Eugene Uginet, to Paris to fetch him. Uginet
told him that if he didn't come quietly *She* would come and
get him herself, and Constant had temporarily caved in.
Uginet had coaxed him as far as Melun, some thirty miles
along the road to Geneva, by the time he came to his senses:

> *Here I am at Melun. It's madness. I'm not accom-
> plishing anything, and I'm thirty miles further from
> the spot where I want to be tonight. And the woman
> I'm so ridiculously afraid of will be none the better
> for this act of weakness that she knows nothing about.
> For the moment there's no way of getting out of it. If
> I go another five miles I risk losing Charlotte. It's fac-
> ing up to Uginet that I'm afraid of. Miserable weak-
> ness. Uginet has come. I've told him I'm going back to
> Paris. Battle with Uginet. I put myself into a rage in
> order to have the strength to stand up to him, and, once
> I was angry, I said a thousand things that were out of
> place. The end product of my journey, my weakness,
> my dodges, and my lies, is that I end up much worse
> off than if I'd been frank and if I hadn't set out. Dis-
> honesty makes one vile, and the feeling that one has
> made oneself vile makes life hard. I've put myself al-
> together at odds with myself. And Uginet had scarcely
> left the room before it all backed up in me. A thou-
> sand memories devastated me. Her good qualities,
> Albertine, so many ties. I cried like a child.*

He spent the next few days in Paris wooing back the
rather shaken Madame du Tertre and waiting for the in-

evitable reactions from Coppet. Madame du Staël sent him
letters that were alternately violently abusive, touching,
and mad, and in the end convinced him that he would,
after all, be better off with the woman who was kind, gentle, and understanding. He left Paris with Madame du
Tertre on the twenty-seventh of June and went as they had
planned to Chalons, where, after a night of memorable
physical pleasures at the Pomme d'Or, they parted in accordance with their original plan. Madame du Tertre wept,
excusably one would think, when they were kissing each
other good-bye. Constant recoiled indignantly at the sight
of her tears. Did she intend to subject him to emotional
blackmail? Had he not promised her that he would have
settled everything with Madame de Staël, once and for
all, by the end of August? Madame du Tertre wiped away
her tears. Her carriage rolled off in the direction of Germany, his cabriolet took the road leading to Dôle—and,
another hundred miles further on, Geneva and Coppet.

When Constant reached Dôle he found a furious letter
from Madame de Staël waiting for him. After his defeat
at Melun Uginet had returned to Coppet only to be sent
back to Paris at once with instructions to bring the recalcitrant to her without fail. She was maddened when he reported that Constant had managed to elude him and wrote
to him at several addresses where he might be likely to be
found in the hope that one of these arrows launched at
hazard might strike him. In her usual manner she abused
him roundly and then proposed that he should come back
to Coppet for two months. Her letter was backed up by
another from Schlegel begging him to resign himself to the
inevitable sooner rather than later. That was on July 3.
On the fourth he had another letter from Madame de Staël
which was all sweetness and promises to be good—and
which he received with scorn. He discussed his intention
of marrying Madame du Tertre with his father that night,
and although the old man took a discouraging line about
women who had been through the divorce court, Constant
ended his day by writing an invocation to Madame du

Tertre in his journal. "Dear Charlotte, all the prejudices
in the world can't stop me from becoming yours." Another
day passed, and then it was the sixth. Constant wrote up
part of his journal before the day's mail reached him:

> *Oh God! How I wish this thing was already over and
> done with! Going back there is pure weakness. She
> won't be any less furious when I leave again, and she's
> certainly not going to kill herself if I don't go back.
> All this stuff about opium is play acting or tantrum.
> Work going not too badly. Even here, I might finish
> my project if it wasn't for that fury, that scourge, that
> hell vomited up to torment me. I've been in a sort of
> fever all morning because I haven't had any letters
> from her....*

The letters came to ease his deprivation pains at midday,
one from Madame de Staël, abominable and abusive, and
another, from Auguste, that achieved a certain dignity.
"I'm tempted not to go," he wrote, at the start of the second
part of the day's entry, and ended by making up a program
for his departure: "Go to Besancon; from Besancon to Orbe,
leave my cabriolet at Orbe; go from Orbe to Lausanne, leave
my manuscripts at Lausanne, go to Coppet with an overnight bag; at the first scene, leave." He hesitated for another two days before leaving, and then, on the third day,
he received letters from both Schlegel and Madame de Staël
that seemed so abominable in contrast with another from
Madame du Tertre that came to him by the same post as to
make him think that he should not go near them. Another
forty-eight hours gave him time to realize that if he just
turned his back on Coppet and walked away from it he
would be abandoning his daughter to Madame de Staël.
He had to go and face her. "The thing has to be finished.
I'll go there, but I'll leave again...." That decision was
canceled on the following day by a letter from Madame de
Staël telling him that she had no intention of breaking
with him. He wrote up in his journal in something like a
panic:

*I've got no further forward than I was six months ago—
ten years ago. I'll be no better off for going near her
again. It will only mean clearing out once more, and I
couldn't have done better than to contrive this breach.
However, it's necessary. I've let myself in for going
back. But let's take steps to get away again as soon as
possible.*

Schlegel arrived the next day, and there was a violent
argument which lasted off and on for the next three days
and ended with their departure for Coppet.

At nine o'clock in the evening on the seventeenth of July
Constant was face to face with his mistress once again: he
was standing in silence in the darkening park as she
screamed abuse at him. She continued to work him over
for the next several days, inflicting nightly tongue-lashings
on him that lasted until four or five every morning. In one
of them, on the night of the twentieth of July, she told him
that even if it would kill him not to be given his freedom
she would rather have him die than let him go. Under her
remorseless pressure his nerve slowly broke and he lost all
capacity to resist. By mid-August he found himself hanging
around Montagny, a large house at Ouchy-le-Petit on the
outskirts of Lausanne, where Madame de Staël had established herself for the height of the summer. She had decided to offer the society people of Lausanne a production
of Racine's *Andromache,* in which she herself was to play
Hermione and Constant was to take the part of Pyrrhus,
King of Epirus. It was a singular notion, since the tragedy
turns on the decision of Pyrrhus to reject the love and devotion of Hermione, to whom he has pledged himself, in order
to marry the Trojan princess Andromache. Constant began
to sweat during the rehearsals:

Rehearsal of Andromache. *I had a certain amount of
pleasure in saying the lines that Pyrrhus addressed to
Hermione. But all that doesn't simplify my life. I'm
enmeshed in a web of execrable falsehoods. It's very
possible that my undertakings to Charlotte will become*

*public property. She will surely have told her family
about them and when she asks for her divorce, as she
may already have done, everybody, everywhere, will
know what it is all about and somebody is sure to
write to Madame de Staël, and all my maneuverings
will become perfidies. It won't be any better the other
way round. Madame de Staël is doing her best to make
everyone believe that we're inseparable. That could
get back to Charlotte and prevent her from acting
[in the matter of the divorce]. But how are you to tell
the truth to a person whose only answer is to swallow
opium?*

With so much on his mind—and on top of everything
else a horrible twenty-one-day stretch in which he had no
word from Madame du Tertre and didn't know whether she
was through with him or whether it was simply that her
letters to him were going astray—Constant hardly noticed
that the day was bearing down on him on which he would
have to stand up in the face of an audience, a large part
of which was to be made up of his cousins and connections,
while Madame de Staël, in the character of Hermione, de-
nounced him for his cruelties and treacheries to her:

*I waited in secret the return of one foresworn
Sure that, remembering your duty soon or late,
You'd bring me back the heart that was my due.
Faithless I loved you, how much more had you been
     true!
And now, even now, when with honeyed words
You tell me, oh so calmly, that you mean me ill,
Ungrateful man, I do believe that I must love you still.
But oh, my lord, if it must be, if angry heaven
Decrees the joy of pleasing you is for another,
Marry whom you will, with my consent, but at the
     least
Let but one day go by. Tomorrow you'll be master....
You've not a word to say?*

You brute I clearly see

*You count each moment lost you waste on me.
Your heart, so wild to see your Trojan once again,*

Can't let you give one moment to another without
  pain.
I'll keep you here no more, get hence—away!
Go pledge to her the faith you swore to keep with me.
Go take the names of all the gods in vain—
The gods, the just gods, who'll not have yet forgot
That these same oaths have bound us with their knot.
                              [*Act IV, Scene 5,*
                              lines 1363–1384]

Having thus put Constant in the pillory, Madame de
Staël returned to Coppet in a state of high glee, after extracting a promise from him that he would follow her at
the end of the month. Constant himself had not found the
public performance very disturbing and had merely noted
in his journal that the house had been friendlier than he
had expected, that Madame de Staël had been quite pleasant, and that he hadn't acted too badly. But his cousin
Rosalie de Constant, who had hated Madame de Staël ever
since the affair of the sale of La Chablière, had been disgusted and appalled by his exhibition of weakness and hers
of cruelty, and by the readiness of both to expose the reality
of their situation to the public in this way. She decided to
save Constant from himself and from his captor, and she
rallied his aunt Madame de Nassau to her side to assist her
in the effort to put some backbone into him and to nerve
him to make the break. They appeared to be succeeding,
and on the thirtieth of the month—the day on which he
had promised Madame du Tertre that he would have freed
himself from his entanglement once and for all—he wrote
Madame de Staël a letter telling her that he refused to come,
tore it up, and went to her.

This was not the surrender that it appeared to be, but
only a preliminary to it. Rosalie de Constant and Madame
de Nassau had nerved him for a confrontation that would
win him his liberty if he proved unable to break with her
without seeing her. Their strategy was a simple one: he was
to tell her that the time had come either to put the relationship on a stable and honorable footing, or to end it;

she must either marry him or let him go. The confrontation was not productive. Madame de Staël flew into a rage when Constant made his show of firmness, and leapt for the bell pull, screaming for help. Her sons Albert and Auguste, her daughter Albertine, Schlegel, and various servants poured into the room, and were told of Constant's infamous proposal: "There he is," she cried, "look at him—the schemer who means to deprive me of my name and of my fortune and who wants to ruin us all." Constant grabbed Auguste de Staël by the shoulder and said: "Look on me as the vilest of men if I ever marry your mother." On this she twisted a scarf round her neck and threw herself onto the floor as she went through the motions of an attempt to strangle herself. When Constant had at length succeeded in calming her and getting her to take her opium and go to sleep, he spent a sleepless night writing her another letter ending it all that he left behind him when he rode away at seven the next morning.

After a two-and-a-half-hour ride through the demure and gardenlike prettiness of the Genevan countryside Constant reached La Chaumière, the house of another of his aunts, Madame de Charrière de Bavois, where, possibly by arrangement, Rosalie de Constant and Madame de Nassau soon joined him to lend him their moral support. While he was recovering from his ride, his sleepless night, and the strain of his encounter, Madame de Staël was organizing a pursuit. Uginet and the men of the household scattered to find out what route Constant had taken and, with that accomplished, sent Madame de Staël off in her famous yellow coach and six with a pretty fair idea of where he was. When it at length rumbled up to the entrance to La Chaumière and discharged its noisily demonstrative owner the three women were sitting with Constant in the drawing room, doing their best to comfort and encourage him. Recognizing from his panic-stricken response to the racket of Madame de Staël's arrival that their kinsman was completely demoralized, Rosalie de Constant and Madame de Nassau attempted to save him by locking him into the drawing room with Madame de Charrière while they went to face Madame de Staël. They found her spread out on the staircase, head downwards, with her bosom bursting out of her dress and her hair all over the place. "Where is he?" she screamed. "I must see him." The two women lifted her up and carried her into the nearest bedroom in the hope of putting another pair of doors between her and her prey. But it was no use. Constant located himself for her by banging on the drawing-room doors in answer to her wild cries and clamoring to be released. The two principal actors in the scene fell into each other's arms as the drawing-room doors were opened, but after the first embraces Madame de Staël flung herself to the ground again and began screaming abuse at her voluntary victim. Not understanding games, and not realizing that a good time was being had by all, Rosalie de Constant now tried to intervene and told Madame de Staël that she had no right to ruin her cousin's life. The full force of Madame de Staël's stream of abuse was now turned upon her. Rosalie de Constant and Madame de Nassau then fled the house, and Madame de Staël presently pushed Constant into her coach and returned to Coppet with him.

"*Journée douloureuse*" are the opening words of the entry for September 2 in Constant's diary.

> ... *I don't have the strength to stick to my guns and to tell her that I want to break with her, and I'm not able to say that I'll come back to her. She is frantic and I suffer. We've agreed that I'll spend six weeks with her, and that then she'll take herself off to Vienna. But what shall I say to Charlotte, who counts on me for the end of September and may set out to join me on the fifteenth. I'm risking all my happiness.*

In this perplexing situation Constant settled down to kill time—the phrase is his own—by translating Schiller's *Wallenstein* and adapting it for the French stage. He kept his nose to the grindstone through the rest of September, October, and much of November, resolutely putting it between him and his steadily increasing anxieties about los-

ing Madame du Tertre. She had made considerable progress
in the direction of securing her divorce during the summer
and was anxious to rejoin him, but he had to keep putting
her off as Madame de Staël repeatedly postponed her departure for Vienna. Toward the end of his remarkable ordeal his misery and confusion became intense, since wish-
ful thinking, or some complex unconscious motivation,
led him to accept a departure date that was purely pro-
visional in Madame de Staël's mind as a definite one.
Under the impression that he would be free by November 2
he wrote to Madame du Tertre telling her to meet him at
Besançon. She hastened to keep this rendezvous, but when
she got to Besançon, after driving on by night and by day
in spite of appalling weather and icy roads, Constant
wasn't there. In his place there were seven coldly unpleasant
letters rehearsing all his doubts and fears about the marriage—and when she had read these she was left to cool
her heels for over three weeks in the cheerless rooms of the
Hôtel National. How much longer she might have had to
wait it is hard to say, but misery and disappointment
lowered her spirits to the point where she became ill. Word
reached him that she was in a serious condition, and he at
last nerved himself to escape, getting away by telling Madame de Staël that it was his father who was at death's
door. When he came to Madame du Tertre's bedside and
found her delirious and almost at the end of her physical
resources, he experienced a great access of an extremely
sinister tenderness for her. She had suffered so much! And
on his account!

As soon as Madame du Tertre could be moved he carried
her off to Brévans to be cared for in his father's house. By
that time Madame de Staël had left for Vienna, accompanied by a representative contingent from the Coppet
household, Auguste and Albertine, Schlegel, Uginet, and
the usual tail of coachmen, grooms, and personal servants.
She was in fine fettle, and quite unaware that the unknown
third player Constant had drawn in to their game had just
taken a vital set from her and developed winning chances.

While Madame de Staël had been putting Constant

through all this she had been keeping up her game with
Prosper de Barante. When he was in Poland on official
business in the early part of the summer she had pursued
him with amorous propositions and blackmailing threats
of her usual brand, and these had brought him, unwilling
but still fascinated, to Coppet in September. He had found
her in a frame of mind that he did not greatly care for: she
had been dabbling in the muddy waters of religious enthusiasm. The thin end of this wedge had been Schlegel's insistence that there was merit and interest in the thought
of even the most gaseous of the romantic metaphysicians
of the German school. His outpourings on this subject had
been well received, and their reception had led the astute
Bonstetten to predict that Coppet would sooner or later
have its religious phase. It had begun, oddly enough, as a
result of the skeptical Constant's sufferings. When he was
in the depths of his miseries his cousin, the Chevalier de
Langalerie, who was a member of a group of well-to-do
quietists called Les Ames Intérieures—"The Inner Souls"—
undertook to show him that he could enjoy the consolations
of religion without the necessity of believing in God or,
indeed, in anything in particular. Constant snatched at
the straw of fatalism that was thus offered to him, the more
enthusiastically because it occurred to him that if Madame
de Staël could be persuaded to accept the idea that the secret of happiness was resignation to God's will, she might
even come to accept his departure as one of its manifestations. She had been immediately enthralled by the obvious
inversion that the idea of resignation offers to the undisciplined and willful egotist, that whatever the individual
wishes to do is God's will. It was as an excited discoverer
of religion as a way of life that she reached Vienna.

Vienna was at that time the most sophisticated of European capital cities. The life of its upper classes had been
untouched by the French Revolution, and the elegant, man-
nered, and formalistic patterns of aristocratic existence
survived there in their integrity. Though Madame de Staël,
who always thought of herself as an aristocrat, was wholly

unaware of it, she was, for the Viennese of the court, the
epitome of the jumped-up bourgeois nouveau riche. While
she might be, for the French nobility, a rather exotic foreign millionairess, she was on her native Teutonic ground
in Austria. "Everyone" there knew that both her parents
had originated in parsonages and that they belonged to the
race designed by providence to supply the owners of great
estates with governesses, tutors, secretaries, and lawyers—
her mother had, indeed, been a governess, had she not? And
her father a bank clerk? And on top of all that Madame de
Staël had never lost the weight that she had put on in Italy
in 1804; she had, on the contrary, gained steadily ever
since, and had become exceedingly unrefined and unaristo-
cratic in her appearance. Her physical vulgarity, which
was given a sort of sparkle by her energy and restlessness,
was much accentuated by her personal style in the matter
of dress. The clothes she wore always seemed eccentric
enough to the French, but in France they were at least tolerable as easily recognizable variations on what was, for the
moment, the fashion. Out of context, as they were in Vienna, they looked like the barbaric caricatures of revolutionary modes that were in current circulation as anti-
French propaganda. It was only the extraordinary thickness
of her skin, and the beautiful manners of the Viennese
aristocrats, that kept her from the wounding realization
that she was considered a grotesque figure. Her relationship
with the aged Prince de Ligne was typical of her relationship with the society. She looked on this embodiment of
the *Ancien Régime* as a dear old dodo, patronized him,
and imagined that she had captivated him by taking a
friendly interest in his writings. He treated her with the
exquisite consideration and the apparent concentration of
interest that had made it easy for him to become the lover
of so many beautiful women in his day, and he never allowed her to guess how little respect he had for her in precisely those regions in which she rated herself most highly.
He thought her imaginative, but not very intelligent, and
profoundly ignorant.

She makes pronouncements, has the last word on every
controversial issue, piles error upon error, and ends by
not knowing what she is saying when she talks about
the arts—of which she knows nothing—and of reli-
gious feeling, which she finds in everything. Her Chris-
tianity makes one wish to be a pagan, her mysticism
makes one love the matter of fact, and her love for
the superior makes one see the good in the common-
place and the vulgar.

The Prince de Ligne put her in touch with Friedrich
Gentz, one of the more important agents of the British
secret service in the German speaking countries, who was
hopeful that some use could be made of her as someone
notoriously at odds with the Emperor. Gentz had two long
conversations with her that led, not to the proposal for
some sort of collaboration that might have been expected
had he been impressed favorably, but to his giving her an
introduction to Adam Müller, a figure on the lunatic
fringe of German mysticism known as the "peasant prophet." She saw quite a lot of Müller in Dresden on her way
home, but when she reached Weimar Goethe, who had been
warned that she was on her way, was not there: he had gone
to take a cure at a spa a safe distance away.

While she was able to blind herself to this aspect of her
Austrian and German experiences in the winter of 1807–8
by dwelling on the numberless dinners, receptions, and
balls to which she had been invited, and the numbers of
distinguished and important people to whom she had been
introduced, there was no denying that her affair with the
Graf Moritz O'Donnell von Tyreonnel had ended in a humiliating defeat. She had first met O'Donnell, a twenty-
seven-year-old Engineer Officer in the Austrian Service,
in Venice when she was on her way back from Italy two
years before, and she had looked him up and pounced at
him as soon as she reached Vienna. He was at first pleased
and flattered to find that a rich and famous woman was
after him, and they soon became lovers. But once the
novelty of the new affair had worn off he became aware

that his mistress was generally considered to be ridiculous and that it was assumed that she was keeping him. He began to back away, and to his considerable surprise and annoyance, she came after him, pleading with him and abusing him by turns, and finally dropping him a broad hint that she might consider marrying him—and that if she did it would be well worth his while: "Do not forget that in my present circumstances I have a yearly income of 120,000 francs and do not owe anyone a penny." If he would only agree to come to join her at Coppet... O'Donnell replied to this offer in a cold fury: it had been rumored in Vienna that he had proposed marriage to her and that she had turned him down, and he believed that the story could be traced back to her; couldn't she realize that she was subjecting him to a persecution that was making him look ridiculous and threatening to damage his career? What could do a young officer more harm than to have a clouded reputation as the mercenary lover of an aging woman?

It was the most absolute refusal of an invitation to join in her games that she had received since François de Pange had turned her down at the beginning of her affair with Constant. Perhaps it was the memory of that check that led her to write to Constant as soon as it became obvious that O'Donnell was going to be obdurate and was not going to play. She wrote to him in May 1808 telling him that she would soon be back at Coppet and that he must join her there:

> I...I'm coming back with the same feeling of devotion for you, a devotion that no worship from others has weakened, a devotion that I feel for no one else on this earth; my heart, my life, everything is yours if you want it—think of that!

Constant thought of it with something in the nature of a thrill of horror. Madame du Tertre had just regained her freedom. The consistory of the Archbishop of Paris had ruled that, the Graf von Marenholz having been still alive when it was contracted, her marriage to Monsieur du Tertre must be considered null and void: she was therefore in a position to marry Constant whenever she chose. And now *She* was coming back, just when everything seemed to have become simple and easy. The only possible way of keeping it that way was for them to get married at once. Madame du Tertre resumed her maiden name Charlotte von Hardenberg, and they hurried to Brévans to tell Juste de Constant that all the obstacles in the way of their marriage had been removed and that they wished to be legally united at once. But in the circumstances a quiet marriage, without publicity, would be desirable—could he help them? He could. His friend the Protestant Pastor Ebray of Besançon was understanding and discreet, and, if the thing were put to him tactfully, he would almost certainly agree to officiate at a private ceremony. Constant was accordingly married to Charlotte von Hardenberg at Dôle on the eighth of June, 1808.

For anyone but Constant this would have marked the beginning of a new chapter in his life, but he had gone to considerable lengths to insure that it would not. The religious ceremony was not, at his request, recorded in the parish register, and it was not followed by the civil ceremony in the office of the mayor that was necessary to complete its legalization under French law. Constant's rationalization for prejudicing the legality of his wedding by these omissions was to say that if these things were to be done there would inevitably be publicity, and he did not care to be responsible for what might happen if Madame de Staël heard from anyone else that he was bound to another woman—she might kill herself or go out of her mind. For the same reason Madame Constant was neither to call herself by her new name—if it were that—or to go on calling herself Charlotte von Hardenberg; she was to revert to the title of Madame du Tertre. This was represented to her as a temporary measure, to be abandoned as soon as he had been to Coppet and had told Madame de Staël how things were. They parted for this purpose at the end of June. He went in fear and trembling to Coppet, she went to Neuchâtel to wait for him in a suite at the Hôtel des Balances.

Madame de Staël found Constant unexpectedly amiable and affectionate on his return, but heard no word of the marriage from him. Face to face with her he simply lost his nerve. Before long he had settled into his usual place in the little clan, the only difference in his situation being that he was now in secret correspondence with his wife, and occasionally stole out with reckless daring to spend a day or two with her—he was in effect carrying on a clandestine affair with the woman he had married while living with his mistress.

Constant would possibly have allowed this state of affairs to continue indefinitely had not his wife's aunt, Frau von Decken, come on the scene late in July, accompanied by her daughter and son-in-law, the Count and Countess von Wangenheim. Frau von Decken could not understand what her niece was doing, hanging about in a second-rate provincial town where there was no society, and insisted on taking her on with her first to Lausanne and then to Geneva. At Lausanne she was introduced, as Madame du Tertre, to Constant's aunt Madame de Nassau, who had been told of his feelings about her but had never met her. Madame de Nassau was very favorably impressed, and wrote at once to Constant to tell him so, and to tell him that he should leave Coppet immediately and come to see her. Constant declined, on the ground that the risk was too great, and that, if he did come just at that moment, there would probably be an outburst that would make the earth speak. It didn't, he suggested, seem worth it, when everything would probably be straightened out peacefully very soon. Madame de Nassau was upset by this cowardly response, and feeling ashamed for him did her best to justify it by telling his wife the story of the horrible scenes Madame de Staël had made at Coppet and in the house of Madame de Charrière de Bavois at the beginning of the previous autumn.

Whatever else Charlotte von Hardenberg may have felt after listening to what Madame de Nassau had to say on that subject, she was not made any the keener to bring herself face to face with the woman who had such a powerful hold on her husband. When Frau von Decken's party moved on to Geneva, and a call on the mistress of Coppet was proposed, she said firmly that the others might go if they wished but that she would not join them. This roused her aunt's suspicions, and to quiet them it became necessary to tell her at least part of the truth—that she had obtained an annulment of her marriage to Monsieur du Tertre, and she was hoping to make Constant her third husband. This roused Frau von Decken's interest and curiosity; she was sixty, and no fool, and it seemed remarkable to her that Constant, if he had serious intentions toward her niece, should be leaving her dangling around Swiss hotels in an ambiguous situation while he stayed at Coppet. She accordingly moved her party into the luxurious Hôtel de l'Angleterre at Sécheron—practically on Madame de Staël's doorstep—to see what he would do, and to see how things were at Coppet. She managed to get herself invited to a meal inside what she now looked upon as the enemy stronghold on the last day of July, and after it had a conversation with Constant in which he showed himself to be shifty and evasive. She tried to pin him down as to what his intentions really were, and he wriggled and dodged in order to avoid telling her what the real situation was. He blotted his copybook still further by showering his wife with agitated notes, carried to the hotel by his manservant, while refusing to run the risk of coming to her in person. Frau von Decken's discontent with all this was turned into outright disapproval after she had accompanied her niece to a dinner given by the Chevalier Jacques Dupuch at which her niece found herself in the same room with Madame de Staël for the first time. Charlotte looked on this long-awaited and much-dreaded confrontation as a challenge, and in attempting to show herself to best advantage, did all she could to interest and amuse the men who were present. She was only too successful in gathering them about her, and at the end of the evening her aunt gave her a tremendous scolding for having been so forward and flirtatious. It was clear to her, she said, that her talk of marrying Constant was ridiculous: if she was so keen on impressing other men he couldn't

mean very much to her, and his furtive and evasive behavior made it just as plain that she wasn't of very much
importance to him. Since the thing wasn't serious she would
be well advised to break it off and the sooner the better.
She could be sure that the whole Hardenberg family would
agree that it would be the right thing for her to do. Taken
aback by her aunt's vehemence, Charlotte blurted out the
truth of her situation. Frau von Decken hugged her, apolo-
gized for having misunderstood things, and promised to
keep her secret.

The story moves into the mode of operetta at this point.
Madame de Staël called on "the German ladies," as they
were now known at Coppet, on the following day. She was
suspicious of them, without knowing precisely why, and
she asked them questions, the drift of which they well
understood. Fobbing her off amused them, it was like playing a children's game, and they foolishly tried to see how
close to the wind they could go. With assumed innocence
Frau von Decken told her how nice to them Madame de
Nassau had been when they were in Lausanne, where they
soon hoped to return. And who would they be expecting to
see when they got there? asked Madame de Staël, knowing
that Constant was planning to go to that place within a
few days. A certain Demoiselle Freymond, replied Frau von
Decken, a delightful woman who had been governess in the
household of her friend the Maréchal von Walmoden.
Madame de Staël nodded and smiled, apparently satisfied,
and left soon afterwards. "The German ladies" laughed a
great deal after she had gone, walked down the sweeping
lawns between the hotel and Lac Leman and went for a
promenade in one of the elegant boats that Monsieur Dejean, the proprietor, provided for the pleasure of his guests.
It glided over the gently rippling surface of the lake pro-
pelled by two oarsmen, dressed in white with colored
sashes round their waists, as the ladies chatted in the shade
of a white awning. A large red-and-yellow flag flew like an
ensign at the stern. The views across the water were enchanting, and for the moment Charlotte felt tranquilly
happy.... But when they returned the figure of Antoin,

Constant's coachman, could be seen waiting for them at the landing stage. He had a panic-stricken letter from his master for Charlotte. Madame de Staël had returned to Coppet in a fury of rage and suspicion and had put him through a prolonged cross-examination about his relationship with the "German ladies." What had they said to her? What had happened? He was at once angry and frightened, and Charlotte had to sit down, without giving herself time to untie the ribbons of her bonnet, to write him a reassuring letter.

This storm blew over, for the time being, and everyone went off to the Fête of the Shepherds at Unspunnen, near Interlaken, where the five hundredth anniversary of the taking of the oath of Grutli was being celebrated by a gathering of some six thousand peasants. The event took place in a grassy natural amphitheater under the walls of a ruined castle in surroundings of great natural beauty. The sun shone, choirs sang, bands played, peasant athletes tossed great stones for improbable distances, the Ranz des Vaches was given an appropriately solemn rendering, there was dancing in the open air, enormous quantities of food were eaten; it was all very enjoyable and touching, and Madame de Staël loved every minute of it. Charlotte, who had a pleasant time herself, saw that she did, and felt that it was a good omen. All might perhaps end happily, with Madame de Staël accepting the situation and allowing her her happiness with Constant. She was an innocently good-natured woman, and she still understood very little of her adversary's twisted nature. Madame de Staël had not allowed Constant to go to Unspunnen because she knew that Charlotte was to be there. She had gone with Schlegel, Sismondi, and Zacharias Werner, and they had all been watching Charlotte during the fête. At the end of the day, when the dancing had begun, Charlotte had been much pestered by an amorous gentleman she didn't know who wished to dance with her, and she had been forced to speak sharply to him to get rid of him. She thought no more about the incident, but it had been observed by the members of the little clan, and they made characteristic use of it. When

Constant returned to Coppet he made a note in his *Carnet:* "Odd stories about Charlotte at Interlaken: I don't want to go into what they're about."

But if he didn't wish to do that, Constant had no hesitation about writing to Charlotte to rebuke her for her imprudence. His extraordinary letter reached her at a moment when she was full of disquiet. She had written to various people before her departure for Unspunnen and had told her correspondents that they could either address their replies to a hotel at Berne where she would be stopping on her return journey, or to an address in Lausanne. She found that Madame de Staël had been at the hotel in Berne before her and had picked up her letters. The same thing had happened to all the correspondence addressed to her as Madame du Tertre at Lausanne. A suspicion, probably well founded, entered her mind that Madame de Staël had got hold of Constant's Antoin, a man she had never found it possible to like or trust, and had bribed him to tell her all that he knew about their relationship. As she read Constant's complaint she felt a dawning awareness of the difficulties of her position as a wife whose husband was living apart from her in the household of a woman who would stop at nothing to poison his mind against her. With a sinking heart she wrote to him to explain what had happened to her at the fête. Her fears were fully justified. A few days later she was writing to him again to tell him that there was no truth in the story that she was behaving indiscreetly with a certain Monsieur de R.

> You say something harsh that has really hurt me. "I love you as I knew you." And as I am, what do you feel about me?—There's no doubt but that you think I am no longer what I was. The whole of your letter, all those five pages in which your dissatisfaction with me comes through in every line, shows that only too well. You criticize everything I've done or felt.

She had wanted to stay on in Lausanne to be near him and to enjoy the company of the friendly members of his

family and the cheerful society of the place, but he would
not allow that—it was too near to Coppet, and the risk that
she would betray their secret in some unguarded moment
was too great. She must remove herself to Neuchâtel, to the
cheerless discomfort of the Hôtel des Balances, and the
limited resources of a society dominated by Monsieur de
Montmollin, the Mayor, and Monsieur Fornachon, the
principal wholesaler. She obediently did so. At Neuchâtel
she found herself being persecuted in a sly way, with
double-entendres, and meaningful hints that he knew
much more about her than she realized, from an elderly
mischief-maker called François Gaudot who was at once a
friend of Monsieur de Montmollin and a regular visitor at
Coppet. Charlotte found her position in the tiny town intolerable and told Constant to tell his father that she would
be coming to Brévans to wait for him to join her, she would
be getting there toward the end of September. Rather sulkily
he agreed and promised to follow her as soon as he could....

When Charlotte at length arrived at Brévans she was
received by an astonished Juste de Constant who had been
given no warning of her coming. His wife was ill; his
daughter was away. It was difficult for him to pretend that
her visit was either welcome or convenient. After a day
or two further explanations for the chilly reception that
she had been given came to the surface. Constant had never
reconciled himself to his father's marriage to Marianne
Magnin, denied its validity, and habitually referred to
the two entirely legitimate children it had produced as
"the bastards." From his strong position as his father's
trustee he was now making it as difficult as possible for
the eighty-one-year-old man to provide for his children
and his wife in the face of an inevitably imminent demise.
He had exacerbated his father's natural annoyance on this
score by churlishly forbidding his relatives in Lausanne
to give any support to the old man's attempt to launch his
daughter in the local society as a preliminary to making
a good match for her. The point he had hatefully decided
to make an issue of was that Juste de Constant was entitled
to call himself Constant de Rebecque and wished his daugh-

ter to be presented and received in Geneva and Lausanne as Mademoiselle de Rebecque. Constant was determined that this should not happen—and to round out the grievances of the Constants of Brévans the visit that Charlotte was proposing to make to them was going to be, to all appearances, a long one. She might think that her Constant was going to appear at any moment, but they happened to know, since he had told them so, that he did not mean to come to Brévans until after his *Wallenstein* had been published, an event that could not take place before mid-November.

As things turned out, it was not until the beginning of December that Madame de Staël closed Coppet for the winter and moved into Geneva. On the sixth Constant wrote a miserable letter to Madame de Nassau:

> *I will, I hope, be at Brévans on Saturday or on Sunday morning. I catch a glimpse of the harbor, but I'm still bumping from reef to reef, and I've two or three more ridges of rock to scrape over. To enjoy a little peace, if there is such a thing, will be a very unusual experience for me.*

He had almost insured himself against the risk of experiencing it by writing a furiously angry letter to Charlotte upbraiding her for betraying him to his father by telling him too much about their affairs and complaining to him of the way in which he was treating her. This provocative tirade was his characteristic way of answering a letter that his father had written him to let him know that his inexplicable behavior had caused Charlotte to fall into a settled melancholy and that it was not right that she should be made so unhappy. Charlotte, however, declined the opportunity to take the offense she had been given. She was now aware that she was in love with a very sick man, and she received him with love and without resentment. He gave her a very rough time throughout the remainder of the winter, being nervous, irritable, compulsively jealous, and once again in the grip of his gambling fever, but in the end her devotion and her refusal to quarrel with him had its effect, and he began to calm down. In the spring it at last became possible for him to concoct a plan for breaking with Madame de Staël that seemed to have some reasonable chance of success.

Constant was not only sick when he came to his father's house in December 1808, he was also suffering from the effects of having been shut up in something very like a madhouse. The Zacharias Werner who had been with Madame de Staël at Unspunnen returned to Coppet with her. He was the wildest extremist on the lunatic fringe of German mysticism; originally a Protestant, he had first become a Roman Catholic convert, and then had passed on to Priapism, preaching the heretical doctrine that sexual intercourse was the true worship, and proving the sincerity of his beliefs by living a life of industrious promiscuity that involved the endless tumbling of maidservants and peasant girls. His mother had been mad enough to believe that she was the Virgin Mary and that Zacharias was the living Christ, and many of his ideas, which required the literal acceptance of the exaggerated metaphors of seventeenth-century religious enthusiasm, suggest that he was just as far gone. It would have been easier to dismiss him as a madman if he had not had a very large measure of personal charm and genuine talents as a poet and a playwright. He was thus very agreeable company, and was able to give his fundamentally ridiculous ideas expression in vigorous and exciting language. He was, indeed, right up Madame de Staël's undisciplined and enthusiastic alley and his visit to Coppet was a tremendous success. It ended with a disagreeable scene in which, no doubt at Madame de Staël's suggestion, he implored Constant, with crocodile tears pouring down his cheeks, never to leave "that poor woman." Constant had promised that he never would.

Another of the autumn's visitors to Coppet had been Julie von Krudener, an aristocrat who had come to religion in her middle years as a result of seeing a gentleman of her acquaintance drop dead in the street seconds after he had raised his hat to her. This had led her to regret her sexually enterprising youth and had driven her into the arms of the Moravian Brotherhood. She had been an orthodox and devoted member of that sect for two years, when she suddenly tired of their insistence on the simple life and the performance of good works and began shopping around for something more immediately rewarding. She had been to Königsberg to sit at the feet of Pastor Mayr who preached the doctrine that all religions and creeds were one (and who had been an inspiration to Zacharias Werner), and she had scouted the whole field of mystical eccentricity in Germany before setting up as an exaltee on her own. She preached quietism and the acceptance of God's will with passion and intensity, and—since her doctrine boiled down to the thesis that God was kind and that if you didn't worry too much, and didn't rush things, and waited to do what you wanted to do until you felt like doing it, you would be doing God's will and would be happy—it will be seen that it would have had a considerable attraction for someone as indecisive and as self-indulgent as Constant, even if he had not been set up for something of the kind by the Chevalier de Langalerie's efforts. Julie von Krudener seems to have been as much of a success with him as the Dionysiac Zacharias Werner was with Madame de Staël, and the only prayers that Constant ever put into his journal were addressed, some seven years later to her *"Dieu de Bonté."*

A curious point that requires explanation is why it was just at this time, when the Coppet circle was clearly in a state of intellectual disintegration, that the Emperor should at last have decided to take Madame de Staël seriously as an opponent. It was in June, when Madame de Staël was exploring the mind of the Peasant Prophet at Dresden, that the Emperor sent minutes from his headquarters at Bayonne on the Spanish border instructing his Minister of Police and his Foreign Minister to take a harsher line with Madame de Staël.

Madame de Staël is in regular correspondence with the man Gentz, and has allowed herself to be drawn

into the clique of London intriguers. I want her to be
watched at Coppet, and desire you to give orders to
that effect to the Prefect of Geneva and the Comman-
dant of the Gendarmerie. Her exchanges with this in-
dividual cannot be otherwise than hurtful to France.
You will let it be known that up to the present she
has been looked upon as mad, but that from this day
forward she is to be considered to belong to a group
detrimental to the public peace.

These instructions to Fouché were repeated in the minutes addressed to Monsieur de Champagny, the Minister
for Foreign Affairs, who was also told to see to it that no
one in the French foreign service in Germany was to have
anything to do with her and that she was to be kept under
constant surveillance.

Since Madame de Staël was now madder, and more inconsequent, than she had ever been, this sudden change
of policy is at first sight hard to account for, but the explanation seems to lie in the tactics of the power struggle
then going on between Fouché, the Minister of Police, and
Savary, the head of the Security forces. Madame de Staël had
become a pawn in this contest because Fouché considered
her unimportant and pathetic, and was inclined to be
tolerant of her childishly conspiratorial efforts to play a
political role. Savary seems to have decided fairly early
on that Fouché had made himself vulnerable by taking this
line and had consistently magnified the scope and importance of Madame de Staël's activities in the confidential
reports which he sent directly to the Emperor and which
were not seen by the Minister of Police. It was almost certainly information about the extent of Savary's interest
in Madame de Staël's movements and activities that led
Gentz to investigate her, and her meetings and subsequent
correspondence with this important British agent then
provided Savary with proof that she was in fact dangerous
and that Fouché had been wrong to take a soft line with
her. His victory in this matter was a small but important
step in the direction of the larger triumph which led to
Fouché's disgrace and his replacement by Savary in 1810.

Ironically enough the Emperor's minutes elevating the mistress of Coppet to the rank of an enemy of the state were written just as she was being written off as a person to be taken seriously by the other side. From the time she reached Vienna at the end of 1807 until she left Germany in the early summer of 1808 she had been under constant sur-veillance by the Austrian secret police, and the reports of their agents, covering every hour of her days and nights, constitute a devastating revelation of the triviality of her interests and pursuits. When she arrived it was thought that she had come as a French agent, a suspicion that seem-ed to be confirmed by her frequent social contacts with the French embassy and its personnel, but as the weeks and months went by the police reports accumulated to build up a mosaic of a life lived without any coherent purpose by an idle-minded and irresponsible woman to whom no sane conspirator would dream of communicating anything that he wished to keep secret.

Between the end of December 1808 and the beginning of April 1809 Constant made a partial recovery from the condition to which he had been reduced by his experiences of the summer. But he was still unable to face the neces-sity of making decisions and taking action. As the day on which he would have to tell Madame de Staël the truth about Charlotte approached he began to hover, and to pro-duce one modification after another to the straightforward plan of attack that he had worked out. This called for a joint confrontation: they were to face *Her* together (they now generally spoke of her and referred to her as *Elle* with a capital E). But as the dreadful moment grew closer Con-stant felt more and more strongly that this would be a mis-take. In the end he even proposed that he should remain at Les Herbages while Charlotte went to Geneva alone to do the job. He was coaxed gently out of this cowardly eva-sion:

> *My poor dear, you would never be able to endure*
> *the loneliness of it. One is always tough enough when*
> *making a plan, but it's another matter when it comes*
> *to carrying it out. How would you be able to stand the*

double strain of our separation and of thinking of the
distress that this brusque way of handling the matter
could cause her. It's I who beg you to give up this idea
for both our sakes. I think our latest plan is the kindest
and best if there's even the slightest chance that
kindness can move her. As to that you know her better
than I do. I'll hold to everything that I've promised.
You know how much I love you, it will see me through.
And besides, I tell you once more, my decision to agree
to whatever she thinks best for her has been taken.
So let's be off tomorrow, and let's put our trust in
heaven.

But in the end he had his way: they traveled to Geneva together, but when Charlotte had been settled into the Hôtel de l'Angleterre at Séheron Constant went into hiding at Ferney. As soon as he was safely out of the way Charlotte wrote a note to Madame de Staël, signing herself Charlotte von Hardenberg, inviting her to visit in order to receive an important communication. The invitation was sent over to Coppet by a valet riding on a horse sometime during the afternoon. Presumably Charlotte expected an answer to be sent to her in a similar fashion, probably on the following morning, and that it would tell whether or no Madame de Staël intended to come, and when she was to be expected if she did come. Thinking along these lines she decided to go to bed early, and, thinking that she might have a cold coming on, she began by soaking her feet in a mustard bath. She was thus engaged, and at a considerable disadvantage, when Madame de Staël burst in on her unannounced at ten o'clock, making the portentous and unintentionally comic remark that "I have obeyed your summons because you are a Hardenberg."

There are two sources for the many reconstructions of this famous interview, which lasted until four the following morning. The most complete is second hand, and consists of Madame Récamier's recollection of what was said to her about it by Madame de Staël. It puts Charlotte, as one might expect, in a contemptible light, and it suggests

that Constant was present. The impression one gets from it
is that he stood by, dumb with terror, while his wife licked
Madame de Staël's boots and made inane remarks about
his sweet nature and her talents, generosity and virtue.
From Charlotte's side there is a long letter written to Constant the following morning which passes over most of the
details of the encounter by saying that she could not possibly get a full account of all that had happened in the six
hours into the compass of a letter:

> I've done everything that it was humanly possible to
> do. I promised everything that could be promised.
> Shall I say it? Over and above all the outrage and dis-
> tress that she displayed I could see that what she wants
> most is a long delay. She gave herself away a thousand
> times on that point. I won't stand in the way of any-
> thing that's a necessity for you both. It is absolutely
> essential that we should speak to each other before you
> go to her house. I swore to her that I didn't know where
> you were because she wanted to send for you.... She
> didn't have even the slightest attack of cramp while
> she was with me. I almost forced her to be calm by the
> way I behaved. Answer me quickly if you can come....
> I beg you to come, because I don't think that I could
> make it to Ferney. Everything will go well, I hope, for
> me, and for what I've done. But come.

What had apparently happened was sufficiently horrible,
even if there had been no scene in the manner of Coppet.
Madame de Staël had come in spoiling for a row, but Charlotte refused to have one and had just let the provocations
slide over her head. Madame de Staël's version of this stage
of the duel was to say that she had been exasperated by
Charlotte's namby-pamby German sweetness, and her insistence that Constant's weakness was really kindness.
Denied the opportunity of beating Charlotte into the ground
in a slanging match, Madame de Staël then changed her
tactics and, with a great show of being reasonable, settled
down to destroy her faith in Constant by reviewing the
whole history of the relationship and by telling her in de-

tail the extent of his commitment to herself. Charlotte was shaken by this, and, since she was also visibly exhausted, Madame de Staël closed in for the kill and extracted various promises from her victim. Before she was fully aware of what she was doing Charlotte had agreed that she was to return to Germany at once; that Constant was to return to Coppet for a period of at least three months; and that the fact of the marriage was to be kept secret, and if necessary to be denied, until Madame de Staël had left Europe and gone to America.

Constant's reaction to this piece of legerdemain was extraordinary. He wrote to Madame de Nassau to say that everything had turned out very well indeed, that Madame de Staël knew of the marriage and was still his friend, and that nothing could be better. He declined to listen to Charlotte's warning that they had been outwitted and that Madame de Staël could keep them apart and the marriage a secret for as long as she wished by the simple device of not removing herself to America. Constant's reply was a shocked reproof to her for not accepting Madame de Staël's word on the matter, and for breaking her word by remaining at Sécheron. She had promised to leave for Germany immediately—why had she not gone? He had returned to Coppet, as his honor required him to do, and he was suffering because *She* was making scenes about this very thing. Charlotte was unsympathetic: she was exhausted and was not ready to leave the comforts of Monsieur Dejean's hotel (which was, indeed, one of the best in Europe at that time), and if *She* had any common decency *She* would not insist on the point. Constant wrote to Madame de Nassau to complain of Charlotte and the humiliating position into which she had put him:

> *For the first time since I have known her, she is finding it difficult to fall in with my suggestions, not out of contrariness, but on account of a kind of weariness and sadness that only permits her a passive submission in place of the active cooperation that she has shown me so often. This gives me the appearance of breaking my word of honor from the very start, of vio-*

*lating a solemn undertaking in the eyes of another
person. I shall be treading on thorns as long as she remains at Sécheron.*

Charlotte presently moved on from Sécheron to Lausanne,
and there she dug in her toes.

*I have to tell you, and you must try to see it for your-
self, that her exigence revolts me to an extent that I
find difficult to express. She is altogether mistaken
if she thinks she can take control of my life as she has,
unhappily, been able to take control of yours.... Don't
be upset, I'll write to her myself, and you'll see my letter before she receives it. It will be up to you whether
you hand it on to her or not. If the truth is to be told,
when I vowed myself to silence I was in the position
of someone who is made to promise to swallow poison
with a knife at his throat. Such a person wouldn't
hesitate to take back the undertaking wrung out of him
in such a fashion just as soon as he was given a moment to think it over. But I'll agree not to use that
right, and to be as scrupulous with her as I would
be with someone who had shown themselves to be
generous, understanding, and proud. I don't want
her to think—and I'm not going to bargain on this
point—that she can ask me for more than my silence.
Granted that much, I'll ask her not to expect to direct
my conscience or my plans, or to lay down the law as
to the places I can or can't go to. At the bottom of your
heart, dear friend, you must expect me to feel this way.
I haven't any reason to blush for what I've done, and to
get me to undertake to hide or to run away at this
moment is to ask me to make a tacit admission that
I've committed some wrong—she has done her best
to make out that that's how it is. I think so differently
from you at this time about this question, that I consider my being here, in proximity to the place where
she is, the best aspect of our situation. I'll talk this over
with you tomorrow, and I have a feeling that we'll be
in agreement.*

This feeling proved to be without foundation, and on

the following day, and on every subsequent day beyond
which she postponed her departure, he made it plain that he
was desperate for her to be gone. In the end, at Madame
de Nassau's insistence, he abandoned his efforts to force her
to leave for Germany—which was then a theater of war—
and agreed to a compromise under which Charlotte would
go off to Brévans to wait for him under his father's roof.
She went there, and, needless to say, waited for him a long
time, and in vain. He did not succeed in getting away from
Coppet as soon as he hoped, and, again needless to say, he
could not in the end bring himself to come to the agreed
place to meet her. His treatment of Charlotte had by this
time disgusted Madame de Nassau so greatly that she had
decided to cut him out of her will, and he was afraid to expose himself to some equally disturbing manifestation of
disapproval if he faced his father with the situation still
unclarified. He accordingly, when he did at last get away
from Coppet on ticket of leave, summoned Charlotte to meet
him at L'Auberge du Cerf at Arbois, a tiny place on the road
to nowhere in particular in the foothills of the Jura where
he hoped that no one would think of looking for them. In
this he was deceiving himself, and the couple had been installed in their hideaway at Arbois for no more than three
days when they were broken in upon by Auguste de Staël.
He was under orders to collect Constant and to escort him
to Lyons, where Madame de Staël wished him to be so that
he could escort her to the theater. The young man was at
first polite and even friendly, but when Constant showed
signs of balking his façade of calm cracked and came
apart.

In the larger world great events were taking place. The
Emperor had marched into Austria for a final settlement
at the beginning of May and had been fought to a stand-
still, and possibly even defeated, at Essling on the twenty-
second of the month. Europe was buzzing with rumors that
the Emperor was trapped on the Island of Libau in the middle of the Danube, and that his army had suffered such
crippling losses that he was at the mercy of the Archduke
Charles. All the Emperor's unwilling allies were preparing

to desert him, and his enemies were rejoicing. And here was the grandson of Louis XV, calling his mother's recalcitrant lover to heel, in a confrontation in a provincial hotel. Constant looked into a face that had suddenly become contorted with unhappiness and rage, and realized that if he did not go he would have to fight a duel with this youth he had known as a child, almost from babyhood. He surrendered, and left Arbois for Lyons in the company of Auguste.

Charlotte was astounded by this betrayal, even though she had witnessed the paroxysms of guilt by which Constant had been wracked between the time he reached his decision to go and the moment of departure. But while she was stunned and appalled, she was nonetheless determined that she was not going to spend her wedding anniversary alone in a provincial backwater, while her husband was making public appearances with Madame de Staël a hundred miles away. Within a few hours of Constant's leave taking she ordered out her own carriage and followed him down the road leading through Lons-le-Saunier and Bourg to Lyons. With courage amounting to foolhardiness she traced Constant to the Hôtel du Parc, where he was lodged with Madame Staël and the bulk of the little clan. She spent the night alone at another inn and on the following morning, that of June 8, the day of the wedding anniversary, she presented herself at the Hôtel du Parc and asked for her husband. To her astonishment he was furiously angry with her for this tactless proceeding and had her turned from the door in the presence of the malignant and triumphant Madame de Staël.

What followed is far from clear. The best-known account, like that of the confrontation at Sécheron, comes through Madame de Staël at second hand, in this case by way of a piece of writing by Sainte-Beuve, who was hostile to Constant and Charlotte and who did his best to make them and the event seem ridiculous. All that can be said with certainty is that when Charlotte had returned to her hotel she took enough opium to make her very ill, and then wrote Constant a note suggesting that she had embarked on an

attempt to commit suicide. Since she sent this note round
to the Hôtel du Parc by hand as soon as she had written it,
and since it ends by urging him to come to her as quickly
as possible, it is permissible to assume that she did not
intend to die, and that her attempt was not genuine in that
sense. It is, however, perfectly clear that it was seriously
made, and that by it she was demonstrating to Constant
the lengths to which she was prepared to go to break out of
the role of patsy for which he had cast her in his three-
handed game. Constant appears to have understood this,
but Madame de Staël either did not, or declined to admit
that the game could be continued on other terms than her
own. She agreed to allow Constant to take Charlotte from
Lyons to Paris, where he was to put her in charge of a Dr.
Koreff, but he was not to hang about her while she recovered
her health and spirits. He was to see that she was in good
hands and to return to the side of Madame de Staël by June
28 at the latest. He was then to stay with her at Coppet, or
wherever else she might feel like living, for a further three
months. While he was still on the road to Paris she sent
a letter after him that can only have been intended to show
him that the game was continuing in accordance with
the old rules:

> Thank you for writing to me from Roanne. That meant
> several hours sleep for me—and that was a change.
> Only my last awakening will be really welcome.
> Thank you for repeating that it's to be the twenty-sixth.
> I believe, and I want it to be so in the depths of my
> being, that these three months may serve to bring my
> wretched existence to an easy end. I'm miserable
> enough to hope so—M. de Lessert has sent four thou-
> sand louis to America on my account. There are ter-
> rible risks in this complete conversion of my fortune
> [into foreign real estate], and I've a vague fear that
> I'm laying up new forms of trouble for the end of my
> life. It has to be done, but what a wrench! For the
> moment I'm someone the world has no use for, and
> what's more I'm not much use to myself.... The hours
> drag by me as if they were days, and everything is dead

inside me—friends, children, thoughts, the sunshine,
they've all become different aspects of my misery.

When I saw you again I thought I was being given a
new lease on life—for the last two days I've been feeling
there's something wrong with my lungs, so I've been
more careful than ever to follow my nourishing diet—
Didn't you tell me that unhappiness killed Madame
Talma in six months? I have exactly that much
time....Oh, Benjamin! To think that you should have
found it possible to use my devotion toward you
against me like a dagger. So it happened on June the
eighth! But let's forget about all that for the time being!
You have prayed, pray for me. Never has one of life's
poor cripples stood in such need of prayers—Abuffar
[sic] was excellent, but who is there for me to talk to
about that sort of thing. All my thoughts are driven
back on themselves, you have Paris to give you fresh
ideas, but I'll have to feed on my own resources until I
die. I think of myself as a Hugolin of the intellectual
world. A wall has sprung up between me and the uni-
verse.

Adieu—I've said more than I really intended to—
I've really nothing to say but "until the twenty-sixth"
and to pray to God that he'll call me to him.

Constant took this letter at its face value, and concluded
that Madame de Staël was suffering appallingly on his
account. The reference to *Abufar*, which shows that she
had been able to go to the theater after Constant's departure
from Lyons, did not give him pause. Nor, apparently, was
he struck by the reference to Hugolin. Madame de Staël's
unconscious was playing tricks on her when she made it.
All she has allowed herself to remember of his story is that
he lived on his own flesh for a time when he had been shut
up in a tower and left to starve. She has forgotten, or re-
pressed, the facts that Hugolin was one of the cruelest
tyrants in the Italy of the thirteenth century, and that he
was punished for his crimes by being locked up in the tower
with his sons and grandsons. He was only reduced to eating
his own flesh after all his progeny had been eaten. But be

that as it may, the effect of this letter was to make Constant
get rid of Charlotte as quickly as he could, and to return to
Lyons in haste after spending only two days in Paris. His
callousness was compounded by the manner of his going:
he slipped away without saying good-bye while his wife
was out for a walk.

All that can be said in extenuation of Constant's truly
lamentable performance on this occasion is that he had
at least warned Charlotte that he felt under an obligation to
return to Madame de Staël for the time being and that he
had promised his wife that if he did so he would come back
to her during August, when he would take her to Les
Herbages. She was thus left with something to hope for,
even if, after what had happened at Lyons, it was almost
impossible for her to trust him. She might very well have
given up at this point, however, had it not been for Doctor
Koreff, a young Jewish medical man, who had been recommended to Charlotte by Constant in 1807. He looked after
her during her convalescence, and, realizing that her doubts
about the nature of Constant's feelings for her were the
cause of her exhaustion and lassitude, he made it his
business to tell her over and over again that Constant was
good at heart, that he really loved her, that she should not
despair of him, and that if she loved him she should stand
by him and help him to escape from his horrible enslavement. Her feelings for Constant had always been strong,
but until she fell under Dr. Koreff's influence they had been
characterized by such things as tenderness, gentleness,
understanding, and tolerance. While she was under Dr.
Koreff's care at this time she developed a certain toughness and realism. But it might have been more difficult
than it was for Dr. Koreff to help her, if she had not been
given a vital insight into the essence of the situation. It
might have seemed a hopeless one—she had been abandoned in Paris and her husband was under the other
woman's thumb three hundred miles away—but the question of motivations put the thing in another light. She had
put it in a nutshell in the note that she had sent to Constant at the Hôtel du Parc after she had taken the overdose

of opium: *"I love you. I am I think, the only person in the world who has truly loved you. The woman who is killing me is hard and feels nothing but what she calls humiliation."*

This was indeed the truth of the matter. Madame de Staël had correctly interpreted *Adolphe* as formal notice of Constant's intention of breaking with her as soon as he could, and ever since he had read its first draft to her she had been fighting desperately to acquire a new lover to put in his place in the little clan, so that it might appear to the world at large that she had tired of Constant and dismissed him to make room for the newcomer, and not that he had dropped her. Her only motive for wishing to hold onto Constant and to have the marriage kept a secret was her desire to shield herself from a blow to her pride. She was simply playing for time in which to get another man.

Since Madame de Staël was not animated by any regard or any true warmth of feeling for Constant, and felt free to tell any lie, or to do anything she felt inclined to that might convince the world at large that he still belonged to her and that the character of their relationship was unchanged, she now began to play herself out of the game. The lethal character of the maneuvers she resorted to slowly came to cancel the value of any of the psychological advantages that Constant might have gained from going on with it.

Madame de Staël's campaign was originally based on a sound intuition that there was something technically wrong with the marriage, based on Constant's reluctance to say where and when it had taken place. Her sense that there was something irregular about it was rapidly transformed into the conclusion that it was invalid, and from there it was an easy step to proceed to the assertion that it had never taken place. In a typical communication forming part of the campaign, it was addressed to that Francois Gaudot who had made himself so unpleasant to Charlotte at Neuchâtel, she was able to say "Benjamin is here," she was writing from Coppet, "which makes me hopeful that all these rumors of his being married are unfounded."

While attacking the fact of the marriage by giving the

widest possible circulation to her claim that it had never taken place, she simultaneously attacked Charlotte's reputation and did all that she could to undermine Constant's faith in her. Stories were put about in such a fashion that they would soon come back to him, to the effect that she had never been properly divorced from Du Tertre, that she was still living with Du Tertre when Constant was not with her, that she had had a multitude of lovers when she was living with Du Tertre in Germany, and that she had become Dr. Koreff's mistress.

The lowest depths were finally plumbed when Madame de Staël sent Juste de Constant a copy of the compact of 1794 and attempted to persuade him that the existence of this parody of a legal document must invalidate any subsequent contract in the nature of a marriage that his son might have entered into. The old man had no idea what to make of the compact and replied evasively that it was beyond him to settle the differences between two people who appeared to have equal claims on his son. Madame de Staël was encouraged but not satisfied by this reaction, and her next move was to drop Juste a hint that if he were to support her contention that Charlotte and Constant could not be considered man and wife in view of his previous commitment to her, she might consider providing for Marianne's children, Charles and Louise. This was well received, and an interested reply suggesting that there clearly was something in Madame de Staël's contention was sent to her, while Charlotte was told that it would be impossible for Juste to recieve her at Brévans until the roof of the house, which had been damaged by a windstorm, had been repaired. Madame de Staël followed up the opening that she seemed to have been given by these indications of complicity by broadening her hint into something like a definite offer. She wrote to Juste to tell him that she would like "to do something for Charles and Louise" as soon as the question of where she stood with his son had been cleared up.

Incredible as it may seem this letter was taken to Brévans by Constant himself when he was enjoying one of the brief

leaves of absence that Madame de Staël occasionally allowed
him. Not that he assumed an entirely passive role while
all this mischief was being made for him: from July onwards he was salvaging his honor by making up small
parcels of his books and papers and smuggling them out of
Coppet in order to send them by carrier to Les Herbages.
But beyond that he was doing very little in the way of preparing for an attempt to break out, other than to solicit
reports of Madame de Staël's earlier infidelities to him that
might justify the argument that she could not use the
famous compact as a weapon against him because she had
long since repudiated it by her own behavior. What he
thought of his own actions at this time is unfortunately
almost entirely a matter of conjecture, as his journals for
the years 1808, 1809, and 1810 are all missing. Since the
section of the *Journal* for the period between November
20 and December 10, 1807, when Constant was also treating
Charlotte with a notable lack of consideration, is also
missing, it is possible to conclude that he didn't feel very
proud of his conduct. He permitted himself to become
jealous of Dr. Koreff and wrote to Charlotte bitterly on that
subject. He again allowed himself the luxury of an outburst of bitterness when she let fifteen days go by without
writing to him at the beginning of October. He complained
of her inconsiderateness: there he was, having a horrible
time at Coppet, and she couldn't be bothered to make it up
to him by writing to him or coming to be near him. This
moved her to a crisp answer:

> *My dear man, it's not really my fault that you've stayed
> at Coppet for four months. You went there of your own
> free will, and if it didn't suit you to be there you could
> easily have found somewhere else to stay.... Your
> father has told you that you might come to him, as
> is natural enough, at any time.... From Brévans you
> could come to me in a matter of hours, and if you didn't
> want to do that I wouldn't have left you alone there.
> You know all that well enough, so let's not talk about
> it any more.*

Constant argued the point, and she replied even more firmly:

> *I will admit that a great many of the things that you have done have hurt me. No, I am not at all sure that you have been acting, where I have been concerned, lovingly, decently, or even kindly. You have, unhappily, put yourself into a position for the last four months which has given rise to a host of false rumors, all of them annoying and discreditable, which have humiliated and distressed me. All this hasn't made me love you any the less, but I have been deeply wounded. I know that what's being said is exaggerated, and sometimes altogether untrue, but I know that it is impossible for people to think otherwise than they are doing. You have put up with this strange situation for so long that people will find it difficult to revise their opinions of your behavior. What I have agreed to out of affectionate consideration for you, or as a willing sacrifice made in the hope of a calm and happy future, has been seen in quite another light by others. I can distinguish very easily between what is true and what is false in the stories which are going round, and in the light of which we are being judged, but the fact that I am criticized unjustly doesn't make the criticisms hurt any the less. Perhaps it is a weakness in me, a mixture of love and wounded pride—define the feeling as you will—I feel it. I will tell you frankly: if this situation should be prolonged, or if I should fall back into it, I shall have the strength to end it.*

What had given Charlotte special offense was a story originating with Madame de Staël and being spread by her friend Constance d'Arlens, one of Constant's cousins, to the effect that he was living at Coppet for mercenary reasons, and that Charlotte tolerated his presence in his mistress's house because this made it easier for her to have affairs in Paris. Her toughness produced results. Constant galvanized himself into action toward the end of October, and, having got away from Coppet to Brévans, presently managed to reunite himself with Charlotte at Les Herbages. At first prickly and suspicious, he soon found himself happy and contented, and in December he had the marriage ratified and registered with the appropriate authorities in France and Westphalia, so that all possibility of questioning of its validity was removed.

At this point Charlotte must have thought she had won and that Constant had been liberated from his enslavement. But in mid-January he became restless and uneasy, and at last admitted that before he had been allowed to leave Coppet in October he had been made to promise that he would be back there by February the first. He had given his word and there was no getting round it, he would have to go. Charlotte was inclined to resist his appeal to his honor. What did it matter if he had been made to promise Madame de Staël, and Schlegel, and Sismondi, and even Miss Randall the English governess, that he would return? A promise made under duress was simply not binding. Constant now admitted the truth to her: he still owed Madame de Staël the thirty-five thousand francs he had borrowed from her father, and over the years he had taken a larger amount directly from her. In all he owed her some eighty thousand francs. Charlotte was horrified to find that Madame de Staël had this real hold on her husband, and urged him to go and settle his accounts with her at once: though the sum was a large one they had the means to raise it, and, although it would mean living economically for two or three years, economies could be practiced painlessly at Les Herbages, and it would be well worth it to be free. Constant left Paris for Coppet at the end of January, and a few days after he had gone Charlotte wrote to him cheerfully, although she had been unwell, to say that she hoped and prayed God that he would soon be back poor. Charlotte remained cheerful through February and most of March, even though Constant's absence meant that she was not able to take as large a part in the social activities connected with the Emperor's wedding to Marie-Louise as she would like to have done. He returned in jubilation at the end of the month: the whole nightmare was over, Madame de Staël's claims had been met in full, and they weren't going to be poor after all. He had managed things very cleverly so that he hadn't been forced to pay her any money at all. Charlotte was so pleased to have him back that she didn't for the moment inquire into the means by which this feat had been accomplished.

What Madame de Staël had done was to offer Constant another of her ingenious parodies of legal documents. This one was craftily designed to have the appearance of giving him a complete release from all his obligations to her, while in fact leaving him in debt to her for the full amount for the remainder of his life. The thing looked very good. It was on the stamped paper embossed with the imprint of the seal of the Canton of Vaud that French law made mandatory for such a legal document as it purported to be, and it was correct in form:

> *Madame la Baronne de Stael-Holstein having lent various sums to M. Benjamin Constant de Rebecque, and these sums having been lent at various times, in part for the personal use of M. Benjamin Constant and in part for the advantage of Mme. la Baronne de Staël, neither the capital amounts nor the interest due can be calculated precisely.*
>
> *The undersigned, however, wishing to settle the matter with propriety and to their mutual satisfaction, M. Benjamin Constant de Rebecque recognizes his indebtedness to Mme. la Baronne de Staël in the amount of eighty thousand French francs, the said sum to be payable only on the decease of M. Benjamin Constant....*
>
> *Mme. la Baronne de Staël-Holstein accepts the proposed method of payment, declaring that the abovementioned sum includes the total of his various borrowings up to the present time, and that the present agreement cancels all previous undertaking whatsoever, in such wise that no one can make any claim on M. Benjamin Constant de Rebecque, so long as he shall live, for capital and interest present or future, for any reason whatsoever.*
>
> *M. Benjan·in Constant de Rebecque undertakes to Mme. la Baronne de Stael-Holstein to make the present*

obligation the first call on his estate by the first clause
in his will, and further undertakes to deposit a copy of
the said testament with Mme. la Baronne de Staël-
Holstein or such other person as she shall devise....

And so on. But for all the formality of its language this
unnotarized private contract had had no legal standing
whatever. It bound neither party and left the situation precisely where it had always been, with the debt unpaid and
Madame de Staël free to claim it from him whenever she
chose. In blissful ignorance of the way in which Constant
had been deceived, or in which he was deluding himself,
Charlotte settled down with him at Les Herbages toward
the end of April 1810. A new chapter in their lives seemed
to have begun, and in May Constant wrote to Madame de
Nassau to tell her how happy he was:

Since I've been here with Charlotte I've become twice
as fond of this place, which I've always loved...my
wife is so easy to live with that I enjoy every minute
I spend with her....She's able to create for me the
orderly routine that I've always longed for and never
been able to establish.

While all this was going on Madame de Staël had been
writing the book that she had first planned when she was in
Germany in 1804, and which was now to serve the double
purpose of repairing the damage which had been done to
her reputation as a serious thinker by the publication of
Corinne and of winning her a place in the Emperor's good
books. He had just married an Austrian princess, and he
was attempting to incorporate a large part of Germany into
his Imperial system, so it seemed logical to her to suppose
that he would approve of a work that was designed to pro-
mote Franco-German understanding. She was also infected
by the same curious prepublication excitement that had
possessed her before the appearance of *Corinne. De l'Allemagne* was going to demonstrate her stature, and make it
impossible for the Emperor to go on insisting that she stay
away from Paris. He would see that she was too admirable,

and too important, to be treated so badly. She had no doubt that it was a great work, and there are those who find it admirable today, but it is difficult for a critical reader to rate it very highly. It is full of generalizations of a rather foolish kind:

> The Germans are in general sincere and faithful; they hardly ever break their word and deceit is foreign to their natures. If this fault ever insinuates itself into Germany, it can only be the consequence of a desire to imitate foreigners, to show themselves as clever as they are, and above all not to be their dupes; but the commonsense and the goodheartedness of the Germans will soon bring them back to feel that their strength is in their unstained character, and the habit of honesty that makes them altogether incapable, even when they want to, of lending themselves to trickery.

In some cases the generalizations are linked with exceedingly doubtful history:

> The Crusades reunited the nobility of all countries, and transformed the spirit of chivalry into a kind of European patriotism which filled every soul with a common feeling. The feudal system, that sad and solemn political institution which to some extent consolidated the spirit of chivalry by turning it into laws, has survived in Germany into the present time. It was destroyed in France by Cardinal Richelieu, and from his time until that of the Revolution the French have been altogether without a source of enthusiasm. I know that it is said that their love of kings provided them with one, but, presuming that such a feeling would suffice, it depends so much on the character of the sovereign that it would have been unlikely, I imagine, that it could have meant much to the French during the Regency and the reign of Louis XV. The spirit of chivalry which emitted a few sparks under Louis XIV, went out after him and was replaced, as a stimulating and intelligent historian has said, by the spirit of conceit, which is entirely opposed to it.

This argument is continued in a manner flattering to the Germans and derogatory to the French:

> *Courage itself, which had formerly been a guarantee of loyalty, became no more than a dashing means for shuffling it off, since it wasn't pertinent whether one was true or not, it was only necessary to kill anyone who denied it in a duel: the rule of society in the great world did away with most of the virtues of chivalry. France thus found itself without any kind of enthusiasm; and, since nations must have this if they are not to decay and dissolve, it is without a doubt this natural need that turned every mind, from the middle of the last century onward in the direction of the love of freedom.*
>
> *The philosophic progress of the human species appears then to be divided into four different eras: the heroic era in which civilization was founded; that of patriotism, which gave antiquity its glories; that of chivalry which was the fighting religion of Europe; and that of the love of liberty, whose history begins at the time of the Reformation.*
>
> *Germany, if one excepts certain court circles, avid in the imitation of things French, was scarcely touched by the conceit, immorality, and skepticism which have transformed the French character since the days of the Regency.*

These views, all expressed in the opening pages of a work which consists largely of extremely superficial summaries of the lives and principal works of an assortment of thinkers and writers, and which leads up to a rather breathless apologia for mysticism and enthusiasm, do not now appear to be very menacing. If the reader of *De l'Allemagne* persists through the essays on the virtues of Talma's acting, the art of conversation, English philosophy, Love in Marriage, Ignorance and Frivolity of mind in their relationship to Morality, and the host of irrelevancies with which its text is burdened, and comes to that apologia, in which Madame de Staël seems to be speaking directly to the reader in her own person, it doesn't seem possible to take it for anything more than a manifestation of intellectual overconfidence on the part of an undereducated woman with an undisciplined mind.

> *Injuries and mishaps, on the physical plane, have something so swift, pitiless, and unpredictable about them that they seem to have the quality of the marvelous. Illness and its furies seem to share an evil life of their own which suddenly takes over our peaceful existence. Our passions make us realize the barbarity of the natural order that we are told is so kindly. How many dangers menace those we love! There's not a day so fine that it may not produce its thunderbolt, not a flower that may not have poison in its sap, not a breath of wing that may not carry some deadly infection, and of wind that may not carry some deadly infection, and to the heart at the very moment when he is intoxicated by its gifts.*
>
> *How to understand the purpose of all these phenomena while we still wear the shackles of our habitual ways of thinking? How can we consider the animals without being bewildered to account for their mysterious existence? A poet has said that they are "the dreams of nature, from which man is the awakening." To what end were they created? What is the significance of those veiled looks they give us, behind which one senses the dawning of a thought? What is their relationship to us? What part do they play in the scheme of things? A bird outlives a man of genius, and I can't describe the bizarre despair that grips the heart when one has lost someone one loves and one sees the breath of life animating an insect which still moves on the earth from which the most noble being has vanished.*

At first sight the Emperor's feeling that the book was a threat to him seems almost as inexplicable as Madame de Staël's conviction that over a hundred thousand words of such pretentious waffle would bring him to her feet.

But the Emperor had created a major problem for himself
in Germany by marching his armies across it, and by anni-
hilating the military power and political influence of Austria. With the destruction of Austrian authority the ghost
of the old Holy Roman Empire of Charlemagne, which had
given Germany a spurious appearance of being a unity,
vanished from the scene, and the full extent of its frag-
mentation into petty kingdoms, dukedoms, bishoprics,
and other nonviable political entities became apparent.
The Emperor's intention, formed as soon as he had grasped
the extent of his opportunity, was to reorganize Germany
administratively as so many departments governed by
prefects controlled from Paris, and, in effect, to incorporate
it into a greater France. But wherever he established his
authority in Germany, and in whatever form, the spirit of
German nationalism flared up and spread like a bush fire.
By 1810 a German aspiration for reunification under
Prussian leadership was recognizable as a developing threat
to the Emperor's plans, and the inspiration for an underground movement of resistance which was of the gravest
concern for General Savary. The power struggle between
Savary and the Minister of Police was reaching its crisis at
the beginning of 1810, and the first sign of the tolerant
Fouché's impending defeat was the installation of a new
government department, concerned with the control and
censorship of all printed matter, under Savary's control.
It was already functioning when Madame de Staël sent the
first volume of *de l'Allemagne* to her publisher in Paris in
April, and when Savary replaced Fouché as Minister of
Police at the beginning of June the book's doom was sealed.
The naiveté of the generalizations, and its scatter-witted
structure could not excuse its intrusion into a sensitive
area of Imperial policy: in the eyes of a thought-policeman,
which is what Savary had become over the years, it inevitably appeared to be a piece of propaganda for German
culture and against the Frenchification of Germany, designed to assist the German nationalists by creating sympathy for them in France. As such it provided a definitive

proof that Savary had been right and Fouché wrong about Madame de Stael and gave him ample ground for cracking down on her.

Blissfully unaware of the extent to which her book was ill timed and likely to be offensive to the regime, Madame de Staël made her preparations for a Parisian triumph. Her first move was to obtain a *laissez passer* entitling her to cross France en route for one of four designated points of embarkation from which she was to set sail for the United States. She had not the smallest intention of doing any such thing, as she demonstrated by simultaneously taking a lease of the extremely picturesque and romantically situated château of Chaumont-sur-Loire, midway between Amboise and Blois. She moved into it with what can fairly be called a motley crew soon after Constant and his wife had taken up their residence at Les Herbages. There were the children Auguste, Albert, and Albertine; there was Schlegel; there was her latest lover, the Russian Baron Balk; there was the Neapolitan guitarist Pertosa; there was Madame Récamier with her two satellites of the moment, the malicious German Baron Voght and the young American John Isard Middleton; there was the epicene Elézéar de Sabran with whom Madame de Staël had once considered marriage; there was the professionally German but in fact French author Adelbert von Chamisso, who had written *Peter Schlemihl*; there was the cold-hearted and pious Mathieu de Montmorency whom she had loved momentarily between Talleyrand and Narbonne back in the early days of the Revolution; there were the Barantes, father and son; and there was Sismondi's distant cousin, Miss Randall, the Englishwoman who had lost a fortune and who had been found a place as Albertine's governess. The extraordinarily intense, and almost entirely pointless, life lived by this remarkably diverse group of people has been ably described in Maurice le Vaillant's book *Une Amitié amoureuse*, which makes it plain why and with what good reason Madame de Staël complained so bitterly and so often of being bored. It was to relieve her from this painful sensation that she sent for Benjamin Constant at the end of May. Her pretext was that the manuscript of the third section of *De l'Allemagne* was almost finished, and that she wanted his help and advice on a number of points before she sent it off to the publisher.

Constant resisted her blandishments briefly and then gave in. At the beginning of June he shut up Les Herbages and settled Charlotte into their apartment in Paris. He said good-bye to her there on the tenth of the month, giving her the usual promises that he would be back in two weeks, but on June 22, just two days before he was to have returned, Charlotte had a letter from him saying that his return was to be delayed, he would be staying on for two weeks more so that he could ride back to Paris in Madame Récamier's comfortable carriage....

Charlotte was thus accompanied by Dr. Koreff and not by her husband when she went to the great ball given in honor of the marriage of Napoleon and the Austrian Archduchess Marie-Louise at the Austrian Embassy on July 1. She was one of the twelve hundred people who had been invited by Prince Schwarzenberg to walk by the ornamental pool in the illuminated gardens, to watch a splendid display of fireworks, and afterwards to dance in a huge temporary ballroom, decorated with hangings of colored muslins and gauzes, which had been erected alongside the Embassy in the angle formed by the junction of the Chaussée d'Autin with the Rue Lafayette. As the dancing began a windstorm sprang up, and before the French windows opening on the garden could be closed one of the hangings lifted in a gust and drifted into the flames of a cluster of candles. A tongue of fire ran up the wall, and in seconds the situation was out of control.

Etiquette held most of those present in their places while Marie-Louise and the Emperor left the room at a measured pace, but as soon as they were gone a panic broke out. Its consequences were vividly described by Charlotte in a letter written to her husband a couple of days later to supplement a first hurried note telling him that she was safe:

*Everyone here is still stunned. You won't find much
about it all in the papers: the motive for the ball means
that they're hushing up as much as they can, but the
steadily growing list of victims speaks for itself. The
cortège of a woman who was trampled to death by the
crowd passed under my window half an hour ago. The
daughter of the poor Princesse de Schwarzenberg,
whose blackened trunk has been found [she had not
found her daughter among those who had escaped into
the garden and had run back into the flames to look for
her], is on the danger list, as is the Princess von der
Leyden. Kourakine [the Russian Ambassador] was horribly burned and trampled. The wife of the Russian
Consul died the day before yesterday. General Toussard
is at death's door. The Duchesse de la Force, who lives
in our building, had her whole face burned...the
Queen of Westphalia escaped by scrambling over the
garden wall, and her two maids of honor, the Coun-
tesses Lowenstein and Buchholz, were burned on their
necks and faces. Furstenstein pulled three horribly
burned and injured women out of the ruins of the stair-
well they'd fallen down. Only their heads could be
seen, and they were screaming with pain. Koreff carried a woman he mistook for me down to the little pool
and washed her face to find out who she was because
she couldn't utter a sound. (I've heard from my servants that he ran from the Embassy to our place twice
to find out if I'd been brought home.) And just imagine
it—Furstenstein saw another poor woman lying stark
naked in the garden, her dress and even her chemise
had been burned right off her, and her body was
nothing but a raw wound.... I swear to you that I still
think I'm living in a nightmare—a bare seven minutes
covered the whole time from the moment we all started
for the doors and that in which there wasn't a trace of
the ballroom left...the flames reached out into the
garden after us...we heard the big mirrors cracking
and the chandeliers crashing down...and through it
all the screams of the wretched beings who were still
inside. To crown the horrors of the night a terrible
gale was blowing....*

Constant's response was to include a few sympathetic phrases in a letter telling her that he wouldn't, after all, be coming back to Paris with Madame Récamier. He had bought a delightfully spirited little black horse, an altogether charming beast, and he'd be riding it back—presently....

Having thus shown Charlotte, who had been quite severely burned on her arms, how little concern he had for her, Constant was ready to be reunited to her and to do what was necessary to charm her back. The first part of that summer was horribly wet, and when they returned to Les Herbages they found that the roads in the neighborhood had become bottomless mires. Constant bought Charlotte a pair to his little black horse, and when the weather opened up toward the end of August they spent some of the happiest weeks of their life together hacking about the countryside paying calls on their neighbors.

Their idyll was brought to an abrupt end when the presses on which *De l'Allemagne* was being printed were stopped, the printed sheets confiscated, and the type broken up by the police. Madame de Staël, ordered to leave France once again, and about to leave for Coppet, sent a message to Constant telling him to meet her at Briare, a small town near Montargis in Burgundy. When she reached Briare Constant was there, as she had expected him to be, but he was not alone. Charlotte, nettled by the contrast between his immediate compliance with her rival's appeal for comfort and support and his failure to come to her after her escape from the Embassy fire, had insisted on accompanying him.

The two-day meeting at Briare was consequently a fiasco so far as Madame de Staël was concerned, and although she extended her scene-making capacity to the full her emotional blackmail failed of its effect, and she had to return to Coppet alone.

Charlotte's victory was, however, a costly one, which provides a text-book example of the dangers run by a player who calls a game before all the parties to it are ready to do so. Constant's reaction to Charlotte's refusal to play her assigned role of patsy in the three-handed match that he had set up was to go on a self-destructive bender. It began with his losing twenty thousand francs at a single sitting at the roulette table on the night of their return to Paris and ended two weeks later with the sale of Les Herbages, its furnishings, and a large part of his library. It was typical of his peculiar brand of dishonesty that when it was all over he had the gall to tell Prosper de Barante that he had been forced to sell his country place because Charlotte found it uninhabitable.

While Constant was carrying out this program of symbolic self-mutilation, presumably with the semi-magical aim of averting worse punishment from Madame de Staël, she was apparently doing her level best to make things as hot for him as she could. She did not, according to a note found among Sainte-Beuve's papers, go directly from Briare to Coppet, but she turned aside to visit the aged and crotchety Juste de Constant at Brévans.

What she can have said to him this time there is no way of knowing, but Constant believed to the end of his life that she went there to incite his father to sue him for the full value of all the family properties that had been made over to him in exchange for an annuity twenty-two years earlier when Juste was about to be overwhelmed by debts and lawsuits. The sum involved amounted to something in the vicinity of 180,000 francs, and, if Juste de Constant had gone ahead with his suit and won it, the result would have been ruinous for Constant and Charlotte.

When Juste moved from Brévans to Geneva at the beginning of the following spring, apparently to initiate proceedings for the recovery of his fortune, Constant, in mortal fear of the outcome, mobilized the whole of his little army of well-disposed cousins to try to bring pressure on the old man to change his mind, but his efforts proved to be unnecessary. By the time the old man got to Geneva Madame de Staël had become interested in something other than her longing to hurt and to be hurt by Constant. She had begun a new affair with a certain Albert-Jean-Michel Rocca, and life had changed for her. Without her to drive him on Juste de Constant soon forgot his project for ruining his son.

Madame de Staël was now forty-five. She had never taken very much care of herself, and the effluxion of time, her irregular habits, and her opium addiction, were all beginning to leave their various marks on her. She now had a noticeably poor skin, her complexion was turning yellowish and she was becoming exceedingly gross. The portrait Madame Vigée-Lebrun had painted four years earlier, depicting her as Corinne, tells most of the story, giving one a little less than the truth about the buck teeth, the weakly greedy mouth, the bulbous nose, and the protuberant eyes, but achieving a complete, and devastating, frankness about the slack spread of the deteriorating stomach, the beefy thighs, and the tremendous width of the hips. Madame de Staël had accommodated her personal style to none of these changes in her person: she still wore the low-cut sleeveless dresses that she had affected when she was a girl with arms and a bosom to be proud of; she still swathed herself in strongly and often extravagantly colored scarves and shawls; and she still wore the enormous turbans that she had taken to wearing in the first place in an effort to minimize the effect of her excessively large and coarsely featured face. Now that she was the victim of an exaggerated case of middle-aged spread these habits of dress all combined to make her a good deal of a figure of fun, and those who met her for the first time at this period in her life were apt to be startled by her grotesque appearance. She was characteristically be-shawled and her head was crowned with an unusually outrageous confection featuring a number of dead birds-of-paradise when she met Rocca that winter in Geneva. He was, however, neither appalled nor amused by her appearance, and immediately fell in love with her.

Rocca was an exceptionally handsome and well-made young athlete of twenty-three who had run away from his aristocratic home in Geneva to enlist in the army of Napoleon when he was seventeen. He had risen from trooper to Lieutenant and had laid the foundations of a promising military career when he rode into an ambush while fighting against guerillas in Spain. He was hit five times, and one bullet smashed his thigh bone in a way that made it almost certain that he would never walk without a crutch again. His manners were those of the camp and the battlefield, and if he had ever read anything his conversation showed no sign of it. (Madame de Staël was moved to defend one of his more fatuous utterances on a famous occasion by saying that "words are not his language.") His one great passion in life, and almost his sole medium of self-expression, was the performance of dashing feats of horsemanship on his splendid Spanish horse Sultan. Although it would be hard to find two people with apparently less to offer each other, this eager stripling managed to convince himself and the deteriorating object of his affections that they were made for each other and should marry.

Madame de Staël held out against his determined assault for several months, but the prolongation of her resistance only meant that she fell the harder when she finally succumbed. Overnight she found herself hysterically and demonstratively in love, and she staged a series of fantastic performances on social occasions that outraged the strait-laced Genevan hostesses and might have been—probably were—designed to advertise the fact as widely as possible. In one typical incident she momentarily disintegrated a dinner party by uttering a scream and fainting dead away at the sight of Rocca with a carving knife in his hand, alleging, when she came to, that she had assumed that he was about to do away with himself despite the alternative, and more likely, course offered by the fowl on the dish before him.

The malicious gossips of Geneva's minuscule and ingrown society were delighted with the comedy. They put all their practiced ill nature into the business of embroidering and enlarging upon every detail of the scandal, while Madame de Staël's little court of parasites and admirers looked on with horror as she exposed herself to their arts. Schlegel, who had nicknamed Rocca "Caliban," was the hardest hit of them all, for the characteristic reason that *her* folly was making *him* look ridiculous. Few of her friends had a thought for what she might be about to do to herself, or for the physical dangers that might be lying in wait for her in Rocca's idiocies, and in the thoughtless egotism of his passion. They could not know that he was already saying to her such things as: "I want you completely. I want you to bear my name, and I want a child from you, a Little Us."

From this demand, so entirely legitimate in form, and so wholly demented in the given case, she had, in her bemused state, no defense. On May 1, 1811, she entered into one of her strange compacts with Rocca, giving it this time the form of pseudo-marriage. In the presence of a Protestant clergyman, and with the English governess-confidante Fanny Randall as a witness, the contracting parties bound themselves to marry "as soon as circumstances permitted," and, meanwhile and forever, to be fine, loyal, and faithful to each other. This seems to have satisfied them both that they were now married in the sight of God, and that the way was clear for her to satisfy his macabre desire. Madame de Staël discovered that she was pregnant that August, and in April of 1812 she gave birth to a son.

The child was born at Coppet, and the accouchement was one of her most astonishing performances. The omnipresent Fanny Randall acted as midwife, but no one else with the household above stairs was let into the secret of what was going on, and none of them found out. Although suspicions that she was about to have a child had been circulating in Geneva for a couple of months and there had been much sniggering and jeering, Schlegel and all the other members of the little clan at Coppet had accepted the story that they had been given to account for her increased size—that she was suffering from dropsy. She looked ill enough to make the claim credible, and those close to her took the epigrams and witticisms on the subject of her appearance that reached them to be slanderous inventions put into circulation by French agents. What was even more extraordinary was that they still remained in ignorance during and after the actual birth of the child. Though the servants, some of whom were paid informers in the French service, knew what was going on, the members of her entourage were still in complete ignorance that anything out of the way had occurred when the six-day-old boy was smuggled out of the house and placed in the care of the pastor's wife in a nearby village.

A week later Madame de Staël rallied all her strength and went the rounds of the Genevan salons, to outface the gossips, looking so ghastly as to convince even the most skeptical of them that her claim to have been ill rather than pregnant had been genuine. Throughout the whole episode she exhibited a degree of fortitude and self-control that she had never risen to before, and would not achieve again. Her conduct was, indeed, so unlike her normal behavior on this occasion that it is to be suspected that she resorted to opium to see her through the crisis of her ordeal. If she did not, and if it were simply grit and determination that enabled her to keep quiet about what she was having to endure while she was in labor, her use of opium was at least helpful to her in so far as it had prepared the household for her disappearance for long enough to be brought to bed of the child and to recover from the effort. The faithful had over the years become accustomed to such fugues of three and four days in which she lay alone in her darkened room in a stupor induced by the drug. Be that as it may, the physical strain of her fourth pregnancy was something from which she never recovered. She was broken in health for the five years of life that remained to her, and when she died, after having had a stroke, at the age of only fifty-one, it was an overdose of opium administered by the devoted Fanny Randall that killed her.

While Little Us, Louis Alphonse Rocca, was getting himself born, the air was full of the electricity generated by the imminence of great events. In May Napoleon summoned the Emperor of Austria and the kings of Westphalia, Wurtemburg, Saxony, Bavaria, Prussia, and Naples to meet with him at Dresden while Monsieur de Narbonne, the son of Louis XV, and now his chief Aide-de-Camp, was delivering his ultimatum to the Tsar at Vilna.

That Monsieur de Narbonne, of all men, should now be at the center of events and even closer to Napoleon than Talleyrand probably contributed more than anything else to Madame de Staël exasperated sense of exclusion from the world of interest and importance at this time. She determined to get, somehow or other, back to the heart of things, and at the beginning of June, as the five hundred thousand

men of the Grande Armée and its endless supply trains began to move through Germany toward their concentration
areas near the Russian frontier, Madame de Staël started out
for London by way of Austria, Russia, and Sweden.

Low comedy involving the unhappy Schlegel took some of
the bloom off the first steps toward the execution of this
grand design. Schlegel had approved of it in outline, but
when he was asked to obtain an Austrian safe conduct for
Rocca, he jibbed. He had, he confessed, only approved the
plan because he had assumed that Rocca, as a French army
officer on sick leave, would have to be left behind. Faced
with his refusal, Madame de Staël felt compelled to tell him
of her pseudo-marriage to Rocca and of the existence of
Little Us. With death in his heart Schlegel then submitted,
and obtained the necessary documents to insure poor Caliban's safe passage through Austria.

It was thus a party composed of Madame de Staël, Rocca,
Schlegel, Albert and Albertine that at last set out. They completed the first part of their journey when, four months
later, having traveled from Vienna to Lvov, from Lvov to
Kiev, from Kiev to Moscow, from Moscow to St. Petersburg,
from St. Petersburg to Abo, and from there, with a narrow
escape from shipwreck on the Aaland Islands, they reached
Stockholm. There had been a moment of near panic in the
Ukraine, when the news of the Grande Armée's swift opening lunge into the Russian void seemed to threaten them
with the possibility of being overtaken. As Rocca stood a
good chance of being shot as a deserter to the enemy in this
event, Madame de Staël considered scrapping her London-
via-Sweden program in favor of proceeding to the Holy Land
via Odessa and Constantinople. She was, after all, writing,
or thinking of writing, an epic devoted to the Crusades, to
be called Richard Coeur-de-Lion, which would more than
justify such a diversion... but all that was forgotten when,
after a respectful reception by the nobility of Moscow, she
was given two private interviews by the Tsar in St. Petersburg.

What passed at these meetings is anybody's guess, but
Madame de Staël was under the impression that the Tsar

had invited her to become his accomplice in an intrigue. Would she, when she reached Sweden, use what influence she had with Bernadotte to persuade him to stay out of the war between the Anglo-Russian alliance and France? She was empowered to tell him that if he did remain neutral Russia would agree to give Sweden a free hand in Norway.

How far Madame de Staël can have understood what the Tsar was saying to her is questionable. What is certain is that by the time she had reached Stockholm she had convinced herself that she was a plenipotentiary in a class with Monsieur de Narbonne, and that she had an important part to play in developing a Swedish-Russian understanding that would be to the disadvantage of Napoleon. The late Mr. Christopher Herold did all he could to lend substance to this fantasy when dealing with this episode in his biography of the lady, but the facts give little support to his arguments in favor of giving her a role of importance in this matter.

Sweden's policy in the event of war between France and Russia had been determined in January 1812 when Napoleon had ordered Davout to march French troops into Swedish Pomerania without giving Bernadotte any warning of what he was about to do. Davout went into the province as if it were conquered territory, commandeering all the merchant shipping he found in the ports, requisitioning supplies, transport, and animals with a free hand, and treating all Swedish troops and officials found on the ground as prisoners of war. Angered by these provocations intended to terrorize him by showing what sort of ruthless treatment the country that had offered him a crown might expect if he didn't see that it remained neutral in the coming struggle, Bernadotte immediately sent emissaries to St. Petersburg and London to propose talks. His overtures led to the signing of a treaty of Alliance between Russia and Sweden at St. Petersburg on April 5, 1812. This was while Madame de Staël was deeply involved in the production of Little Us, and nearly two months before she left Coppet for her end run round the advancing French army.

But, even if the Tsar can have had no doubt of where he stood vis-à-vis the strangely adopted son of the Swedish king

and Sweden as a power when he talked to Madame de Staël
in August, the question remains of whether Madame de
Staël played a part of any significance in persuading Bernadotte to go further and abandon a policy of what might be
called neutrality against France in favor of active participation in the anti-French war. Although she was, in this
case, on the scene when Bernadotte made his decision, there
are no grounds for thinking that she had any hand in deter-
mining what it was to be.

Bernadotte had two strong motivations for staying out of
any coalition based on the Anglo-Russian alliance against
France. He had his residual emotional attachment to France
and to the French cause, and he had the obligation to put
Swedish interests above all others which fell upon him
when he accepted the rank of Crown Prince and the position
of heir to the Swedish throne. Sweden had nothing to gain
from participation in the war, and popular opinion was
strongly against it, the general feeling being that the Anglo-
Russian alliance wanted to draw the country into the war
merely in order to increase the supply of warm bodies available to them as infantry replacements. If Bernadotte were to
ignore this feeling and take Sweden into a war that involved
her in heavy losses of men and matériel, there was a good
chance that he would lose the throne which was almost his.

On the other hand the Anglo-Russian alliance was as dedicated to the obliteration of the consequences of the French
Revolution as it was to the defeat and destruction of Napoleon. In the event of an Anglo-Russian victory Bernadotte,
who had been a Jacobin before becoming one of Napoleon's
most successful army commanders, might well assume the
character of one of those legacies of the Revolution that the
alliance was pledged to destroy. In that case the possibility
of his removal from the scene would become a probability.

All the evidence goes to suggest that Bernadotte considered the problem throughout as one of a balance of risks.
That he postponed his decision until the liquidation of the
Grande Armée in the course of its retreat from Moscow
made it clear that participation had become the least dangerous course. Bernadotte signed the Anglo-Swedish Treaty

of March 1813 when, and only when, he could no longer
stay out of the anti-French coalition without raising suspicions that he was activated by a residual attachment to the
French cause, and at the last moment in which he could
hold out for *douceurs* that would sweeten the pill for the
Swedes. His signature to the treaty finally cost the British
government undertakings to produce a subsidy covering the
monetary cost of participation, to limit her demand for Swedish troops to the provision of an expeditionary force of thirty thousand men, and to give Sweden a free hand to absorb
Norway, if she could.

The terms of the Anglo-Swedish treaty and the timetable
of the military and political events of the winter make it
perfectly clear that Bernadotte was animated by prudential motives possesing an objective reality when he went
over to active participation in the war, and that he would
have had to do just what he did just when he did it whether
or no Madame de Staël had come to Stockholm.

It cannot be denied, however, that while Madame de
Staël was in Sweden she was exerting some influence on
the rather peculiar mind of the Tsar Alexander, and that she
was in constant communication with him through diplomatic channels. But what she was doing was attempting to
enlist Russian support for a wild scheme designed to prevent
the achievement of the principal war aim of the anti-French
coalition and to preserve as much as possible of the creations
of the revolution and of French power. These aims, directly
contrary to the Anglo-Russian purposes, were to be achieved
either by making Bernadotte Regent of France during the
minority of Napoleon's infant son or by placing him on the
French throne as a constitutional monarch. The theoretical
justification for this visionary project was that when Napoleon had been defeated the French would be found to be so
determined to retain their postrevolutionary institutions
and to resist the reestablishment of the political structures
of the *Ancien Régime* as to make the restoration of Louis
XVIII impossible. In that event, the former Jacobin who had
become the adopted son of a legitimate monarch belonging
to the old order of things might be an acceptable middle-
of-the-road candidate for the position.

The extreme improbability that this fantasy, originating in the fevered brains of a Swiss lady and a German gentleman, would find favor with the French people in their hour of defeat was not immediately apparent to the Russians, and when they showed signs of taking it seriously Bernadotte allowed himself to be seduced. His own experiences had corrupted his judgment in this region, and there seemed nothing unlikely in the proposition to a man who had already had one crown come to him out of the blue. It was not immediately apparent to him that there was an essential difference between the processes involved in being offered the Crown of Sweden by the Swedish monarchists and being put on the throne of France by a foreign power after taking part in the defeat of French armies in the field. He had no inkling of the extent to which he was compromising himself in French eyes by what was fairly generally seen as a double treachery: to France itself, and to the leader who had made him.

Hopelessly unrealistic as Madame de Staël's schemings for Bernadotte had been from the start, they ceased to have any meaning whatever after Napoleon's fate had been sealed by his defeat in the two-day battle of the nations at Leipzig in November 1813. The turning point in this vital fight had come when the Saxon regiments in Napoleon's army learned that they had been put into the line opposite Bernadotte's Swedes and that he was with them. The Saxons had fought under Bernadotte's command at Wagram, and rather than fight against him on this occasion they went over from the French to the Anglo-Russian side *en masse*. Their defection, so far as French public opinion was concerned, convicted Bernadotte of final responsibility for the French defeat at Leipzig and all that followed from it.

Wholly unaware of the strength of feeling against him in France, Bernadotte allowed the intrigue initiated by Madame de Staël to go forward, and when the armies of the anti-French coalition entered Paris at the end of March 1814 he was sufficiently dazzled by the prospect that she had held out to him as to go to Paris in order to be available if the call should come. He reached the city on April 13 and was horrified to find how far he had been deluded and

to what extent he had deluded himself. Those of his old
friends and former associates who were willing to receive
him did so coldly, and most of them wished to have nothing
whatever to do with him. The occupying forces, once they
had realized the extent of his unpopularity and were
satisfied that the French were too stunned by the collapse
of the Napoleonic regime to be able to oppose the restoration
of Louis XVIII, had no further use for him, and the op-
portunists with careers to make who might have hedged
their bets with him as a dark horse shunned him as a sure
loser.

The most telling of all signs that he had blundered came
from the arch-opportunist, Benjamin Constant. Madame de
Staël had persuaded Constant to attach himself to Bernadotte as a political adviser during the winter of 1813–14,
and after a series of meetings with the Crown Prince he had
smothered his doubts and plunged. When he arrived in
Paris, on April 15, the *Journal des Débats* had carried a report of his arrival in which it was stated that Constant was
in Paris as "personal-private Secretary to the Crown Prince
of Sweden." The day after this item had appeared in its
columns the paper carried Constant's cool denial that he
was attached to Bernadotte in any capacity whatsoever.

At the end of two weeks of such experiences as a political
leper Bernadotte made haste to return to Sweden, realizing
that all he had done by going to Paris in pursuit of Madame
de Staël's fata morgana was to imperil the credibility of his
commitment to Swedish interests and his chances of being
seated on a real throne. His wife, that Desirée Clary who
had been Napoleon's first marriage prospect in the days
before Josephine de Beauharnais, remained behind in
Paris where she presently received some thoughtful advice:

> *If Madame de Staël should come to see you, be kind to
> her; let her have her visit, but, whatever you do, don't
> talk politics with her. She is a likable and essentially
> good woman, but she's so passionately for her friends
> that she often does them a great deal of harm by the
> unrealistic way she talks of them. I don't doubt that
> she'll be one of the leaders of the opposition when she*

*gets to Paris, and our situation makes it absolutely
essential that no one should ever be able to lay so much
as the appearance or the shadow of a fault at your door.
The unjustified suspicions that people have built up
on the foundation of my grand designs should be
warning enough to you, along with all those who have
my best interests at heart, to be careful to avoid giving
the smallest cause for alarm to the government which
has just been set up and which is going to be touchy
for a long while.*

Bernadotte might well have been furiously angry with
Madame de Staël for her part in putting him in the unpleasant position in which he had found himself; but he
was a genuinely great-hearted man, and in the midst of
this humiliation he was big enough to realize that it could
never have happened to him if he had not been greedy
enough to take the golden bait that had been offered to
him.

For Madame de Staël herself the years of Napoleon's
defeat and downfall had been increasingly unhappy. She
had not, in the end, gone down well in Stockholm. In the
face of the legend of herself that she had created in *Delphine*
and *Corinne* the predominantly golden and well-made
Swedes found her almost spectacularly unimpressive, and
in making their entry into the formal mazes of Swedish
society her Albert and Albertine gave a display of gaucherie
and awkwardness that spoke volumes as to the way that
their upbringing had been neglected. The noisy, ill-man-
nered, and self-congratulatory family seemed more ridiculous than important, and Madame de Staël found herself
more laughed at than respected. It was hard for her to bear
social failure in a provincial backwater, and as 1812 drew
to an end she became determined to escape to England and
to make her way to the center of things once more.

She sailed from Göteborg in May of the following year,
accompanied by Rocca, Auguste, who had come from
France to join her, and Albertine; but when she reached
England she found herself little the better for the move.
She had the disagreeable experience of being lionized with-

out being taken seriously. She was invited everywhere by
people who wanted to see her, but who had no intention of
listening to her. For the past three years she had been
intermittently at work on the historical epic that had
almost persuaded her to turn south for Odessa and the Holy
Land during her passage through the Ukraine. Its subject
was "that great epoch in English history" in which, according to her, enthusiasm for the Crusades had been replaced
by an enthusiasm for due process and constitutional
government that had led to the signing of Magna Carta.
Hypnotized by her thesis, she had ultimately convinced
herself that the war was being carried on by an idealistic
people dedicated to a struggle for European freedom in
general, and for what was best for France in particular.
She found herself in a country as deeply divided on the war
as the United States was later to be divided on its war in
Vietnam, and run by a reactionary war party cynically
and cold-heartedly in pursuit of a very narrow conception
of the national interest. They did not wish to have her views
on what would be the ideal government for France after
the war; they wanted the legitimate line restored to the
throne, and they hoped to achieve the maximum destruction of France's capacity for waging offensive war at the
lowest possible cost to themselves. They looked on Madame
de Staël as noisy, ill-informed, and unrealistic; flattered her
with tributes to her intelligence and acumen; and disregarded everything she had to say.

But Madame de Staël soon had other things than the
degree of importance that was attached to her views to
cause her pain. When Austria bolted from the ranks of his
allies and joined the Anglo-Russian camp, Napoleon dis-
graced Monsieur de Narbonne, who had been his Ambassador at Vienna, and sent him to be governor of the melancholy fortress at Torgau on the Baltic shore. There he very
soon died of typhus. A few months after his death his son
Albert, who had been given a commission in a Swedish
cavalry regiment by Bernadotte, and who had been behaving ever since with a compulsive aggressiveness that led
many of those around him to conclude that he was delib-

erately trying to get himself killed, either in action or in
a duel, succeeded in achieving the latter aim. After pro-
voking a Russian officer to challenge him he had his head
virtually cut off with the first sweeping blow of his opponent's saber.

On top of these grievous losses Madame de Staël was
also having a hard time with her young lover. Rocca had
never properly recovered from the wounds he had received
in Spain, and his always-precarious health had been under-
mined by the jolting and bumping that he had had to endure during their long *chevauchée* round the head of the
advancing Grande Armée in 1812. He was now in continuous pain from his old wounds and showing alarming
signs of being in for serious trouble with his lungs. As an
ex-officer in the French army, and in his heart still a passionate admirer of Napoleon, he found the strength of anti-
French and anti-Bonapartist feeling in England and the
coarseness of its expression—both a function of the tensions of the long-drawn-out war—extremely hard to bear.
It was also hard for him to accept the fact that English
conventions required the concealment, if not the denial,
of the nature of his relationship with Madame de Staël.
To the sick and irritable Rocca it was exasperating and
humiliating to find himself being packed off to Bath and
similar retreats at frequent intervals to keep up a fiction
of their independent existence in which no one believed.
He spent half his time exploding into fits of rage, and she
spent half hers wheedling him out of them.

And in the midst of these private vexations and distresses
Madame de Staël was further tormented by the realization
that she could no longer evade the truth she had been
refusing to face ever since she had become one of Napoleon's enemies. She did not really want to see *that man*
brought down, whatever he might stand for, because his
defeat involved the defeat of France. Monsieur de Narbonne
had been right, and she had been wrong: to be *for* France
one had to be for Napoleon. In her desperation she found a
formula for aspiration that would enable her to have it both
ways. In a conversation with an English cabinet minister

she said pathetically that she wanted Bonaparte to win
and to be killed in the decisive battle—a solution that
would leave France free of the tyrant but unoccupied and
unhumiliated.

Her distress grew as Napoleon's position crumbled.
"One must not speak ill of France when the Russians are
at Langres!" she wrote in a letter to Constant. "May God
exile me from France rather than let me return with the help
of foreigners. And as for *the man,* what free spirit could
wish to see him finished off by Cossacks?" But for all that
she returned to Paris in the wake of the allied armies in the
middle of May in 1814.

And it was there, in her beloved city, the only place in
which she felt truly at home, and the center of her universe
of meaning and interest, that she received the *coup de
grâce.* After half a year of intriguing and scheming, much of
it devoted to the lost cause of saving the crown of Naples
for Murat, Madame de Staël received official notification
that she had not succeeded in fulfilling Bernadotte's
prophecy by making herself a leader of the opposition. Her
son Auguste's curiously witty and complicated cousin
Louis XVIII sent an emissary to her with a personal message
far more cruel and far more devastating in its effect than
any of the punitive actions to which she had succeeded in
driving Napoleon:

> *We attach so little importance to anything you may
> do, say, or write that the Government wishes to know
> nothing of it and, further, neither desires to give you
> any anxiety on this score, nor intends to allow anyone
> to do anything to interfere with your projects and
> mystifications in any way.*

What made this shrewd thrust at Madame de Staël's
self-esteem so particularly telling was that, according to
vulgar report, her influence had never been greater. Her
acquaintance with the Tsar, with such British magnates
as Lord Liverpool, with the great Wellington himself; the
debts of gratitude owed her by the Constitutionalists she

had rescued in the days of the Terror; her "standing" as an opponent of Buonaparte and a victim of his hostility; the reputation of her writings; her reputation for shrewd political insight—all these persuaded those who did not know her or her work, the nature of her ideas, or who were remote from the real centers of political power, that she was among the most powerful people in the new France. Harold Nicolson accepts this strange view of her position in the Paris of 1814 in his short biography of Benjamin Constant and, having claimed that she possessed a unique influence under the occupation, repeats the contemporary boutade to the effect that there were three powers in the Europe of the day, Russia, England, and Madame de Staël. But we have seen the line that Louis XVIII felt able to take with her, and there are Constant's own reports of her. He noted that she had changed from head to foot, that she had become thin and pale, and that she was absent-minded and inattentive to what was said to her. She was in fact dying, of the knowledge of her political insignificance, of her anxieties about money, and of her fear that poor Rocca might die before her and leave her alone.

In view of her position and her possessions it seems absurd that Madame de Staël should have been seriously concerned about her financial situation at this or any other point in her career, but she had always been a very rich woman, and like most very rich people she thought she was facing impoverishment whenever she had to modify her expenditures. In 1812, before leaving Coppet to make her long swing through the Ukraine and round the Baltic, she had prepared for all eventualities by turning one large part of her fortune into ready cash, investing another large part of it in real estate in Pennsylvania, and making substantial deposits in a number of Italian banks. In 1814 the deposits in the Italian banks were frozen and untouchable, the real estate in Pennsylvania was unsalable, and the ready cash was shrinking rapidly as a consequence of her constitutional inability to regulate her daily expenditures. Her situation became critical, at least in her eyes, when Albertine fell in love with the gifted and handsome Victor de

Broglie, and it became necessary to provide her with a
dowry. He was a duke, but an impoverished one, who belonged to a noble family which had lost everything but its
pride in the Revolution. His parents could not be expected
to approve their son's marriage to anyone of such notoriously irregular origin as Albertine de Staël—unless she
were to be given a really substantial dowry. Madame de
Staël's first thought when faced with the problem of raising
a capital sum without going to the length of reducing her
own levels of expenditure was to petition the King for the
repayment of the two million francs that her father had
lent to Louis XVI. Louis XVIII recognized his obligation
to repay the loan in principle, but the handing over of so
large a sum under the prevailing conditions involved certain difficulties that could not immediately be overcome:
for the moment the Crown had more pressing calls on its
limited supplies of ready money.

It was at this point, in August, that Benjamin Constant
drew her attention to himself by falling head over heels in
love with that beautiful and ageless goose Madame Récamier. She was one of Madame de Staël's oldest friends, and
one of her very few women friends; but a certain coldness
had invaded their relationship during the winter of 1812–13
when Auguste de Staël had fallen for her, and she had done
rather more than she should to encourage him to dangle
after her in France when his place had clearly been at his
mother's side in Stockholm. That her Constant, her Benjamin, should now be following in Auguste's footsteps was
more than she could bear. Her salon in the Rue Lamoignon
began to ring with denunciations of his behavior, and then
suddenly it occurred to her that Albertine was Constant's
daughter and that he still owed her eighty thousand francs.
It was providential, the dowry problem was solved, Constant could put up the money....

When he heard of this solution of the problem Constant
was infuriated. In his mind the matter of the debt had been
settled long before—in March of 1810 when he had undertaken to leave Madame de Staël or her heirs the sum owing
with accumulated interest. So far as he was concerned the

debt had been paid by that agreement, and he now owed her nothing. That his conscience wasn't altogether clear is evident from the entry that he wrote into his diary when the question of the dowry had been put to him:

> *Madame de Staël is a serpent of ferocious vanity;*
> *fundamentally she loathes me as much as I detest her.*
> *I must protect my money from the claws of that ferocious harpy.*

That he could quite easily have raised the money if he had given up gambling doesn't seem to have occurred to him; nor did he, apparently, feel under any obligation to his daughter in the matter. Confronted with his indignant refusal of the entire sum asked for Madame de Staël cut her request by half. Would he put up forty thousand francs? He would, he replied, be glad to do anything he could for his beloved daughter, but not that—he just didn't have that much to give away.

At this point, in March 1815, Napoleon escaped from Elba and returned to France. Madame de Staël, along with most of those who had come to Paris in the baggage of the foreign armies, took to her heels and fled away to Coppet. She was accompanied by Rocca, now a living skeleton who spent most of his time in bed, Schlegel, and Albertine. Constant stayed in Paris, and announced his intention of dying in the fight against the tyrant in the *Journal des Débats* of March the eleventh. He noted in his diary that publication of this article would in itself put his life in danger if Napoleon's bid to return to power should succeed. On March 17, when Napoleon had already passed through Auxerre and was approaching Paris, Constant renewed his defiances, again in the *Journal des Débats*. In this new article he compared Napoleon to Attila and Jenghiz Khan, and rallied all good men to oppose him:

> *Those who desire no more than to become the servants*
> *of a despot can readily transfer their services from one*
> *system to another, confident that under a new despot-*

*ism they can renew their servitude as obedient tools.
But those who love liberty will prefer to die upon the
steps of a throne by which that liberty is safeguarded
and assured....*

*I am not the man to crawl, a miserable turncoat,
from one seat of power to another, I am not the man to
justify evil with sophistry, or to mumble shameful
words in order to save a life that I would feel ashamed
to have preserved.*

Napoleon installed himself in the Royal apartments in
the Tuileries on the following day, and Constant took refuge with the American Minister. He escaped from Paris
on March 23, and after hiding in Angers for three days
had second thoughts. He returned to Paris on March 28,
and on the same day presented his pledges of support for
Napoleon to General Sebastiani. Sebastiani handed him on
to the Minister of Police, and two days later he was being
given an audience by Joseph Bonaparte at the Palais Royal.
On April 13 he had an interview with the tyrant himself.
He was then assigned to the task of liberalizing the Imperial Constitution, and after further interviews with the
great man on the fourteenth, fifteenth, seventeenth, eighteenth, and nineteenth he was officially recognized as a
member of the administration and appointed a Counselor of
State.

His traverse from the position of dedicated opponent to
eager personal collaborator in the space of thirty days
shocked Constant's friends, delighted his enemies, and
infuriated Madame de Staël. Such a performance by the
man who was her most intimate political associate in the
world's regard could only reveal that no question of principle had ever been involved in her opposition to Napoleon.
On the twentieth, the day that he obtained the splendid
new gold-embroidered uniform that went with his office
and noted in his journal that now that he had made it he
would have to give up gambling and frequenting prostitutes, he received a letter from her roundly abusing him
for selling out *and* demanding repayment of his debt to
her at the earliest possible date in order to avoid prejudic-

ing his daughter's marriage to de Broglie. Constant, who
was exhausted by overwork (he had never in his life been
driven as Napoleon was driving him in his haste to have
the revision of the constitution completed) and sick with
frustrations induced by his realization that his new master
was not going to go an inch further than he had to in the
direction of constitutionalism, sent her a curt refusal. She
replied threatening him with a lawsuit and with exposure.
She might not, she told him, win her suit, but when it was
over the evidence of his conduct would have revealed the
baseness of his character to the world:

> The remembrance of your past life will rise before you
> and make you tremble. However, all is now over be-
> tween you and me; between you and Albertine; be-
> tween you and all men of decent feeling. In future I
> shall only address you through my lawyers and in my
> duty as my daughter's guardian. Adieu.

"It's war!" Constant wrote in his journal. "I shall wage
it with pleasure." And he slipped, effortlessly, into the pos-
ture of a blackmailer, asking her if she had thought what
impression her letters to him were likely to make if they
were to be read out in open court. This frightened her into
an explosion of fury:

> I did not mean to write to you on this horrible sub-
> ject again, but the letters that my son has brought to
> me demand a final reply. You threaten me with my
> letters! This last stroke is worthy of you! I repeat it—
> worthy of you! To threaten a woman with her private
> letters—letters that might compromise her and her
> children—in order to avoid repaying the money you
> owe her.

And so lamentably on. The letter was written a week before Waterloo and the end of Napoleon's hundred days. It
would be a mistake, however, to suppose that this squalid
obsession had occupied the whole of her mind during this
dramatic episode. Before it ended Madame de Staël had

further demonstrated her complete lack of political judgment, and of ordinary common sense, by writing to Lord
Castlereagh, the English Secretary for Foreign Affairs, to
try to persuade him that it would be in everybody's interest
to leave Napoleon on the French throne. She had also written to Louis-Philippe, Duc d'Orléans, to try to persuade him
to come forward as a liberal candidate for the throne that
would become vacant if Napoleon were to be, once again,
deposed. While both these suggestions would have been entirely reasonable in the context of an ideal world, they were
simply fatuous in relation to that of 1815.

Strangely enough, one of the things that the government
of Louis XVIII found it possible to do in the late autumn
of that year, after Napoleon had been finally disposed of,
was to extinguish its indebtedness to Madame de Staël.
With her two millions safe in hand at last she went off to
Italy in January 1816 with her little band, Rocca, Auguste,
Schlegel, and Sismondi, to marry Albertine to Victor de
Broglie at Pisa in February. She then returned to Coppet,
free from most of her cares, to spend a long and happy summer entertaining an enormous number of distinguished
and important people with all her old lavishness and inconsequence. In October, when the stream of visitors had
at last dried up, Pastor Gerlach came to the house and ended
the life of Madame de Staël by transforming her into Madame Necker de Rocca in the presence of Fanny Randall
and John Rocca's brother Charles.

Gerlach was, however, persuaded to keep the marriage
secret, as Swiss law entitled him to do, on the grounds that
the difference in the ages of the contracting parties, and
the existence of their five-year-old son, might make it a
matter for scandal if it were made public. Madame Necker
de Rocca was thus able to return to Paris for her last winter
under her old name and to set up an establishment in the
Rue Royale as Madame de Staël. She was still living at
that address and under that name when she was felled by
a stroke at the end of February 1817 (characteristically, the
blow fell on her when she was in full evening dress as she
was about to make her entrance at a reception given by

Louis XVIII's minister, Decazes). A month after that event she was moved, still as Madame de Staël, to the house in the Rue Neuve-des-Mathurins in which she was at last to die in the middle of July. Rocca, himself dying and too weak to stand or walk unsupported for more than a few minutes, stayed at her bedside by the hour, calming her fears that if she were to fall asleep she might wake to find that he had gone. When she was dead he dragged himself to Coppet to see her coffin carried into the appalling mausoleum in which her mother and father lay pickled in alcohol like medical specimens. He was spared the experience of entering the tomb and seeing her laid at the feet of those two strange beings whose passionate self-regard and inability to love anybody but themselves had blighted her childhood and her life; but he was present at the reading of the will that she had made two days after their marriage before Pastor Gerlach. When that was over Madame de Staël had ceased to be Madame de Staël at last; she had signed both the document-in-chief and the codicil attached to it, as Madame Necker de Rocca, and had accompanied each signature with the declaratory phrase "my real name."

John Rocca was thus given the second of the three things he had asked for during their courtship six years before. She had already given him the child he had asked for, and she had now taken his name. But the first of his three wishes, that she should belong to him completely, was to be explicitly denied him. Her will contained no word of tenderness or of regard for him, and the preamble, where such an expression of feeling might have been expected, consisted of a eulogy of someone else:

> *I commend my soul to God, who has lavished his gifts upon me in this world, and who has given me a father to whom I owe what I am and what I have, a father who might have saved me from all my errors if I had never turned away from his principles. I have but one counsel to give my children, and this is to have ever present in their minds the example of the conduct, the virtues and the talents of my father, and to imitate*

him, each according to his calling and his strength.
I have known no one in this world who equaled my
father, and every day my respect and love for him be-
come engraved more deeply in my heart.

It would be naïve to assume that these words refer to the
real Monsieur Necker or to suppose that they describe her
feelings for the human being who bore that name. They
refer to the ideal figure identified with her father which
had taken shape in her mind after the real Monsieur
Necker's death. In this tribute to the father of her invention
she discloses the psychological function of that posthumous
adulation, by claiming so much for the dead man, and by
giving him the central position in her life she could reduce
every other man who had aspired to play a part in it to just
such a nullity as she had made of Monsieur de Staël, and so
to take vengeance on the entire male sex for her father's
crime of abandoning her and leaving her defenseless in the
hands of her frozen-hearted and coldly self-regarding
mother.

Madame de Charrière

Benjamin Constant's friend Madame de Charrière was very much Madame de Staël's superior in talent and intellect; but her career followed another course. She was born in Holland in 1740 as Agnes Isabella Elisabeth van Tuyll van Serooskerken van Zuylen. Her father, Jacob van Tuyll van Zuylen, Baron of Serooskerken and Westerbroeck, was the descendant of a long line of aristocrats, who had lived in the four-towered Chateau Van Zuylen since feudal times, but he departed from his family's traditions and married the daughter of a wealthy bourgeois from Amsterdam. He was twenty-three and his bride was sixteen at the time of the marriage. Agnes was born just under a year later, and she was followed into the world by another girl and four boys.

While she was growing up, Belle de Zuylen, as she came to be called, wrote of her father that his only fault was that he set "a standard of morality so high that one feels always at a disadvantage with him...our family vocabulary is molded upon his attitude. No lively expressions, nothing shocking." He was an extremely conventional and slow-witted man, and his unusually intelligent and quick-witted daughter had little difficulty in making circles round him from a very early age. He seems to have been impressed by her performances and even to have encouraged them, and by the time she was twelve she had developed a habit of showing off and had a rather priggish sense of her own superiority to the common run of humanity.

What had happened to Agnes Isabella in her earliest years is not a matter of record, but for some reason she felt that she had never known what it was to be loved or happy until she was sent away to Switzerland to learn French under a Mademoiselle Prévost when she was in her eleventh year. She had been educated at home by governesses and tutors up to that point, and she found the experi-

ence of being one of a crowd of children at the Institut
Pierre Colomb in Geneva liberating and delightful. When
the time for her to go home for the summer holidays came
round she felt the oppressive weight of her straitlaced
family hanging over her like a thundercloud, and she
begged to be allowed to stay in Switzerland with Mademoiselle Prévost rather than go home.

The Baron van Serooskerken and his wife were somewhat
taken aback by this request; but, after taking outside advice,
(from a gentleman who had been tutor to George III and
his brother the Duke of Gloucester), they granted it. The
few months that followed were fantasized by Agnes Isabella
into a visit to Paradise, and they had a decisive influence
on the rest of her life. To her enormous pleasure Mademoiselle Prévost carried her off to her country cottage, and
there treated her like a perfectly ordinary little girl. When
they went picnicking she carried one of the baskets, and
she washed the plates in a brook afterwards; and when they
went to fêtes and concerts in Geneva they went as ordinary
people. She tried to convey the essence of her delight in
her letters home: "The cook at Zuylen lives in the lower
depths of the house, like a whale in the great deep. But
the cook here in Switzerland is in and out of the rooms like
sunlight and fresh air. She comes to borrow a copy of the
Gazette or to ask for advice about the dress she is making...." The cook's dress was being made to be worn at the
village fête celebrating the completion of the *vendange*. The
time for the grape-picking and the feeding of the wine
presses soon came round. "Everyone is having such fun
drinking and dancing. Nobody cares whether meals are
properly served or the rooms are done during the *vendange*;
all of them, masters and servants, are among the vines."
Her parents were upset by these letters and called her
home.

Any hopes that they may have had that Agnes Isabella
would be returned to them were destined to be disappointed.
Every morning when she got up while she was staying at
Mademoiselle Prévost's cottage she ran out onto her balcony
to salute the sunlit waters of Lac Leman and the distant

alps with a theatrical *"Bonjour, ma Suisse chérie! Bonjour, le monde!"* Good morning, my beloved Switzerland! Good morning, world! She said this in French, not in Dutch, and although French was the language of the international society to which she, as an aristocrat, belonged, the point is significant. Dutch was the language normally spoken by her father and mother, and by her brothers and sisters, at home, and she was rejecting it as her private mode. When she returned to Zuylen after her stay with Mademoiselle Prévost she had adopted a new French persona. She had ceased to be Agnes Isabella, and had become Belle de Zuylen. Part of her adolescent struggle to assert her right to an independent identity was devoted to a successful effort to have this change recognized, and by the time she was eighteen she had officially established herself as Mademoiselle de Tuyll or Mademoiselle de Zuylen, even though her parents and her brothers and sisters were always known as Barons and Baronesses van Tuyll, or van Zuylen. She paraded the fact that she was a Voltairean skeptic, that her literary admirations were French, that she aspired to speak and write the language of Versailles, that hers was a free and enlightened spirit which had no real connection with the heavy clay of Holland. Her brother Diederick, the only member of the family who really loved and understood her, warned her against the consequences of indulging in this fantasy. "Be careful, Belle, you are more of a Tuyll and more Dutch than you know."

The trouble of which he was giving her warning began to mature as she passed into her twenties. She "came out" and was presented to society when she was fifteen, and was then discovered to be physically very attractive and formidably well educated. But although she was good looking, amusing, and rich, she passed eighteen without being in even momentary danger of entering the married state. At this time she wrote a collection of portraits of her friends, in which, particularly in her own self-portrait, she exhibits herself at her priggish worst. She nevertheless manages to say something extremely revealing about herself in this *Portrait of Zélide:*

...She is patient only in the interest of good manners: When she is indulgent and easy be grateful to her; for it is costing her an effort. When she prolongs her civility with people she holds in small esteem, be doubly grateful to her; she is in torment. She is vain by nature, but experience has doubled that vanity: closer acquaintance with mankind and scorn of them has made her feel superior to most people. Yet this vanity is excessive, even to her own way of thinking....

Excessively emotional, and not less fastidious, she cannot be happy either with or without love. Perceiving herself too sensitive to be happy, she has almost ceased to aspire to happiness and has devoted herself to making others happy instead. She thus hopes to escape repentance and to be amused at the same time.

Have you guessed her secret? Zélide is sensuous. Emotions too vivid and too intense for her organism, an exaggerated activity without any satisfying object, these are the source of all her misfortunes. With less sensitivity, Zélide would have the mind of a great man; with less intelligence she would have been only a weak woman.

She allowed this to be published along with the other portraits in the collection, and the publication created something of a scandal in the social circles in which she moved. Those who were shocked by the book were outraged by the excess of vanity involved in the mock modesty of her confession that she felt superior to most people, and by the admission that she was sensuous. That the portrait is, in fact, a declaration of reluctance to enter upon a sexual commitment, and a proclamation of her unnegotiability as a wife, escaped the attention even of those whose criticism took the form of saying that its publication would damage her chances of getting married. Not long after she had written this self-portrait Belle de Zuylen wrote a somewhat more direct letter to her cousin, Lady Athlone:

To tell the truth, I'd rather not marry. I'd rather be a Ninon de l'Enclos.... But I cannot be a Ninon, because I am a Tuyll. Ergo, I must have a husband.... I

shall never find my great establishment, or the hus-
band who must go with it, here in Holland. To live
in Holland, one must either be unlucky or else ex-
tremely stupid, and I am neither, I hope. I cannot like
Holland just because it happens to be my native land.
I should prefer France above all else; but as things
are, I am unlikely to meet a Duc de Choiseul or a
Marquis de Bellegarde.

Tell me, who will be at the Duke of Brunswick's
ball on Christmas Eve? All the Hague, I suppose, but
who new...? I am getting desperate, for I am getting
old. I am almost twenty. Twenty, and still unmar-
ried.

I remind myself of Penelope with her suitors. But
I am far from being a Penelope. I want to be married.
Having to live without love is too much of a privation
to be endured.

A woman who really wishes to get married does not take
the first step toward matrimony by ruling out every man
of the country in which she lives as a possible partner.
And, having specified a class of persons who might be
acceptable, she doesn't then rule out all of its members
but the two least likely to be available. Belle de Zuylen
was, of course, joking with Lady Athlone, but the nature
of her facetiousness, in itself strained, tells its own story.

...love is bound to be a bed of thorns for a woman;
the thing is, to find a man who knows how to put a
few roses among the thorns...the roses of my bed
of thorns must be all that goes with a great establish-
ment; and that I am resolved to have. When I am a
great lady, I shall have a menagerie about me, but
not one of dogs, cats, and monkeys, with or without
Dutch crops and starched ruffs; I shall have a menag-
erie of queer people. By queer people I mean people
without titles of nobility but with talents—such
as the little boy Mozart, who has composed the most
enchanting minuets and is already a clavecin virtuoso,
at only four years of age. They say his father drives
him, and makes him work too hard, not through un-

*kindness, but because they need money. Will little
Mozart live very long if he does not find a patron,
such as I mean to be?*

While giving her credit for wishing to do the right thing
by Mozart, it has to be said that there are two sides to the
ambition: the woman who wants to marry so that she can
maintain a private court of dependents, or who is prepared
to put up with being married to do so, can only be called
inadequately motivated for anything in the nature of marriage as such. The letter as a whole leaves an ineffable
impression that it is a piece of gallantry on the part of a
woman who is repelled by the idea of marriage, and who
is under tremendous pressure to get married, imposed on
her by her family, her social position, and the expectations
of her society. She wants to be a Ninon de l'Enclos:

*... She remained a great lady despite her morals, be-
cause she was born such. She gave Voltaire his first
encouragement; what does it matter what else she
did? But if I were Ninon de l'Enclos, I should not have
quite so many lovers; in fact, I would be faithful to
the first if he would be reasonably faithful to me....*

It is significant that after saying that she wants to be
like a woman who was famous for her unabashed sexuality
she proceeds to justify that woman in terms of what was
her most marginal and nonsensuous interest. She then
announces a program of being as unlike Ninon in her
sexual behavior as it would be possible to be.

The contradictions of her attitude extend beyond her
letter to her behavior at the Christmas Eve ball to which
it refers. She arrived at the ball late, so that her entry would
be spectacular, and she dressed for it in a flesh-colored dress
that was generally thought to be indecent by the standards
of the time, since at a little distance it gave her the appearance of being naked to the waist. In a society which placed
a premium on virginity and inexperience in brides (a
product of the practice of entailing landed property on

heirs male, rather than of any psychological kinkiness), this performance was in itself an advertisement for her undesirability as a wife. She compounded it with another by ditching the partner to whom she was committed for the first dance of the evening, and crossing the floor to offer herself to David Louis de Constant d'Hermenches de Rebecque, the colonel of a Swiss regiment in the Dutch service.

Constant d'Hermenches was one of the four sons of Samuel de Constant de Rebecque, a general in the same service, and he was brother to the Juste de Constant who was Benjamin Constant's father. He was eighteen years older than Belle de Zuylen, he was married, he was a notorious womanizer, and, although he had a small income from an estate in Switzerland, he was largely dependent on the pay he earned as a soldier. It may be added that although he was a good-looking and well-made man he had been badly wounded in the head at the battle of Fontenoy and had suffered ever since from severe migraine headaches and from occasional prostrating spells of acute nervous exhaustion. The nature of his profession, and dependence on his earnings, were important factors in the picture. His commanding general was the Duke of Brunswick who was not only a personal friend of Belle de Zuylen's father, but also in an official relationship with him. The Baron van Serooskerken van Westbroeck was Deputy of Utrecht and as such part of the body that voted the funds for the army in which Constant d'Hermenches was a mercenary. Since anything in the nature of a serious complaint about d'Hermenches's conduct from the Baron to the Duke would almost certainly result in his speedy dismissal from the service, he was not in a position to take physical advantage of the offer that had apparently been made to him. Even if this had not been so, the circumstances in which it was ostensibly made were such as to alert Belle de Zuylen's parents to the fact that something untoward was going on. They removed her from the Ball while supper was being served and before the cotillion had begun and, by returning from Utrecht to the Hague on the

following day, made it impossible for her to meet him that
night at a gala performance of the Opera House as she had
promised she would. For the next several years they exerted themselves to insure that, whatever else might happen, their daughter should not be seduced by Constant
d'Hermenches. She told him, rather early in the relationship, just about what she was doing.

> *I have sought first your notice and then your esteem.*
> *But to what end? We can never see each other freely*
> *nor write to each other openly. You are for me one of*
> *those rare and precious possessions which one is mad*
> *enough to wish to obtain and to keep at any price,*
> *though one can put them to no use, once acquired.*

What she had acquired was a lover with whom it was
most unlikely that she would ever find herself making
love, and for the next ten years she managed to keep this
nonphysical affair between her and the necessity for entering into something in the nature of an adult relationship.
Constant d'Hermenches did not wish to play the game that
way, and he developed a long-term plan for changing it.
Although it would be impossible for him to risk the seduction of the Baron van Serooskerken's unmarried daughter,
there would be nothing in the least dangerous about having
an affair with a Belle de Zuylen who had become another
man's wife. He therefore embarked on a well-considered
campaign to get her married to a friend of his, who, by a
truly remarkable coincidence, happened to be François-
Robert-Eugène, Comte de Cursinges, Marquis des Marches,
and Marquis de Bellegarde. Monsieur de Bellegarde was
very much a man of the *Ancien Régime.* He had no wish
to marry, but he was fifty, he had no heir, and his extensive estates were encumbered with debts. He was quite prepared to marry a good-looking woman with a fortune on
the understanding that once the business of his heir had
been attended to she would be free to do as she pleased—and
he would have the same liberty.

Rosalie de Constant, daughter of Samuel, the third of

Constant d'Hermanches's brothers, once made a written assessment of her uncle's character:

> ...he had every quality necessary for a successful life. But vanity and ambition gave him no rest. He wanted to be everything—courtier, author, soldier, farmer, voluptuary, and saint; and he wanted to continue everything, business with pleasure, magnificence and economy, wife and mistresses. He had every possible ambition: to dominate society; to rule his friends; to crush his enemies; to eclipse his rivals. He often succeeded, but there are many things in which he failed.

Constant d'Hermanches's scheme for making Belle de Zuylen first the Marquise de Bellegarde and then his mistress was one of these. She first thought that he was being noble and disinterested in finding her so magnificent a husband, but as she slowly came to understand the nature of Monsieur de Bellegarde's views on matrimony and realized that the primary object of the transaction, in his view, was the exchange of the amount of her dowry as a lump sum for a mortgage on his real estate, she at length divined d'Hermanches's motive, and with a good deal of forensic skill forced him to say precisely what it was. When he had admitted to his program for a *mariage à trois*, she told him that if her children were going to appear in the stud book as Bellegarde's, Bellegarde's they would have to be, and that if the marriage went through he would have to be satisfied with a pen-friendship that would exclude seeing her. Physically he would be put right out of her life. Their conversation, which took place in her sister's house, was interrupted as soon as she had delivered this ultimatum. She expected that it would be resumed on the following day, at the house of her cousin Lady Athlone, but at the time appointed for the rendezvous a manservant appeared with a letter. D'Hermenches had resigned his command, left the Dutch service, closed up his house, dismissed his servants, and gone into France. Now that she was absolutely safe she could afford to throw her bonnet over the windmill:

*I shall go to parties, I shall seem gay, and no one will
guess how much my heart is paining me. I shall be
following you in my imagination, caressing you, and
longing for you even in my dreams. Ah, Hermenches,
a sensual and sensitive woman should be careful before she becomes the friend of a man. I don't put the
gloves you left behind my pillow at night, and I don't
kiss your letters, but I have all the feelings that I would
have had we been lovers, nothing is lacking except the
memory of those caresses which have made it sweet to
live and joy to love since the world began. Do you know
what I should have done had I come to your house? I
should have asked you for an embrace....*

This letter, which reached d'Hermenches in Paris, went
unanswered for some time, but was ultimately parried by
his earnest recommendation that she should marry Bellegarde, without further delay. The story becomes a farcical
one at this point, because the negotiations for the marriage
had been carried forward to such a point that they had generated a species of inertia of their own, and rolled on for a
considerable period regardless of the fact that none of the
principals—Belle de Zuylen, the Marquis, or the Baron
Serooskerken—had the smallest intention of ever letting
it actually take place. There was even some doubt, and
heavy legal expenses were incurred in clearing up the point,
as to whether the parties, being Protestant on the van Tuyll
van Zuylen side and Roman Catholic on the other, *could*
be legally married in either Protestant Holland or Roman
Catholic France.

The farce had nonetheless to be played out, until the
point was reached where it became necessary for the parties
to commit themselves to some kind of contract. The Marquis de Bellegarde—all aristocratic lightness, cynicism,
and hard-fisted avarice—came to the severities, austerities,
and fierce rectitudes of Zuylen, wheedled and pushed by
Lady Athlone, to discuss the terms of the marriage settlement with Belle de Zuylen's father. The two men met in a
rather constrained atmosphere, and remained deeply suspicious of each other until they had retired to the Baron's

study for a serious discussion. From this both men emerged beaming and relaxed. For a few hours Belle de Zuylen believed that this meant that they had reached an agreement favorable to the marriage, and she prepared fatalistically for her transformation into her fantasy self as a French Marquise. But while she was writing notes to her friends saying that it was all settled, he was telling his intimates that it was all off. The two men had emerged from their conference radiant with relief: the Marquis had been delighted to find himself let out, and the Baron as much so to find that he wasn't going to have to give his daughter away to a Roman Catholic Frenchman. The Marquis had found that, in spite of all her efforts to be French, Belle de Zuylen was in essence, as her brother had warned her, very Dutch, and as a French aristocrat familiar with the great houses of France he had been unimpressed by the splendors of Zuylen: "I don't want to spend my days visiting a parcel of pennypinching Dutch patrician in-laws." Being what he was, the Baron did not feel under any obligation to discuss the outcome of the exchange with his daughter—since nothing had been arranged there was, indeed, strictly speaking, nothing for him to let her know. As for Bellegarde, he did not have quite the face to tell her that it was all off himself, and he hit on a remarkably novelistic and possibly sadistic way of doing so. He wrote a letter addressed to Constant d'Hermenches—who, now a major in the French service, was with his regiment in Corsica, taking part in the supression of an insurrection—and gave it to her as he was leaving Zuylen, unsealed, with a request that she should have it forwarded to him. She could not resist the temptation, and opened it and read it as soon as he had gone:

> *Give my compliments to General Paoli and tell him that he's a fool to be fighting the French when he could make friends with them and be made welcome in Paris, where he could enjoy the beautiful French ladies and adept little mistresses that one can find there—all the things, in short, that I am counting on enjoying there next winter.*

*I'm leaving Holland soon, though I had thought of
looking up that widow of whom there could be no
question while I still had a chance of bagging that
inestimable treasure the sublime Agnes. But, that
widow being Dutch, I have decided to go back to
France where there is a treasure who is only fifteen,
and whose many quarterings and portion make her
more suited to a man of my rank, with the living habits
and tastes that I have acquired in my half century of
life. I have renounced the idea of marrying Agnes only
because I am not worthy of her. But then, what man
could be? I have a few confidences to share with you
on that topic, but they must wait until we meet
again.*

de Bellegarde

In the background of the comedy of Franco-Dutch manners which had ended by delivering her this nasty jolt,
there was the purer farce of her involvement with the simply ridiculous James Boswell, who was so unexpectedly to
achieve a kind of greatness as the biographer of Dr. Johnson.
Very plain and enormously conceited, Boswell learned,
soon after his arrival in Utrecht, that the still unmarried
elder daughter of the house of van Zuylen was the best
catch available on the Dutch marriage market, and he determined to go after her. Introducing himself to the Baron
van Serooskerken as the son of Lord Auchinleck of Auchinleck, he managed to get himself invited to Sunday night
dinner at the Zuylens' own house in Utrecht. Being Boswell,
he prepared for this visit by spending Saturday night whor-
ing and drinking in the rougher stews and taverns of the
town and arrived at the Baron's house with an appalling
hangover. Hulswit, the Baron's wine butler, and Belle de
Zuylen were the only people present who realized the nature
of his condition, and it amused them to enter into a compact to abuse his drunkard's raging thirst and to see how
much they could pour into him. At some stage in the evening. Boswell spotted that signals were being exchanged between the daughter of the house and the butler, and he
twitted her in a thick and angry voice for being unduly

familiar with a servant. His aggressive manner of speaking alarmed the Baron and the Baroness, but Belle de Zuylen, having brought him to the brink of trouble, decided to get him out of it, and explained Boswell's incoherence as "only his delightful Scotch brogue." She handled him so skillfully for the rest of the evening that all ended well, with the van Zuylens concluding that he was charming, if a little rough in his manner, and his deciding that they were very genteel people indeed and that their daughter showed signs of developing a tendre for him.

He did, in fact, become a Sunday evening regular at the van Zuylen house for as long as he remained in Utrecht. He had one view of his visits, she had another. She was amusing herself by seeing how far his conceit would take him when he had a few drinks in him, and he was convinced that, while he was saving her from the pernicious influences of Calvinism and preparing her to undertake the duties that the wife of a son of Lord Auchinleck would be expected to perform, she was falling in love with him. There came a day at last, shortly before he left Utrecht, when he made an approach to a proposal, and funked it at the last moment. "I might even marry you," he began, and hurriedly added, "to a friend of mine in Scotland." "Oh, Jamie, Jamie Boswell!" she exclaimed, and buried her face in her hands to hide her explosion of laughter. He thought she was crying, and when she looked up at him again took the tears on her cheeks for tears of humility.

When Boswell left Utrecht they began a correspondence, wholly serious on his side, teasing and frivolous on hers. He could not see it, and went about Europe showing her letters to such people as Jean-Jacques Rousseau and his friend Paoli the Corsican rebel, telling them how he had captured the heart of this well-born and enormously rich Dutch girl. They warned him that she was playing with him, but he declined to even admit the possibility, and wrote letter after letter to her, preparing her for the serious role of wife of a Scotch laird in which he was sure that she would find her true happiness. At last he had to challenge her to admit how she truly felt:

*I charge you once and for all be strictly honest with
me. If you love me, own it. I can give you the best advice. If your love is all over by now, tell me. If you love
another, confess it. Answer me this one question: If
I had pretended a passion for you, which I might easily
have done, had I not been a man of the highest honor—
for it is not difficult to make believe what we already
please to imagine—would you not have gone to the
world's end with me? Supposing even that I had been
disinherited by my father, would you not have said:
"Sir, here is my portion. It is yours, we may live gen-
teely on it!"*

He was astonished when she replied that so far from being ready to go to the world's end with him she was not even
prepared to live in Scotland for his sake, but he soon reconciled himself to the apparent rebuff by telling himself that
this was just another example of her "enchanting humility"
like the tears she had shed when he failed to propose to her.
He was jolted again, a year later, when he found that this
extraordinary woman had spent the whole winter in England without letting him know that she was there or asking him to come and see her. Could it be that...? But no.
He cleared up a disturbing point. She had, it appeared,
spent several days in a disreputable lodging house in Shep-
herd's Market with a seafaring man and while there had
invited the philosopher Hume to dinner. Hume had been
startled to find himself being served dishes sent in from a
tavern instead of being offered a formal meal and shocked
when Mademoiselle de Zuylen had fed her little dog with
scraps from her plate. Could any of this be true? Belle de
Zuylen explained that she had been visited in London by
her brother Diederick, and that they had wanted to spend
some time together without the constraints that being guests
in a great house inevitably placed upon them; and yes, she
had given the dog a few scraps from her plate—and why
not? Perhaps, after all, none of it was really of any importance.

Boswell thought matters over for a year, then took the bit
between his teeth and made his formal proposal, coupling

it somewhat perversely with an adamant refusal to give her any freedom whatever in the matter of editing and abridging his book on Corsica, a translation of which she was then preparing. While waiting for her answer to his proposal, as to the nature of which he had no doubt, he wrote confidently to his friend and confessor the reverend William Temple:

> *I have bid her be my wife. I have written to her, and have told her all my perplexity. I have put it in the plainest light what conduct I shall absolutely require of her, and what my father will require. I bade her comfort me with a letter in which she shall show me at once her wisdom, her spirit, and her regard for me .... You shall see it. I tell you man, she knows me, and she values me as you do!*

What his letter to her was like, or hers to him, is, with the song that the sirens sang, a matter for conjecture, but the nature of the exchange can be guessed at from the accounts of it sent by her to Constant d'Hermenches and by him to his clerical friend.

> *I will with a good deal of pleasure write out what you request; it will be a brief epitome of an interesting book that I am fond of but which I am no longer translating. I was far advanced in the task, but I wanted permission to change some things that were bad and to abridge others that French impatience would have found unmercifully longwinded. The author, though at the moment he had almost made up his mind to marry me if I would have him, refused to sacrifice one syllable of his book to my taste. I wrote to tell him that I had decided once and for all never to marry him, and I abandoned the translation.*

> *... I told you what sort of letter I last wrote to her. It was candid, fair, conscientious. I told her of many difficulties. I told her my fears from her levity and infidel notions, at the same time admiring her and hoping she was altered for the better. How did she answer?*

Read her letter. Could any actress at any of the theatres
attack one with a keener—what is the word? not fury,
something softer. The lightning that flashes with so
much brilliance may scorch. And does not her esprit
do so? Is she not a termagant, or at least will she not be
one by the time she is forty? And she is near thirty now.
... I have written to her that we are agreed. "My
pride," says I, "and your vanity would never agree. It
would be like the scene in our burlesque comedy, The
Rehearsal. *I am the bold thunder, cries one. The quick*
lightning I, cries another. Et voilà notre ménage."

Whether the prospect of becoming a termagant ever gave
her any concern or not there is no way of knowing, since
she never expresses herself on that topic. But it did bother
her that, when she had her falling out with the ridiculous
Boswell, and again when the magnificent Monsieur de
Bellegarde walked out on her, that she was twenty-eight
and unmarried. When she had read the latter's wounding
letter to d'Hermenches, she took to her bed for three days
and then got up to talk the whole thing over with Charles-
Emmanuel de Charrière, a thirty-six-year-old Swiss gentleman who had been a member of the van Zuylen household
for ten years as tutor to her younger brothers Willem and
Vincent. He was a sweet-natured and kindly man whose
family had been ruined and stripped of all its properties,
but the ancient manor of Colombier as a punishment for
adopting the religious heresy of quietism and refusing to
take part in formal church services as the citizens of Berne
were legally required to do. He was a good listener and over
the years he had become a comforting presence and a confidant for her. She now asked him what he thought Monsieur de Bellegarde had meant by those hateful sentences:
"I am not worthy of her. But then, what man could be?"
What was lacking in her, she asked him, what quality was
it that she did not have, that could make her lovable or even
acceptable in the eyes of a man? He offered her what comfort he could, and as he did so the germ of an idea presented
itself to her. This man understood her, she liked him. He
was gentle, simple, and unworldly, and he could be trusted

not to try to dominate her or interfere with her in thoughts, words, or deeds.

It is doubtful if this germ would ever have taken root and become more than a passing fancy if she had not at this point been subjected to an appalling psychological assault. Her mother fell ill of a fever at a time when a smallpox epidemic was raging through Holland, and since Belle de Zuylen knew all about the discoveries of Dr. Jenner, she insisted on having an English doctor who practiced the art of inoculation brought in to treat the case. She had her way. A Dr. Cooper came, and Helena Jacoba was inoculated. She rallied, but then collapsed, and died, though not until she had said that her daughter had killed her. Belle de Zuylen's situation became very unpleasant indeed.

> *My father cannot bear the sight of me. My brothers will not speak to me unless it is absolutely unavoidable. I can't blame them. My father has lost his life's center, the only human being he ever really loved. My brothers can't forget that the inoculations were my idea. I was so distracted the other day that I spilt boiling water on my poor dog Zephyr and scalded him severely. I was horribly upset when I saw how much pain I had inflicted on the helpless creature. I dressed his wounds, and asked his pardon, wept, put him on my bed, and spent the rest of the night caring for him. Vincent said I was mad. Willem came into my room, threw the dog off the bed and booted him into a corner. Oh, Ditie, my friend, is there any mercy or forgiveness, or love, in any of these Tuyll men? I must get away from Zuylen somehow. I can't bear it much longer.*

In her unhappiness she remembered the dazzling days of happiness in Switzerland with Mademoiselle Prévost, the free-and-easy life at the cottage among the flowery meadows. At Colombier, with Charles-Emmanuel, it would be like that. In her letters to d'Hermenches in Corsica she began to drop hints about a surprising attachment that she had formed and which might provide the solution to all her problems. He caught their drift almost immediately.

Am I right in thinking that you are talking about your
brothers' tutor? Monsieur de Charrière is no doubt a
perfectly amiable and worthy person. But what plea-
sure could you get out of life with him? He is too much
of a sobersides, too regular in his habits, too phleg-
matic a man for you. And his home is in the most bor-
ing village in Switzerland, Colombier....

D'Hermenches went on to say that as the dull and impoverished husband of a rich and brilliant woman Monsieur de Charrière would find himself in an embarrassing
position.

[He] would be far less happy with you than you would
expect him to be, and you would be bitterly disap-
pointed. You would try to make it up to him by exag-
gerating your manifestations of regard for him, only
to find in time that you were doing him no good at all.
He would become less amiable with every passing day,
and you would soon find yourself as good as a widow
even though married.

She tried to explain what she was about to do to him and
why she felt she had to do it, but the more that she said the
less d'Hermenches could see it. One of the most brilliant
and good-looking women he had ever known was planning
to turn her back on the international society to which her
wealth gave her the entry in order to set up house with a
dullard, his senile father, and his two spinster sisters in a
rundown farmhouse, in a boring hamlet a few miles from
Neuchâtel (in his view one of the most boring small towns
in Switzerland); and all she could say in favor of this project was that the dullard was to hand, that he was harmless,
and that she would be living near her brother Diederick
who, having been forced to give up the sea for reasons of
health, was now living in Lausanne. He begged her not to
do it, to give herself time to think, to do nothing rash,
particularly while her spirit was under the shadow cast on
it by the circumstances of her mother's death.

D'Hermenches was not altogether frank with her, and he

did not tell her that he was pleading with her on his own account. She learned of it through her cousin Lady Athlone of Amerongen, who was an acquaintance of a certain Louise de Corcelles who, in turn, was a new neighbor of Madame d'Hermenches and an indefatigable letter writer. Mademoiselle de Corcelles wrote to Lady Athlone, as she wrote to many other people, to tell her of the state of unspeakable despair to which Madame d'Hermenches had been reduced by her husband's sudden request for a divorce after nearly thirty years of marriage. Lady Athlone passed the news on to Belle de Zuylen, as she was almost certainly intended to do, and she wrote to d'Hermenches in an evident panic asking him to deny it and reminding him that he was under an obligation to his wife that he could not fittingly escape however much he might wish to. He wrote back defensively, sending her a classic husband's letter. He had not known what he was doing when he married at twenty-two. It had not seemed important, then, that his wife was eight years older than he was. He had not realized that she was going to become a hypochondriac, that she lacked commonsense, that she would not be able to run a house, that she was going to become embittered, and lazy.... He had, God knew, tried to make her happy and to do the right thing by her....

Belle de Zuylen, becoming every inch a van Tuyll, replied that it was no wonder that Madame d'Hermenches had become embittered, since they lived apart even when they were living in the same house together. Had he not denied her the love and affection he had promised her when they were first married? D'Hermenches replied to this accusation with an even more desperate self-justification.

> Older women who no longer have the power to attract love no longer desire it. That is a kindly provision of nature. They concentrate their affections upon themselves. All that matters to them is their own well-being, their cherished comfort. In the case of my poor wife the only person she really loves is the maid who keeps her comfortable—and she loves her dogs, who give her an abundance of love that she

> *doesn't have to do very much to earn. The maid and*
> *the dogs constitute her real family. She's happiest*
> *when I am away from home, because the presence*
> *of a man in the house involves a disturbance, and*
> *disturbance is painful to her. All she really wants is*
> *to be allowed to stay in bed all day drinking hot choc-*
> *olate with whipped cream by the bucketful. In the*
> *afternoons she sometimes summons up the energy*
> *to play a game of whist with her poisonous relatives,*
> *who delight in reminding her of my faults but who*
> *never tell her that she has responsibilities—as the*
> *mistress of my household and mother of our children.*
> *As a wife she is simply the shadow of what she was.*

This cry of discontent did not have the hoped-for effect;
with it d'Hermenches only succeeded in giving Belle de
Zuylen a further argument in favor of mistrusting him.
He had once loved the woman he now spoke of with such
bitterness and contempt, had he not? "Wax that has melted
once can be melted again." Rather than run the risk of
betrayal involved in loving, she determined to commit
herself to a loveless marriage. She turned her back on
d'Hermenches and in her thirtieth year proposed to Monsieur de Charrière. He refused her for two good reasons:
that she did not love him, and that there was no possibility
that her father would give his consent to her marriage to
a man who was in effect one of the house servants.

Faced with this impasse she thought of a brilliant strate-
gem. She recalled that one of those who had cast his eye
on her as a desirable parti in the past had been a Jacobite
peer called Lord Wemyss, and she now maneuvered him
into a renewal of his suit. He had come into exile on the
continent with an evil reputation for having mutilated
the English prisoners taken by the forces under his command during the rebellion of 1745, and he had soon added
to it by his outbursts of ungovernable rage, his brutal ill-
treatment of his servants, and his drunken lechery. When
in funds he lived a life of spectacular debauch in Paris,
and when he was in low water he retired, by a curious
coincidence, to Monsieur de Charrière's native village in

Switzerland. As soon as Belle de Zuylen heard from the pastor of the Scottish church in Utrecht that Wemyss was still interested, she announced her intention of accepting him as soon as he offered.

Her announcement shook her father into a realization of the cruelties that had been inflicted upon her since her mother's death: "Have we hurt you so much that you would make as abominable a marriage as this to get out of the house?" he asked her. "Can you really want Lord Wemyss?" She then told her father that she would accept Monsieur de Charrière if he disapproved her choice of Lord Wemyss. The Baron van Serooskerken recoiled at this suggestion: Why would she not marry the eminently suitable Count Wittgenstein, who had recently made an offer for her through intermediaries in Utrecht? Because, she replied, the Count was a good man with the right to a wife who would be a credit to him and might make him happy. She was not such a woman, and she deserved Lord Wemyss, as he deserved her.

The Baron now became desperate. He would, he told her, agree to any proposition that she might make, except that she should marry Monsieur de Charrière. In that case, she replied, she would marry Lord Wemyss.

The deadlock was broken by two outsiders. Monsieur de Charrière consulted a friend of his as to where his duty lay: was he not under an ethical obligation to overcome his objections to the marriage that had been proposed to him, in order to save Belle de Zuylen from Lord Wemyss? His friend was the same gentleman, a Monsieur de Salgas, that the Baron had consulted years before when his daughter had wished to spend her summer in Switzerland with Mademoiselle Prévost. He now came foward to assure Monsieur de Charrière that he would be doing the right thing if he accepted Belle de Zuylen's offer, and to carry his request for formal approval of the match to the Baron. The Baron rejected the proposal out of hand as a gross impropriety and would have continued to do so indefinitely had not Lord Wemyss at this point sent him such a brutally mercenary letter announcing the terms on which he was

prepared to marry his daughter as to shock him into surrender. He withdrew his opposition; but he compensated
himself for his disappointment and the wound to his pride
by cutting her dowry in half. The wedding, and the wedding reception, passed off well enough, but the wedding
night was a fiasco. When the time came for the newly
married couple to go to bed Madame de Charrière was in
the throes of an agonizing attack of toothache, and Monsieur de Charrière was drunk.

It was later to appear that Monsieur de Charrière had
good reason to wish to postpone a test of his manhood. Sex
had never played an important part in his life, and he was
the last person to deal with a woman who was both fascinated by and desperately afraid of her own sexuality.
He had neither the address that might have calmed her
fears nor the ability to satisfy her natural appetites once
they had been overcome. Monsieur de Charrière had read
in the pages of Plutarch that one of the wisest of the Greeks
of antiquity had recommended men to service their wives
three times a month if they wished them to be physically
happy and had further understood from the same authority
that this was all that a chaste and virtuous woman should
require of a man. Monsieur de Charrière's unworldliness
seems to have led him to adopt this recommendation as
a program, and his natural inclinations, or lack of them,
are said to have resulted in his execution of it dutifully
and without warmth. Madame de Charrière hinted that
she had attempted to change his mind on these matters,
and that she had tried to persuade him to make his love-
making more spontaneous and enthusiastic, and more
frequent, but without success. It is hard to believe that
she did anything of the kind in view of the record of her
evasion of passionate entanglements over the greater part
of her life, and more particularly in view of the evidence
of the portrait bust that Houdon made of her while she
was on her honeymoon in Paris in 1771. It is very obvious
from this that the sculptor was repelled by his subject, to
whom he gave the face of a cold, bloodless, and frightened
young man, whose expression suggests that he is contem-

plating some disagreeable prospect. There was, in fact, something that she found disagreeable to contemplate on her mind when the portrait was being made. She had just learned, from her brother Diederick, that although she was married d'Hermenches had not abandoned his ambition for her:

> He has not, in spite of your sacrifice, gone back to his wife; he is going ahead with the divorce and Madame d'Hermenches is broken in health and spirits. The worst of all this is that people here are blaming you for the divorce, so that when you come to take up your abode in your new country you will find that everybody has been turned against you. And how can people know the facts as opposed to the fictions of what there has been between you if he himself has not talked of it, or quoted your letters, or shown them about?

Horrified by the implications of Diederick's letter, Madame de Charrière wrote to d'Hermenches to beg him to abandon the course of action on which he seemed to have embarked:

> If you will give back to Madame d'Hermenches her dignity as a married woman, her fortune, and her peace of mind, if you will prove to your children that you are not a deserter, and restore to your friends the reasons that they once had for respecting you, you will, Hermenches, give me such release from distress, such serenity in my friendship for you, such joy in believing in you again, as I have no words to describe.

D'Hermenches had replied uncompromisingly that the divorce was a necessity and that he could not go back on it. She was forced to recognize that she had not succeeded in putting Monsieur de Charrière between them, but only in setting up the situation that would have come into existence had she married Monsieur de Bellegarde. She still had to make the decision whether to accept or reject the

involvement to which her senses urged her and of which
she was so mortally afraid. The cards were again stacked
against her, and her sense of guilt was reenforced at the
critical moment by the critical event. Constant d'Hermenches obtained his divorce in 1772, and Madame d'Hermenches almost immediately died, so that it could be said that
she had been killed by it. After a suitable interval d'Hermenches wrote to Madame de Charrière to propose that she
should come to see him at Ferney where he was staying with
Voltaire, who was fond of him and who had given him a
place of refuge from the slanderous gossip of Lausanne
and Geneva. Ferney was only an hour's carriage drive from
Colombier, and the visit could be made with little risk
of gossip or scandal. Madame de Charrière had, however,
made her decision. She pretended to believe that d'Hermenches had asked her to come and see Voltaire:

> You want me to come to Ferney, but I have no wish
> to be there. Voltaire is a bad lot, for all his brains.
> I'll read him, but I won't be coming to Ferney to burn
> incense before him.

She did not go.

Diederick came to Colombier for a while and then went
away to Naples to die. Monsieur de Charrière's aged father
died. Madame de Charrière's father died. The long spell
of mourning that these deaths then demanded added to the
isolation and obscurity in which the once-dazzling Belle
de Zuylen had enwrapped herself. The buzz of conjecture
about her extraordinary marriage that had resounded
through the salons of aristocratic Europe died down, and,
though there were occasional rumors of her to the effect
that she had been seen doing the communal laundry of
the household in the courtyard of her undistinguished
husband's house, or that she was living on one floor of
the building in her own suite of apartments while he was
living in another, she dropped out of sight of everything
but the limited societies of Neuchâtel and Lausanne for
thirteen years.

At the end of that time she suddenly emerged from her obscurity to become, for a few years, a successful and much-talked-about writer. She had made her first splash in this field with a tiny novel when she was twenty-two. It was called *The Nobleman,* and its feline caricatures of aristocratic pretension in general and of her race-proud father in particular made it a *succès de scandale* and let to its being banned by the Dutch authorities. It had come to the attention of Frederick the Great, who had been so much taken by it that he had instructed one of his gentlemen to marry her so that she might become an ornament of his court. It is a charmingly light-hearted work which can still be read with pleasure today, and its combination of crisp wit and a pellucid *bon enfant* style suggest that if she had been born in a later age she would have gone on to become a writer in a class with Ada Leverson or Nancy Mitford. But the writing of novels was not by then established as a suitable occupation for a young woman of quality, and she published nothing between 1762 and 1784. By then she had become a different person. Her style was still sharp and laconic, but what she wrote was no longer lightly amusing. Although she adhered to an obsolete eighteenth-century form, in which a narrator tells all in a series of letters to a confidant who makes an occasional reply, she had broken through to the world of interest of the modern novel. *Mistress Henley,* her first publication of 1784, describes the developing unhappiness of a mismatched woman. It has a special and unusual quality of its own rising from the fact that there is no right or wrong in the situation: it is not that the husband treats the wife badly, or that she feels wronged by him; it is simply that there is a want of essential sympathy and understanding—they are not suited. There is no conclusion to the book, which ends in the manner of a Japanese novel, on a dying fall, as the woman recognizes that there is no escape from her situation, and that incomprehension and lack of warmth are what she must learn to live with.

This tragedy of the interior life was followed by *Letters from Neuchâtel,* also of 1784, and *Letters from Lausanne,* of 1785. There was then a two-year interval, at the end of which *Caliste* appeared. The *Letters from Neuchâtel* is a lighter book, but still an exceedingly unhappy one. It is a disillusioned adult's view of the world of simplicities and sensuous delights that had captivated Madame de Charrière during her enchanted summer with Mademoiselle Prévost when she was eleven. She has learned by coming back to it that it is possible to suffer from both intellectual and emotional starvation in what had seemed to her to be a paradise. The effect of the *Letters from Neuchâtel* is disconcerting; reading the volume is rather like being taken into a tranquilly beautiful picture by some genre painter with Vermeer's gift for investing the ordinary with beauty and finding that he is pointing out how desperately provincial and stultifying an existence goes with the scene. The *Letters from Lausanne* is its natural, and heartbreakingly sad, pendant. It concerns itself with a very tenuous subject indeed, a mother's concern for her daughter's happiness. The girl, who is a member of the upper class of Lausanne, becomes involved in a flirtation with a visiting Englishman. Is he serious, or is he not? Neither mother nor daughter can be wholly sure. The cool flow of beautifully simple sentences gives a first impression of triviality, and then, abruptly, the reader becomes aware that there is real desperation behind the uncertainty of the two women. They both know that there is something terribly wrong with the local society, which condemns its women in particular to lead lives of a singular aridity and pointlessness, and that the Englishman represents the girl's only chance of escape. It is not a very good one, because her mother is not rich and cannot provide her with a big enough dowry to make her a *bon parti*. The story is, in fact, about precisely the desparation that filled the heart of poor Suzanne Churchod when Gibbon jilted her. But there is no probability for Madame de Charrière's heroine, of the miracle that produced Monsieur Necker, his millions, and Versailles for Mademoiselle Churchod; when the Englishman's carriage rumbles off at the end of the story Cecilia is left with the choice of spinsterhood or marriage to someone like the muscular young clod of a country parson from the shores of the Lac du Joux who will carry her off to the loneliness of his parish and a life of childbearing and pennypinching.

Between the time of the publication of *Letters from Lausanne* and the appearance of *Caliste* in 1787 two events had a shattering effect on Madame de Charrière's life. At the beginning of 1786 she learned that Constant d'Hermenches had died, alone and in poverty, in Paris at the beginning of the winter. The second event seems to have been in some way related to the first, though its precise nature is a matter which is wrapped in an almost impenetrable obscurity. During the summer of 1786 Monsieur de Charrière, feeling that his wife had begun to find the winters at Colombier insupportably lonely and sad, arranged to rent an apartment in the Rue Beauregard in Geneva. It was a very agreeable apartment, and its salon was hung with *couleur de rose* Aubusson tapestries that made it a perfect setting for the still beautiful green-eyed and fair-haired woman. But before the winter had properly begun something had happened that made them leave for Colombier at a few hours' notice. Whatever it may have been, it left Madame de Charrière with no desire ever to see Geneva again, and her husband with some memory so painful that he could never afterwards hear the place named without wincing. A remarkably handsome young man, a great deal younger than herself, is said to have been involved, but neither Madame de Charrière nor her husband ever mentioned his name or left any record of it or of what passed between them. All that is certain is that two days after their panic flight from Geneva, Monsieur de Charrière returned to their apartment there with two servants to close it up and sell all its furnishings before leaving Geneva forever.

This crisis, whatever it may have been, was followed by a purely horrible winter in the house at Colombier. Monsieur de Charrière's spinster sisters saw their brother and his wife were desperately unhappy, and, assuming her guilt, did their best to make her life as much more miserable as they could. They were aided in their evil work by

the official Christian of the village, Pastor Chaillet, who
used to visit the house frequently for the sake of the money
he could win from the two sisters at the card table. Although
he was given to signing his letters "J. Chaillet, Servant of
Christ," he was without charity, and pursued Madame de
Charrière with envious spite, covertly encouraging the two
sisters to torment her on the ground that she had no moral
principles and no religion, and, therefore, no right to happiness. He was delighted to find that there was real trouble
in the house, and the gloating entries in his diary recording the winter's miseries at Colombier provide yet another
revelation of the depths of nastiness to which the professionally good can sink. At the end of this melancholy season
Madame de Charrière escaped from the house and the
household and took refuge at the Château de Chexbres in
the country above and behind Lausanne. For a time she
made work for herself there by teaching in the village
school, but after a few weeks she sat down and began to
write *Caliste*, a story which is set in England and is the
apologia for his mysteriously evasive conduct that the
Englishman who has jilted Cecilia promised to deliver at
some future date in the concluding pages of the *Letter from
Lausanne*.

The opening chapters of the novel are concerned with a
rigmarole about twin brothers which at first sight appears
to be no more than a pump-priming exercise, written while
Madame de Charrière was warming up for the real business at hand. This view is initially confirmed, since once
the redundant twin has been killed off the book comes
alive and one finds oneself in direct contact with the substance of Madame de Charrière's distress. The heroine of
the book is motivated by a profoundly neurotic conviction
of her own worthlessness and sense that she does not desire
to be loved. Since Madame de Charrière was writing before
the days in which unconscious motivations were well recognized other than intuitively, she had to rationalize her
heroine's low view of herself. This she did by thinking up
a cock-and-bull story of how Caliste was first put on the
stage by a vicious mother and sold off it to a noble lord

who had her in keeping until he died, leaving her with a
small income and a house. The narrator, who is the surviving twin, meets her as an independent woman, and she
falls in love with him. As he has clearly fallen in love
with her, all should now be plain sailing, but he, as it turns
out, cannot quite bring himself to give a woman the place
that his brother once had in his heart; a species of loyalty
to the dead twin makes him feel that he should reject her
love, and, although he manages to overcome this feeling,
the shadow of the dead man is never altogether lifted from
the relationship. Madame de Charrière's treatment of this
aspect of the story is oddly strained, and there is no accounting for the degree of tension that surrounds the point on
internal evidence alone. But if her biography is examined
it is not necessary to look very far for a likely clue. When
Madame de Charrière was born her father was pleased to
have a child but disappointed not to have an heir; he would
have much preferred his firstborn to be a boy. This disappointment was modified when his wife presently gave
him a son, but it was renewed sharply when that son was
drowned in a bathing accident while swimming in the river
near the Château van Zuylen when he was still a small
boy. It is tempting to assimilate Caliste's feeling that she
has been tainted permanently by her sexual frailty with
her lover's feeling that he must deny himself much of the
happiness that life has to offer in order to atone for surviving his brother, and to relate both to Madame de Charrière's probable reactions to the death of the boy that she
ought to have been.

Be that how it may, the story takes an odd turn when
Caliste has succeeded in breaking down the male narrator's
reluctance to commit himself to her. She will not consent
to become his mistress, and she uses considerable ingenuity
to prevent the occurrence of situations in which she might
be left alone with him. But she agrees to marry him, if he
can obtain his father's consent to their union. She knows
that it will not be forthcoming, and he applies for it in
terms that will leave his father no alternative but to refuse:
identifying her flatly as "the mistress of the late Lord

L——." The father rises to the occasion and returns the son a nicely calculated blasting that concludes with the line "I will have no son if he can take such a wife." The narrator passes the letter on to Caliste. She reads it in his presence, and although he saw its "every word pierce her heart like a dagger" he permits her to let herself in for more of the same by writing her own personal appeal against the father's decision. They wait three days for an answer, and it is a very odd one when it comes. The father argues that he cannot possibly agree to let his son *marry* her, because he would not find it supportable to have it said of his son that "He is the husband, they are the children of a woman of that sort." But he will not object to their living together (and presumably raising up a crop of bastards), "on condition that neither he nor you ever speak to me again of the marriage now in question." An interesting situation has now been set up:

> *"Let us at least be to each other all that we can be," I said to her, speaking very low and almost as if I feared that she might hear me. I was able to remain in doubt whether she had heard me or not; to believe for a moment that she might consent, for she did not answer and her eyes remained closed.*
>
> *"Caliste," I said, "let us change this sad moment to a moment of rapture."*
>
> *"Ah," she replied, opening her eyes and casting upon me looks of sorrow and fear, "I must then become again what I once was."*
>
> *"No," I said after some moments of silence.*

They settle down to a life of such standoffs, but it is hard going for them, and they are both cursed with an excess of insight:

> *"Let us make an end," I said one day carried away by both love and anger. I locked her door and led her away from the harpsichord.*
>
> *"You will not, I know, do me any violence," she said gently, "for you are my master."*

Her speech and tone quieted my vehemence, and I could only seat her on my knees, support her head on my shoulder, and, moistening her beautiful hands with my tears, ask her forgiveness again and again. She continued to pour out her thanks to me in a manner that showed the reality of her alarm. Yet her passion and her suffering were in truth equal to my own, and she would have liked to be my mistress.

One day I said to her, "You cannot decide to give yourself, and yet you wish that you had given yourself."

"That is quite true," she said.

But there was nothing more for me to obtain, or even to attempt, from this avowal.

Madame de Charrière rescues her characters from this impasse by a plausible succession of events which leads them both into prudent but loveless marriages. The narrator's marriage disintegrates because his wife cannot stand being married to a man suffering from a degree of indecisiveness approximating to paralysis of the will, but Caliste's falls apart for another reason. She becomes physically repulsive to a husband who has up to that point adored her when she has a miscarriage and loses his child on learning of the narrator's marriage. Madame de Charrière's account of Caliste's husband's behavior is astonishingly acute, as is her description of what happens when Caliste has a chance meeting with the narrator at the theater where she had once been an actress after their marriages have broken up. They talk for a while, and then prepare to part. Caliste has her moment of common sense:

...If you don't want the reports of those who have seen us here at the play tonight to be believed, and to make sure that no one will pay any attention to this meeting, go back to the country tonight or tomorrow— then it will be thought that you must have been quite unmoved by finding me again....

As soon as she has said this she repents of it:

With trembling fingers she cut a lock of my hair
and placed it in her bosom; then, putting both her
arms around me, she said, "What shall we do without
each other? In half an hour I shall be as I was a year
ago, as six months ago, as this morning: what shall
I do if I still have some time to live? Shall we go away
together? Have you not obeyed your father sufficiently?
Have you not a wife and child of his choosing? Let
us return to our real ties. Whom should we injure?
My husband hates me, and will not live with me, your
wife no longer loves you!... No! Don't answer me,"
she cried, putting her hand over my mouth, "don't
refuse, but do not either consent. Until now I have
only been unhappy—let me not become guilty! I could
support my own guilt, but not yours—I should never
forgive myself for having degraded you! Oh, how un-
happy I am, and how I love you. Never was any man
so beloved as you!" And holding me in a close embrace,
she burst into a flood of tears.

The narrator's answer to this is characteristically to take
to his heels. He returns to his country house on the following day and, after talking things over with his father, leaves
England almost immediately as the escort and guide of a
young nobleman who is setting out on the Grand Tour.
Caliste does not recover from the blow of this final desertion, and presently dies, somewhat in the manner of
Camille.

The book now seems to the last degree amateurish in its
structure, but there had been nothing like its absolutely
truthful account of the irrational element in the behavior
of supposedly rational persons in the European novel before,
and it made a considerable stir in its day both by virtue
of its novelty and the depth of its perceptions. But while
Caliste was a great success in Paris and in other places
abroad, it completed Madame de Charrière's ruin at home.
The *Letters From Neuchâtel* had resulted in her ostracism
by the local society, and every salon in Lausanne was closed
to her by the publication of the letters from that city, both
because it was so frank about how women thought about

men and because it was so critical of the quality of the life depicted by implication. *Caliste*, with its unusually direct approach to questions of sexuality and sexual mores, finished the process of her social isolation. Monsieur de Charrière saw how it would be before he was halfway through his task of copying out the manuscript and realized at the same time how good the book was. He decided that it was essential for her future happiness that she should enjoy the success that it would be bound to have in Paris rather than face the hostility and criticism with which it would be received in Switzerland. He accordingly lured his wife out of her retreat at Chexbres and installed her in an apartment in the Rue Thérèse in the spring. It was a kindly and well-meant idea, like so many of his ideas, but Madame de Charrière was forty-seven, and it was too late for her to conquer the city which had once been the focus of all her dreams and hopes. She was wiser, too, than she had been, and she was no longer dazzled by the glitter and splendors of Versailles and the salons. She sensed an underlying desperation and saw wretchedness round every corner. She felt ill at ease and at a loss until one day she found herself being introduced to a gangling young man with red hair, Benjamin de Constant de Rebecque, the nineteen-year-old nephew of Constant d'Hermenches. They looked at each other and were instantly friends, he knew that he would be able to say anything to her and be understood, she saw at once that he was the child she might have had by d'Hermenches and that he was desperately in need of love and understanding.

> The cast of her mind delighted me and we spent whole days and nights in talk. She could be very cutting in her criticisms of the ideas and the personalities that surrounded her. I, too, was given to mocking. So we were a perfect match. Madame de Charrière's view of life was so original and so very much her own; her intellect was so powerful, and her superiority to the average human being so marked and certain that I, twenty years old, and as much of an oddity and an

*enemy of shams as herself, found in her company a
sheer joy such as I had never known before. And it
was not long before we found ourselves in a relationship that was more genuinely and essentially intimate.*

They explored Paris by day, talked to each other for most
of the night, and shared what was, to them, the delicious
comedy of *Les Pourrat.* Juste de Constant had decided that
the best he could do for his troublesome son was to give him
a good start in life by marrying him to a sixteen-year-old
heiress. How Juste de Constant formed the idea that the very
pretty but also very frivolous Mademoiselle Pourrat was
available is hard to say, but he did so, and ordered his son
to court the woman of his choice. Constant did as he was
told, and was not immediately told that he was wasting his
time by Madame Pourrat, even though she had already
arranged a marriage wholly satisfactory to herself and her
daughter. She found Constant amusing and interesting and
was fascinated by the letters he wrote to her daughter. She
accordingly told Mademoiselle Pourrat not to do anything
to upset the "half-mad but very lovable" young man, and
settled down to enjoy the acquaintance for as long as she
could. This situation did not at all please Monsieur de
Sainte-Croix, who was Madame Pourrat's lover, and he became convinced that the passionate love letters Constant
was addressing to the daughter were really intended for
the mother. As luck would have it the moment chosen by
Monsieur de Sainte-Croix to break in upon them for a confrontation was one in which Constant had chosen to put
on a performance as a desperate lover. He had burst into
tears as he explained the intensity of his passion for Mademoiselle Pourrat, and Madame Pourrat was consoling him
with a motherly hug when the suspicious lover burst in on
them. There was then a fine scene which culminated when
Madame Pourrat asked Constant to explain how things
really were and to tell Monsieur de Sainte-Croix that she
had been comforting him because he was so distressed by
her daughter's unresponsiveness. This touched a raw spot
in Constant's rather strange brand of vanity. He found it

maddening to have to tell an unknown man that he was an unsuccessful lover. It didn't make matters any better for him to realize that, although he had begun the courtship as a joke, he had created a real situation which might lose Madame Pourrat her lover and Mademoiselle Pourrat her husband-to-be. In an excess of self-disgust he whipped out a phial of opium that he happened to have in his pocket and swallowed its contents. Monsieur de Sainte-Croix and Madame Pourrat then spent the rest of the afternoon administering emetics and taking the necessary counter measures. Mademoiselle Pourrat then appeared in full evening dress to remind them that they had a box at the opera for the first night of Beaumarchais' *Tarare*. Constant leapt from the couch on which he had been reclining and hurried off to change for the theater, as did Monsieur de Sainte-Croix and Madame Pourrat. At the Opéra Constant was in the highest spirits and the evening was a great success. But during the night Madame Pourrat thought the whole thing over, and in the morning she sent Constant a sharply worded note to say that he had abused her hospitality and must not come to the house again. The Pourrat-Constant marriage was at last definitely off.

When Juste de Constant heard the news his fury knew no bounds. He attributed the disaster entirely to Madame de Charrière. The woman who had ruined his brother had now got her hooks into his son and was threatening to ruin him. He sent a Lieutenant Benay to Paris with orders to find Constant and to bring him back to the regimental headquarters at Bois-le-duc without delay in the carriage that he had left there in the care of a hotelkeeper who had a large coach house. Constant's reluctance to go with the Lieutenant to face his father's anger was much increased by the fact that he had sold the carriage and converted the proceeds to his own use, and after leading poor Benay a devil's dance through Paris he managed to shake him, borrow some money from Monsieur de Charrière, and slip away, after spending a night with a prostitute, to England. Constant spent nine weeks there, cadging and borrowing his way from London to Edinborough and back again, and returned

sooner than he intended because he was overwhelmed by
guilt on reading the most pathetic and affectionate letter
that his father had ever written to him. He wrote to Madame
de Charrière to say how touched by it he had been, but went
on to say that he knew just what would happen. As soon as
he got to Bois-le-duc his father's love for him would evapo-
rate and would be replaced by anger. Constant did his best
to make sure that it would be so by arriving at his father's
quarters unannounced, travel stained and in rags at such
a time as to break up a card party. His father declined to play
and received him with a rough tenderness that he found so
disconcerting that he absconded four days later and made
his way to Colombier and Madame de Charrière, who received him, as he put it, with "transports of delight."

Whether it was a matter of desiring to atone to his father
for his flight from Bois-le-duc, or whether it was another
instance of the working of the psychic machinery that had
given him time to spend the night with a whore but not
time to say good-bye to Madame de Charrière when he left
Paris, he now removed himself from Colombier after two
days, and went to stay at Beausoleil, the house near Lausanne at which his father was keeping Marianne Magnin.
He remained there until a raging gonorrhea he had acquired
in one of Lausanne's seedier brothels made it possible for
him to return to Colombier as an invalid. This was the
strange beginning of the happiest eight weeks in his life.
Madame de Charrière gave him a room at the foot of the
spiral staircase leading up to her suite on the first floor,
she found the perfect valet to look after him, and she took
over the supervision of the kitchen, which had until then
been the responsibility of her husband's sister Henriette,
so that he should have proper food. Monsieur de Charrière
exerted himself to get him all the books he needed, and his
other sister, the gardening Louise, made his room a bower of
flowery plants. The whole house revolved about him, and
when the acute phase of his complaint burnt itself out he
spent more and more time talking about anything and
everything with his benefactress. During the day they talked
in the big upstairs room which she kept in such a state of

chronic untidiness that her husband could hardly bear to
enter it; and in the night they sat beside the fire in the big
country kitchen until long after everyone else in the house
had gone to bed. It was the perfect relationship for Madame
de Charrière, a nonphysical blending of intelligences, but
it was one that Constant was bound to outgrow as he left
his sexual uncertainties behind. These were, however, very
great, and for eight years Colombier was the center of his
life and the secure retreat to which he could return whenever he felt threatened by the necessity of assuming an adult
masculine role in a relationship with a woman. When
Constant's marriage with Wilhelmina von Cramm and his
first involvement with Charlotte von Hardenberg had both
come to nothing, Madame de Charrière seems to have entertained for a while the hope that he was never going to be
able to assume such a role, and that they would be able to
go on, as brother and sister, forever, or at least for a considerable period.

> You cannot live far from me, nor I without you. I know
> that in theory and in the eyes of the world things can-
> not be equal between us. And yet what is to be gained
> by thinking of that? Come back! No one loves you or
> understands you as I do; no one prizes you so deeply
> or so truly; and if I die, as in nature I must, before you,
> then you can form other habits; there is no need to form
> them yet.

She was fifty-four when she wrote these line, and Constant was twenty-seven. When Madame de Staël met
Constant a few months later she was twenty-eight, and she
was without sexual inhibitions of any kind: that Madame
de Charrière would lose him to her was inevitable. When
she had lost him, Neuchâtel had its revenge. Her consolation was the devotion of her personal maid Henriette
Monachon, but soon after the final rupture this young
woman gave birth to a second illegitimate child. Under the
laws of the place she could be expelled from the commune
for this offense, and they were enforced. Madame de
Charrière appealed to Pastor Chaillet to help her to get the

sentence released when her husband refused to intervene. The Pastor replied by releasing the pent-up resentments of years in a savagely worded sermon denouncing Madame de Charrière and her ways and by writing her a letter announcing that he could have no more to do with her. She felt herself becoming lonely and queer, and to combat her tendency to eccentricity she began to take young girls in distress or want into the house. Henriette l'Hardy, whom she had befriended earlier, returned and became the nucleus of a little group of younger girls, Thérèse Foster, Isabelle de Gélien, Marianne Ustricht, and a Dutch girl. But she subjected them to an austere regime and the strictest discipline, so that her relations with them were those of a stern headmistress to her pupils and their presence did little to warm the house or soften her manner. The aging Monsieur de Salgas, who had recommended her to the care of Mademoiselle Prévost so long before, came to stay and, having had his head bitten off for mentioning that he had recently seen Constant, conceded that she had become a frightening woman. Her unhappiness was poisoning her and infecting her with a perverse desire to live in such a way as to increase her unhappiness.

> My sojourn at Colombier has always been hateful for me. Sojourn? A life sentence. Every time I have left it my return has filled me with a sense of despair. So I am resolved never to leave it again and thus to save myself the misery of coming back. I am still as lively as ever I was, and perhaps more impressionable than most people; nevertheless, with resolution and will power, I shall make Colombier endurable.

Monsieur de Charrière had a stroke and developed a senile passion for Henriette l'Hardy, by whom he had been attracted from the first. His longing for her made him furious with his wife for not having gone off with Constant and left him a free man before it was too late. Madame de Charrière herself fell ill, and she would have been in an evil case had not the spinster Mademoiselle Henriette de Charrière, who had been so unpleasant to her in the past, nursed her with devoted kindness to the end, which came in the last days of December 1805. Mademoiselle Henriette took charge when she had gone. It was found that between the Dutch wars and her generosity almost all the fortune that Madame de Charrière had brought with her to Colombier as her dowry was gone. It was necessary to send away the grooms and stable boys and to sell off the horses, the carriages, the plate, the fine furniture from Paris, the hangings, the objets d'art, and all the things that she had brought in to enrich the sparse life of the house. Three years later, when Monsieur de Charrière died, there was little to show that she had ever lived in it but for some Directoire decorative painting, a chandelier, and a large Aubusson carpet that testified to her vain attempt to turn a large loft or attic into a summer drawing room.

George Sand

T here's nothing in my private life for which I have to blush, nothing, nothing, from A to Z," George Sand wrote in a letter to a friend in 1852, and fifteen years later she told another correspondent that if he wanted to know who she was he should read the ten-volume *Histoire de ma vie:* "there you have, unvarnished, all the facts of my life.... I'm really no more than a good woman." At about the same time she told Juliette Adam that she might have lost the right to be judged as a woman, but she could still claim to be judged as a man, and that in love she had been more honest than any "of you." She had, she claimed, never deceived anyone, and had never had two affairs going simultaneously—all that could be said against her was that she preferred the moral standards of the male to the female.

The extraordinary thing about her is that she was probably entirely sincere when she wrote and said these things, and if she were aware that she was now being described as a pioneer in the Women's Liberation Movement who had fought hard to bring a new candor and and honesty into the relationship between men and women, she would probably consider that she was being given no more than her due. And if she could be asked why, if she had always told the truth about herself and her actions, she had felt called upon to destroy, or edit, or mutilate so many letters and documents relating to her affairs, she would almost certainly reply by saying that these lost pieces of evidence were written by people who had not understood her, and that she had removed them from the record in the interests of truth and justice....

George Sand was born Aurore Dupin. She was the child of a Colonel Maurice Dupin and a certain Sophie-Vic-

toire Delaborde. He was the son of a wealthy business
man who had owned a textile mill and a landed estate
in the province of central France known as Le Berry;
but she was something else again, the daughter of a man
who, having failed as the proprietor of a bar and pool-
room, had drifted into the business of selling caged birds.
Monsieur Delaborde had followed his trade in that part
of Paris now known as Les Halles which was then largely
devoted to prostitution and brothel-keeping. It was less
a matter of a tendency to vice or lack of morals than of
uncomplaining conformity with local custom that led
Sophie-Victoire to become what was euphemistically
described as a "dancer" in a neighborhood café-concert
in her early teens. She was, however, no longer a working
prostitute when she at last met the man who was to
become her husband. This, it is necessary to add, was
not because she had fallen in love with virtue, but more
simply because she was then being kept for private use
and enjoyment by the somewhat elderly general to whose
staff young Colonel Dupin had been attached as an aide-
de-camp.

So far as his military career was concerned Maurice
Dupin did himself no good when he committed the
tactical error of involving himself with his commanding
officer's mistress. The affair might not have done him
too much harm in an ordinary army in ordinary times,
in which it would have been a trifle to ruffle the surface
of the social life of an officers' mess for a few weeks or
months, and the cause of more laughter than grief. But
this was Napoleon's army and he was against such fri-
volities: his army was the instrument with which he
was making his career, and he made it his business to
know everything that went on in the ranks of its officer
corps. When he learned of Maurice Dupin's indiscretion
he was infuriated, not because he had any strong feelings
about the morality of the situation, but because Maurice
had shown that he was not serious about the *métier*. It
was unprofessional of him to allow a personal matter
to get out of hand to the detriment of his utility as a

staff officer and of the efficiency of the staff to which
he had been attached. The tyrant wrote off his twenty-
three-year-old colonel as an unreliable fool, relieved him
of his appointment, and saw to it that he did not get
another posting. This meant that the price Maurice
Dupin had to pay for his liaison with Sophie-Victoire
was consignment to the peculiar limbo reserved for the
militarily unemployed officer: he was on the strength
and in receipt of pay, but he was completely side-tracked
professionally. He had to sit by as a spectator while all
his contemporaries of promise were rocketing up the
ladder of promotion.

When Maurice Dupin had spent three exceedingly long
and exasperating years cooling his heels in idleness and
living in cheap lodgings while he curried favor with a
variety of up-and-coming general officers in the hope
of getting them to "ask for him," Sophie-Victoire found
that she was pregnant, and the unlucky liaison became
a marriage. The auspices for this union cannot be called
propitious. At the time of the wedding the groom was
twenty-six, the bride was thirty, and both parties had
had illegitimate children by previous connections, the
groom having fathered a son on one of his mother's
housemaids, and the bride having had a daughter by the
Lord knows whom...and then the Colonel's mother
loathed Sophie-Victoire with a passionate intensity. This
lady, Madame Dupin de Franceuil, had married a gentleman of sixty-four when she was in her thirtieth year.
She had always spoken of her elderly husband as "Papa,"
and had lived happily with him until he died, leaving
her with her eleven-year-old son, Maurice. Once her
husband had vanished from the scene her son became
the center of her physical life and of the obsessive fantasy
that dominated it....

It is necessary to understand the nature of this fantasy, and its origins, if one is to understand what happened to George Sand in her childhood, and how she
came to be what she was. Madame Dupin de Franceuil
was largely a fabrication. She was christened Marie-

Aurore de Verrières, but she had no particular right to
this name. It had been adopted quite arbitrarily by her
mother, an actress who had been born plain Marie
Rinteau, when she became the mistress of the Maréchal
de Saxe in her eighteenth year.

This famous soldier, who holds an important place
in military history as a tactical innovator, and who was
the most brilliant field commander of his day, was also
a man with an obsession. His father was Frederick-
Augustus, Elector of Saxony, King of Poland, and Grand
Duke of Lithuania, and his mother was the beautiful
but fiery-tempered Swedish countess Maria-Aurora von
Konigsmark. This pairing makes it sound as if the Maréchal had been fortunate in his birth, but the glory of
it all was largely nullified for Maurice de Saxe by the
fact that his parents were not married. The usual psychological problems created by illegitimacy were reenforced in his case by the further complication that his
mother Marie-Aurore was an exceptionally close friend
of Frederick-Augustus' wife, Christine-Eberhardine. The
two ladies both became pregnant by Frederick-Augustus
at the beginning of January 1696, and both gave birth
to sons within a period of days nine months later. But
while Christine-Eberhardine's boy was from the start
heir to all his father's powers, titles, estates, and belong-
ings, and in the long run his only legitimate child,
Marie-Aurore's son was heir to nothing very much beyond
the appellation de Saxe, and a place in a regiment of
his father's bastard offspring which was to have at the
final count no less than 355 members. Maurice de Saxe's
situation filled him with an intense longing for titles
and honors that might put him on an equal footing with
his legitimate half-brother.

At thirty Maurice de Saxe almost achieved his goal,
by coming within a hair's-breadth of marrying a granddaughter of Peter the Great of Russia and establishing
himself on the throne of the Duchy of Courland, then
an independent sovereign state. Had he succeeded in this
design the King of France would have addressed him as

mon *cousin*, and he would have been, diplomatically speaking, the equal of any monarch in Europe. But the marriage fell through at the last minute, and Maurice's election by the boyars of Courland was annulled by the tramping feet of Russian troops who marched in to enforce the extinction of Courland's independence. Maurice escaped from his principality alone but for a single man-servant carrying a small box containing the now-worthless certificate of his election. He was to cling to this document, and to what it represented, for the remainder of his life.

After this check Maurice de Saxe devoted himself, somewhat paradoxically, since he was a Saxon and a Protestant, to the service of the crown of Roman Catholic France. In due course, after he had rounded out his career by whipping a British Army led by the Duke of Cumberland at Fontenoy, he retired. But he still cherished his obsession, and after his death the draft of a remarkable petition was found among his papers.

> *The Comte de Saxe, Marechal General of the King's Camps and Armies, would humbly beg to remind His Majesty that he is the son of a great King who was head of one of the most august sovereign houses in Europe and that he has been legitimately elected Duke of Courland....*
>
> *Every European court with the single exception of Vienna ... has always accorded the Comte de Saxe the princely honors due to his birth, independently of his election to the throne of Courland....*
>
> *The Comte de Saxe does not ask Your Majesty to recognize him as Duke of Courland, since this would be attended by a political awkwardness that the Comte de Saxe would wish to spare His Majesty....*
>
> *His Majesty has assured him, however, in terms too flattering and too generous to bear repetition, that he has had the good fortune of serving His Majesty usefully....*
>
> *Dare he hope, therefore, that he might be accorded*

the favor of enjoying the treatment, rank, and honors
possessed by the Princes of the Blood of France....

Though Maurice de Saxe was never accorded these privileges and may never, indeed, have had the nerve to put
forward his request for what was in effect adoption as a
child of the royal house of France, he was assigned a palace
second only to Versailles in its splendors when he finally
yielded up his military offices and retired from active
service. The palace was François Premier's Chambord, the
great house of 441 rooms, 74 staircases, and innumerable
towers and turrets which stands beside the delightful
River Cosson in a park surrounded by the longest wall
in France. Maurice de Saxe, who had those twenty-four
miles of wall built to surround his private kingdom, lived
there in royal state. He exercised his regiment of cavalry
in the enormous park and lived surrounded by armed
guards. He dined in public once a week just as the king
did at Versailles, and when his own company of players
put on their shows in the palace theater he watched them
from the Royal box seated on the thronelike chair on which
Louis XIV had sat to watch Molière acting in his own
plays when the royal company had come to Chambord.

Like many other royal patrons of the theater before him
and after him Maurice de Saxe had been as much interested
in actresses as he was in acting, and in 1748 a young woman
of eighteen called Marie Rinteau who had recently come
from Paris to join his company attracted his attentions.
She presently bore him a daughter. The Maréchal was infatuated with his young mistress at this stage in their
relationship and was so delighted to be the father of her
child as to depart from the practice of a lifetime and recognize the child as his. He permitted her to name the child
Marie-Aurore in honor of his mother and went so far as
to attend the christening ceremony in person. Marie Rinteau did not apparently consider her family name sufficiently distinguished for her child on this occasion and so assumed the more aristocratic one of de Verrières, by which
she was thereafter known. Unhappily for her daughter,

she was as foolish as she was amiable and before her child
was a year old she had muffed all her chances. She took
advantage of her elderly lover's temporary absence from
Chambord to give herself to his resident poet, Marmontel,
for no better reason than that he was a nice fellow and that
he wished to enjoy her. When the Maréchal found that she
had been to bed with his poet his fury knew no bounds.
She tried to make him believe that there had been no more
to the affair than some private lessons in elocution, and
this silly lie did not improve matters. The Maréchal swore
that he would have nothing more to do with either the
mother or the child, and he was still of this bitter frame
of mind when he died some fifteen months later.

In death the French court and all Europe at last, now
that it could no longer give him any pleasure, recognized
Maurice de Saxe as the Duke of Courland. To show the
world that he had been a sovereign and one of the company
of Christian kings, a silver crown was placed on the lid
of his coffin as it lay in regal state in various churches in
the course of his long-drawn-out obsequies. But his only
acknowledged child had been cut out of his will and all
traces of his connection with her had been, so far as was
possible, effaced. All that Marie-Aurore de Verrières received in the way of a legacy from her father was the description that was to be attached to her name in every legal
reference to her existence during the first half of her life:
natural child of unknown parentage.

The route that Marie-Aurore was compelled to travel
in order to reach the social level on which she felt that
she belonged was a tortuous one. Her mother gave her
little help in the pursuit of what was in effect respectabil-
ity. When turned off by the Maréchal the former Marie
Rinteau had decided to exploit her skill in the arts of pleasing and giving pleasure rather than to attempt to pursue
her career as an actress, and had sought a protector rather
than a place in another theatrical company. She soon found
one in the person of a Monsieur D'Epinay and was before
long maintaining, with the help of her attractive younger
sister Geneviève, an elegant establishment on a fashion-

able street in Paris. There she ran an open drawing room in which gentlemen of means could count on meeting a mixed company of amusing intellectuals and charming and readily accessible young women. This somewhat ambiguous setting provided a background for Marie-Aurore's earliest years and lent her adolescence a peculiarly schizoid character. As soon as she reached the age of puberty and could look forward to marriage as a prospect, she became aware of the many social disadvantages that went with the phrase "of unknown parentage." She accordingly began to make strenuous efforts to have herself recognized as her father's child. She received partial satisfaction from the *parlement* of Paris after a long siege; but that body was representative of the third estate, and its proceedings cut no ice with the aristocratic landed gentry into whose ranks Marie-Aurore intended, come hell or high water, to marry. What was vital to her peace of mind was recognition from the court, the true fountain of nobility. French law was then inveterately hostile to the conception of *la recherche de la paternité,* direct legal action to compel a father to recognize his illegitimate offspring, so that Marie-Aurore had to resort to indirect means of approach to her objective. This was to petition the court for a grant of the pensions and allowances that she would have received had she been her father's legally recognized child. In her petitions she labored the point that she was "la Demoiselle Aurore, natural child and only daughter of the Maréchal de Saxe," while the court bureaucrats replied by inviting her to get lost for a consideration in such a way as to dodge the issue of her paternity: *"The King grants to Mademoiselle Aurore an allowance of eight hundred livres for such time as she shall remain in a convent to be named by Madame la Dauphine...."* A string of such limited successes meant that the youthful Marie-Aurore's life alternated between the genteel, correct, and somewhat austere settings provided by the various convents under the patronage of Madame la Dauphine and the louche and easy-going establishments in which her mother functioned as a superior procuress.

Marie-Aurore's first attempt to better her situation by marriage was not a success. When she was in her twentieth year she married a forty-four-year-old captain of infantry who died within five months of their wedding, leaving her with a new name and very little else. As Aurore de Horne she petitioned the court for support once again, and once again was offered the usual invitation to disappear into a convent in return for a small allowance. She retired into that gray enclosed world for as long as she could stand it, and then returned to her mother's house for a stay of several years.

What followed was extremely curious. Marie de Verrières's protector did not allow his relationship with her to prevent him from being jealous and possessive where his own wife was concerned. His wife, feeling bored and neglected, took up musical composition as a hobby, a step that involved lessons in harmony from a good-looking dilettante of her acquaintance, Claude Dupin de Franceuil. Monsieur D'Epinay did not care for this development, and in the hope of breaking up what had very soon become an affair, introduced his wife's lover into his mistress' establishment. The maneuver was wholly successful, and before long Monsieur Dupin had dropped Madame D'Epinay in favor of Marie de Verrières' sister, the golden Geneviève. It was not long after this foursome of good friends had been set up that Marie-Aurore returned from the convent, to which she had withdrawn as a widow and resumed her role as the charming and talented unmarried daughter of the house. Things ran along in this way for several years, until Marie de Verrières suddenly and unexpectedly died. Monsieur D'Epinay thereupon took her sister Geneviève away from the man who had been his wife's lover, and, after a short period of retreat in a convent, Marie-Aurore became the wife of the man who had been living with her aunt.

It is not altogether surprising that Marie-Aurore, now nearly thirty, should have wished to put all this behind her as soon as she was safely married. She persuaded her elderly husband to leave Paris and to set himself up as a country gentleman in the province in which his business

interests were concentrated. The couple settled into one
of Monsieur Dupin's properties at Chateauroux, a massive
but undistinguished early Renaissance building with rather
more character than charm called the Château Raoul which
looks out over the lush meadows beside the River Indre
with the air of being a castle. Here Marie-Aurore bore her
husband a son, significantly christened Maurice, in honor
of the father who had turned his back on her when she
was a baby rather than for the husband to whom she owed
so much. This little family lived happily in the Château
Raoul until Claude Dupin died as France was sliding into
the confusions of the Revolutionary years. When these
were over Madame Dupin had much to remember, for she
had been in prison and in fear of her life for a time in Paris
during the Terror and had experienced other vicissitudes.
But in those years of anxiety and tension she also managed
to keep moving up the social ladder. When they were at
last over she was found to be living as the lady of the manor
on a landed estate in the village of Nohant-Vicq near La
Châtre, a property she had bought for a song during the
bad times from a member of the minor nobility who had
been in trouble with the Revolutionary tribunals and
wished to emigrate. The house on the property, though
not distinguished as a piece of architecture, was still very
much an upper-class dwelling despite certain rustic simplicities and living in it surrounded by portraits of her
noble kinsmen and ancestors and her father the Maréchal
completed the process by which the actress's bastard, and
granddaughter of a Parisian lemonade vendor, was transformed into a member of the upper class and a gracious
relic of the *Ancien Régime.* In this setting Marie-Aurore
raised her son Maurice to be a soldier. When he achieved
his colonelcy at twenty-three his mother was sure that he
was embarked on a career that would establish the truth
of the old saying that blood will tell, and would also give
the world a final and overwhelming proof that she was
her father the Maréchal's daughter.

In view of all this it was natural that Marie-Aurore
should have been enraged when she learned that her be-

loved Maurice had formed an association that threatened
to undo all that she had been working for over the years.
She did all that she could to break up the liaison in its
initial phases, and when she was told of the marriage as
a *fait accompli* she made a major effort to have it annulled.
When that failed she compromised by maintaining a chilly
relationship with her son that involved ignoring the existence of his wife and his child, the Aurore Dupin who
was to become George Sand. Marie-Aurore kept up this
front of implacable hostility until the baby girl was a year
old and then became frostily reconciled to the realities
of the situation.

Three years later, when Aurore was four, Colonel Dupin
at last received a military appointment, and found himself
attached to the staff of General Murat as an aide-de-camp.
As he went off to Spain with his showy, demanding, ambitious, and almost invariably successful general, he had
a lively sense of being on his way at last. Where Murat
was there was sure to be action, and there would be the
opportunities for advancement he was looking for...or
sincerely believed he was looking for. The outcome suggests
that either Napoleon was right and he was simply incapable of taking the *métier* seriously, or that he was deeply
involved in a quest for misfortune.

When Maurice Dupin set out for Madrid with his new
chief he had just been told that Sophie-Victoire was pregnant again. She was left behind him in Paris on the understanding that she would join him as soon as she could after
the birth of the expected child. The time seemed unendur-
ably long, and before she was halfway through her pregnancy she set out in pursuit of her husband. She arrived
in Madrid, accompanied by the four-year-old Aurore, in
her eighth month, and gave birth to a son there in June.

Colonel Dupin was overjoyed by this event, and in his
euphoria fell into one of those fugues of fatuity and self-
deception to which men are prone when they have received
such flattering certifications of their virility. He managed
to persuade himself that his mother's coldness towards
his wife would be bound to turn to a friendly warmth as

soon as she saw her with a man-child of his fathering in
her arms. In order to bring about the necessarily joyous
confrontation as rapidly as possible he immediately obtained a leave of absence from his general, bought an enormous Spanish traveling coach, packed his family into
it, and set out for Nohant in the mounting summer heat.

In the course of the seemingly endless journey, behind
plodding horses, across half Spain and all of southwestern
France, both children became ill. By the time they reached
Nohant they were not only yellow as parchment and wasted
with fever, they were also crawling with lice picked up
at one or another of the wayside inns in which they had
stopped at night. The baby boy died shortly after their
arrival, and Maurice Dupin was killed a few days later.
The magnificent charger that he had acquired in Spain
and ridden home alongside his lumbering coach threw
him one evening as he was riding between Nohant and
La Châtre in a failing light. The beast shied away from
the shadowy menace of a heap of material left on the
verge for the roadmenders. Maurice was pitched head first
onto the pile of broken stone and his skull was shattered.

Given a reasonable minimum of love, understanding,
and concern, Aurore Dupin could easily have put this series
of traumatic events behind her. Many people have lived
through worse. But her grandmother and her mother were
far more interested in hurting each other than they were
in making her happy. The grandmother's first thought
was to get rid of the mother so that she might secure exclusive possession of her son's child. She achieved this
aim by refusing to allow Sophie-Victoire to bring her illegitimate girl to live with the family at Nohant. She calculated, correctly, that her daughter-in-law would not be
able to bring herself to abandon her older child, who was
unprovided for, to the care of strangers. She also foresaw
that Sophie-Victoire would far more readily be able to leave
her second child, Aurore, behind her, not only because
she would be leaving the little girl in a place where she
would be well cared for and made much of, but also because she would think it foolish and sentimental to jeop-

ardize Aurore's chances of inheriting her grandmother's estate by removing her. Sophie-Victoire knew that Maurice's illegitimate son Hippolyte Chatiron lived on the property, and it would occur to her that the elder Madame Dupin might very well take it into her head to recognize him as her heir if Aurore were not present to remind her of her existence and innocence of any such crimes as she herself might be considered to have committed in marrying and ruining her son. When Aurore begged her mother to take her away to Paris with her and not to leave her alone at Nohant, Sophie-Victoire appears to have treated her to these arguments, but they do not seem to have been well received. The child could not appreciate their force and felt only that she was being abandoned without sufficient cause.

The older Madame Dupin's rationalization for her daughter-in-law's expulsion was that she was saving her son's child from the corrupting influence of a horribly vulgar and loose woman. She assumed, to judge by her subsequent behavior, that she had laid the foundation of a more or less complete victory when she succeeded in maneuvering the younger woman out of the house. But the arrangement made to sugar the pill of Sophie-Victoire's apparent defeat was that her child would be allowed to pay her a certain number of visits each winter when the older Madame Dupin shut up the house at Nohant and moved into town. Such arrangements have become familiar enough to us in the age of easy divorces, and so have their pitfalls; but Marie-Aurore had no inkling of the tremendous advantages possessed by the absentee in such a situation if there should be anything in the nature of a contest for the child's loyalties and affections. It never entered her mind that while Aurore seemed to be happily getting into the vein of life at Nohant she could be thinking of the place as a prison and longing with all her heart and soul for a reunion with her deplorable and disreputable mother and the shabby rooms and lodgings that were her normal habitat. The old lady was rudely brought up against the realities of the situation when a spying servant broke it to her

that the apparently contented child was secretly accumulat-
ing a little hoard of trinkets and semiprecious objects that
she hoped eventually to sell for enough to get her to Paris
and to set herself up in business with her mother. She was
given to understand that Sophie-Victoire had encouraged
her daughter to believe that, if it could be financed, they
might live and work together as the joint proprietors of a
dressmaking shop.

As soon as Madame Dupin, who had recently had her
first stroke, learned of this nebulous and pathetic scheme,
she staged an appalling scene. She made her granddaughter
kneel at her bedside while she told her everything that she
knew or had chosen to believe that could be alleged against
Sophie-Victoire. If she did not tell the girl in so many words
that her mother had been a prostitute she left her in no
doubt that this was the implication of what she was saying.
She rounded out her brutal assault on the girl's sensibilities by telling her that she was sending her to Paris to be
confined for the rest of her adolescence in the convent of
the Dames Augustines Anglaises. The English nuns, she
hoped, would save Aurore from sinking back to her mother's level, and might even cure her of the taste for the mud
of the gutters which she seemed to have inherited. What
gave this program a more weirdly sinister character than
Aurore can have realized was the fact that, when her grandmother had been imprisoned during the Terror, it was in
just that convent of the Dames Augustines Anglaises that
she had been locked up.

But although this was a blow there was a worse to follow:
when the mother and daughter met briefly in Paris before
Aurore was handed over to the nuns, the girl was undoubtedly expecting sympathy and comfort, perhaps even an offer
of rescue, from an ally and confederate. But she found her
mother coldly indifferent. It was made clear to her that
her mother had never been serious about the dressmaking
project and that she was thought to have been a fool to
take it seriously. Sophie-Victoire also let her daughter know
that she had not the slightest intention of reordering her
life, or any part of it, for her sake. She was, indeed, well

pleased to have been relieved of her responsibilities in that region, and she said so in language that Aurore found peculiarly desolating in its flat lack of sensitivity. She went on to tell her daughter that she thought she had been exceedingly foolish to antagonize and annoy her grandmother, and that she had no one to blame for her troubles but herself. In the circumstances, she concluded, the convent was probably the best place for her.

With this painful and disillusioning episode Aurore's childhood may be said to have come to its dismal end. Her passage from adolescence into womanhood was almost as unpleasant. Three years after Aurore had been committed to the convent, the older Madame Dupin became aware that she had not much longer to live. She also realized that if her death were to take place before her granddaughter reached her majority the odious Sophie-Victoire would, unless the girl were married, become her legal guardian. This would give the hated destroyer of poor dead Maurice control of everything that Marie-Aurore was planning to leave to Aurore: Nohant and all its farms, her house in Paris, the money in the funds, and all the rest of the apparatus for keeping up a social position that meant to her just about what that certificate of election to the Duchy of Courland had meant to her father. In order to avert this obscenity the old lady pulled Aurore out of the convent and brought her home, simultaneously launching a campaign to find her a husband. But before she could saddle her victim with any of the debt-burdened adventurers and battered old soldiers who turned up in response to the handsome offer of a fresh young girl and a substantial estate that she was advertising as widely as she could, she had another stroke and collapsed into senility and incompetence.

Aurore Dupin then experienced a period of tranquil happiness that lasted for some eighteen months. During this time she was, for once, in the care of someone who was genuinely fond of her, Deschartres, the steward of the Nohant estate, a kindly old man who had originally entered Marie-Aurore's services as Maurice Dupin's tutor. He al-

lowed Aurore to do very much as she pleased, and although
she enjoyed the experience of being indulged it may not
have been the best thing for her at this particular moment
in her development. She had attempted to seduce the convent's hierarchy into approving of her by a parade of religious enthusiasms, but neither the nuns nor the male
religious advisors and supervisors concerned were deceived.
Rebuffed by the institution, Aurore had then turned to its
inmates and had bought a large measure of popularity
with them by becoming a good deal of a buffoon, assuming
for her purpose a hearty, rompish male persona with an
English flavor derived from parody of the English nuns
in charge and the English material in the syllabus. Aurore
Dupin might well have left this precursor of the "George"
of George Sand behind her in her adolescence, as many
girls do, had she not moved on from the convent to Nohant
and the relaxed regime of Deschartres. But during this
interregnum she was able to move on from a phase of fan-
tasy-building to one of acting out: she spent a good deal
of her time during these eighteen months dressed as a boy
and pretending to be one—occupying herself for much
of the day with what were then regarded as exclusively
masculine pastimes outdoors, such as rough shooting.
While the main direction of her future development had
clearly been determined long before this, it is plausible
to suggest that a habit of externalizing her resentments
by means of aggressive displays of transsexual behavior
took hold of her in these unguarded months and seeded
the conversion of "George" from a private fantasy to the
public performance which dominated the middle of her
life and added greatly to its difficulties and complications.

How far the transvestite public performance was associated with the private practice of lesbianism is not clear:
this aspect of the record is one that has been almost entirely
obscured by the editorial interventions of "George," her
descendants, the families of her probable partners, and
the devoted Vicomte de Spoelberch who bought up so many
of the papers relating to her in order to be able to withhold
them from publication. But whatever doubt may exist to-

day, her contemporaries were sure that she was a practicing lesbian, and that she was the lover as well as the friend of the actress Marie Dorval.

Be that as it may, death at last came to take away the poor lady who had been lying helpless in the great four-poster bed in the ground floor bedroom for so long, and Sophie-Victoire, accompanied by a sister, descended on Nohant to take charge and to exact vengeance for the slights and rebuffs of nearly twenty years by exerting every ounce of authority over Aurore and her inheritance that was given her by the law. Aurore's situation was not made any easier to bear by her mother's condition. She was in the middle of her change of life and making very heavy weather of it. She was barely sane for days at a stretch, and in her confusion of mind she created scenes in which she heaped abuse on her late mother-in-law, her daughter, and, indeed, any other person whose name occurred to her. Scenes of exceptional squalor and violence broke out when poor Deschartres' accounts were found to be in disorder. He was accused of embezzlement, and sent packing under threats of prosecution. He was only saved from arrest by Aurore, who swore that the missing funds had been given to her.

From this singularly unpleasant situation Aurore Dupin escaped, after two years of bickering and recrimination, by plunging into marriage with a young man she hardly knew, a certain Casimir Dudevant. In view of the obsessions of both Maurice de Saxe and Madame Dupin de Franceuil, and the shadows they had cast on Aurore's infancy, it was only to be expected that the man of her choice would be another illegitimate child. Casimir was in fact the natural son of a man who had been one of her father's friends, Colonel the Baron Dudevant, and of a housemaid he had seduced. It was also inevitable, given her history and his, that they should give each other a hard time. Though Casimir had been legally recognized as the Baron's son, his mother had not been thought good enough to marry his father and had been supplanted by another lady who was considered fit to bear the title of Madame la Baronne.

She was a cold woman who did not care for Casimir and was condescendingly kind to him while he was growing up. He reached manhood encumbered by a profound sense of his own inferiority and by the awkwardness and shyness that is apt to go with such a sense.

Each member of this pair was, in fact, a classic example of that species of human being known to the psychiatrists as a deprived child, that is to say, an adult who has been so effectively traumatized in infancy by the sudden loss or withdrawal of the love and affection of one or both of its parents as to be marked for life. The damage done to the child is so great that there can be no subsequent compensation for the injury. Such permanently maimed persons are organized psychologically to reject as inadequate whatever may be offered to them in the way of love and affection. What is more, they are largely motivated in their personal relationships by a desire to visit upon others just such a sense of loss and desolation as they have experienced themselves. They spend their adult lives in the ritualistic construction of situations in which they can blackjack their emotional dependents with sudden withdrawals of support. It is part of the dismal fate of such beings that they show a marked tendency to seek out their own kind in order to form sadomasochistic compacts the function of which is to produce guaranteed dissatisfactions. The theme song of the typical marriage between deprived children is "nothing you can do for me can ever be right," and the partners tend to trade accusations rather than the customary endearments. The games played are played in deadly earnest so that these accusations generally go directly for the vitals. The woman will accuse the man of being either financially or sexually inadequate, and the man will accuse the woman of being either frigid or insatiable, or the financial equivalents of those things, but whatever form these attacks may take, they all have the same functional aim, to damage the partner-enemy's belief in himself and demonstrate that he or she is worthless as a man or as a woman. The hard player of the games involved is out for more than the mere emotional satisfaction to be derived from inflicting pain; he is playing for keeps and will not let up until his partner has committed suicide or taken some similar step, such as becoming an alcoholic. George Sand was such a hard player of her chosen game, and her goal in her personal relationships was always the symbolic emasculation of her partner. The husband she had chosen for herself was in many ways the ideal man for her, since his muscular sense of guilt led him to seek the same goal.

The marriage lasted, formally at least, from 1822 until 1836, when the court at La Châtre gave Aurore Dudevant a separation and custody of the children. The judgment was handed down in May, and Casimir's appeal against it was heard in June in the district court at Bourges. Aurore went there for the hearing, and on the night before it was to be held engraved something in the nature of a prayer on the paneling in the room in which she was to sleep. "Grand Dieu!" it began. "Almighty God! Protect those who wish for what is right, cast down those who mean to do wrong...confound the scribes and pharisees, and clear the way for the traveler who seeks Thy Holy Places...." On the following morning she appeared before the tribunal, dressed all in white to emphasize her innocence, and listened as her lawyer told the court in the language of moral outrage that she was a cruelly wronged and irreproachable wife who had been forced to leave her home by the infamous behavior of a miserly and licentious husband. The lawyer went on from this to argue that in view of all that she had suffered, his client should not only have her divorce and custody of the children, but also monetary compensation to the amount of a hundred thousand francs. What is peculiarly disagreeable about all this is that Aurore had secured the services of the lawyer who was putting her case to the court by becoming his mistress and that she knew perfectly well that her husband, who had spent half his small fortune on indulging her whims and fancies during the first three years of their marriage, had nothing like that sum, and would have serious difficulties in raising it.

But it had taken a long time to bring the marriage into

the divorce court. At the beginning of it all Aurore had
been delighted with Casimir, and her letters written at
the time are full of happiness. This state of affairs lasted
through her first pregnancy, was reinforced when she bore
her husband a son—Maurice—and went on until Casimir
realized that he had been spending money like water and
that half his capital had gone. It had never been very much,
no more than sixty thousand francs, but it had been enough
to give him his independence. While he was coming to grips
with this unpleasant fact, he also became aware that his
wife's estate at Nohant had been very badly managed and
that it was not producing anything like as much income
as it should. Casimir reined in his expenditures sharply
and began scrutinizing the family accounts more carefully.
By a truly remarkable coincidence it was just at this junc-
ture—when Aurore was required to put something into
the marriage for the first time—that she discovered that he
was made of some coarser and less sensitive fiber than herself and that he was unworthy of her. In that state of mind
she began a series of flirtations with other men, finally
settling on a certain Aurélien de Sèze for something a little
more serious.

In later life, when Aurore Dudevant had completed her
transformation into George Sand, she wrote up this episode
and invested it with a good deal of emotional substance.
But the letters she wrote at the time suggest that it did not
go much further than a little kissing, a certain amount
of heavy breathing, and a functional *coup de théâtre* in
which Aurore contrived to have herself caught in her
Aurélien's arms by the unhappy Casimir. The discovery
scene was an absurdity, and its only purpose can have been
to learn, before she put herself too far into the wrong, how
much Casimir would be willing to take when it came to it.
Her husband's abundant distress and anxiety on being faced
with the possibility of her infidelity, and his willingness
to behave as if he were as much at fault as she was, showed
her how little cause she had for worry—he was abject and
completely at her mercy. In her triumph she fairly let him
have it, and the relationship became an exceedingly grisly

one. Its new tone can be judged by an incident that occurred a few weeks after the discovery scene, when Casimir took Aurore to stay for a while with his father, the Baron Dudevant. Casimir told a story that fell flat when they were at dinner one night, and Aurore felt sufficiently sure of herself to crown his failure by saying, "My poor Casimir, you really are unusually stupid. But never mind, I love you as you are."

While infidelity is not a necessary consequence of such an attitude, at once patronizing and contemptuous, it certainly becomes a probability rather than a possibility once it has been adopted. In this case the probability became a certainty with some rapidity. Not long after that wounding remark was made Casimir's father died, and his will, which had been expected to make Casimir Aurore's equal financially, left him in a very inferior position. By this instrument he was made the Baron's heir, but Madame la Baronne had a life interest in the estate and he could not touch any part of his inheritance until she was dead. Casimir was left to maintain his position as the husband of a wife with more than fifteen thousand francs a year on an income derived from just twice that sum. Casimir would be rich one day, but for the present he was poor. Aurore did not care for this situation and was soon telling her friends as much in letters that saw the birth of the ugly myth that she had suffered hardship because Casimir had wasted her money and mismanaged her properties. "We are terribly hard up this year, having put in hand the building of some new barns—at a ruinous cost...."

But Aurélien de Sèze was not to be the beneficiary of Aurore's growing sense that Casimir, having shown himself less than her intellectual equal, was now failing her financially. She made both men look foolish by embarking on a second pregnancy with the help of Stéphane Ajasson de Grandsagne, an assistant of Cuvier, the great systematizer of vertebrate anatomy. Since she had been playing the two men off against each other they were thunderstruck to find that there was a third in question. Aurélien was so upset by this discovery that he had something like a

nervous breakdown, and Casimir began to drink heavily
and to console himself with the maids at Nohant. By the
time the pregnancy reached its term every one in the family
was happily giving everyone else a hard time. When Aurore's labor began both Casimir and her half-brother Hippolyte, who was by way of being her husband's crony, had
been drinking themselves silly for days, and shortly before
the delivery took place she overheard her husband tipsily
making up to one of the maids in an adjoining room in
earthy language that made it clear that they were already
lovers.

This performance, by means of which Casimir Dudevant
managed to put himself in the wrong even in a situation
as clear cut as that in which his wife was bearing another
man's child, shows better than anything else how intent
upon his own destruction he was. But he was soon to go
further, by "investing" all but five thousand francs of what
remained of his capital in the purchase of a freighter from
a vendor who did not in fact have title to the vessel, of
which he was at best a part-owner. When Aurore found
out that Casimir had lost this money she let him have it
in a letter in which her complete contempt for him fairly
brimmed over.

> *Cannot you ever carry through a deal without get-*
> *ting yourself caught up in a tangle of trickery? You*
> *never have any luck with this sort of thing, so why*
> *go on trying? We should get much better results by*
> *combining our practical talents—all of us, I mean—*
> *than by each going off on his own and making deci-*
> *sions on our separate judgments. Dutheil understands*
> *business, and Hippolyte—though I know you think*
> *him a bit mad—has more sound horse-sense in matters*
> *of this kind than you and me put together. Why not*
> *let him regulate the household expenses? You can*
> *look after the cabbages and the roots....If you want to,*
> *and can, you may buy a few more parcels of ground*
> *every year, though I think I ought to warn you that*
> *you are a byword in the neighborhood for always*
> *paying higher prices than anybody else....*

In due course, though she was never to acknowledge it, Casimir's additions to the Nohant estate and his management policies were roughly to double Aurore's income. But that was a matter for the future, and meanwhile she was able to trample his pride into the dirt. Presently she had it arranged to her satisfaction that he should remain at Nohant with the children while she went off to Paris with freedom to do as she liked. She left Casimir, in short, in the position of an abandoned wife.

In Paris Aurore Dudevant, who was now twenty-six, became the mistress of Jules Sandeau, a young man of nineteen who was embarking on a career as a writer. He interested Aurore in his profession, and she was soon collaborating with him on various journalistic and literary projects and frequenting literary and bohemian circles as his companion, generally in male costume. He was effeminate, delicate, and idle, and she was soon mothering him and doing most of the writing that was appearing over the team signature of J. Sand. But although all their acquaintances and friends took it that the affair was a romantic idyll it presently became apparent that there was something wrong. Before much more than a year had gone by Aurore was denying rumors to the effect that Jules was consumptive; the truth, she was afraid, was that there was something else, which might be much worse, the matter. She confided the precise nature of her fears to her friend Emile Regnault.

> Would it be better if I sent him to sleep at your house?
> ... It is frightful to see him growing thinner and thinner and more exhausted, to realize that I am bringing death ever closer to him...that is a hideous thought, which Jules refuses to understand...he merely laughs and says that such a death is what he longs for...many and many's the time I've seen him in a half-fainting condition and have resisted his desires. But I have always yielded in the long run, for fear of killing him....
> I now tremble at the thought that I have done him more harm by my devotion than by my resistance. I am killing him, and the pleasure I give him is bought at the cost of his life.

She gave this fantasy its airing in the winter of 1831, and in the following spring published a novel to which poor Sandeau had made no contribution and which was all too plainly much more interesting than anything he could have written. Having once again established her physical and intellectual superiority over her lover to her satisfaction, she proceeded to his humiliation—the extreme one in this case of leaving him not for another man but for another woman, Alfred de Vigny's mistress, the actress Marie Dorval, to whom she made an almost comically chappish approach:

> *Do you really think you can endure me? That is something you can't know yet, nor I. I am such a bear, so stupid, so slow to put my thoughts into words, so awkward and so dumb just when my heart is fullest. Do not judge me by externals. Wait a little before deciding how much pity and affection you can give me. I feel that I love you with a heart rejuvenated and altogether renewed by you. If that is just a dream, like everything I have ever wanted in life, do not wake me from it too soon. It does me so much good. Goodbye, you great and lovely person. Whatever happens, I shall see you this evening.*

Having driven Alfred de Vigny wild with jealousy by dangling around Marie Dorval booted and trousered in the height of male fashion of the day, George Sand, as she was now almost invariably calling herself, had a reconciliation with the man she was now thinking of as "poor little Jules" in order, it may be suspected, to organize the final breach on lines wholly satisfactory to herself. When it came she was striding about in her tasseled boots taking care of the practical details, getting little Jules his passport, making reservations for a trip to Italy, canceling the lease on his apartment, and so on, while he, poor fellow, was sitting about weeping. At this stage in the game she wrote another letter to Emile Regnault:

*Please look up Jules and do what you can so far as
his bodily health is concerned. His heart is broken and
beyond help. You can do nothing for it, so do not try.
I need no attention, in fact I would rather be left alone.
Life no longer holds anything for me. Do what you can
to bring Jules back to life. He will suffer terribly for
a long time to come, but he is very young. One day,
perhaps, he will cease to regret that he has lived....*

The very strange nature of the participants in these
extremely sophisticated parlor games is indicated by the
fact that Jules Sandeau, having come back to life, in the
fullness of time became one of Marie Dorval's many lovers.
And the twenty-nine-year-old woman who was so patronizingly saying that "poor little Jules" was "very young"
was on the brink of an affair with another twenty-three-
year-old man—Alfred de Musset.

George Sand finally broke with Jules Sandeau and met
de Musset in April of 1833, a few months before the publication of *Lélia*, the singular novel in which she proclaimed her frigidity to the world. George and de Musset
did not immediately become lovers, and when she sent
him a set of galley proofs of this bizarre and pretentious
work there was still nothing between them but a light and
almost entirely jocular flirtation. That a reading of *Lélia*
should have inspired de Musset to take the initiative that
turned the flirtation into a liaison raises a number of questions about him and his psychic necessities. In the unre-
vised version in which de Musset read the book there is
a sudden change of tone when one of the characters describes the torments she has had to endure because she can
readily be aroused sexually but can never enjoy the sexual
act. The description is unambiguous, despite the highfa-
lutin language in which it is couched:

*Sometimes when I was asleep, and prey to the wild
ecstasies that fill the heads of dreaming ascetics, I
would feel that I was being borne off with him among
the clouds by scented breezes, or that I was swimming*

through waves of an unspeakable sensuality, and,
putting my nerveless arms about his neck, I would
lay my head upon his breast murmuring words I barely
understood myself. But then he would wake and that
would be the end of my happiness. In place of that
airy being who had cradled me on the wind from his
wings, I would find myself faced with a man as brutal
and as voracious as a wild beast, and I would flee him
in horror. He would not let me go and, insisting that
he was not to be wakened from his sleep for nothing,
would take his coarse pleasure from a woman who
was half-fainting and half-dead.

There is no doubt that George Sand has stepped out of
the character and is speaking to her readers in an unusually
direct and personal way in this passage. But the question
is not so much one of whether the words are supposed to
be applicable to her or not—one can safely take it that they
are—but a matter of what they in fact mean. Was George
Sand in truth constitutionally unable to enjoy the sexual
act? Or did she have a very strong need to have it believed
that she suffered from this disability when she wrote this
novel? All the evidence goes to suggest that the second
possibility is the likely one. The evidence for her frigidity
is all manufactured and exists in the form of recollections
written some time after the events by which the issue was
raised. The evidence in favor of the view that she enjoyed
sexual pleasures in the normal way exists in the form of
letters written when the events were taking place, and
before she had developed a "policy" about this aspect of
her life. There can be no doubting that some of the uncon-
sidered and spontaneous letters that she wrote in the first
months of her marriage to Casimir, and about her affairs
with de Grandsagne and Sandeau, are those of a woman
who has been physically pleased and is looking forward
to the renewal of her physical pleasures. The question that
remains to be answered is why she should have wished to
advertise this nonexistent defect in her physical being?
The answer lies in the technique of games-playing: wom-
en players of the kind of games in which the woman in-

flicts the full weight of her hostility toward men in general upon her partner-opponent get an added satisfaction from conducting their proceedings more or less openly, and from offering them a losing game with a disarming air of frankness. A very common invitation to take part in such a one-sided game has the structure: "Well, all right, I'll go to bed with you, or even marry you, if you like, but it will give me no pleasure, and I can promise you that you won't like it either."

There are good reasons for supposing that George Sand was attempting to set up a game situation of just this type when she embarked on her affair with de Musset, and that the passage quoted from *Lélia* was in the nature of a manifesto announcing the kind of game that she would be playing in future. The chief of these reasons is that she had resorted to the use of precisely this formula in initiating her brief contest with Prosper Mérimée in April 1833, in the course of a walk beside the Seine.

In matters of this kind Mérimée was virtually a professional male, priding himself on his efficiency as a seducer of women and on the skill with which he got them to give themselves to him on his terms with the minimum of concessions. Mérimée had disregarded Sand's clear warning that if he became involved with her he would be playing a hand from the bottom of the deck and had insisted on the trial of his virility—presumably taking the greenhorn gambler's position that "with me it will be different." He doubled his stakes by making his pursuit of her a public matter, going so far as to stage a scene in which he appeared in the role of deputy father to Sand's daughter Solange. Although the gesture does not seem to mean very much by the light of the relaxed and "natural" norms of the present day, Mérimée was doing something very pointed when he showed himself at the head of the grand staircase of the Paris Opéra with Solange in his arms as the audience was letting out after a performance of *Robert le Diable*. In an age of formalized social behavior, his action was declaratory and unambiguous. It meant, the rules of the games being what they are, that his humiliation also would have to be a public matter—a thing that was accomplished easily enough by confiding the details of the inevitable fiasco to Marie Dorval, who could be relied upon to spread the word.

What actually happened is no longer to be learned with any certainty, but such evidence as there is suggests that the affair went on for from a week to ten days before Mérimée had finally accepted his defeat. But almost as soon as it was over a friend of Marie Dorval's, the novelist Dumas père, was happily broadcasting his version in the form of a neat anecdote. According to Dumas, he had been riding in a cab with Marie Dorval when they had been hailed by Sand from a vehicle which had pulled up alongside theirs. He alleged that Sand had called across to them to say "I had Mérimée last night, but it wasn't anything very special...."

The story went round the circles frequented by the parties with the usual rapidity, and by July Sand was writing to her friend Sainte-Beuve to explain what had really happened, why it had happened, and why Marie Dorval was not to be blamed for spreading a travesty of the truth. This letter, a curiosity in itself, is made even more of an oddity by the tenacity with which Sand attaches the assertion that "I am utterly and completely Lélia" to her explanations. It is as if she took a pride in having been unmoved, and in being immovable.

Be that as it may, de Musset must have heard the story by the time that Sand sent him a set of the galley proofs of *Lélia*, presumably as a challenge and warning of the kind that she had given to Mérimée, at the end of the same month. His reaction was to write her a declaration in which he said that he had been in love with her ever since their first meeting three months earlier. She replied with a communication that can only be called coy, inviting him to prove it and thus to set himself up, as Mérimée had done, for a short game with a quick end played entirely on her terms. De Musset replied with a masterly rejection that was simultaneously an invitation for a much more serious contest. In this letter he suggested that he was just as much of an emotional cripple as she was: "You should love only those who know how to love. I know only how to suffer. ..." He went on to make the beautifully calculated claim that he loved her "like a child." This settled the issue, and in August the woman-man and the man-child became lovers, the relationship being made "official" by means of a formal announcement to her confidant Sainte-Beuve toward the end of the month: "I have fallen in love, and this time very seriously, with Alfred de Musset..."

The child took the opening rounds with some ease. He was a great deal more experienced than she was in sexual matters and was able to wound her rather easily, by telling her that she hadn't got as far as C in the alphabet of love-making, and by comparing her performances with those of his other women. This was especially galling for her because most of his other women had been professionals, and the message of his apparently light-hearted teasing was to the effect that what she was giving him was of less value to him than what he was used to getting from the prostitutes he had frequented. Before long, however, George Sand seems to have got the hang of her partner-opponent's game and to have found a way of nullifying its effectiveness by coming on as the eager learner willing to be taught whatever there was to know. Then already having done her best, she could let him know that *his* best still wasn't much good for her and start constructing a position with winning chances. De Musset reacted to this change in the balance of the game by changing his ground to that of the young captive of an older woman, and, even more effectively, to that of the aristocrat degrading himself by forming a connection with a vulgar woman of the people. De Musset was, indeed, well bred from the aristocratic point of view, and in a position to snub the daughter of Sophie-Victoire, great-granddaughter of Marie Rinteau, and wife of a Napoleonic Baron's by-blow. He found it easy to keep her off balance in this phase of their game by flirting with younger women and by keeping up his connections with houses that she was not thought fit to enter; and her letters of the time are filled with an uneasy sense that she is being outmaneuvered, and that the game is going so much in his favor as to be only dubiously worth playing. The indications are that she was thinking of breaking it up from October 1833 onwards, but that she was uneasy about admitting to a lost game while they were in Paris and very much in the public eye. She accordingly decided upon a visit to Italy, with a program in mind. They would go to Venice and, having broken up there, would separate. He would return to Paris alone, and she would go on to Greece, and perhaps Turkey, on a trip that would last for several months. When she was ready to return, Paris would have forgotten that they had ever been lovers. There is little doubt that this was her plan—or that she saw herself as being in control and kindly but firmly giving de Musset his marching orders and sending him home from Venice. But when they reached that city she was very ill, and de Musset found himself dangling round the sickbed of a woman who seemed to him suddenly and shockingly old and plain, for nearly three weeks. It was more than he could stand, and before she was fully recovered he abruptly called the game. "George—it's all been a big mistake— forgive me—but I don't love you."

Having made this winner's gambit, which left George Sand with the limited options of either ending the affair or going on with it, on his terms in either case, de Musset no doubt relaxed. But whatever his feelings may have been, he incautiously accepted George's unconditional surrender, and instead of a breakup there was a kind of victory celebration that he came to describe, nearly twenty years later, as "eight days of youth and passion regained." In his euphoria he had forgotten the important point that George's illness had played in creating the necessary conditions for his victory, just as he had forgotten that he might himself fall ill. Nevertheless this honeymoon came to an abrupt end at the beginning of February 1834 when George woke to find him with a raging fever and the beginnings of delirium. She sat down and dashed off a hurried note, in schoolroom Italian, to a doctor Pietro Pagello who had been recommended to her by the French Consul when she herself had been sick. She was not so much, she said, afraid for de Musset's life as for his reason: *"Io temo per la sua ragione più che per la sua vita."* Could Dr. Pagello please come *at once* and do all he could for this young and promising writer who was *"molto adimirato"* in France, and *"la persona che amo il meglio del mondo."* Dr. Pagello came at once. He was a hefty, athletic young man of twenty-seven, with a pleasantly open expression and powerful hands. He came again, and when de Musset's illness reached its crisis between the seventh and tenth of February, he stayed at the bedside day and night, with George watching beside him. De Musset was considered to be out of danger by the fourteenth, but he was weak and helpless until well into the following month, and by the time he was up and about George and the doctor had been lovers for quite a while.

Who took the initiative? He said that she did, she said that he did. He said that he had been the prey of a seductive ghoul, she said that a cry of horror had escaped her when she first realized that he was making a pass at her, but that she had succumbed to the mixture of daring and humility with which he had implored, tormented, and persecuted her for hours at a stretch until she gave way to him. By her own account the seduction or courtship or whatever it was took place in the sickroom and in the presence of the invalid, and the decisive event in it was a letter written by her to him. The text of this letter, which she wrote at one end of the sickroom, with de Musset lying sleeping at the other, and Pagello sitting watching her, has a false title *En Morée,* presumably put at the head of the document so that, had Alfred woken up and asked her what she was doing, she could have shown it to him and told him it was part of a story or novel she was writing. What it is, however, is a request for reassurance in the form of a statement of the lingering doubts of a woman who has been propositioned by a foreigner she hardly knows and has made up her mind to go to bed with but doesn't quite know where the decision will take her. "Am I to be your friend or your slave? What is it you feel for me—desire or love? When your passion has been satisfied will you give me thanks? When I have made you happy, will you know how to tell me so?" And so on. When she had done she put the lengthy communication into an envelope and sent him off to read it. Since he couldn't know that it was full of eloquent phrases that she had already used, or would later use, in letters to her various lovers, he was very much impressed and touched, and hastened to give her all the assurances that she asked for. They met on the following day, and as they walked up and down on the great square in front of St. Mark's he told her all his love, and she told him that everything had been over between her and de Musset long before he fell ill. And so they became lovers.

It is hard to make out just what followed even though this can be described as one of the most lavishly documented triangles of all time. Alfred de Musset was the first to give a fictional account of it in his self-serving *Confession d'un enfant du siècle,* in which Brigitte Pierson represents George; Smith, Pagello; and Octave de T, himself. Then, when Alfred had been dead for a year, George wrote the wildly mendacious *Elle et lui,* a novel in which she figures as Thérèse Jacques, Pagello as an American called Palmer, and Musset as Laurent de Fauvel. Sand undoubtedly hoped to have the last word with *Elle et lui,* but she had forgotten that Alfred had a brother, Paul de Musset, who could write. Paul replied to *Elle et lui* with a novel of his own called *Lui et elle* in which Sand figures as Olympe de B, Pagello as Palminello, and de Musset as Eduard de Falconey. Little as Paul de Musset's countermove was to her liking, she had a more bitter pill to follow when de Musset's last mistress, Madame Louise Colet, wrote yet another reply to *Elle et lui* called *Lui* which not only showed anyone who cared to see that the poet had disclosed all the most intimate details of their relationship to another woman, but also that he had come to look upon her with a large measure of contempt. And in due course Pagello's journals, and the letters she had written to him, came to light....

But all that lay a long way ahead. For de Musset and

for Sand the important thing for the moment was the complete reversal of their situation. When de Musset took to his bed he had had a mistress who was prepared, for the time being at any rate, to submit to almost any humiliation in order to keep him and to preserve the appearance at least of a happy relationship, but when he recovered he found himself in what is from the male point of view the classic loser's position, that of the man who has lost his woman to another man with nothing in his favor but a superior physique. De Musset was Pagello's superior in every way but one: whereas de Musset was a weakling and anything but a fine animal, the doctor was physically magnificent. A glance at the two of them would show in an instant why Sand had preferred the one to the other and, further, would make it plain that Sand valued animal grace and muscle above all the things that gave de Musset his distinction and interest. Faced with the problem of playing this unplayable hand de Musset simply blew up, and began presenting point after point to his opponent. There was after all no way of escaping the fact that, whatever he might do or say about it, part of his record was going to be that of "the man who took George Sand to Venice and lost her to the local doctor."

It is a measure of his desperation that he tried to evade the irretrievable consequences of the deterioration of his position by pretending that he thoroughly approved of what had happened. In a letter of early April 1834 he wrote to George Sand to say that "As soon as I saw Pagello I recognized in him the best part of myself, but exempt from the irreparable soilings that have made it go bad on me. That's why I saw that I had to bow out...."

But George Sand had already anticipated this attempt to retrieve the completeness of de Musset's defeat by making out that he had willingly collaborated in it, and had written to some friends to explain that she had been forced to part from de Musset, just as she had been forced to part from Sandeau, because she had overpowered him sexually. "I'm brokenhearted, but I've done what I had to do," she told one of them, "his lung condition made complete abstinence mandatory, and his nerves, always on edge, made his deprivation insupportable; it was necessary to put an end to these dangers." She had to send him away for fear that she would let him have her, and so kill himself.

Unaware of what she was up to, de Musset continued to attempt to play out the grotesque hand he had dealt himself until the end of the month. On the thirtieth of April he wrote to George to say: "Tell P that I bless him for loving you and watching over you as he does. Was there ever such a ridiculous thought in the world as that? But I love him, that boy, almost as much as you. Make whatever you like of that. On account of him I've lost everything of value in my life, and I love him as if he'd given it me. I wouldn't want to see you together, and yet I'm happy to think that you are together. Oh my angel, my angel, be happy, and then I'll be happy." Not that he was without his suspicions. In the same letter he asked her if she was not doing something behind his back. "There's a lot of talk about my return. What I find incomprehensible is that, only fifteen days after my arrival, everybody already knows that we've separated.... You haven't, by any chance on an evil day, written a little something to Buloz...?"

By voicing this suspicion de Musset, without realizing it, opened a new phase in the game. George Sand's mother had already written to her to warn her that unpleasant things were being said about her in Paris, but she had an entrenched habit of disregarding anything her mother might say, and she had not taken the warning seriously. De Musset was another matter, however, and when he said that the end of their affair was being discussed on all sides she experienced a return of the panic that had visited her when he had threatened her with a walkout at the end of her illness. Suppose that everything was to come out, and that the whole story of the past eighteen months in her life was to be broadcast? Where would she be if "everyone" became aware that she had had affairs with Sandeau, Planche (the critic), Marie Dorval, Mérimée, de Musset, and now Pagello in that brief period?

Sometime in May she appears to have decided that the

correct strategy for her to follow was to dump Pagello and to reinstate de Musset, a switch that could only be accomplished by reopening their game on a new basis. An invitation to him to join her in a round of "let's get Pagello" was written on May 12 in a letter containing the significant phrase "good old P hasn't read *Lélia* and I'm pretty sure that even if he did he wouldn't understand a word of it." This signal, "He's not really one of us," was followed by a virtuoso display, the theme of which can be interpreted as "Look, I can do anything I like with the big booby." She began by saying, in effect, Pagello is going to write to you, he doesn't want to, but you'll see, *he* will, and ended by delivering a letter that only a clown could have written, containing such splendid things as "we haven't either of us written to each other yet, perhaps because neither of us wished to be the first. But that hasn't been any barrier to the mute correspondence of affection which will always bind us in its knots, sublime for us, incomprehensible to the rest of the world." It ended with the salutation "farewell, my good Alfred, love me always as I love you. *Vostro vero amico*, Pietro Pagello."

When the ground had been fully prepared by much more of this sort of thing Pagello was brought from Venice to Paris, dumped, and sent home. He was a realist, and before he left Venice told his father that he expected precisely this to happen. But he was an honest man, too, and he had expected to be dealt with honestly. He was not prepared for connivance and unnecessary lying that were put into his deception, and he was shocked by it and by discovering the extent to which he had been used as a pawn in the game between George and de Musset. He had, after all, only come to Paris to be kind to her, and she had responded by doing her best to make an egregious fool of him—even going so far on one occasion as to attempt to inveigle him into paying a visit to Nohant as Casimir Dudevant's guest. With a good deal of amiable gallantry he put on a show of accepting his fate with good grace, but inwardly he felt extremely bitter and he made some scathing comments on George's conduct to those few of his French acquaintances

whom he felt able to trust. He was wrong to do so, as it
turned out, and soon found himself being rebuked for what
he had said by George, on whom he at last turned. But
he was now, more than ever, a subsidiary character in the
game, and her reaction to the confrontation was to write
to de Musset about it. Pagello, she told him, had wounded
her to the bottom of her soul, and she went on to say: "I
loved him like a father, and you were our child...and
here he is once again a feeble being, suspicious, unjust,
making quarrels out of nothing, and in general upsetting
the apple cart."

George was at this time doing more than writing de Musset privately; she was also addressing him publicly through
the medium of a series of communications published in
the *Revue des Deux Mondes* under the title of "Lettres d'un
voyageur" and writing something that she called a *Journal
Intime*, which was in effect a forged piece of evidence to
be brought forward in support of a completely false account
of the relationship. De Musset too was busy writing his
side of the story—as if the relationship were already a
matter of history—in his *Confession d'un enfant du siècle*,
and both parties to the affair were also unburdening themselves less formally in letters and statements to their friends.
In the confusion created by the intensity of these exchanges
and the elaboration of the moves and countermoves of the
game being played, Pagello, now angry as well as bitter,
was able to slip away and return to his pleasant Venetian
life almost unnoticed. With the "official" bone of contention removed de Musset was free to concentrate on
George's dishonesty: she had lied to him, terribly, about
Pagello. She defended herself by saying that she had lied
to him only because she loved him, no one had ever loved
anyone so intensely, or so purely. He won this part of the
game insofar as he made her go to extravagant lengths
to get him back, but she took the match. They became lovers
again in October 1834 and she walked out on him the following March. They were living together in Paris at the
time and she was at pains to make sure that the blow should
be as surprising and crushing to him as possible; she kept

all her plans for departure secret, was there one day and gone the next, leaving him with no idea where she might be...

She was, as it happened, at Nohant preparing for a new campaign of a rather different kind that would settle her outstanding business with the unlucky Casimir Dudevant. In the course of her games with de Musset and Pagello she had become aware of an increasing weakness in her position. She was becoming notorious, and a distinct possibility that Casimir might divorce her had to be reckoned with. If he succeeded in such an action he might not only get custody of their children, but, the law of married women's property being what it then was in France, he might also be awarded all but a bare minimum of her inherited wealth and possessions. Her lawyer of the moment gave her the cynical advice that she could avoid these risks if she took the precaution of becoming her husband's mistress whenever she went to stay at Nohant; but she felt that such an arrangement would smack of prostitution, and she rejected this solution to her problem out of hand. A formal legal separation was what she wanted, and what she was determined to have. Her lawyer, recognizing the considerable difficulties lying in the path of a female plaintiff in a divorce case who has abandoned her husband's domicile to take five lovers in eighteen months, recommended her to someone tougher and less scrupulous. There was such a person, he suggested, in practice in Bourges, Louis Chrysostom Michel, known as Michel de Bourges, a lawyer and politician from Provence who was of peasant stock and was a formidable histrionic orator. George, who had broken with Alfred de Musset between March the sixth and the ninth, met Michel de Bourges on April the seventh and became his mistress on April the ninth. There was nothing impetuous or capricious in this, she told him in a letter written at the end of the month, because: "It's you I've loved since the day I was born, notwithstanding all the will-of-the-wisps in whom I've thought, for an instant, to have found you and possessed you." If he had known that she had said precisely the same thing to poor Pagello a year

earlier he might have been better prepared for what was
to happen. Exactly two years later, at the end of April 1836,
she was telling a charming young Swiss gentleman, Charles
Didier, that she had not been to bed with anyone since she
had left Alfred de Musset, and that her relationship with
Michel de Bourges was purely intellectual. Then there
was Pierre Leroux, a radical mystic who preached a species
of groupie philosophy and tinkered with an automatic
typesetting machine, and after him Maurice's handsome
new tutor, Eugène Pelletan. A year after he had won her
court decree for her and secured her property and children,
Michel de Bourges had had enough. "Things can't go on
like this…there is something unspeakably beastly in sex
warfare." The phrase is an interesting one and shows that
he had realized why she felt compelled, while having
almost any young man she fancied, to tell him that she
was incapable of being unfaithful to him:

> …and yet there is not a man, no matter how young
> or how handsome, who could tempt me to be unfaith-
> ful to you in spite of your forgetfulness, your contempt,
> even your infidelity. When the fever takes me I get
> the doctor to relieve me of a pound of blood. He tells
> me that it is a crime, that it is tantamount to suicide,
> and that in any case it won't help me much. What I
> need, he says, is a lover, failing whom my life will
> be in danger from the very excess of the demands it
> makes on me. Well, no matter how much I might
> wish to take his advice, I cannot. The mere thought
> is intolerable to me.

This fantasy about bloodletting as a substitute for sexual
activity is preceded by a boast:

> I, alas, am younger than you: I have hotter blood in my
> veins, stronger muscles, tougher nerves than you, and
> a constitution of iron, as well as a superfluity of energy
> for which I can find no outlet.

The compulsive nature of this claim is evident when it

is related to her expressed conviction that she was over-powering Sandeau in one case and de Musset in another. The parallel becomes even more exact in a later paragraph in the same letter:

> *Ah! Whither are my memories wandering? Once when I revived your failing senses with my sighs, I thought I should have died, so hard did I try to impart to your failing powers something of the life that filled my breast. How sweet I should have found it then to die in the very act of injecting into you some of the rich sap of youth that was to me so heavy a burden!*

When these lines were written Michel de Bourges was a worn out old man of thirty-nine and George was a young girl of thirty-three, so that she would seem to have been making rather more of the age difference than was, strictly speaking, warranted. The point has a certain significance, however, since she had been precisely six years older than both Sandeau and de Musset and was nine years older than Félicien Mallefille, the young playwright who was to suc-ceed Pelletan as Maurice's tutor and her lover—her bed-mates were, indeed, almost always younger than herself, and in some way in need, or arguably so, of care and protec-tion. Michel de Bourges is the one exception of importance to this rule.

Mallefille, a promising young writer who had used up all his talent by the time he was twenty-four, stands on the dividing line between the two parts of George's life. She had scarcely overcome an initial physical repulsion and made herself his mistress late in August 1837 when she heard that her mother was dying. She hurried to the bedside of the woman who was now calling herself Madame Dupin de Nohant and spent several days with her until she at last died in her sleep. While she was performing this daughterly duty she had a panic: word reached her in Paris that Maurice, who had been left behind at Nohant, was missing, and she jumped to the conclusion that the boy had been kidnapped by the wicked Casimir. Mallefille was sent to investigate and found that Maurice had been taken in by a neighbor who was an old friend of his mother's. But although this was a false alarm, George's intuition had been correct. Casimir had come into his own not long before on the death of the Baronne Dudevant, taking possession along with much else of Guillery, his father's country house in Gascony. Now comfortably settled into that pleasant place, he was beginning to hanker for the company of the children, and late in September of that same year he did in fact commit the folly that George had credited him with a month earlier, though it was Grandsagne's daughter Solange and not his son Maurice who was carried off. George, Mallefille, and a lawyer rapidly organized a pursuit and soon had the little girl back; but, although the mother's victory over the father seemed complete and easy, it was, as Marie-Aurore's first triumph over Sophie-Victoire had been, merely the beginning of a long struggle—but this time between mother and child—and for something undefinable. The world at large has made up its mind that the part of George Sand's life that followed her mother's death was dominated by the relationship with Frédéric Chopin which was central to it for more than eight years. But it was Solange whose intuitively Machiavellian machinations—teaching one the lesson that neither intuitions nor little girls of eight should in any circumstances be underrated—whose words and actions determined the shape of the relationship almost from the beginning, and it was Solange who created the difficulties that brought it to an end. When it was over, the failure of Solange's marriage, and her extraordinary subsequent career, provided George with a diet of exasperations and irritations that colored much of her life and kept her daughter in the forefront of her fantasies.

George Sand had met Chopin sometime before she made the acquaintance of Mallefille. At the time she was staying at the Hôtel de France in the Rue Lafitte with Liszt and his mistress, the icily beautiful blonde Marie d'Agoult, and the three of them went round together to Chopin's new apartment at 38 Rue de la Chaussée d'Antin. Chopin could not have known that he was living only a few doors away from the house in which Marie de Verrières had lived with Monsieur D'Epinay, but he felt there was something louche about George that he did not like. He was offended by her cigar-smoking, by her trousers, boots, and chappish behavior, by her parroting of Pierre Leroux's mystico-socialistic ideas, and by the company she was keeping. Gossip had told him of George's lesbian affair with Marie Dorval, and also that, having had a brief liaison with Liszt, she was now to all appearances making an effort to seduce Marie d'Agoult.

Popular legend has Chopin typed as a romantic rebel, but this is not in the least true. He was a rebel only against the extinction of the liberties and freedoms that the Polish upper classes had enjoyed as Russian subjects before the nationalist rising of 1830, and he interpreted those liberties and freedoms in an extremely conventional sense. It was not a revolution of a progressive, radical, or socialistic character that he supported, but a liberation movement that would restore to Poland the establishment of the status quo ante to which he had been emotionally and practically attached.

When Chopin met George he was in a complicated frame of mind since he was in the difficult situation of the self-made man who has reached the top only to find himself rejected by the establishment that he feels he has conquered. By remote origin Chopin was of French peasant stock, his upward climb had been prepared for prenatally when his father, working as a tutor for one of Poland's noble houses, had married a poor relation. His first published work was dedicated to the head of the family into which his father had married, "Her Excellency the Countess Victoria Skarbek," and he grew up as a protected person under the wing of the Polish nobility, his precocious genius and his father's professional talent as a teacher combining to secure them a series of grace-and-favor apartments in its great houses and palaces. When he became an exile it was not so much for ideological reasons as because the nationalist insurrection of 1830 and its brutal repression had temporarily

destroyed the conditions that had made his series of drawing-room successes possible, and had raised questions,
already existing in his mind, about the possibility of sustaining a musical career in what was essentially a provincial society. Before the outbreak occurred he had left
Poland for France to further his musical career, and had
been accused of betraying Polish culture in intention even
before he left. He did not return to Poland during the insurrection or after it because his father had written to him giving him prudential reasons for not doing so. And thereafter
his career kept him abroad. There is something forced about
his patriotism that may well have stemmed from its fundamental lack of depth, and from his lack of any commitment to the revolutionary ideology that became attached
to Polish nationalism among the exiles in Paris. His feelings
of unease on this whole question were exacerbated by two
things. In his first years in Paris Chopin had a musical
success but a materialistic failure, and he was on the brink
of going to America to try his luck there when he accidental-
ly ran into Valentin Radziwill in the street. The Radziwills
had always taken an interest in Chopin, and Valentin was
distressed to find him in a mood to accept his rejection
by the Parisians. He knew that the remedy for that situation
was a drawing-room success in the right place, and he took
his protégé to play at a reception at the Baron de Rothschild's that same evening. His physical beauty—he was
extremely handsome—and the combination of the emotionally charged nature of his music with the beautifully restrained and cool character of his technique made him an
instant success in this setting; within a week his situation
was transformed. The Baronne de Rothschild led an army
of her friends and rivals to him for music lessons at the
top rate of twenty gold crowns an hour, and with the money
earned in this way, and from playing in salons, he was soon
liberated from the brutal business of trying to win concert
audiences round to the acceptance of an intimate art that
they did not understand. As Liszt put it, "He knew...that
he could not move the masses, because, although they are
like a sea of lead and their waves can be molded by any fire,

they are no less heavy to move and require the strong arm of the athletic workman." They wanted, in short, a lot of noise, all that could be got from that astounding new instrument the concert grand, and they were disappointed by a virtuoso who obtained his best effects by playing with such delicacy that the hammers seemed at times to be just stroking the wires, and whose performances were, essentially, personal communications.

Chopin celebrated his release from poverty and uncertainty by becoming an elegant perfectionist both in his dress and in his way of life. The whiteness of his cambric shirts, of his gloves, the polish on his patent leather boots, the cut of his superb pale gray, lavender, and powder-blue frock coats, and the swing of his black capes lined with gray silk became famous. He kept his own carriage and hired servants. His apartment was spotless and always in order, and furnished with austerely beautiful eighteenth-century pieces of the kind that he had learned to admire in the great Polish houses. The dedications of his compositions became a kind of supplement to the *Almanach de Gotha*, there was no room for the names of his friends on the list of such persons as the Baronne de Rothschild, the Princesse de Baveau, the Princesse Czernichev, the Comtesse de Lobau, the Comtesse Esterhazy, and Mademoiselle de Noailles. His politics fell into line, if they had ever really departed from it, with his dedications: "I am in sympathy with the Carlists—I cannot stand the supporters of Louis Phillipe." He was expressing his preference for the aristocratic-royalists—and absolutists—of Spain over the parliamentarian bourgeois-monarchists of France. For a moment he was able to believe that he had crossed the social barriers on the wings of his gifts and had indeed become an aristocrat. When a member of one of the families who had been his patrons in Poland, the Countess Wodzinska, sent him an invitation to come to see her in Geneva in the spring of 1834, he allowed himself to take it as a proposition between equals. He did not go there, but joined the family in Dresden the following winter.

At the height of his success, and to all appearances radiantly strong and healthy, Chopin made a more than favorable impression on the Wodzinskis. The Countess was soon calling him her fourth son, and within days her sixteen-year-old daughter Maria was in love with him and he with her. They reached a secret understanding, and when he left Dresden for Paris in the middle of October he was dreaming that they would one day be married.

Or was he? Behind the Countess there had been the disapproving presence of Maria's uncle, the Palatine Wodzinski, radiating hostility toward the base-born intruder, and Chopin had been well aware of it. The family had petitioned the Tsar for permission to return to Poland and for the restoration of their confiscated fifty-thousand-acre estate. What would his position be if their petition were successful? And how secure a hold had he established on the sixteen-year-old girl's heart? These nominal worries opened some gateway of self-doubt in Chopin, and his health collapsed. Although no one has ever been given tuberculosis by anxiety, this disease has often been released from latency by just the sort of strain that Chopin was now called upon to bear, and blood in his sputum was soon telling him that there was something profoundly wrong with him. When, after keeping his understanding with Maria alive by correspondence for nearly two years, he next met the Wodzinskis, he was still the same elegant and manifestly successful figure externally; his confidence in himself, however, was virtually gone. Maria was still in love with him, and her mother raised no objection to their becoming formally engaged, provided that there was no announcement for the time being. But the hostility of the Palatine was more obvious than ever, and there were rumors in the air that there was soon to be a favorable answer to his petition. After this second visit to the Wodzinskis, Chopin returned to Paris more doubtful than ever. His behavior had bewildered the mother and daughter, who had expected him to be elated by the engagement, and had left them wondering if he really wished to go through with the marriage. The half-hearted and uncertain letters that then came to them from Paris increased their perplexities, and when the news presently reached them that their petition had been granted and that they were free to return to their estates the Palatine had little difficulty in persuading them that Chopin should be dropped. His congé was given him with aristocratic brutality, when he sent a Pleyel piano to the Wodzinskis' estate at Sluzewo as a gift for Maria he was asked to send a bill for the instrument to the Countess. Chopin then became very ill indeed, and his friends exerted themselves to distract him. They did not realize that he was suffering from a real complaint and thought that he could be cured of his distemper by diversions and happiness.

It was when he was in this state, and undoubtedly to amuse him, that Liszt and Marie d'Agoult took George Sand to see him. She fell for the "poor sad angel" at once and hungered for a chance to minister to his weakness and distress. He was utterly repelled: "How unsympathetic she is, that Sand woman! Is she really a woman? I am beginning to doubt it...." Liszt, who had a profoundly religious sense buried in the depths of his worldly personality, could recognize the extent to which Chopin was conventionally Roman Catholic at heart, and Marie D'Agoult, who was fundamentally cold sexually in spite of the warmth of her feeling for Liszt, could see that there was something in him, just as there was in her, that shrank from the mechanical aspects of the act of love. They were partly amused and partly distressed when George showed every sign of falling for a man to whom she could only be disgusting morally and physically, and out of pity they fixed her up with young Mallefille.

George accepted him, but although she was soon to say that she was as good as married to him, she adhered to her determination to get Chopin if she could. She installed Mallefille at Nohant as substitute husband and lived there with him—and Maurice and Solange—in a sort of parody of healthy bourgeois bliss. But every so often she slipped away to Paris, leaving him in charge of the children, to continue her courtship of Chopin.

After nearly a year and a half, in which she had got nowhere, she took the extraordinary step of writing a five-

thousand-word brief in favor of the liaison she was proposing and submitting it to Chopin's friend and confidant,
the Count Albert Gryzmala. In this strange document she
defended the morality of her way of life against the criti-
cisms that a good Catholic might make of it; undertook to
take the best possible care of Chopin's health; and promised
to accept a sexless relationship if that should be what he
really wanted—but she made it clear that she would do her
best to make him change his mind on that issue if his desire
turned out to be based on the idea that there was something
wrong with sexual relationships as such:

> ...is it that some wretched woman has left him with
> this view of physical love? Has he had a mistress who
> was unworthy of him? Poor Angel! I should like to see
> all women hanged who have dirtied in men's eyes the
> thing in life most worthy of respect, the most sacred
> fact in all creation, the divine mystery, the most
> serious of all human actions, and the most sublime in
> the whole universal range of life.

Strangely enough this almost dazzlingly insincere
performance, full of calculation and less than candid
franknesses, had the desired effect. George, who had gone off
to Nohant and Mallefille and left the two friends to talk
over what she called her ultimatum, was summoned back
to Paris in terms that suggested unmistakably that the
liaison was on. When she received the call she packed
Mallefille off to the Channel coast with Maurice and, taking
Solange with her as a blind, went up to town, ostensibly
to stay with a Madame Marliani. But while Solange slept in
that lady's apartment, she did not. She slipped away every
evening to spend the night with Chopin in the Rue Chaussée d'Antin.

What she thought she was doing is not clear: at first
sight the arrangement appears to have been made for reasons of discretion. But Madame Marliani, as George well
knew, already had a reputation as one of the more irresponsible gossips in Paris. Short of putting up fly posters adver-

tising the matter she could hardly have found a more certain way of giving her new affair publicity than by launching it with Madame Marliani's help. Her handling of Mallefille was also a riddle. Although she knew that he had challenged a visitor to Nohant who had seemed too attentive to George to a duel during the winter, she assured Count Gryzmala that there was nothing to be feared from him. "He is so good and so wise that, given time, I shall be able to let him know what has happened...he is wax on which I have set the imprint of my seal, and when I want to change the superscription I shall, if I go carefully and have patience, succeed." At the same time she wrote with a good deal less confidence to her former lover Pierre Leroux, knowing that Mallefille was planning to visit him: "When you get around to talking about women with him, put it to him as directly as you can that men can't make them their own by the use of brute force, and that cutting throats proves nothing." The weaving of such webs of confederacy and deception always creates suspicions, and it was not long before Mallefille, like Pagello before him, found that he was being made to look ridiculous and became furiously angry. He came to Paris and made a scene in the street outside Chopin's apartment in which Gryzmala had to intervene to keep the two lovers from coming to blows. Nothing spreads more rapidly than a piece of gossip that can be given the form of a good story, and this episode was made to order for the anecdotal scandalmongers. When George and Frédéric left Paris for Majorca in October 1838, accompanied by Maurice, Solange, and a woman servant, it was already common knowledge that they were lovers. And Chopin, upset at finding himself in an ambiguous position, was once again having trouble with what he liked to call his chronic bronchitis. His cough was worse than ever, and there were ominous flecks of blood in his sputum.

With all this in its baggage, so to say, George's little group was headed for an ultraconservative community of devout Catholics whose prejudices against sexual irregularities and departures from established convention in general were almost as strong as their superstitious horror of consumption, a sickness looked upon by the islanders as a divine punishment for loose living. A woman of George Sand's reputation, arriving in Majorca with a lover and her estranged husband's children in tow, would not have been given a very warm welcome at the best of times. In 1838 their chances were not improved by the fact that a civil war, with the right-wing conservative followers of Don Carlos on one side and the liberal and anticlerical adherents of Queen Maria-Cristina on the other, was dragging out its dismal course on the Spanish mainland. Palma, the metropolis of Majorca, and indeed the only sizable town on the island, was crowded with Carlist refugees from Catalonia and elsewhere who had been received with more than sympathy by the Majorcans. Since the amount of mystico-socialism and propaganda for freethinking and libertarianism in George's novels had been steadily increasing since the days of her affair with Pierre Leroux, she was, quite simply, one of the enemy and wholly unacceptable to the majority of the upper class in Palma. These were precisely the people by whom she was accustomed to being welcomed and made much of wherever she went, both as "one of us" and as an artist of distinction for whom the rules binding upon ordinary folk should be waived, and she was quite unprepared for dealing with the practical consequences of social ostracism. And while George's behavior and opinions saw to it that there was no place for them in the drawing rooms of Palma, Chopin's state of health meant that they had the greatest difficulty in finding anywhere to sleep. According to Majorcan usages all the bedding, upholstered furniture, and textiles from a house in which a consumptive had lived would have to be burned after his departure, just as all the woodwork and wooden furniture would have to be scrubbed down with vinegar and the walls and ceilings whitewashed or replastered. George's party consequently found themselves being turned away from all normally available furnished accommodations as soon as Chopin's condition was recognized. They presently came to rest in a two-room apartment in a disreputable quarter. It was above the work shop of a barrel-maker, and there was nothing in it beyond a couple of straw-bottomed chairs and some apologies for beds made of boards laid down on trestles.

When the whole group had become throughly demoralized and was on the brink of reaching a decision in favor of going home without more ado, one of George's few well-wishers in the town came to the rescue. He had got hold of a Señor Gomez, who had never heard of George and who knew nothing of Chopin, and had persuaded him to let them have the tenancy of one of his properties, a summer villa called Son Vent out in the countryside to the northeast of Palma. It stood among stone-walled barley fields and olive and almond orchards at the foot of a romantically beautiful range of limestone mountains. Neither George nor Chopin had been in such a remote and tranquilly lovely place before, and as the autumn drew to an end with an unprecedented spell of warm weather they spent three idyllically happy weeks exploring the neighborhood with the two children and watching the eagles soaring above them in an immense transparent sky.

But then, toward the end of November, the rainy season began, and the cold weather set in. The dry gullies running down from the mountains filled with roaring torrents, and everything became wet and damp. There were no fireplaces, and the only way of getting warm was to huddle round the Majorcan charcoal braziers that no one knew how to manage and which filled the rooms with choking fumes. Nothing could have been worse for Chopin, and it soon became obvious that they must move without delay to quarters built for winter occupation. By chance they found what they wanted almost at once in the shape of an apartment in the recently secularized Carthusian monastery at Valdemosa a few miles away at the head of a wild gorge leading up into the mountains. When they had come to terms with the owner of this spectacular retreat they left Son Vent and returned to Palma for four days in which they returned the keys of the summer villa to Señor Gomez, purchased various things they would be needing up at Valdemosa, and consulted the best doctors available as to what should be done for Frédéric's persistent cough.

These four days in Palma were to be a turning point in
Chopin's life. Until then he had been able to deny his illness because no doctor had been straightforward enough to
name it to him. He continued to deny it when the Palma
doctors, whom he affected to despise, had told him that he
had consumption, and went on insisting that his trouble
was bronchitis. But the resonance of what the doctors had
said nonetheless reverberated in his heart. What each of the
three men who had been consulted had told him really
meant that he was dying, and would die sooner rather than
later. The message was brutally reenforced by the actions of
Señor Gomez. The doctors were apparently indiscreet and
word of their findings reached the owner of Son Vent.
Already irritated by the brusque termination of what he had
been led to expect would be a half year's tenancy, he was
now aggrieved. He sued for the value of the household
effects in Son Vent that he felt called upon to destroy and for
the cost of the whitewashing and replastering that Chopin's
passage through his house had made necessary. This sordid
dispute brought it home to Chopin that his condition was
no longer definable in terms of his own feelings about it;
he was forced to admit that he was a dying man in the eyes
of the world.

Son Vent is within easy walking distance of Valdemosa,
and the story of George's dispute with Señor Gomez, and the
reasons for it, must have reached the village at the gates of
the monastic buildings in which her pseudo-family now
took up its abode almost as soon as they got there. George
was thus an object of aversion to the villagers from the very
first, not only because she was an adulteress living openly
with her lover, but also because she was exposing her children to the risk of catching his deadly and, in their view,
loathesome disease. Their feelings about Chopin as a victim
of the disease had another dimension altogether.

Before the group moved to Valdemosa Chopin, who was
intoxicated by the beauty of Majorca, wrote a letter to a
friend in Paris in which he touched lightly and in passing
on an important aspect of the matter:

"In a few days I shall be living in the loveliest spot on

earth: sea, mountains...all one could wish. We are going to live in an old ruined and abandoned Carthusian monastery from which Mendizábal seems to have expelled the monks expressly for my sake...nothing could be more charming: cells, a most poetic cemetry."

Mendizábal had, when he was the Prime Minister and leader of Queen Maria-Cristina's government a few years earlier, persuaded her to allow him to confiscate the church's lands in order to split the Carlist rebels. He knew that if these valuable properties were put on the market at sufficiently tempting prices large numbers of their wealthier supporters would be unable to resist the lure, and would change sides in order to benefit by the opportunity. The dodge worked and large numbers of Carlists sold out. The whole business had been bitterly resented by devout Catholics throughout Spain, nowhere more than in Majorca. For a woman of George Sand's reputation to move into an expropriated church property in her circumstances was a provocation which would almost certainly have had serious consequences had she offered it to any less good-natured and kindly people than the Majorcans. But if her new neighbors did not resort to violence, and to other overt manifestations of their disapproval, they were nonetheless outraged by what she was most conspicuously doing in what was to them a holy place, and they talked about the matter a great deal. It was obvious to them that George, with her cigars and cigarettes, and her outrageous style, was the bad lot, and that Chopin had been led away by her. It seemed to them a terrible thing that she could go on with their affair when he was obviously dying and expose him to the appalling risk of dying in mortal sin.

Some of the village women worked for George as maids and kitchen servants, and they talked these matters over as they did their work and minded the ten-year-old Solange. Solange was a remarkable child, and she still had the privileges that go with the assumption that young girls are innocent. She was the one member of the party who was not considered by the village to be involved in its wickedness, and she had a free relationship with the village children

that some of them could recall as long as sixty years later.
All the evidence suggests that she was the only member of
the group who could speak Mallorquin and consequently
the only one who really knew how it was regarded by the
villagers. George Sand had a smattering of Spanish, but
this was only the official language of the administration
and hardly anyone in the Valdemosa of those days could
have expressed an idea of any complexity in that tongue—
and, if they could it is more than doubtful if George would
have been able to catch it. At Valdemosa Solange simultaneously discovered an area in which her mother was ignorant and powerless—and another in which her mother's
lover could be reached.

The romantic beauty of the spot, the presence of the
monk's cells, the proximity of that "most poetic cemetery,"
and the brutal reminders of his mortality that he had just
received were the preconditions for her success, but when
Solange approached Chopin as the one person she knew who
was likely to be able to tell her what it was all about, to ask
him what the Mallorquin servants meant by the things that
they were saying to her in their well-meant efforts to win the
little infidel round to their faith, she succeeded in reawak-
ening his beliefs by reminding him of their fundamentals.
When she went further and let him know what she had
picked up of the local criticism of his relationship with
George, he abruptly realized the extent to which he had
departed from the path he had chosen to follow as a good
Catholic. He was not living a good Catholic life, and if
he went on as he was doing he would make a bad death. He
would have to change his ways.

What followed is entirely a matter of conjecture, since
nothing is known of the means by which Chopin made
peace with his church. What is certain is that Liszt, who
knew the inner workings of his mind very well indeed,
wrote that "The memories of the days passed on the lovely
island of Majorca, like that of an entrancing ectasy which
fate grants but once in a life time even to her most favored
children, remained perpetually dear to Chopin's heart. He
always spoke of this period with deep emotion, profound

gratitude, as if its joys had sufficed for a lifetime, and without hoping that he could ever again find such felicity." George Sand, however, republished in 1855 a little book called *A Winter in Majorca,* which she had written in 1840 and published a year later. This work describes the visit as a cruel ordeal that nearly killed Chopin, and makes an extraordinarily bitter attack on the Majorcans at large and the Valdemosans in particular, most of the latter being alleged, by a pretty touch, to be illegitimate children of the monks of the charterhouse. Most biographers of George Sand, André Maurois included, have taken this harrowing production as gospel truth, and it has only been lately that Robert Graves and others have thought to compare her account of things with what Chopin had to say about them in his letters from the island. These show that he was delighted with the place and very happy to be there because he was able to work so well. The discrepancy is inexplicable until it is related to the fact that during January 1839 Chopin broke off his sexual relationship with George. It was never to be resumed, and for the next eight years they lived together as brother and sister or, as she sometimes put it, like mother and child. A great deal that is obscure becomes less so when it is remembered that this would have been the only condition on which a confessor or spiritual advisor, if such a person had been controlling Chopin's actions, could have permitted the association to continue. The further point that should be made is that from the beginning of 1839 until the day of his death Chopin was unshakably devoted to Solange, and stood by her through the thick and thin of a tumultuous growing up, until at last, when it came to making a choice between trusting George and trusting her, he took Solange's part and ended the relationship with her mother. The only explanation for this apparent perversity that will hold water is that which has been advanced by Robert Graves, who argues that Chopin felt that his spiritual regeneration had been accomplished during his winter in Majorca and that he believed that Solange had been the agent of his salvation. But all that George could know was that she had suffered an exasperating and incomprehensible defeat.

The years that followed, dominated by the routine of
long family summers at Nohant and social winters in
Paris, are commonly represented as predominantly happy
ones by George Sand's biographers, and, while there was an
enormous amount about them that was to the good, there
has to be something else in the picture to explain the fre-
quency with which she found it necessary to relieve her
pent-up aggression and hostility by plunging into quarrels
with her enemies and friends, and in particular with
Solange. These wars between mother and daughter steadily
increased in their violence and intensity until finally they
reached the point, when Solange had just turned sixteen,
that she was thrown out of the house and sent off to stay
with a certain Marie de Rozières, who had never been quite
right in the head since she had been seduced and dumped
by one of the Wodzinskis. There she remained until George
discovered, or thought she had discovered, that Solange's
custodian was talking to her about *men* and, incredible as
it might seem, interesting her in *sex*. Her reaction was to
snatch up her pen and write a letter, scolding the woman
for her crime, forgiving her, and then suddenly finishing
her off with a grotesquely vulgar insult: "All the same, I
have decided that Solange had better not see quite so much
of you—until this little nervous trouble of yours is over, and
you have taken either a lover or a husband *ad libitum.*

Chopin was the only member of the household who
passed unscathed through it all, in spite of his moodiness,
his patrician contempt for her bohemian and socialist
friends, and his jealousy of her children. But there were
things going on in her mind, and presently she began writing a novel called *Lucrezia Floriani* at him. Lucrezia was a
beautiful Italian actress who managed to combine a virginal
purity with an industrious promiscuity by a number of
semantic devices that are not altogether convincing. In her
middle years, at a time when she has reached the conclusion
that her sensuous life is over, she meets a sickly young man
with the beauty of a melancholy woman. He is called Prince
Karol, and she falls in love with him because he is so frail
and so charming. They become lovers, and at first it is en-

tirely marvelous. But then she discovers, little by little, that
he is not quite the man she thought. He believes that virtue
is abstention from sin, and he is without charity. He is
willing to give the poor alms, but he cannot think of them
as his equals and has no wish to associate with them. He
does not believe that social reforms can make a heaven on
earth. And worst of all, he does not lose his temper when he
is angry:

> *It was at these moments that he was truly insupport-*
> *able, because it was then that he tried to argue, to force*
> *real life—which he had never begun to understand—*
> *into the mold of principles which he was incapable of*
> *defining. The mood bred in him a false and brilliant*
> *wit, and with this he tormented those who loved him.*
> *He assumed the airs of a mocker and a prig. He became*
> *mannered. He affected to view everything and every-*
> *body with disgust. It was as though he were indulging*
> *in a game of wild biting for his own amusement, but*
> *the wounds he made went very deep. When he lacked*
> *the courage to contradict and jeer, he took refuge in*
> *disdainful silences and fits of heartbreaking sulkiness.*

Life with such a man is naturally unpleasant, and it is
far too much for Lucrezia. She loses her looks, wastes away,
and when she at last realizes that the odious Prince Karol
despises her, gives up and dies.

While writing this astonishing attack on the man with
whom she was sharing her life, George was widening the
front of her psychological warfare upon Solange by adopting
a substitute daughter who had been dredged up from the un-
savory world of Sophie-Victoire's origins. She was the pretty
child of a prostitute called Adèle Brault, and George inter-
vened in her affairs just as her mother was about to realize
the cash value of her virginity by, in effect, selling her to
a brothel-keeper. This was a usual beginning for a career in
the trade, and its unpleasant possibilities were much increased by the prevalence of a species of clubman's super-
stition that intercourse with a virgin was a cure for syphilis.
George Sand was at her kind-hearted best when she paid

Adèle Brault something a little better than the going price for the girl and took her into her home. But she was at her compulsive worst when she began calling Augustine Brault her "real daughter" and lavishing upon her all the love and affection that Solange felt had been denied her ever since she was born. The tension between the two young girls mounted steadily throughout the long hot summer of 1846 as George worked away at *Lucrezia Floriani* and bickered with Chopin, at first over such little things as the firing of a dishonest gardener and then over larger matters. Chopin's feeling was that since the gardener had been stealing (as estate gardeners almost invariably did in the loosely organized world of the land owning gentry) for over twenty years, it was too late to fire him. But George was merciless in her defense of bourgeois rectitudes when it came to this sort of thing, and would not give way. Though the point at issue was a small one, it showed significantly how the "brother and sister" were drawing apart in the matter of social identifications, which were to become all important in the autumn when Maurice and Solange both became engaged.

Solange agreed to marry a neighbor. George had to admit that Fernand de Préaulx was, in her phrase, "as beautiful as an antique statue," but beyond that she was derisive. She told one correspondent that:

> *His intelligence is not very apparent, especially when it comes to talking...he certainly will not set the Seine on fire. He knows nothing of our modern civilization. He has spent his life in the backwoods with horses, wild boars, and wolves, whose heads he cracks with his whip handle.*

and wrote to another to say:

> *I confess it had never occurred to me that my son-in-law would be an aristocrat, a royalist, and a hunter of wild boars. But life is full of surprises.*

But to Chopin it seemed altogether right that the daughter of the Baron Dudevant should marry a man of her class, and he gave the match his whole-hearted approval. His feelings were, however, altogether different when he learned that Maurice was planning to marry Augustine Brault. But before he could give full expression to his views on the subject Maurice had jilted the girl. Maurice proposed to her, and having been accepted, went off to Guillery to tell his father what he had done. If George Sand is to be believed, he next wrote to Nohant, with the unthinking cruelty of the very young, to say that "my father does not much care for the idea, and he could be right." When he returned to his mother's house the atmosphere was charged with electricity, less because he had broken off the engagement than because in the course of the agitated discussions of it that had been taking place in his absence Solange had seen fit to tell Chopin that Maurice had seduced Augustine and made her his mistress during the summer. Chopin managed to be furiously angry with them both—with the girl for having been weak enough to give in and with Maurice for having taken advantage of a girl five years his junior who was under his mother's protection. As soon as the opportunity arose he lit into him in a cold fury, and said things that made the younger man threaten to leave the house for as long as he should remain within it. George managed to patch things up between them for the time being, and the appearance of harmony had been restored when Chopin left Nohant for Paris in November. But he was never to return.

Substantially the relationship between George Sand and Chopin had ended when she saw him assuming the role of a father with her beloved son in the matter of Augustine's seduction. But it remained to find some way of terminating it that would give her either the appearance or the reality of some kind of victory over the man who seemed in the world's eyes to be her lover. In the course of the row about Maurice's relationship with Augustine it had become apparent to her, perhaps for the first time, that there was some kind of confederacy between the pianist and her daughter. It must have struck her that she could obtain what she wanted by breaking that up and demonstrating that the center of power in her family lay with herself, not with the intruder. What better way of doing these things could she find than that of getting Solange to break off her engagement to the booby who had won Chopin's approval, and married to someone from her own world?

Her mind turned to Auguste Clésinger, a ferociously good-looking former cavalryman turned sculptor with a dashing manner who could be relied upon to teach Solange what passion was. When she took her eighteen-year-old daughter to Paris in February 1847, ostensibly to order her trousseau, it was to meet Clésinger. He did a portrait bust of her as a bacchante, and the necessity of going to his studio for numerous sittings made it easy for him to seduce her. The day before the marriage contracts were due to be signed she broke off her engagement to the Vicomte de Préaulx. Though George now learned that Clésinger was a drunkard and heavily in debt, and that he had an ugly reputation as an ill-tempered brute, she did everything she could to hurry on his marriage to her daughter, always to the tune of "not a word of this to Chopin; it does not concern him." And on May 20, four months after their first meeting, Solange and Clésinger became man and wife.

The announcements that preceded this coup were characteristic of the woman, since they not only served their ostensible purpose of summoning the guests to the wedding, but also added a little something to the process of the formal annihilation of the still-hated Casimir. Monsieur le Baron Dudevant had, they made it appear, nothing whatever to do with the event: *"Madame George Sand a l'honneur de vous faire part du mariage de Mademoiselle Solange Sand, sa fille, avec Monsieur Clésinger...."* And, in a letter to a friend written the day after she had brought it off, she mentioned his presence as a measure of the extremities to which she had been willing to go: "Never was a marriage carried through with such determination and promptitude. Monsieur Dudevant spent three days under my roof.... Now it is all over and done with, and we can breathe freely." The thing had been accomplished, and Chopin still knew nothing of it. She decided to let this other superfluous and unnecessary male know how completely he had been dispensed with by indirection, and wrote his sister a chatty letter that disclosed that the one marriage had only been the preliminary for another: "I've neither paper, nor pen, nor time. I don't know what to turn to next. I've so many things to do, because I'm marrying my adopted daughter next week, and I'm scarcely done with all the fuss and bother of the last marriage."

That something had been going on in the background of their wedding had become evident to Solange and Clésinger while they were at Nohant, but they had not been able to figure out what. Throwing their suspicions to and fro between them on the honeymoon they reached the conclusion that it was a matter that they shouldn't ignore, and they hurried back to face George with a demand for explanations. They found that all through April and May George Sand had been promoting a marriage between Augustine Brault and Maurice Sand's friend, the painter Théodore Rousseau. The deal had been clinched during the week before Solange's wedding by the offer to the debt-ridden but up-and-coming artist of a dowry of a hundred thousand francs—a far more substantial wedding settlement than George had been willing to give to her own daughter.

The psychology of her readiness to do more for the prostitute's child she had arbitrarily brought into her life than for Solange is as transparent as that of the attack of hysterical paralysis of the legs which had afflicted her on the morning of her child's wedding and made it necessary for her to be carried to the church of Nohant-Vicq to attend the ceremony. Solange interpreted it as the act of aggression that it undoubtedly was, and she hit back by telling Théodore Rousseau a few things she felt he ought to know: about his fiancée's background, her affair with Maurice, and a more recent entanglement with Clésinger's younger brother, who had refused to marry her.

For Rousseau to marry his friend's adoptive sister was

one thing, but marrying his discarded mistress when she was on the rebound from an affair with another man—that was quite another story. Beside, Adèle Brault did not impress him as a desirable connection. Feeling, with some justice, that he had been sold a bill of goods, he began to back out. Certainly, he admitted, Augustine was attractive enough (he had been attracted by her), but marriage—marriage was an important step—and when it came to choosing a wife...

George hit the roof. Did Rousseau imagine for a moment that she had raised and cherished her adopted daughter in order to provide one of her son's friends with a mistress? What sort of abominable slanders had he been listening to? She could tell him that the girl was an angelic creature who had in her nobility of spirit refused to marry her son because she did not believe that he could give her the love to which she felt entitled. She could tell him, too, that she was beginning to wonder if he was quite sane—he seemed to be afflicted with emotional hallucinations. Overwhelmed by the pressure that was being put on him, Rousseau decamped.

The situation then passed rapidly out of George's control: Maurice, having learned that Rousseau had gone without saying good-bye to him, received an explanation for his departure from a weeping Augustine, who told him that her Théodore's mind had been poisoned against her by Clésinger. Maurice went to have the matter out with his brother-in-law. Voices were raised. George came on the scene, and with her hysterical support Maurice became insulting. The cavalryman snatched up a hammer, if one is to believe George's account of the incident, and was only restrained from killing Maurice with it by her quick-wittedness in throwing herself between them and slapping his face. According to her he then struck her on the chest, but it seems more likely that he brushed her aside in order to leave the room. But, whatever may or may not have brought this sordid exchange to an end, its sequel was that Solange and Clésinger, after packing up a few things from her room that she thought of as her personal possessions, cleared out and went to Paris. To one correspondent George described them as going off "laden with booty like highwaymen," and she used even stronger language in a letter to Marie de Rozières (who had been back in her good books for some time):

> *The diabolical couple took themselves off yesterday evening, crippled with debts, glorying in their impudence, and leaving behind them a scandal, the effects of which they will never be able to live down....* *I never want to see them again. They will never cross my doorstep. This is the end! Dear God, what have I done to deserve such a daughter?*

A new dimension was added to her fury when she learned that Solange had turned to Chopin for moral support and had told him the whole story of her marriage and its grotesque sequel. The pianist (who had, in spite of George's communication to his sister, known nothing of the matter until the Clésingers presented themselves to him as man and wife) was appalled to learn how completely George had excluded him from the life of what he still thought of as his family. But, recognizing the seriousness of the situation and the undesirability of a complete breach between George and her daughter, he wrote her a letter such as he might have written if nothing had changed. What it contained there is no way of knowing, as George later destroyed all that he had written to her that might conflict with what she wished to have believed about the relationship, but her angry comments on it suggest that he made the mistake of saying that there was probably something to be said on both sides and that it would be better to make up the quarrel rather than take up absolute positions that would make a later reconciliation difficult and perhaps impossible.

> *...sick as I was, I was about to go [to Paris] to see why I hadn't heard a word. And then I had a letter in the morning post from Chopin. I saw that, as usual, my*

soft heart had made a fool of me, and that while I'd been spending six sleepless nights worrying about his health, he'd been passing the time tearing me to pieces with the Clésingers... his letter is laughably pompous, and his sermon in the style of a good-hearted family man would, indeed, serve me as a model... there are a great many things in back of all this, and I know what my daughter is capable of in the way of slander, just as I know how Chopin's poor old brain is when it comes to jumping to conclusions and credulity.... But my eyes have been opened, and I'll act according- ly.... I'm amazed that Chopin should go on seeing and supporting this Clésinger, who struck me because I tore the hammer he'd raised against Maurice out of his hands, Chopin, the man the whole world was telling me was my most faithful and devoted friend. It's astonishing! Life is a bitter worry, my child, and those who are naive enough to love and trust can count on ending up with a hollow laugh and a despairing sob.

Having fired this off at Marie de Rozières, who had also been guilty of speaking up for Solange and saying that she was not quite as wicked as all that, George settled down to hit Chopin as hard as she could. There are those who contend that her farewell to him is a dignified and even noble document; but Delacroix, to whom he read it and who knew them both as well as anyone, was not favorably impressed:

One must admit that she is atrocious. Cruel passion and a long-repressed impatience come out in it; and by contrast (which would be amusing if the subject were not so sad) the writer usurps the place of the woman and lets herself go in tirades which seem to have been borrowed from a novel or a philosophical homily.

The cruel passion and the impatience were directed at Solange as much as at Chopin:

As for my daughter—she has the bad taste to say that she needs the love of a mother whom, in fact, she hates

*and slanders, whose most sacred actions she befouls,
and whose house she fills with her own atrocious talk!
You have allowed yourself to lend her a willing ear—
and perhaps you even do believe what she tells you.
I won't argue the point—it fills me with horror to even
think of it. I would rather see you go over to the enemy
than take up arms against that same enemy who was
born from my body and nourished at my breast.*

George brooded over all this through what remained
of the summer and the early autumn, until in November
she felt able to put something close to her final version
of the end of her affair with Chopin on paper for the benefit of Madame Marliani and posterity:

*Chopin has taken Solange's side against me, and that
without knowing the truth, a thing that speaks of
ingratitude to me and of a crazy infatuation for her.
Please act as if you knew nothing about it. He has
changed so much that I can only take it that she has
worked on his jealous and suspicious nature, and that
it is by her and her husband that this absurd slander
has been spread about concerning a love affair, or an
exclusive friendship, on my part, involving the young
man you mentioned [Victor Borie]. That's the only
explanation for such a ridiculous story that comes to
me. I've no wish to get to the bottom of this particular
piece of trivial nastiness.*

*I don't mind telling you that I'm a long way from
regretting that he should have decided to relieve me
of the burden of managing his life. He and his friends
were beginning to put much too much responsibility
on my shoulders. He was getting more and more embittered as time went on, and it had got to the point where
he was making scenes in front of my children, and my
friends. Solange turned him to her own account with
the low cunning that is natural to her, and Maurice
was beginning to lose patience with him. He knew,
from the evidence of his own eyes, how chaste our
relationship was, but he couldn't help seeing, too,
how the poor invalid behaved as though he were my
lover, my husband, and the master of my every ac-*

> *tion—without wishing to, and perhaps without being*
> *able to help himself. Maurice was on the point of fac-*
> *ing up to him and telling him that he was making*
> *me—a woman of forty-three—ridiculous, and that he*
> *was taking advantage of my goodness of heart.*

By December she was quite openly living with Victor
Borie, a young socialist journalist she had met through
Pierre Leroux, and she was hard at work on the ten-volume
Histoire de ma vie that she had contracted with her pub-
lishers to finish within a twelvemonth. As this extraordinary mixture of half-truths, exaggerations, distortions,
outright lies, and occasional lapses into honesty poured
from her pen, the winter passed away, and it was spring
almost before she knew it. At the beginning of March she
found herself facing Chopin on the threshold of Madame
Marliani's apartment. Mildly and gently he asked her if
she had recently had any news of Solange. "I heard from
her a week ago," she said defensively. "Not yesterday, or
the day before?" he asked. "No." "Then I am happy to be
able to tell you that you are a grandmother. Solange has
had a daughter, and I am delighted to think that I am the
first to inform you of the fact." They exchanged a few more
words about the young mother's health, all of them confirming the fact that she had turned to him and not to George
at this important moment in her life, and then parted forever.

It is difficult to say how George would have reacted to
this humiliating termination to her connection with Chopin if she had been left to brood over it without distraction.
But France was at that moment on the brink of a revolutionary upheaval, and she was able to evade contemplation of
the mess her personal life had become by plunging into
politics. At first it was all the greatest possible fun, since
the collapse of the monarchy had been brought about by its
own defects rather than by the efforts of an organized opposition prepared to take over the state machinery. There
was an interregnum, between the time of the disappearance
of the power of the crown and the appearance of aligned

forces capable of producing a substitute for it, a void filled
in by a carnival of playacting and posturing in which the
political bohemians of the left pretended to be carrying
through a socialist revolution. By virtue of her connections
with her former lovers Pierre Leroux and Michel de Bourges,
and with Victor Borie, and with such leaders of the revolutionary movement as Louis Blanc and Ledru-Rollin,
George Sand was able to get into the thick of it, and to fancy
that she was playing a leading role in the comedy. She believed that she had earned her position at the heart of things
by backing a left-wing periodical called *La Revue indépen-
dante* as a vehicle for Pierre Leroux, and when Ledru-Rollin
appointed her to the post of editor of the *Bulletin de la ré-
publique* she took it as no more than her due rather than as
a measure of his complete inability to come to terms with
reality. She was delighted to find herself up to her ears
in work for which she possessed no qualifications whatever, and three weeks after her last meeting with Chopin
she was writing jubilantly about the fun she was having
to Maurice, who had been installed as the republican mayor
of Nohant:

> Here I am, doing the work of a statesman. I have just
> drawn up two government circulars, one for the Min-
> istry of Education and the other for the Ministry of
> the Interior. It amuses me to think that they will go
> out addressed to "All Mayors," and that you will be
> getting instructions from your mother through official
> channels. Ho-ho, Monsieur le Maire, you had better
> step carefully, and begin by reading out one of the
> Bulletins of the Republic to your assembled National
> Guard at Sunday parades.... I don't know whether
> I'm coming or going. There's somebody after me all
> the time. But this kind of life suits me.

She was not wholly without political acumen, and by
the time she had got to Bulletin Number Sixteen she had
become aware that, although the revolutionaries had
succeeded in taking control of the machinery of the government because no one else had been ready to do so, they

had no backing to speak of outside Paris or among its masses. It was in effect a revolt of the intelligentsia acting in isolation from both the upper and lower classes, and without more than partial support of the middle class. George Sand saw all this and concluded rightly that the revolutionaries would certainly be defeated in the elections that they were committed to hold. She accordingly began to think along these lines: "The ideal expression of the sovereignty of the people is not *majority* but *unanimity*... there are times when unanimity is arrived at in the face of heaven, and mere majority, in comparison with it, counts as nothing...." Such glib sophistries finally found their way into Bulletin Number Sixteen and were distributed throughout France:

> *If these elections do not assure the triumph of social truth, if they express only the interests of a caste, and if the trusting loyalty of the people is deceived by violence, then there is no doubt that they will sound the death knell of the Republic instead of being its salvation. Should that happen there can be but one road to safety for those who have already built the barricades, and that will be for them to make it known for a second time that it is their will that the decisions of a false national representation shall be annulled. Does France wish to force Paris to resort to such an extreme, such a deplorable remedy?*

To clear the ground for precisely what she was proposing the left-wingers attempted to expel the moderates from the revolutionary administration in mid-April. They failed because the National Guard, supported by the mass of the middle and working classes in Paris, took to the streets against them to the cry of "Long live the Republic and Death to the Communists!" George hastened to explain what had really happened, and what it really meant, to Maurice; if the plot had succeeded, she told him, it might

> *have saved the Republic by proclaiming an immediate reduction in the poor man's taxes, and by introducing*

*measures that would have brought the country out of
its financial crisis without bringing ruin to those
whose fortunes were honestly acquired. Success would
also have made it possible to change the electoral laws,
which are bad as they stand because they can only
produce parish pump elections, in short to do everything possible to rally the People to the Republic with
which they are already disgusted as the result of bourgeois machinations, and to give us a National Assembly which would not have found it necessary to employ
force.*

It is an indication of the extent of George's political
naïveté that she was really capable of believing that a
revolutionary government faced with the problem of a
constituency averse to violence and eager for reform, and
without the support of the armed forces, could have solved
it by expelling its moderates. That it had made the effort
was in itself fatal to it, and the election results were even
worse than its supporters had expected them to be. The
majority in the new National Assembly was well to the
right of center. George's friends rose to their ultimate folly
in the face of this situation, and tried to rally popular
support to their side by calling for a war with Russia in
defense of Polish freedom. Their supporters attempted to
rush the National Assembly building on May 15 to cries
of "Long live the Republic!" and "Long live Poland!" But
the National Guard turned out. The Government's supporters bolted in a panic, and the whole country was given
convincing proof of its weakness and futility. A little later,
in June, it was put out, and the carnival of unreality came
to an end amid massacres and deportations. But by then
George Sand was well out of the way, lying low in lodgings
in Tours.

She was not having a particularly agreeable time. At the
end of 1847 her friend Victor Borie had found a husband
for Augustine Brault, a thirty-six-year-old Polish exile
called Karol de Bertholdi who was scratching out a living
as a drawing master in the town of Tulle. George had put
up a dowry of thirty thousand francs (she had embarked

on the *Histoire de ma vie* to raise the sum), but she had
been too busy with her political affairs to attend the nineteen-year-old girl's wedding when it took place on May 6.
Augustine was disgruntled at finding herself married off,
after having been given much greater expectations, to a
man she looked upon as an elderly mediocrity, and her
feelings were not improved by the fact that it was Maurice,
in his capacity as mayor, who officiated at the ceremony
and pronounced them man and wife. Whether or no she
communicated something of her feelings directly to her
legal father, the tailor who was married to Adèle Brault,
a version of the story of the marriage reached him that
led him to write and publish a pamphlet entitled *One of
Our Contemporaries—The Life Story and Schemes of George
Sand.* This accused George of having procured Augustine
to serve as Maurice's concubine, and of marrying her off
to the first comer once she was done with. George got some
satisfaction out of shutting Brault's mouth on further
slanders that he was planning to circulate—but none from
hearing that Chopin knew of the libelous pamphlet and was
confirming its essentials: "The father has behaved disgracefully, but his story is no more than the plain truth. So much
for that 'act of charity' which I condemned as forcefully
as I could from the moment that young woman entered the
house." Her rejoinder was to say that anything coming
from him could be disregarded as the utterance "of a sick
child who has become bitter and unbalanced."

By the time this ugly business had been straightened
out George had taken advantage of the lessening of political tensions to return to Nohant, but things did not immediately improve for her. She was upset by the deaths
of the man who was Solange's actual father, the Vicomte
de Grandsagne, and of Marie Dorval, who had been overwhelmed by failure and poverty after Jules Sandeau had
left her in order to marry a rich wife. There were bickerings
with Maurice about a marriage project of which she disapproved, and an unwise proposal for a reconciliation
coming from Marie d'Agoult, with whom she had not been
on speaking terms for over ten years, only led to a flareup

of old resentments and a renewal of the original quarrel. And beyond all that the Clésingers were a continuous source of worry and annoyances. They had mortgaged the Hôtel de Narbonne, the house in Paris that had formed part of George's inheritance, and which had been given to Solange as her dowry, and had lost it when they proved unable to meet the interest payments. The bloom was off their original physical interest in each other, and they were fighting like cats and dogs. What was particularly galling about this was that it had been Chopin who had warned her of Clésinger's evil reputation when the cavalryman had first come on the scene. He was now drinking heavily, spending money as fast as he could get hold of it, and getting into one scrape after another. From time to time Solange left him, and the crowd of process servers and bailiff's men who surrounded him, to take refuge with the patient and gentle Casimir at Guillery; but then there would be a reconciliation and the pair would be back together in Paris living more extravagantly than ever. George followed their affairs as closely as she could in order to keep her hatred of them alive, and so learned, almost as soon as she had the news of Chopin's death, in October 1849, that Solange had been sent for and had been with him at the end.

In the following year two things happened that took the relationship a stage further. The self-reliant and active Victor Borie—on his way away from his left-wing past and on toward the Directorship in a thriving banking business and the twenty-five thousand francs a year that was waiting for him ahead—dropped out of George's life and was replaced by another of her lover-children, Alexandre Manceau, an engraver friend of Maurice's with a weak chest and poor physique who was thirteen years her junior. At about the same time Solange took her first overt step in the direction of prostitution by putting herself under the protection of the Count Alfred d'Orsay. He was a rich and politically powerful member of a small group of men who were behind Louis Buonaparte, the nephew of the Emperor Napoleon who had been brought to the Presidency of the Republic by the continuing drift to the right which had

begun in 1848. Since d'Orsay had a conscientious conception of his role as Solange's protector which embraced
adopting a measure of responsibility for the well-being
of her mother, George was now relieved of all fear that
she might be arrested and deported as a prominent member
of the left. Her fury at finding herself under an obligation
to her daughter probably lies behind the following awful
warning, of March 1851, addressed to Maurice:

> *I don't like the idea of your eating with those people....*
> *Clésinger is as mad as can be. Solange is without any*
> *natural feelings. The pair of them are both so utterly*
> *amoral...that there's no knowing what they might*
> *not do in certain circumstances.... It would be very*
> *much in their interest if you were to cease to exist,*
> *and with them interest is everything. Solange has*
> *always been eaten up with jealousy...you must act*
> *with extreme caution. Once again I say,* do not eat or
> drink at their table.... *Burn this letter but memorize*
> *its contents.*

Those who are unfamiliar with the mechanics of games
will assume that the state of feeling revealed by this letter
would make it impossible that George should have had
anything more to do with Solange for a considerable time.
But those who have looked into the matter will realize
that two games-players who were so responsive to each
other's gambits, and who could get such predictably satisfactory results in the way of license for outbursts of hostility and aggression, would have been unable to stay away
from each other for very long. The mother had to have the
daughter on hand to make her feel the denial of love and
affection that she felt that she had been denied by Sophie-
Victoire, and the mirror image of the same necessity pulled
the daughter toward the mother to meet with the inevitable
refusal of what she considered to be her emotional birth-
right. Their need for each other brought them together
again within two months of the time at which this extraordinary warning was put on paper, and at the end of February 1851 George was writing to Augustine de Bertholdi

to tell her that Solange had been staying with her at Nohant. Solange had, she said, "come with the intention of being agreeable, and agreeable she was in an artificial sort of way, like a great lady without a heart. That is all I can tell you: for what the purpose of her visit was, or what she hoped to get out of it, is beyond the ingenuity of mortal man to discover." After running her daughter down for another four or five hundred words she went on to say: "She writes me letters full of the most pretentious expressions of affection. I've decided on the best line to take in all this, and I'm sticking to it. I'm no longer angry, miserable, or deluded. I'm quite calmly facing the facts of the situation, and they are not likely to change...." Time passed by, and, at the beginning of December, on the eve of the coup d'etat that made Louis Buonaparte dictator and a year later Emperor of the French, George, Manceau, and Solange made up a little family party and went to the circus together.

The coup d'etat had a curious effect on the relationship because it placed George more than ever under an obligation to Solange. It was the culmination of France's drift to the right, and the Buonapartists consolidated their seizure of power by a savage repression of the left that was designed to break the opposition once and for all. Thanks to Solange's position as d'Orsay's protegée George had complete immunity from the persecution and harassment that drove many of her friends into exile and put others behind bars. Thanks to d'Orsay's political astuteness she soon found herself in a relation to the regime that made it possible for her to render it an important service without either recognizing the fact or making any apparent sacrifice of her integrity. D'Orsay recognized that she was completely harmless as a socialist ideologue because she understood nothing about either politics or power and had no influence whatever on the working classes. He further saw that by leaving her alone the regime could get credit for its tolerance and liberalism with her section of the reading public. She thus became one of those "outspoken" opponents that dictators like to have around as walking advertisements for their ability to respect the virtues of honesty, goodheartedness, and so on wherever they may be found. D'Orsay saw to it that the regime's "good" socialist had access to the Prince President and the Ministries and that a high percentage of the petitions on behalf of detainees and deportees—and in some cases of people in more serious trouble—should be successful. When she saved four young soldiers from a firing squad by taking up their case she obtained a good deal of publicity. Her socialist friends warned her that she was being used in a skillfully managed public relations campaign by which the regime, having broken all resistance by terrorism, was now demonstrating that it could be merciful and responsive, if nicely approached by nice people, but she would have none of it. Would her friends have had her stand by while those four young men were shot? The argument, while not answerable from the long-term point of view, is almost impossible for a normal person to reject when real people are being sent to face real firing squads, and, humanly speaking, George was in the right when she followed a line of conduct that earned her such titles as *The Saint of Le Berry*, and *Our Lady of Succor*. But when her daughter, to whom she owed the whole of her ability to function in this field, turned to her for support and reassurance when her marriage with Clésinger finally broke up in 1852, it turned out that this public performance had exhausted all her reserves of kindness, and even of common decency. Not that Solange, as a committed and ritualistic games-player, had failed to supply ample grounds for her rejection. Having written her mother a letter to tell her that, her life with Clésinger having become insupportable, she had run away from him and had taken refuge from his threats and violence within the walls of a convent, she went on to say that she found it worse than dull being there:

> *Having to live in this isolation, with the sound and movement of life all around me—people laughing together, horses galloping, children playing in the sunshine, lovers being happy—it's not so much a matter of being bored as of being made to despair.*

People wonder how it is that girls without minds of
their own or any sort of education allow themselves
to drift into a life of pleasure and vice! Can even
women with judgment and warm affections be sure
of being able to steer clear of all that...?

George, or perhaps one should say George's unconscious,
read this as a threat, interpreting it to mean "If you don't
give me everything I want I'll become a prostitute." It made
her explode into a fury in which she produced, virtually
by return post, one of the most memorable rockets that
has ever been written by virtue of the unique challenge
it contains. George warmed up to this by brusquely de-
molishing her daughter's claims to sympathy:

*I spent many of the best years of my own youth living
in what you call "isolation" working hard between
four dirty walls, and let me tell you that, though I
regret a great deal, I don't regret that.... It may be
that your husband does not wholly deserve to be so
bitterly disliked or so impulsively put aside.... In
my view it is not very pretty of you to complain of the
immediate consequences of a resolution which you
took entirely of your own accord. The only thing which
will console you is money...and a great deal of it... I
could only give you what you need by working twice
as hard as I do now, and if I did that I'd be dead in
six months, since even my present program is beyond
my strength—besides, even if I could work twice as
hard and keep at it for a few more years, what is there
to say that it's my duty to turn myself into a galley
slave or a complete hack merely to supply you with
money to burn? What I can give you, you shall have.
You can treat this house as your home, on the sole
condition that you don't upset everybody with your
idiotic behavior, or drive them to distraction with
your ill-natured ways.... What I will not do is to
pretend to sympathize with the difficulties and pri-
vations that you will have to endure in Paris.*

Having thus cleared the ground George got down to her

real business of responding to the challenge that had been put to her:

> So you find it difficult, do you, being lonely and poor, not to step into a life of vice.... It's all you can do to endure being cooped up within four walls while women are laughing and horses are galloping outside? "What a horrible fate!" as Maurice would say.... All right then, just try a little vice... just try being a whore. I don't think you would make much of a success of it...a woman has got to be a great deal more beautiful and more intelligent than you are before she can hope to be pursued, or even sought out by men who are eager and anxious to pay for her favors...men with money to spend want women who know how to earn it.

Having gone this far, and having ingeniously found a socially acceptable way of saying "Go ahead—see if I care," George made her challenge irresistible by adding a rider showing that she would feel that it would be in some degree a reflexion upon herself if her daughter did in fact follow in the footsteps of Marie Rinteau and Sophie-Victoire Delaborde:

> I have known young women who have fought down the impulses of heart and body, scared to death that domestic unhappiness might trick them into giving in to the mad impulse of a moment, but I've never known a single one of them, brought up as you have been in an atmosphere of personal dignity and moral freedom, who has dreaded unhappiness and isolation because of such dangers as you talk of.

Here, again, the naive observer would expect a complete breach, but in fact the two women spent most of the following year and a half in a close collaboration for the purpose of keeping Solange's small daughter out of Clésinger's hands. They managed to hold onto this unlucky creature until Clésinger got a court order committing her to the neutral care of a boarding school. He had got the drop on his wife by seizing a number of letters addressed to her by a Piedmontese gentleman, the Count Carlo Alfieri, which left no doubt that their connection was a sexual one, and was vindictively exploiting the opportunity given to him of coming to the courts as the wronged spouse. Worn down by frustrations and worries, Solange turned to the Church for comfort and actually went so far as to make a retreat under the direction of her spiritual advisor, Father de Ravignan. (Interestingly enough for the light it throws on the strength of the conventional French sense of family and family obligation, she was recommended to him by Gaston de Villeneuve, a grandson of a Comtesse de Villeneuve who had tried to rescue George from the clutches and the evil influence of Sophie-Victoire when she was eighteen, and who had been a child of Claude Dupin de Franceuil's first marriage.) Under Father de Ravignan's influence Solange began to utter noises of a pious nature: "My child can only be restored to me by a miracle. God can bring such things about, but what have I ever done that he should work one for my benefit?" Superb games-player that George was, she could not let this opportunity pass: "If your piety is genuine, now is the time to make peace with Augustine." Solange kissed that rod and was ill rewarded for it. She was first lifted up when, either in answer to her prayers or in response to the wire-pulling done by her powerful friends with influence in the Ministry of Justice, the court adjudicating the terms on which her marriage was to be dissolved gave her custody of the child. This ruling was handed down in mid-December, and it filled the mother and daughter with delighted thoughts of having her back at Nohant for the Christmas holidays. But Clésinger's lawyer, acting on the instructions of his bloody-minded client, dashed their hopes by applying for a stay of judgment pending an appeal against the decision. Jeanne Clésinger was still in the boarding school in mid-January when she caught scarlet fever and died. Utterly cast down Solange took to her bed, and, while she lay there in a stupor of grief, George sat down and began to write a long essay: *After the Death of Jeanne Clésinger.*

When the spring came, the household at Nohant broke up.
George, accompanied by Maurice, Manceau, and her man
of business Emil Aucarte, went off on a trip to Italy, and
Solange went up to Paris to launch herself on her new career as a prostitute.

Ironically enough, when George returned from Italy she
found that her adopted daughter Augustine, whose good
looks had improved with maturity, was thinking of doing
the same thing. Tired to death of the life in the provinces
to which she was condemned by her marriage to the insignificant de Bertholdi, she asked her foster mother to in-
troduce her to the Emperor's nephew, the Prince Napoleon,
whose womanizing was notorious. George saw what she
would be at but took the suggestion with a large degree
of calm, perhaps because her mothering instinct was now
focused on another young girl, a certain Marie Cailland,
a Nohant-Vicq girl who had originally been hired to look
after the hens; she had subsequently been made a sort of
family pet on the strength of her good looks and her talent
for the amateur theatricals that had played more and more
important a part in the Nohant routine ever since the original flareup between Solange and her mother over Augustine's marriage to Rousseau. When calming herself down
on that occasion George had been inspired to knock down
the wall dividing Solange's old bedroom from the adjoining
apartment in order to make a private theater for Maurice....
But for whatever reason she turned Augustine down without giving her any kind of tongue lashing:

> I don't want to introduce you to the Prince. It wouldn't
> suit me at all to put a pretty woman with favors to
> ask in his way...and don't expect me to give you a
> letter to him, either. It wouldn't be at all suitable for
> me to be sending a young and pretty woman to have
> an audience with a man who is all too fond of sex. I
> have no wish to do any procuring.... Maurice is still
> with us.... He sends you his love, as does Manceau.

Between the mother and the real daughter there was

a truce of sorts. Solange was successful in her new profession and keeping her mother posted on the more amusing aspects of the good time she was having. Her mother responded with restraint:

> I'd like to be able to laugh at the fantastic travel adventures that you tell me of with such relish. But I can't help feeling that there may be a great deal of sadness and difficulty lying in wait behind all your gaiety...do at least keep me informed of your whereabouts, and when you're tired of your never ending search for amusement—come here and be bored. At least it will give you a chance to catch your breath.

She renewed this invitation of midsummer in the autumn, pressing Solange to winter with her, but making the proviso that if she did come she wasn't to bring her saddle horses with her. Solange, realizing that she was being invited to take part in another round of the mother-daughter game, replied in a way designed to show George that while she was still in form she wasn't going to play: she had won their last set by calling her mother's call of her bluff and actually becoming a prostitute, and she had no intention of coming back into the game until she had got to the very top of the tree and proved that she did *so* know how to please men:

> I frankly confess that Le Berry—explored on foot—has lost a good deal of its charm for me. Unhappily, I'm only twenty-seven, and, though I'm often out of sorts, my blood still flows too fast, and my nerves are still too young to make it possible for me to spend an entire winter doing wool work, playing the piano, or giving all my attention to my vast correspondence. I need to be active in some way or another.

As a woman of quite unusual beauty with an iron will and an unaffected enjoyment of sex and high living, Solange was almost ideally equipped for success in her profession, but while she had handled very large sums of money

by the time she was forty she was still as hard up as ever,
and ultimately dependent on the allowances she took from
both her parents. George finally called her back into their
game-playing by writing a novel at her. Called *Mademoiselle Merquem*, it consists quite simply of an exceedingly
ill-natured account of Solange's broken engagement with
the Vicomte de Préaulx and of her capture by Clésinger
hung on a portrait of her daughter which can only be described as a vicious caricature. After this demonstration
of power ("I can do whatever I like to you because you take
money from me—and *need* it"), George organized a round of
the interesting but disgusting game that the late Dr. Berne
christened "Let's you and him fight," with Maurice, Solange, and Casimir Dudevant as the principals. It was by all
odds the most atrocious performance of her career.

From the time that her children had grown up George had
become increasingly aware that Casimir had in some extraordinary way survived his annihilation, and had somehow reconstituted himself as a human being. He had inherited a very large acreage with Guillery but very little
cash, and he had done a remarkable job of climbing out of
a difficult position. His neighbors respected him for the
skill with which he had handled a tricky problem in estate management, and for the gentleness and intelligence
that were his leading characteristics in company. Solange
and Maurice both liked him, and as they grew up came to
look on him as a tower of strength who could be relied upon
in times of trouble and stress. He was exceedingly helpful
to Solange in all her troubles with Clésinger, and Jeanne
Clésinger had been born at Guillery. And when Maurice
had his great row with Manceau—over the growing for-
wardness and impertinence of a by then thoroughly spoiled
Marie Cailland—that led to the temporary break up of the
Nohant establishment in 1863–4, it was to Guillery that
he went with his young wife and their small son. The mechanics of that affair had been simple. At the height of
the dispute Maurice had told his mother: "You must choose
between him and me. One of us must leave Nohant." Initially George had chosen her son, but after a night's re-

flexion she had decided to leave the place with Manceau. When she did, in due course, actually leave, Maurice shut the house up and went to stay with his father. Outcast of paradise, George had scarcely settled into her new home, the villa George Sand in suburban Palaiseau just outside Paris, when she began to receive a series of telegrams about the health of Maurice's son. He was ill, he was dying, she should come at once if she wished to see him alive. She reached Guillery some hours too late....

It was exasperating to her to be received by a Casimir who was far from being the coarse and drunken brute of the legend that she had put so much energy and skill into creating, and who was quite evidently a functioning father, not only for her son, but also for Rose Dalias, the daughter of Jeanne Dalias, the pleasant woman who welcomed her to Guillery, and who had been his wife in everything but name for a great many years. George spent her time at the house wrapped in silence, and smoking cigarette after cigarette, taking in the facts of Casimir's happiness and success, and renewing the passion of her ill will for him. She returned home to brood over what she had seen, and five years later discovered a way of striking at him through the old Baronne Dudevant's will. It could be argued that it had been misinterpreted in Casimir's favor and that Guillery had not been left to him outright but to him *and* his children. She persuaded Maurice and Solange to sue for an immediate division of the property on the grounds that if they did not he would in all probability cheat them out of their inheritance by leaving Guillery in its entirety to Rose Dalias. They pressed their case to a victorious conclusion, and there was a forced sale which produced a hundred and fifty thousand francs for Casimir, and a hundred and thirty thousand for division between Maurice, his son and the heir to Nohant and its estates, and Solange, daughter of the Vicomte Stéphane de Grandsagne. Ousted from the property he loved, Casimir retired to a small house in the nearby village of Barbaste where he died of frustration and unhappiness within the year. In the distress of mind which preceded his end he applied to the Emperor for the Légion d'Honneur on grounds that are unique in the history of that order and which testify to the completeness of George's success in encompassing his final destruction:

> *I feel that the time has come for me to address myself to your Majesty's good heart, that I may obtain an honor to which it is my sincere belief that I have a right. Now in the evening of my days, there is but one ambition left to me, namely to obtain the Cross of the Légion d'Honneur. This is the supreme favor which I solicit from Your Imperial Highness. In asking for such an award I base my claim not only on those services which, since 1815, I have rendered my country and to its Government by law established—services in themselves, perhaps, of no great brilliance, and possibly even insignificant—but also on those of my father during the period from 1792 until the return from Elba. Still more do I venture to invoke those private misfortunes which are now matters of history. Having married Lucile Dupin, famous in the literary world under the name of George Sand, I have suffered cruelly in my feelings both as a husband and as a father. I am sure that I have deserved the sympathetic interest of all who have followed the miserable occurrences of that period of my life....*

Poetic justice was done to George for pushing this wretched and innocent man to the point at which he could make this application for a decoration as the most spectacular cuckold in France. She had rejoined the household at Nohant after Manceau's death in 1865, and Solange now used her share of the proceeds from the breakup of the Guillery estate along with the residue of her professional earnings to set herself up in the Château de Montgivray, a property within walking distance that had formerly been the home of George's half brother Hippolyte Châtiron. George responded to this act of aggression by cutting off her allowance and ordering that the doors of Nohant should be permanently closed against her. But she couldn't be prevented from dropping in unannounced and making her presence felt more or less whenever she felt like it, and dread of her descents filled the last three years of her mother's life with apprehensions and irritation. She brushed Maurice aside the minute that George was dead, and while he was paralyzed with misery she made all the necessary arrangements for this professed freethinker and Voltairean skeptic to have an orthodox Catholic funeral. The Prince Napoléon, Flaubert, Renan, and the younger Dumas were among the limited number of people who came to the ceremony, and Victor Hugo delivered a superbly meaningless oration at the graveside:

> Can it be said that we have lost her? No! Great figures such as she may disappear—they do not vanish. Far from it. One might almost say that they take on a new reality. By becoming invisible in one form they become visible in another. Sublime transfiguration! The human form eclipses what is within, masking the true, the divine visage, which is the "idea." George Sand was an "idea." She has been released from the flesh and now is free.

Flaubert was impressed by this fantastic nonsense and added his mite to it in a letter describing the event that he wrote to Turgeniev: "She will remain one of the splendors of France, and her glory will be unrivaled." But what is impressive today is only the strength of the imperatives that drove her, on the one hand to give up the hours between midnight and six in the morning almost every night of her life, from the time she was thirty until a year or two before she died, to producing between fifteen and thirty pages of it hardly mattered what; and on the other to destroy everyone who asked for her love and came anywhere near to obtaining it. At the end of their lives her devoted enemy and former friend Marie d'Agoult summed her up:

> She has a species of contempt for those to whom she has been generous.... She treats her lovers as sticks of chalk that she's used for writing on a blackboard.

As soon as she's done with it she treads the chalk under foot, and in a moment it's nothing more than a fine powder that blows away.

And in the end she came to regret having given her lovers anything: "If I had to start my life over again," she told Juliette Adam, "I would choose to remain chaste."

Postscript

I t may seem to some that I am unwise to base a general theory about writers and writing on the case histories of three women who had so much more in their lives than the devotion to the craft of fiction which is said to play so great a part in the existence of such truly professional writers as Flaubert or Henry James. Such committed lives, I am assured, do not show the direct relationship between the day-to-day existence and the work produced that I propose. Of this I am far from convinced. It was Henry James who pointed out the central flaw in Flaubert's work—that he had no tenderness or regard for any of his characters—and it has since been amply demonstrated by his biographers that he gave his life to the creation of imaginary persons precisely because he was to so large an extent unable to enter into satisfactory relationships with real ones, particularly when they were women. The primary situation that disabled him in this regard is not known, but can be guessed at. One indicator of what is likely to have been the source of his trouble will be found in Dr. Flaubert's quite evident hostility towards his son, symbolically expressed by his easily rationalized, but nonetheless transparent, decision to have a grave prepared for him in the family's plot in the local cemetery when he was still a child. Another is to be found in "Quidquis Volueris," a story written by Flaubert when he was fifteen—soon after he had blocked off the possibility of the attachments normal to a person of that age by committing himself to the emotional dead end of a fixation on the unattainable Elisa Schlesinger. This jolly little yarn had its origin in an account, published in a paper directed by one of his friends, of an incident in Paris in which an orangutan from the Jardin des Plantes attacked a woman. The story described an imag-

inary sequel to such an event, the suicide of a half-breed—
half-ape and half-man—who has inflicted horrifying injuries on a woman while raping her. When one reads this
disagreeable piece of fantasy it is hard not to feel that one
is getting a sight of the scar tissue surrounding the psychic
wound which made Flaubert what he was, and which made
Madame Bovary what she was too: a being isolated from
the real world and trapped in a world of fantasy. His work,
on the one hand, formed a protective barrier between him
and the potentially lethal involvements of which he lived
in dread by preempting much of his time and most of his
energy, and, on the other, provided him with a substitute
for the experience that his timidity denied him.

The reader who plows his way through the melancholy
chronicle of mediocre activities, mediocre interests, mediocre associations, hesitations, and small-minded cattinesses
which fill out the baggy amplitudes of Mr. Leon Edel's
life of Henry James will probably come to a very similar
conclusion about him. It is evident from what Mr. Edel
permits himself to admit that the history of the developing
turgidity and obscurity of James' style is in fact the history
of his gathering awareness of his own bisexuality and the
surfacing of his homoerotic tendencies, and it is as evident
that what one has taken for his devotion to his craft was
something other than that. When one reads of James, who
was nothing if not middle class, flying into a tantrum when
reminded of it by an English woman who presumed to
assume that she was socially his equal, one is amused by
the endearing naïveté of his snobbery. But then one discovers that in the course of his last illness James dictated
a letter, written as from the Tuileries, which he signed
Napoleone.

This extraordinary communication from his fantasized
self is addressed to certain members of his immediate family
who seem to be troubling him by their inability or their
unwillingness to rise to the level of the greatness to which
he has attained. To read this pathetic document is to experience an immediate illumination: it is to recognize that
the central theme of James' professional life, the creation

of a conception of the art of the novel that will rule out of consideration as serious contributions to its development almost all work other than his own, or work modeled on it, is an exercise in narcissism that has had few equals. In his famous saying that it is "Art which makes life, which makes interest, which makes importance..." he appears to be making a stirring claim for the nature of something outside himself, and greater than himself, of which he is the humble instrument or servant. But what if the claim is more candidly stated? "It is what I do, or what I choose to lend myself to, that makes life, makes interest, makes interest, makes my importance...." However willful this subject is followed by a meaningless predicate. But the whole thing becomes crystal clear if it is made into a personal statement. "It is art that makes my life, makes my interest, makes my importance. . . ." However willful this revision may seem, there is a point of substance here that even the most convinced believer in the absolute importance of the art of fiction will have to take into account. Narcissism, and of a sufficiently infantile variety, must play a large part in any process involving the polishing, refinement, and perpetuation of what an individual produces from within himself. The ancients may have been simple-minded enough to believe that Narcissus was overwhelmed by the discovery of his own beauty and that, but for his bad luck in being so beastly handsome, he would have lived and died a straight. But we know now that anyone who sets out to be self-sufficient to that extent is the traumatized victim of some infantile disaster who has been left in mortal fear of interpersonal relationships. We would suppose that he had been programmed to avoid the risks inherent in such relationships by becoming both parties to the central one in his life. The conception of narcissism has to be a vital element in the construction of a theory of the motivation underlying a Flaubertian or Jamesian dedication to the art of fiction. There *are* novels by men in which all the characters are men, and there *are* novels by women in which all the characters are women; but they are atypical. Characteristically the novel concerns itself

with what are, roughly speaking, balanced populations
of men and women, and the authors of novels "come on"
as often in the person of a member of one sex as of the other.
In extreme cases writers act out the opportunities for impersonation that the form licences.

Prosper Mérimée, whose brief passage with the transsexually named and often transsexually dressed George Sand
has already been described, originally came before the
public under a female pseudonym, Clara Gazul, in a book
which had his portrait in drag for a frontispiece; and there
is the even more striking case of the massively built and
splendidly bearded nineteenth century editor of the *Times
Literary Supplement* who found it necessary to dress as a
woman in order to write the novels which he published
under the pen name of Fiona Macleod.

It may seem a far cry from these examples of marginally
psychotic behavior to the intense seriousness about writing
of Henry James, but the distance is not all that great. It
is only necessary to turn to the opening pages of *The Wings
of the Dove* to find the master himself deeply involved in
a female impersonation. For two or three pages before her
father comes to her Kate Croy is alone in the room and
James tells the reader what she is thinking: it is a classic
example of the nobody-here-but-us-chickens situation by
which the novel has been haunted throughout its history,
and from which there is, ultimately, no escape.

It shouldn't, however, be supposed that what is involved
is a simple matter of dressing up physically or metaphori-
cally in order to assume the otherness of the alternative
mode of being with the clothes. What is at issue is the basic
narcissistic urge to eliminate the other by becoming both:
a man who has taken on the appearance and manner of a
woman is in control, for as long as he enacts the role, of
a woman who is without the menace of femaleness, and
the same object is attained when it is the woman who comes
on as a man. The motivation for the impersonation is not
the desire to be but *the fear and loathing of,* and its pathology is made perfectly clear by the extreme case of the male
transsexual who enlists the aid of surgeons to complete his

performance. When he has undergone his castration and had his penis removed he is still in secure possession of his original identity, but there is no way in which a woman can take anything more from him. He is absolutely safe at last.

While the brutalities of surgical intervention are exceedingly remote from the hesitations and tentatives of Henry James, it has to be remembered that his Kate Croy has a singular appetite for dependency, and strange ambitions for her lover. She makes three proposals for their future: in the first they are to live with, and off, her entirely disgraceful father; in the second they are to live on the bounty of an aunt whose way of life involves the complete negation of everything which gives meaning to her lover's existence; and in the third they are to live on the proceeds of a coup which is to involve him in marriage to a dying woman of means if it is to succeed, and which will be entirely dishonorable to him. At the conclusion of the book Kate Croy lets her lover go in a curiously apathetic fashion. Their breakup is generally ascribed to lofty moral considerations: the coup has gone oddly awry. The rich object of Kate's machinations has died before the marriage can be brought off, having been killed prematurely by her discovery of the scheme. But she has had the time and the thought to change her will before her death, so that by it Kate's partner is to inherit the money he must have if he is to marry her, an action which has the long-term consequence of dissolving the compact between the schemers. The dissolution of their alliance is formally achieved in the course of high-flown exchanges which manage to suggest to such critics as R. P. Blackmur that what has happened is that the rich girl's "absolute goodness and beauty" have in fact redeemed the schemers. But it is significant, to me if not anyone else, that Kate's interest in pushing her lover into the dishonorable situation she has designed for him collapses just when her beastly father's ego structure disintegrates in a spectacular fashion and he is reduced to total dependence on his daughters. (Kate's sister, it should be noted, has the very ugly name, if one allows for the not unlikely possibility

that James' unconscious spoke Franglais, of Mrs. Condrip.)
When Kate Croy has "got" her father, in a demoralized state
in which he lies in bed, weeping and prey to nameless ter-
rors, all day, she no longer needs her other subject to operate
upon and can afford to let him go with no more than a per-
functory effort to hold him.

My feeling is that the ruined father is brought back just
at that point in the story, and in that condition, in order
to show the reader exactly what the consequences of sexual
involvements are likely to be, and from what Kate's lover
has had a lucky escape. This reading is in part based on the
occurrence of an extremely odd phrase in Kate's original
indictment of her father in the opening section of the book:
she says that her father has inflicted a *bleeding wound* on
the family name. She goes on to imply that however this
may have been done—the extent of her knowledge, so far
as she is willing to own to it, is that he has "done something wicked"—it has, somehow, had the consequence of
making her a "penniless girl." It is, of course, because she
is a "penniless girl" that she involves her lover in the wickedness that brings about the rich girl's death: the rich girl's
death is in the end a payment deferred for the parent's wickedness. If this picture of the thing is accepted, it will be
seen that *The Wings of the Dove* has at its core a structure
closely resembling that which is to be found in Flaubert's
"Quidquis Volueris," in which a lethal sexual involvement
figures as payment deferred for the wickedness of the original rape of the man-ape's mother. It is also to be found in
Mérimée's grotesquely detailed story of the Russian gentleman whose mother has been raped by a bear on her wedding
day and who in due course savaged his wife on *her* wedding day.

The story of the misbegotten or woefully begotten child,
Tristram, whom it is death to love, is indeed a familiar
one: it is perennially reinvented, and psychiatrists tell
one that it is native to the fantasy of the child who has become prematurely acquainted with the mechanical aspects
of the act of love and of the process by which the young
human comes into the world through the bleeding wound

between its mother's legs. This child does not fully understand what it has been confronted with, and may have divined what has shocked it rather than been given the information, but it does receive the impression that a great wrong
has been done for which *someone* has to atone, as Flaubert's
ape-man and Mérimée's bear-man do, by being killed or
locked up.

Henry James had before him the example of an oddly
emasculated father, an object of pity to his family, who
very obviously played second fiddle to his wife and had had
his leg cut off after being terribly burned while fighting a
fire. This burning and amputating followed not long after
an episode (the details of which aren't clear), which gave
the poor man a reputation that he was never able to shake
off in his family of having "done something wicked." He
contended with this reputation until he was well on into
middle life, and then suffered some kind of moral collapse,
after which he seemed to accept it that he had to live with
the fact of his being, in some way, no good.

That the example of his father marked James isn't purely
a matter of conjecture, since when he was on the brink
of manhood he ritualistically repeated his father's experience. His accounts of what in fact happened to him on this
occasion are so portentous and so, in the pejorative sense
of the word, Jamesian, as to make the nature of the event
undiscoverable while promoting the most bizarre of con-
jectures. These have ranged from severe shock to actual
physical castration, with a largish body of opinion favoring
a hernia so severe in its effect as to rule out any possibility
of normal sexual relationships thereafter. Mr. Edel shows,
however, that the record of James' activities immediately
and for some time after the event are incompatible with his
having suffered anything worse than severe muscle strain
in the region of the lower back. Whatever may or may not
have occurred is, however, of less importance than that
James, finding himself in a situation parallel to that which
had caused his father's mutilation, should have leapt at the
chance it offered him of taking up the role of someone who
had undergone a permanent disablement. He enthusi-

astically embraced the idea that the effects of the catastrophe were to be long lasting, and in all probability, irreparable, almost as soon as it occurred to him that he had been injured, and from then on looked on himself as being excluded from a whole region of human experience.

It doesn't seem to me possible to consider this episode, in conjunction with the rest of what one knows about the structure of the James family as it was when he was in his infancy, without reaching the conclusion that *The Wings of the Dove* is, whatever else he may have intended it to be, a very direct and unguarded statement about the origins of his drive to demonstrate his potency and fertility, or "greatness," in a way that wouldn't ever take him anywhere near the bleeding wound that had proved to be so dangerous for his father. What is fascinating about the book if it is read as a statement of this kind is not what is exceptional or special to Henry James in it, but the extent to which it remains typical of the fantasies associated with the specific behavioral patterns of which his life is exemplary in spite of all his efforts to make more of it than that.

It is in this matter of being in essence typical that Henry James has in common with D. H. Lawrence, who, if he never saw himself as a Napoleon, certainly identified himself with Jesus, and thought of himself as an isolated and exceptional figure. The available information about his family background and early years, however, gives one a standard picture of the characteristic family structure associated with a specific form of sexual maladjustment. In Lawrence's home one finds an aggressively masculine father who doesn't deliver on his masculinity and the classic dominant and domineering mother who, by filling the male role in the household as well as her own, provides the children with a bisexual model for their behavior and a nice set of identity problems. The children raised in families of this type do not, of course, grow up to be writers who produce *The White Peacock, Sons and Lovers, The Rainbow,* and so on, or even versions of these novels, but they do grow up to express verbally and in their actions the ideas about the relationships between men and women, and about masculinity and femininity, that are given formalized literary expression in Lawrence's writing. Given the family background it is predictable that a reader will be responsive to the content of the writings of Otto Weininger, Edward Carpenter, Madame Blavatsky, and Walt Whitman that Lawrence responded to, and that if he should be a writer and a man he will produce similarly ambivalent writing about women, and will show in his personal life the same intense desire to identify with them coupled with the same vehemently expressed fear of them as emasculators.

Psychiatrists commonly encounter the ideas that Lawrence gathered from these sources and made his own, in the context either of an adolescent identity crisis, in which his patient has found it impossible to relate to members of the opposite sex in any productive way, or, later, in the context of a marriage which is on the rocks because the man is in competition with the wife's femininity and uncertain of his own performance as a male.

When the psychiatrist investigates the total situation in the latter case he generally finds that the wife has been well chosen to produce the situation that has brought him his patient. She is almost certain to be a woman nicely calculated to make him feel sexually insecure or inadequate, and even more likely to be someone too impatient with, or at odds with, the traditional feminine role to be able to fulfill it gracefully or effectively. Her refusal to undertake the household chores or to be conventionally houseproud gives her husband the ideal pretext for taking over most of the functions traditionally assigned to the wife in the home, and for setting himself up as the bisexual head of the family on the lines of the model provided for him by his own mother. As his mother did a great deal of complaining about the martyrdom inflicted upon her by the father's failure to fulfill his fatherly functions, the husband will be at pains to let the wife know how ill used he feels by her failure to function as a woman. She will resent this and prove that she is indeed a "real" woman by showing her husband that she can attract and satisfy "real" men, and she will take care to see that her husband knows what she is doing.

The interesting thing about this type of marriage, so

far as psychiatrists are concerned, is that although logic might suggest that it would invariably come to an explosive end in a very short time it only rarely does so, and generally lasts either for a period of several years or for the lifetime of one or other of the parties to it.

The marriage of Frieda and Lawrence was just such an arrangement, and like all members of the class it poses the riddle of why the parties should wish to go on with it when it is, at least as seen from the outside, so evidently productive of discomfort and suffering.

The answer to the riddle is to be found in a consideration of the model on which the bisexual husband's performance is based. Being seen to suffer was an essential part of the mother's performance, and she briefed her children so as to make sure that they would recognize that she was suffering and being made to suffer by their father. The suffering is an essential part of the role, and a necessity if a complete performance is to be given. As the goal is to duplicate the mother's performance in its entirety a situation which is not productive of suffering is positively disadvantageous: the last thing that the husband wants in this type of marriage is an accommodating wife who will go along with the role reversal and do her best to be a good husband to him, or to match his performance with one of her own that might be smoothly complimentary to it. If she does respond in this way the marriage very rapidly breaks up.

The answer to the problem presented by this apparently paradoxical element in such situations is a simple one. The suffering represents, or is, a positive psychological gain or advantage: it is part of what the man has worked for, or sought to obtain, by marrying that particular woman or a woman of that kind. The marriage lasts because it is productive of what is desired and continues to last until it ceases to be so. The operating base of the marriage is a deal or transaction. "If you do this and I respond by doing that, you will then have grounds for doing your thing, and that will give me grounds for doing mine." The marriage lasts as long as the transactions yield worthwhile results for both parties.

It is perfectly clear from the available accounts of Frieda and Lawrence's behavior that their marriage was of this nature, and it is also perfectly clear that Lawrence's transactions with Frieda provided the model on which the descriptions of the relationships between men and women that occur in his later novels are based. It is also perfectly clear that transactional relationships as a class are immature, and that they have their foundation on models provided by infantile experience.

The baby's world is largely a transactional world. It is not to be supposed that the newborn child conceptualizes a universe of deals in such terms as "If I cry Mummy will come back" and "If I cry I will get something to eat," but repeated experience teaches it that crying is followed by attention and solace. Its subsequent experience, in the years in which it is learning to form concepts, reinforces this lesson. It is very hard to avoid making toilet training a form of schooling in blackmail, and even harder to prevent a child from gaining the impression that tantrums and similar attention-getting devices and coercive maneuvers are as effective means towards the achievement of desired goals as any others, and often more effective.

It may be hard for the average parent to realize how things are, but the toddler he has to deal with—who has not as yet acquired full control of his muscular organization, and who is so obviously much less experienced and much less informed than he is—may be his equal and perhaps his superior in intelligence. It will be repulsive for him to face the possibility that his child is capable of assessing a situation and of reaching cynical conclusions about it ahead of him.

The assessment in such a case may not be put into words, but there can be no doubt, in view of the observed behavior of children of under five, that these little operators are fully capable of basing an action program on a logical formulation, such as "If I can get him to lose his temper or to hit me I will have this one made." When the roar of fury has been released, or the blow has been delivered, the child dissolves into tears and the parent is instantly transformed by his guilt and remorse into a suppliant for the child's forgiveness.

The next step for the child who has discovered that it can manipulate a parent in this way is to construct a scenario for transforming an unsatisfactory situation into a more acceptable one: "There is Momma or Papa paying me no heed; if I set up a situation which leads to his or her shouting at me or hitting me things will soon be different and I will be getting the attention and cuddling I need."

All this is straightforward enough, and may not seem to take one very far. But if the child's parents are so wound up in their own conflicts and tensions as to be incapable of responding to the child's demands for love and affection without that stimulation, the child will grow up to assume that warmth can only be introduced into human relationship by preliminary exercises in mutual outrage, and that the normal pattern of exchange between lovers has to be "I annoy you, we have a row, and when we've hurt each other we can make love." Effectively the subject making such an assumption will have been programmed to require a row as the license for the release of tenderness: he will be unable to give or to receive emotionally without a preliminary release of aggression and hostility.

It is difficult for anyone who has read the body of Lawrence's oeuvre not to conclude that he has been programmed in just this way, and that the bulk of his work consists of fictionalizations of the effect of such programming on someone who, having been raised by Mrs. Lawrence, then elected to spend the rest of his life with Frieda. From *Women in Love* onward descriptions of his current transactions with her play a larger and larger part in his work, and in the end it assumes the character of a series of situation reports on the development of the relationship.

It is also apparent, when the external and internal evidence is put together, that the transactional pattern in which Lawrence was trapped was producing less and less in the way of psychic advantage for Frieda toward the end, and that once her children had grown up and established themselves as emotionally independent entities unlikely to make further demands on her, the role of Frieda Lawrence lost much of its point. A study of *The Plumed Serpent*, in conjunction with the large amount of information that is at hand about what the Lawrences were saying and doing at the time, forces one to the conclusion that Lawrence's physical collapse was his answer to the unmistakable hints to this effect that she was giving him by her behavior.

The individual who has been programmed to live as an emotional blackmailer will very often die as a blackmailer, making his death and the manner of it his final retributive and coercive act. The interesting thing about Lawrence's final, doom-laden years is that his conduct was extravagantly foolish in the light of what was known of his complaint at the time. It is not hindsight but an objective reading of the details of his movements, the regime he adopted, and the kind of advice that he sought and regarded that shows him going to the wrong places, doing the wrong things, and consulting the wrong medical advisors. He was hazarding his life on his ability to maintain himself in a condition in which it would be impossible for Frieda to leave him and move on to the next phase of her existence.

"The Man Who Died," a story about a Jesus who survives his crucifixion and comes off the cross to enjoy the favors of a woman who really knows her place in the scheme of things as a docile and supportive ministrant to male necessities, throws a good deal of light on the transactional process that he had in mind. It defines the terms on which he would have been willing to come off *his* cross, at any rate.

The *"Virgin and the Gypsy"* of the same epoch, with its infantile central fantasy of the defeat of a grown-up conspiracy to deny a child sexual satisfaction and the drowning of all the conspirators in the flood of the achieved release, is another straw in the wind—the gypsy, who is the deus ex machina, comes mysteriously into the virgin's world from outside to give her what she wants and then vanishes, leaving her desolate among its ruins. It seems clear that Frieda was to get the message from this that she would be very sorry if her liberator was to pull out. She would find, then, that she had nothing worth having left, either.

There is deep water in this neighborhood, because tuberculosis is a lethal clinical entity and an objective reality. Those of an eighteenth-century rationalist habit of mind who believe in one-to-one patterns of cause and effect find it very hard to swallow the concept of complicity where such a thing as death from tuberculosis is concerned. He had the disease and he died of it, what more is there to say? This disease, however, is an extremely interesting one to both medical men and psychiatrists precisely because there is a lot more to say about the very wide variation of response to infection; most people who are infected with the potentially lethal complaint handle it as a minor episode. It is only autonomously lethal in the case of very old people and very young ones.

For persons between the ages of six and sixty-five the disease is very rarely fatal unless the infected individual is in serious trouble emotionally or in some kind of developmental impasse from which the role of tuberculosis victim offers him as means of escape. In that role he can count on social sanction for lying down and dying, and while so engaged, he can count on getting a full measure of supportive response from those with whom he is emotionally involved.

At the present time death by tuberculosis for anyone in the age group mentioned is almost as much a matter of election as committing suicide with a firearm. It was substantially already so when Lawrence was dying of it. Had he gone to Switzerland and followed the advice of the conventional practitioners treating the disease as soon as he became aware of it in himself he would almost certainly have lived on for another thirty to forty years. But he required his death as a final emotional assault upon Frieda before she escaped him, just as his mother had required her death as a final emotional assault upon him before he slipped away from her.

However fanciful and extravagant this account of Lawrence's end may seem to the reader, he will find ample warrant for it in the available accounts of the event and its antecedents. All this leads up to the bald statement that D. H. Lawrence, having been produced by a family structure of a kind that characteristically gives rise to a specific deformation of the personality in its male children, was receptive to, and expressed, the concepts of maleness and the nature of male-to-female relationships characteristic of the deformation, and was, further, programmed to relate to the men and women with whom he became emotionally involved along lines predetermined by the deformation. If this statement is true, as I think it is, it follows that Lawrence's writings, all as closely related to his immediate experience as it is possible for writing to be, must be so profoundly affected by the deformation as to be incomprehensible when it is not taken into account. The question of their value raises itself with some insistence when the point is understood, and not only in this case.

Between the worlds of Lawrence and Proust there would seem to be an even wider gap than that which divides the Nottingham coalfield from the America inhabited by the married and insecurely genteel children of immigrants who had made good which produced Henry James. But the sophistication of Proust's mode of expression and the high social shine on much of the content of his work and on his literary persona can't, in the end, hide the large extent of the common ground he shared with the miner's son. Those who doubt its existence should refer to the first line of the text of his "Contre Sainte-Beuve:" "Every day I set less store by the intellect. Every day I see more clearly that if the writer is to repossess himself of some point of his impressions, reach something personal, that is, and the only material of art, he must put it aside." What follows is a prolonged argument in favor of instinctive responses and intuitions that is in other language precisely what Lawrence has to say in favor of blood consciousness as against reason. The route that is followed by this argument passes through some sufficiently peculiar, and extremely personal, countryside. There are conversations between Proust and his mother:

"What is my silly billy thinking of, what nonsense is this?"

"I should be so happy if I never saw anyone again."

"Don't say that, my lamb, I am very fond of those people who are nice to you. In fact I would like to see you with more friends who would come in and talk, without being too much for you."

"All I want is my mamma."

"But your mamma would rather think of you seeing other people, who could tell you things she doesn't know, things you could explain about after they had gone..."

As an exchange between a mother and her grown-up son this is on the verge of the pathological, both parties are so clearly clinging to a state of things that they should have outgrown. The tone becomes even more manifest after we have been treated to a little flashback in which Reynaldo Hahn comes to the apartment in which Proust's parents live and sings for them some of the "ravishing" choral settings that he has composed for a selection of passages from Racine's *Esther*. As soon as Hahn has sung his last song we return to the undefined "now" in which the mother and son are having their heart-to-heart talk:

"Darling Mamma, I must have one more kiss."

"Not really, my lamb, this is silly, you mustn't over-tire yourself. When I come back I shall want to hear that you are in blooming health and feeling as strong as a horse."

She leaves me but my thoughts return to my article, and suddenly I have an idea for another one. "Contre Sainte-Beuve." When I re-read him not long ago, I made, contrary to my usual habit, a great many rough notes and put them away in a drawer, and I have some interesting things to say about him. I begin to think out the article. More and more ideas occur to me. Before half an hour the whole article has taken shape in my head. I want to ask mamma what she thinks of it....

Well, anyway, he calls her back and presently their dialogue is renewed:

"Listen! I want to ask your advice. Sit down."

"Wait till I've found the armchair. It is not very easy to see in here, I must say. Should I tell Felicie to bring the electric lamp?"

"No don't, I might not be able to go to sleep again."

"Still Molière" she said laughingly. "Forbid the torches to approach, sweet lady."

"You're settled? Good. Now this is what I want to tell you about, I've had an idea for an article, and I want your opinion of it."

"But you know that I can't give you advice about such things. I'm not like you. I don't read great books."

"Now listen! The subject is to be: objections to the method of Saint-Beuve."

"Goodness! I thought it was everything it should be. In that article by Bourget you made me read he said that it is such a marvellous method that there has been no one in the nineteenth century who could make use of it."

"Oh, yes, that's what he said, but it's too fatuous. You know the principles of that method?"

"Go on as if I didn't."

Chapter VII having concluded with this dazzling glimpse of the interior of Proust's workshop, we come at last to "The Method of Sainte-Beuve" and the heart of the argument. This is a hysterical piece of scolding which seeks to refute the critic by the simplistic device of asserting that his views must be wrong because they are not correct. It is not necessary to argue the case for rejecting his views: "We have only to let him speak for himself." There follows an eminently reasonable statement from Sainte-Beuve to the effect that the behavioral approach to literary criticism can't work where the writers of antiquity are concerned because the necessary information about their lives and opinions are lacking. "With the moderns," Sainte-Beuve goes on, "it is quite different." Not only is the information accessible, but there has been an accretion of knowledge about the meaning of behavior that opens up interesting possibilities. The passage that Proust finds especially Sainte-Beuvian, and, presumably, ridiculous, goes as follows:

The moral study of character is as yet a piecemeal affair, confined to the description of individuals or, at most, a few types: Theophrastus and La Bruyere go no further. A day is coming, of which I believe I have caught glimpses in the course of my studies, when scientific knowledge will be established, and the major family systems of the intellect and their chief subdivisions will be determined and known. Then, being given the leading characteristics of an intellect, we shall be able to deduce several others from it. With man, of course, we shall never be able to proceed exactly as with animals or with plants: a moral being is more complex: he is what is called a free agent, which in any case presupposes a great versatility of possible combinations. Be this as it may, we shall come in time, I fancy, to constitute ethical science on a more ample scale: today it is where botany was before Jussien, or comparative anatomy before Cuvier—at the anecdotic stage, so to speak. For our own part, we compose simple monographs, but I catch glimpses of links, and affinities, and an intellect more far reaching, more enlightened, but retaining its grasp of detail, may one day discover the great biological divisions that correspond with the family system of intellect.

Of this one can only say that the language is of its time — one in which the intellectual systems of the eighteenth century were collapsing under the weight of an accumulation of new knowledge with which they were not equipped, terminologically or conceptually, to deal, and that the insight is a shrewd one. Although the French had been in advance of the rest of the world in psychological studies since the sixties of the previous century it was still not clear when Sainte-Beuve was writing that what was considered to be primarily a consideration of mental disorders and abnormalities might lead to the establishment of a generally valid anatomy of motivations and behavioral patterns such as he proposes.

But the question here is less one of whether Sainte-Beuve was being reasonable or not than one of why Proust should have been as disturbed as he was by what Sainte-Beuve was saying. The tremendous piece of abusive scolding which forms the core of the essay begins with a quotation from, of all people, Carlyle: "An artist is sent hither specially that he may discuss for himself, and make manifest to us, this same Divine Idea which lies at the bottom of all Appearance."

Proust passes on from this to say that:

> *At no time does Sainte-Beuve seem to have understood that this makes it different in kind from what busies other men, and, at other times, busies writers.... But Sainte-Beuve remained unable to understand that world apart shuttered and sealed against all traffic with the outer world, the poet's soul.... And so by failing to see the gulf that separates the writer from the man of the world, by failing to understand that the writer's true self is manifested in his books alone, and that what he shows to men of the world...is merely a man of the world like themselves. Sainte-Beuve came to set up that celebrated method...which consists, if you desire to understand a poet or writer, in greedily catechizing those who knew him, who saw quite a lot of him, who can tell us how he conducted himself in regard to women, etc. precisely, that is, at every point where the poet's true self is not involved.*

It is curious that this passage, which has begun with an invocation of Carlyle, the whole structure of whose thought is related with a singular directness to the fact of his sexual impotence, should end as it does, with the isolation of Sainte-Beuve's contention that a male writer's approach to women in life may explain some of the things that he says about women, and about their relationships with men in his work. But that is not all that is odd about it. When one reads that small talk about a writer's personal life is irrelevant to a consideration of what he has written, one is compelled to ask why Proust has regaled his readers with the very personal account of his transactions with his mother which constitutes the greater part of the preceding chapter. It is also unsettling to find that, having advanced this particular argument, Proust should immediately proceed to show how Sainte-Beuve's career was affected by his financial situation and to give us a malicious caricature of his professional life which is based entirely on gossip.

This rather disagreeable performance is followed up by two violent attacks on Sainte-Beuve for his failure to do justice to Baudelaire, in one instance, and to Balzac, in the other (attacks which ignore the fact that it would be hard to find two writers who were as hard-driven by their compulsions, or who as straightforwardly made their work the mirror of their private necessities) and by a mysterious piece of chatter called "The Balzac of Monsieur de Guermantes," which leads, in its turn, to a discussion of the homosexuality of the Marquis de Quercy under the title of "A Race Accursed." This sinister outpouring, which is the original version of a very similar passage in *Remembrance of Things Past,* begins to drift off course as it proceeds, rather in the manner of one of those four masters which in certain circumstances would take charge and refuse to answer to the helm until their canvas had been reset and brought into balance with the force of the wind. It is with astonishment that one realizes, quite suddenly, that one is reading a passage in which Jewishness is being equated with homosexuality. The first statement of this theme slips by as a resort to metaphor:"…a contempt of the least perverted for the most perverted like that of the most desemitised Jew for the little Jew in the slop shop…."

But when it comes up for the second time it is a thing without any kind of ambiguity:

> … Because if in the depth of almost every Jew there is an anti-Semite whom we best flatter when we attribute every kind of fault to him but treat him as a Christian, so in the depth of every homosexual there is an anti-homosexual to whom we cannot offer a greater insult than by acknowledging that he has talents, virtues, intellect, heart, and in sum, like all human characters the right to enjoy love in the form that nature allows us to conceive of it, though respect for the truth meanwhile compels us to confess that this form of love is strange, and that these men are not like other men.

This is followed up by a second resort to metaphor, a reference to "those bearded Levites, who in their dread of contumely, will only associate with those of their own race, who are the bureaucracy of perversion...."

This equation of homosexuality with Jewishness carries one back to the extraordinary introduction to the attack on Sainte-Beuve in which Proust's parents are seen with Reynaldo Hahn:

> *Of all Racine's plays, it is* Esther *that Momma loves best, and after these quotations from it, she begins to hum—diffidently and as though she were afraid that too loud and bold a voice would scare away the tune that is in her mind like a heavenly presence.... She tried over a solo part, diffidently, as though she were one of the young girls at Saint-Cyr rehearsing before Racine; and her beautiful Jewish features stamped with Christian sweetness and Jansenist fortitude made her a very Esther in this domestic, almost cloister-like little performance...*

He is, indeed, telling the reader in this curious fashion that his mother was Jewish, a fact which is not perhaps without significance when it is related to the equation made in "A Race Accursed." The crude facts of Proust's tie with that "Combray" that was to emerge in its entirety from his cup of tea at the bidding of the madeleine are that Adrien Achille Proust, his father, was born there in 1834, as the son of a small shopkeeper who kept a general store.

Adrien Proust escaped from this "Combray," which was in fact Illiers, a town of three thousand inhabitants in the department of Eure-et-Loir, by way of a scholarship to the Collège de Chartres and medical school in Paris. He qualified in 1862, and in 1866 had the good fortune to be sent to Persia as a member of a government commission inquiring into the causes of the rapid spread of epidemics of cholera. This diverted his ambitions in the direction of a "political" career in medicine, in which he could not hope to succeed without money and influence behind him. In 1870, when he was thirty-six, he successfully married these things in the person of Jeanne Weill, a young member of a prospering cousinship of Weills and Neubergers who had moved on from wholesaling to finance and who had developed useful leverage in the two chambers and the ministries. With this clan behind him Adrien Proust proceeded to climb to the top of the tree in his chosen field, that of administrative medicine in the domain of public health, and so elevated his branch of the family to the level of the professional section of the upper middle class. When he died in 1903, he was a commander of the Légion d'Honneur, a member of the Academy of Medicine, occupant of the chair of Professor of Public Health, and Inspector General of the Public Health Services.

It becomes quite clear to the reader of Dr. Robert Le Masle's biography of Adrien Proust that to escape from the limitations, social and economic, embodied in the description "son of a shopkeeper in Illiers," had been a principal aim in his life and that his marriage to Jeanne Weill was an instrumentality of major importance in achieving it.

It is just as clear that for Marcel Proust the connection with the Weill-Neuberger cousinship, which had been so useful to his father, was an immediately recognizable handicap, blocking him off from all hope of realizing his ambition of escaping from his father's world of government functionaries and successful professional men into that of "society." To be the son of a Jewish mother, in addition to being the grandson of a shopkeeper, was a fatal defect in a social climber who aspired to win recognition from an aristocracy for whom pride of race was all important in the face of the mounting tide of xenophobia and anti-Semitism that was finding its mode of social expression in the controversy over the Dreyfus case.

That the point was of capital importance with Proust is demonstrated in his lifelong habit of telling anti-Semitic anecdotes, and of larding his conversation and his letters with straightforwardly anti-Semitic remarks—such as that in his letter to Robert de Billy in which he warns him that the Grand Hotel at Cabourg is full, and with awful people: "not a soul you could put a name to—and a few Israelite wholesale dealers (who) are the haughty aristocracy of the place...."

His insecurity on this issue also forces him to exchange the soggy rusk of the trial passage concerning involuntary memory in *Contre Sainte-Beuve* for the madeleine which is the trigger for its release in the key passage in *Remembrance of Things Past*. The substitution had to be made because the rusk could only carry him back to the home of his Jewish relative Nathe' Weill at Auteuil, whereas Illiers-as-Combray and the world of his Christian connections could be summoned up by the unpolluted Madeleine.

Those familiar with the transactional theory of behavior will recognize in Proust's Jewishness one of those grievances, composed of a combination of subjective and objective elements, which are cherished as the justification for long sequences of the class of transaction described by Dr. Berne as games. The characteristic pattern of these sequences is that displays of aggression and hostility justified by the grievance alternate with excessively emotional displays of love and affection, the latter being guilt offerings in atonement for the immediately preceding display of hostility, and so on. Berne describes these things as games because they are artificial constructions designed by the players either to stand between them and the necessity for expressing their genuine feelings, or to fill voids in cases in which the players have been traumatized into emotional impotence. A rather usual indication of this last condition is a complete inability to relate to siblings, and it is striking that Proust's account of his relationship with his mother-grandmother in *Remembrance of Things Past* is that of an only child. Robert Proust is as shadowy and marginal a figure in the novel as he is in the biographies of the author.

It is apparent, too, that there was something badly wrong with Jeanne Weill in this region; she was as apt to make anti-Semitic remarks as her son, and her absorption in classical French literature, of which Proust makes so much in his accounts of their Genji-like quotation swappings, involved a repudiation of Jewish culture parallel to that repudiation of her Jewishness of which her marriage was an expression.

Her relationship with her son Robert was almost as poor in its emotional content as Marcel's with him, and the foundation of Marcel's relationship with her was his "ill health." He was to complain, toward the end of her life, that he was never permitted to enjoy good health *and* her affection simultaneously, and there can be little doubt that his "attacks" and collapses were extractive maneuvers designed to force an appearance of concern and affection from her.

His choice of a profession appears to have been a maneuver of the same order, and even his most sycophantic and supportive biographers, André Maurois and George Painter, have to concede that his adoption of the role of writer and artist enabled him to remain in a state of infantile dependence on his parents until he was into his thirties. When his father died he was still living in their apartment and occupying the bedroom which had been his when he was a child, and this pattern of existence was only broken up by his mother's death four years later.

It is striking, when one looks into the matter, that he had done no serious work up to that time, and that the sum total of his achievements before his mother's death was rather less than the bare minimum that would have been needed to make anything other than the most indulgent and permissive of families go along with his claim to be a writer. The greater part of his published works at this time had, indeed, appeared on the society pages of *Le Figaro* and other daily newspapers under a variety of pseudonyms—Horatio, Echo, and Dominique—and had consisted of such stuff as this from his account of the salon of the Contesse Potocka:

All her faithfuls, the Dowager Duchesse de Luynes, Madame de Brantes, the Marquise de Lubersac, the Marquise de Castellane, the Comtesse du Guerne, the great singer whom I can do more than mention today, the Marquise de Ganay, the Comtesse de Bearn, the Comtesse de Kersaint, monsieur Dubois de l'Estang the Marquis de Lau, one of those first rate men who have only been prevented from coming to the fore

*and shining in the highest places by the vicissitudes
of politics; the charming Duc de Luynes, the Comte
Mathieu de Noailles, whose superb portrait, so full
of distinction and life, by the Duc de Guiche has just
been exhibited at the Salon; the Comte de Castellano
(of whom we've already spoken in connection with
the salon of Madame Madeleine Lemaire and of whom
we shall have more to say presently), the Marquis
Vittellerchi, Monsieur Widor, and last but not least,
Monsieur Jean Béraud of whose brilliance, talent,
prestige, charm, and kindliness we have already said
something—in connection with that same salon of
Madame Madeleine Lemaire—they'd all go to the end
of the world to fetch her back, because they couldn't
be without her.*

While buying his entry into society with his ability
and willingness to write chitchat of this kind, he had compensated himself by writing a novel, which he wisely left
unpublished, called *Jean Santeuil*. It is, as a matter of fact,
an abuse of language to describe this work as a novel, since
it consists of a number of pieces of "fine writing" that have
no organic relationship with each other, embedded in a
wish-fulfillment fantasy in which the narrator conquers
the noble house of Reveillon by sheer charm, achieves the
most glorious putting-down of a society hostess who snubs
him, and finally plays the central role in a drama of *le high
life,* a card-sharping episode modeled on the Tranby Croft
scandal.

One has to be very deeply immersed in the Proustian cult
to take *Jean Santeuil* as anything other than a demonstration of the completeness of the divorce of his ambition
to be a writer from the desire to write any particular thing
that characterized his literary behavior up to the time of
his mother's death. It seems reasonable to conclude from this
that the declaration of the ambition was functional, as was
his commitment to the doctrine that, for the artist, the
periods of quiescence in which he devotes himself to the
refinement of his sensibilities and the enrichment of his
interior life in preparation for the creative act are just as

important as those in which he is visibly working: as a
writer whose creative hour had not yet come he could
remain in his state of infantile dependence on his parents
indefinitely.

The accounts of the death of Proust's mother and of her
lying-in-state given by his biographers have an element
of the comic in them, recalling that scene in which Hamlet
steals the central role from the corpse at Ophelia's funeral.
According to the Painter biography, he lay in bed "weeping
incessantly and entirely deprived of sleep" for a month after
the event. At the end of that month he managed to get up
and leave his bedroom, but he had still not been outdoors
a month later, and finally, on December 6, his mother having died on September 26, he was taken off to Dr. Sollier's
private nursing home at Billancourt, where he spent six
weeks undergoing a form of psychotherapy rather mysteriously described as isolation-treatment (since he was
allowed to receive visitors from two to four in the afternoon on three days in the week). It is this brief period of
partial seclusion which is described as "long years in a
sanitarium, during which I had completely renounced my
idea of becoming a writer" in *Time Regained*, a distortion
which is justified by Mr. Painter by the following ingenious,
if somewhat overwrought, argument:

> Yet the significance of the brief real and the long imag-
> inary stay in a nursing home was the same. The six
> weeks under Dr. Sollier marked a fundamental divi-
> sion between the two eras of Proust's life, between the
> past twenty-four years with his mother and the coming
> seventeen years without her.... The year of half life
> that followed Billancourt formed a moorland plateau
> from which the rivers flowed on one side to his child-
> hood, on the other to his death. He had reached the
> watershed between time lost and time regained.

This is very elegant, but it is doubtful if it means anything very much. As soon as Dr. Sollier began work with
Proust he recognized that he was dealing with one of those

patients who have no intention of seeking any benefit from the psychotherapist and do not even intend to be frank with him. The essence of Proust's relationship with Dr. Sollier was its nullity, and when he left Billancourt he was in precisely the same state as that in which he had arrived. It may seem perverse to say this, when the Proust who went to the sanitarium was the nonentity known as Horatio, Echo, and Dominique to most of his readers and to the remainder as the perpetrator of a refined form of academic fraud, the translation of Ruskin's *Bible of Amiens* (which he had produced without knowing a word of English), and the Proust who came away from it was to become the almost universally admired author of *Remembrance of Things Past.* The conventional interpretation of these events would be that Proust's mother's death and the retreat at Billancourt were indeed the peaks of a watershed, in that on one side of them his creativity had been blocked and on the other the inhibitions that held him back had been removed.

This interpretation of the situation holds as long as one thinks in terms of Proust's reputation and the critical standing of his novel, but it does not stand up in the face of an examination of the content of the novel itself, or of that of Proust's other writings written on the creative side of the watershed.

When Proust first began to write again after his mother's death he committed himself to a somewhat bizarre project, a collaboration with a playwright, René Peter, on a drama for which he had supplied the plot; it was to be about a man who loved his wife but who at the same time frequented prostitutes. This character enlivened his commerce with these commercial ladies by saying very vulgar things about his wife to them and encouraging them to speak of her in the same way. The wife was to find out about these transactions and to make them her reason for leaving her husband, who was then to commit suicide. Mr. Painter does his best to distract his readers from the fundamental oddity of this story as a part of the interests of a mature adult by saying that "this was an actual occurrence (except

for the suicide in the liason of his (Proust's) father's colleague Dr. Albert Robin with the courtesan Liane de Pougy."
By the curious fatality that pursued Proust's Albertine when
she was attempting to be less than frank with his narrator,
Mr. Painter finds himself compelled to mention Madame de
Clermont Tonerre on the very next page to that on which
this statement occurs. It is from that lady's reminiscences
that we learn what really happened between Dr. Robin and
the courtesan.

Liane de Pougy was one of those women at the top of her
profession who only sold themselves to people they liked,
and who sometimes became fond of their regulars. Dr.
Albert Robin was at heart very much the family man, and
even when with Liane de Pougy could not deny himself the
pleasure of speaking with his customary pride and devotion of the wife and daughter he adored. This made her
jealous, and to punish him for it she insisted that if he
was going to speak of those people when he was with her it
could only be on condition that he would refer to his wife
as "the monster," and to his daughter as "the little monster," when he did so. He kept to the terms of the agreement,
and it became a running joke between them.

It will be seen that the actual occurrence is at several
removes from the thing that Proust had made his own, and
that in making it his own he has introduced something
nasty which is also something childish into the story. There
is something essentially infantile in the conceptual field
involved: from Proust's version of the story one would deduce that bad men go to bad women to do bad things with
them, of which saying bad things about nice people is a fair
sample. It is Benjamin Bunny's idea of sadism.

Mr. Painter relates the topic of this uncompleted play
to that of a piece of writing that Proust had produced ten
years earlier, in 1896, the fantastic "Confession of a Young
Girl" in *Les Plaisirs et les jours*. Of this singular work Mr.
Painter writes:

> He had used the theme, long before the misdemeanour
> of Dr. Robin made it come true, in *The Confession of*

*a Young Girl...where the girl, who is so evidently
Proust himself, kills her mother by allowing her vice
to be detected, and then kills herself; and he was to
use it again, reversing the sexes, in Mlle. Vinteuil's
desecration of her dead father.*

Mr. Painter's use of the phrase "her vice" is strange: what
happens in "Confession of a Young Girl" is that the girl is
seduced by a young man. Her downfall begins when she is
fourteen and a distant cousin who is fifteen tells her
"things" that make her shiver with remorse and sensual
excitement. Scared to death of what appears to be about to
happen to her, the girl tells her mother what her cousin is
up to, but her mother listens with a "divine incomprehension" of the importance of what is being said and dismisses
the matter with a kindness that lifts the weight from the
poor girl's conscience. Presumably the girl made the tactical
error of saying "my cousin is saying horrid things about sex
to me" instead of saying "the horrid things my cousin says
about sex to me are making me want to do what he suggests." Her mother's "divinely uncomprehending answer"
is then, naturally enough, "Oh you mustn't let that worry
you, dear, all young men say horrid things about sex." This
would explain why the mother did nothing to break the
thing up at that stage, a point that is made much of by a
number of critics hostile to Proust, notably Charles Briand,
who have been bothered by this piece. Be that as it may, the
next step is for talk to become action. When the young girl
reaches the age of sixteen she begins to have gentlemen
callers.

*One of them was perverse and naughty. His ways were
at once gentle and bold. It was with him that I fell
in love...he induced me to do wrong, almost before I
was aware of it, then he made me accustomed to allow
wicked fancies that I hadn't the will to resist to awaken
in me....*

Once the poor girl had gone over the falls the whole world
became a darker place.

Never have I been to so many concerts, or been pro-
foundly less aware of music. I listened but I heard
nothing. If it did so happen that I heard I no longer saw
what music has to make visible. My walks also became
meaningless. Things that had once filled my days with
happiness—a ray of sunshine gilding a meadow, the
smell of leaves after rain, everything of that kind had
lost its bright charm just as I had. The woods, the sky,
the streams and lakes seemed to turn themselves from
me....

After this comes the terrible moment of truth when
mother at last realizes how things are.

I saw myself in the looking glass. I saw that the anguish
that was troubling my soul had left no mark on my
face, all that I could see there, in my shining eyes, in
the flaming cheeks that I was offering to his mouth,
was a stupid and brutal sensuality. I thought at that
moment how horrified anyone who had just seen me
kissing my mother with a melancholy tenderness
would be to see me transformed into a beast in this
fashion. Then all at once the glass showed me, opposite
my face, Jacques' mouth avid under his moustache,
Troubled in the profoundest depths of my being I was
drawing my head closer to his, when I saw before me,
yes, I'm telling you how it was, and you must listen be-
cause I can tell you, on the balcony, outside the win-
dow, I saw my mother who was watching me in utter
bewilderment. I don't know if she cried out, I heard
nothing, but she fell backward and lay there with her
head wedged between two balusters of the balcony....

The mother dies, of course, and the daughter, overcome
with guilt, puts a bullet into her chest.

Although I find it impossible to agree with Mr. Painter's
contention that this piece of nonsense is related to the plot
of the unrealized play and the description of the mysterious
transaction between Mlle. Vinteuil and her lesbian friend
at Montjouvain in the way that he suggests, it does seem
interesting to me. For Mr. Painter, and most of those who

have considered it, its importance resides in the obvious
point that it is clearly not the confession of a girl who has
been caught having her first affair with a man, but that of a
boy who has been seduced by another boy and caught with
him in a situation that suggests that he is a willing victim.
For them what is important is that the story shows that
Proust intends to make literary use of his homosexuality,
the feelings of guilt that it gives rise to in him, and its complication of his feelings about his mother, and that it shows
him adopting the strategy, for dealing with this topic as
part of the experience of the narrator in *Remembrance of
Things Past*, which will make Albertine a girl.

It has quite another significance for me. It does not appear
to me to be the account of a real event, or of a real state of
mind, but seems to me to have all the earmarks of a fantasy.
I don't think that it can be correctly described in terms of its
stated contents: "Confession of a Homosexual, or how I hurt
Mummy terribly by letting her find out, wicked creature
that I am, that I am one of the Accursed Race." My suggestion is that the story itself is the event, and that its writing
and publication constitute a single functional act of hostility and aggression directed at the writer's mother. Its basic
content is stated in its conclusion, and may be summarized
in the simple statement "I wish you were dead," and its
secondary level of content consists of the disclosure of the
secret, knowledge of which is shown to be lethal in its effect
on the mother inside the story, and which may be presumed
to have been calculated to cause her pain and distress in
"real life."

I am not sure how much weight should be given to the
question of the mother's "divine incomprehension" of what
is going on in the early part of the story; it looks as if Proust
was intending to saddle her with responsibility for what was
to happen later on, but if the suggestion is made it isn't
followed up.

What does seem clear, at least to me, is that the story was
part of a behavioral pattern, of which Proust's homosexual
practices were also a part, which is recognizably that of
the game Dr. Eric Berne has described under the name of

"Let's Make Mother Sorry," a point that becomes significant
when one finds that the first piece of writing that Proust
produces on the "creative" or "liberated" side of the watershed proposed by Mr. Painter is uncannily close in substance and spirit to the functional "Confession of a Young
Girl."

The essay concerned had its origin in a chance encounter.
When he left Dr. Sollier's sanitarium at Billancourt Proust
established himself in temporary quarters in the Hotel des
Reservoirs at Versailles. While he was living there he often
went into Paris for the day to see his friends, and on one of
these excursions he made a great effort to pick up an attractive young railwayman in the Gare Saint Lazare. The young
man wasn't keen and he slipped away after fobbing Proust
off with a false name and address. Proust made a number of
unsuccessful attempts to trace this person over the next
two months, and then by chance received a letter from
Henri van Blarenberghe, who was chairman of the Chemins
de Fer de l'Est, the railroad corporation which operated the
Gare Saint Lazare. Proust thought Blarenberghe might help
him to run down the missing man, and wrote to him asking
him to make the necessary inquiries. On January 17, 1907,
Proust received van Blarenberghe's reply, saying that he
could find no trace of any person bearing the name he had
been given in the company's records. Just over a week after
he had been given this bad news, Proust opened his morning newspaper and learned that Henri van Blarenberghe,
whose father had died earlier in the winter, had murdered
his mother and killed himself. Within a week Proust had
talked the editor of Le Figaro into giving him space for an
article on this subject, and had sent his new secretary-
friend, Robert Ulrich, down to the newspaper office with the
finished product, an essay entitled "Filial Thoughts of a
Matricide," slightly expanding Oscar Wilde's thought that
"each man kills the thing he loves" to the more elaborate
notion that as we all kill our mothers by causing them so
much pain and anxiety the only thing that distinguished
Henri van Blarenberghe as a criminal was that he had used
a knife to do what we all do with our heartless egotism.

Proust went on to compare Blarenberghe with the tragic heroes of Sophocles, Shakespeare, and Dostoievski, in a passage which the subeditor of the paper declined to print on the grounds that any reasonably sane reader would take it to be eulogy of matricide.

It is hard for a dispassionate reader to disagree with the subeditor—a Monsieur Cardane—and harder still for him to agree with Mr. Painter when he says that the essay represents a point of departure at which Proust's work can be seen to be taking a new direction.

> It was as if he saw van Blarenberghe's crime, and his own insight into its real nature, as an act of mythological, almost ritual dignity, as a moment of truth. The night on which he wrote Filial Feelings of a Matricide was a turning point in Proust's life. For the first time he acknowledged his guilt, and was therefore able to forgive his mother; he had gone back beyond the evening at Auteuil where Time Lost began, into the world outside Time where his novel awaited him.

I find this quite impossible to accept. The essay seems to me to be an obsessive recension of the content of the "Confession of a Young Girl," duplicating the original demonstration of hostility and aggression. If it means anything it is that Proust is going to go on playing the game of "Let's Make Mother Sorry" in spite of her disappearance from the scene.

Many readers will feel that this contention must be wrong because there can surely be no psychological gain for anyone who plays this game if the target figure is not available to take punishment. While this might be so if the player could be assumed to be making a series of rational decisions about what he was doing, the patterns of behavior involved are in fact compulsive, and the courts where the games are played are situated in the *terrain vague* between the domains of reality and fantasy. In this uncertain countryside symbolic acts and real ones are of equal value, and imagined or fantasied consequences are as good as real ones. The game of

"Let's Make Mother Sorry" can thus be played perfectly
satisfactorily in the absence of any direct line of communications with the target. All that is necessary to make the
game "work" for the active player is for him to have a sufficiently vivid sense of what the effect of a knowledge of his
activities would have if Mother were possessed of it. There
is thus no difficulty in going on with the game indefinitely
with a dead person in the role of dummy.

There are, however, other reasons for thinking that Proust
came through the experience of his mother's death with a
determination to go on playing the old game in the old way
than the mere fact of his having been thrown into an excited state by learning of van Blarenberghe's crime. When
the lease of his parents' apartment in the Rue de Courcelles
fell in a year after his mother's death Proust at last acquired
a place of his own. The building he chose to move to, of all
those in Paris that might have received him, was that on the
Boulevard Haussman which had once belonged to his
mother's uncle, Louis Weill, the naughty old man who had
shared the favors of Laure Hayman, a woman of the same
type as Liane de Pougy, with Dr. Adrien Proust. It seems unlikely that it was purely by chance that he should have
celebrated the anniversary of his mother's death by moving
out of the house in which he had spent the first thirty-five
years of his life beside her and into the one in which he had
first made the acquaintance of his father's mistress. It was
also hardly by chance that when he at last got up, after
spending nearly eighteen months in bed mourning for his
mother, it was to leave Paris for the Grand Hôtel at Cabourg where she had taken him for his summer holidays
when he was a child and his grandmother was still alive.
It was while he was on this sacred ground that he made the
acquaintance of the chauffeur, Alfred Agostinelli, with
whom he was to have the long, drawn-out affair which is,
in a complicated way, the foundation of the story of the
narrator's affair with Albertine in *Remembrance of Things
Past*. It is again no accident that Proust should have gone to
a place rich in association with a period of innocent happiness in his relationship with his mother to achieve a further

stage in his commitment to homosexuality, and of a more sinister kind.

Before the time of his mother's last illness and death Proust had unquestionably had occasional affairs with young men of the lower classes who had been bought, but most of his lovers had been friends in his own walk of life who had given themselves to him for the pleasure of it and because they liked him or were interested in him. After his mother's death he began more and more to look beneath him for his partners and to require them to be uneducated and mercenary. There is something extremely pathetic and sad in the thought of his making his return to the place where he had once been so contented to be what he was with his Jewish Maman and nou-nou, in order to acquire the experience that he would need to justify the terrible equation made in the Accursed Race. Agostinelli was neither very wicked nor very contemptible; indeed he was almost as nice as a young man who can be bought can be, but there were others who came from lower levels and were of another kind.

It is only when one has realized the nature of Proust's nocturnal associations during the winter that followed his first visit to Cabourg after his mother's death that one can understand the full significance of the exchange recorded in *Contre Sainte-Beuve* that has been quoted above:

> "What is my silly billy thinking of, what nonsense is this?" "I should be so happy if I never saw anyone again." "Don't say that, my lamb. I am very fond of these people who are nice to you, in fact, I would like to see you with more friends who would come in and talk without being too much for you." "All I want is my mamma." "But your Mamma would rather think of you seeing other people who could tell you things she doesn't know—things you could explain to her after they had gone. . . "

I would suggest, however ridiculous the suggestion may seem at first sight, that the majority of Proust's works—his

"Confession of a Young Girl," his "Filial Thoughts of a Matricide," his *Contre Sainte-Beuve,* and his *Remembrance of Things Past*—have to be considered primarily in the light of a series of statements forming part of the game called "Let's Make Mother Sorry," which have as their central content a body of knowledge answering to the description of "things mother doesn't know and would rather not hear about." Some elements in *Remembrance of Things Past* are less closely related to this main structure than others, and some are barely connected with it at all, but all the important interpersonal relationships described are integrated with it, and so are most of the truly memorable and effective scenes.

Those who are reluctant to consider the idea proposed, and find themselves inclined to reject it out of hand, should pull the sample thread from Proust's elaborate tapestry which first shows itself in the scene at Montjourvain, between Mlle. Vinteuil and her lesbian friend, which is so implausibly witnessed by the narrator. The donée is, one cannot say anything else, marvelously absurd. The delicate narrator, who is already haunted by his fear of those mysterious attacks of breathlessness and suffocation, so useful in manipulating the terms of his relationships with his father and mother, lies down (although there has just been a shower) on the ground in the shrubbery immediately outside the drawing room window of the Vinteuil's house. When he wakes he finds that darkness has fallen and that he is looking into the now-lamplit room in which he can see Mlle. Vinteuil standing, dressed in deep mourning. Because the ground in front of the window has, conveniently enough, a sharp upward slope to it, Proust's narrator is placed slightly above Mlle. Vinteuil and so positioned as to be able to see the whole room and to hear everything that is said within it. Mlle. Vinteuil is in mourning because, by a remarkable coincidence, she has recently disposed of her father by the very means with which the heroine of the "Confession of a Young Girl" killed her mother. She is in consequence a murderess in the sense that we are all murderers according to the argument advanced in the "Filial

Thoughts of a Parricide:" she has in fact killed the poor old man by taking no trouble to conceal her lesbianism from him or, for that matter, from anyone else. She is now awaiting the arrival of her butch lover, the hearty, strapping girl her father disliked so much while he was still alive. When this lady's carriage is heard to arrive Proust's narrator sees Mlle. Vinteuil performing a routine which, by a truly remarkable coincidence, duplicates something that he saw when fate brought him to the very same spot on a previous occasion. The narrator had then been allowed to slip round to the back of the house while his parents were waiting on the front door step to pay a formal call on Mlle. Vinteuil's father. Gazing into the drawing room from this same coign of vantage he had then seen Monsieur Vinteuil hurrying into the room to place a sheet of music on the rack above the keyboard where his visitors would be sure to see it. With this done the old man had withdrawn to greet his visitors, and on returning with them had claimed to be surprised and embarrassed to find the music where it was. The narrator now sees Mlle. Vinteuil doing just the same thing with a small photograph of her father. She places this object on a small table by the sofa on which her friend is soon making love to her. As the fondling begins Mlle. Vinteuil draws her friend's attention to it with an exclamation of dismay:

> "Oh! There's my father's photograph looking at us:
> I can't think who can have put it there; I'm sure I've
> told them twenty times that it's not the proper place
> for it."

To this the friend replies:

> "Let him stay there. He can't trouble us any longer.
> Do you think he'd start whining, do you think he'd
> turn you out of the house if he could see you now,
> with the window wide open, the ugly old monkey!"

From this it is a short step to the point at which she spits

on the father's photograph. Tlhe narrator does not see this
happen, because Mlle. Vinteuil closes the shutters and shuts
off the view before the deed is done.

Left in the dark, and under the necessity of extracting
himself from the garden and making his way home to
Combray, the narrator muses on what he has seen:

> I knew now what was the reward that Mlle. Vinteuil
> had received posthumously from his daughter, as a
> recompense for all the suffering that he had been
> through in her account during his lifetime.

This is a reference back to some times in the text that
appear at the point at which the narrator is spying on Mlle.
Vinteuil before her friend's arrival. He stares at her and
recalls an utterance of his mother's:

> "'Poor M. Vinteuil,' my mother would say, 'he lived for
> his daughter, and now he has died for her, without
> getting his reward. Will he get it now, I wonder, and in
> what form? It can only come from her.'"

My own feeling about this episode, with the prolifera-
tion of technical absurdities in its writing, and the accumulation of implausibilities in its action, is that it is incomprehensible if it is not related to some such general pattern
as the one which I propose, and to what is known of Proust's
obsessions. Disregarding the intervening links in the chain
of similar incidents scattered through the various volumes
of the novel, in all of which the narrator spies on various
people who are engaged in compromising activities from
places of concealment of extreme unlikeliness, one can
proceed from this point near its beginning to that near its
end, in which, in the male brothel in the Tansonville
chapter of Time Regained, Proust's narrator runs across
Jupien once again, in the blacked-out Paris of the war years.
The narrator has no previous knowledge of this institution;
his curiosity about it is aroused by the numbers of soldiers
he sees entering and leaving the building, and by the

ambiguity of such of their remarks as he is able to overhear. He goes in, and asks to be given a room, giving as his pretext for making the request that he is unable to reach his own home because the air raid which is in progress has driven all the cabs from the streets. He gets what he has asked for, but when he reaches the room, number 43, which has been assigned to him, he finds it unpleasantly stuffy, and begins roaming about in the corridors of the establishment. He has reached the top floor when he hears stifled groans coming from "a room situated by itself at the end of a corridor." He walks rapidly toward the sounds, and putting his ear to the most likely door is soon aware that someone inside it is being beaten. How will he find out who it is? There is no difficulty about that:

> At this moment I noticed that there was a small oval window opening from the room onto the corridor and that the curtain had not been drawn across it.

The narrator looks in and there before him is his old friend, Monsieur de Charlus, being whipped by a young man. As soon as he has made this recognition he is faced with another.

> Suddenly the door opened and a man came in who fortunately did not see me. It was Jupien.

The mechanics of this are a little hard to envisage. The narrator had his ear to the door through which Jupien has just passed when he saw the convenient window that he is now glued to—how, pray, did Jupien get down the corridor and in through the door without seeing him?

But no matter. Monsieur de Charlus next tells Jupien to send the young man with the whip away, and that person leaves, again without seeing the narrator. This seems just possible, but what follows is wholly inexplicable. As Monsieur de Charlus and Jupien are talking—in this room at the end of the corridor on the top floor of the hotel—a bell is heard to ring. As soon as he hears its summons Jupien

knows instantly that it is a customer in room number 3 who
is ready to leave, and he goes downstairs to see him out.
To give a moment's thought to this bell is to realize how
architecturally impossible this baudy house is, in which
everything that passes in the rooms can be seen and heard
from the corridors, and in which the bells ringing in the
ground floor *bureau de service* can be heard in the top floor
rooms. When the passage is reread the architecture is found,
too, to be marvelously flexible. It produces extra closets
and rooms to hide in and internal windows and ventilators
for the use of eavesdroppers whenever and wherever they
become necessary. Such intentions are not such as to gen-
erate respect for the inventor; they are clearly creations
of necessity which attempt to explain how it is that the
narrator has knowledge of transactions that only a participant could acquire without having been engaged in them.
But however implausible the physical properties of this
establishment may be, it does not come as a surprise to the
reader who moves on from the novel to the biographies to
learn at last that Proust was very much involved in the
affairs of just such a house and was, indeed, in partnership
with its proprietor. This person was a Breton called Albert
Le Cuziat, a man who had turned to brothel-keeping after
having had a long and successful career as a male prostitute.
Proust first met Le Cuziat in 1911. The latter's career in
prostitution was then drawing to a close, and he was
making his first tentative moves in the direction of pro-
curing so that his earnings would not fall off too sharply
when he finally lost his looks. Proust was immediately
drawn to Le Cuziat for two reasons: the procurer was not
only useful to him in the obvious way, but also because
he was a tremendous snob who had acquired a unique
fund of the lore of society. Le Cuziat had come to Paris
in 1881 at the age of sixteen and had practiced his dubious
calling while working as footman for a succession of noble
masters and mistresses: Prince Constantine Radziwill, the
Prince d'Essling, the Comtesse Greffulhe, Count Orloff,
and the Duc de Rohan. Proust found the fund of anecdote
and the knowledge of protocol and etiquette that Le Cuziat

had acquired while holding these positions endlessly fascinating, and frequently asked him up to his apartment
on the Boulevard Haussman to pump him for more, much
to the disgust of his devoted servant Celeste. There seems
to have been a break in their intimacy while Proust's affair
with Agostinelli was running its course, but when, in 1917,
Le Cuziat found that he had an opportunity to buy the
Hôtel Marigny in the Rue de l'Arcade that would enable
him to satisfy his ambition to set up a brothel for homo-
sexuals he turned to Proust for help. Proust not only found
a part of the money that Le Cuziat needed to swing the
deal, but went further and helped him to furnish the place
when he had taken possession—giving him for this purpose
a large part of the furniture that he had inherited from
his mother, which had been in storage ever since the lease
of the apartment in the Rue de Courcelles had fallen in.
As an *ami de la maison* Proust had a privileged position
among the clients of the Hôtel Marigny and within its
walls. Surrounded by the chairs, tables, and sofas with
which he had been familiar from his earliest childhood,
he was able to do all the things, and to act out all the infantile ritualizations that are ascribed to Monsieur de
Charlus in *Time Regained.* He also amused himself at the
Hôtel Marigny with a more pathetic routine in which he
showed photographs of his mother, and of other women
who had been given to believe that he liked or admired
them, to young male prostitutes who had been briefed
beforehand by Le Cuziat, and who consequently received
them with derision and contempt and then spat on them.
    It seems to me to be either impossible or foolish, and
perhaps both, to disregard this information when one is
considering what manner of thing Proust's novel may be,
what he may be supposed to be doing when he describes
the desecration of Monsieur Vinteuil's photograph by his
daughter's friend, and the narrator's visit to Jupien's brothel. What it seems to demonstrate beyond any question is
that Proust's compulsions were far from being under control
when he sat down to write and that, in these instances at
least, they, rather than his aesthetic sense, determined what

went into the book. Further questions as to the extent of Proust's conscious control of his material rise from his falsification of his knowledge of this experience for what may, or may not, have been artistic purposes. I have already questioned the process by which the sodden rusk of *Contre Sainte-Beuve* became the *petit madeleine* of the novel so that it could allow his involuntary memory to bring back Illiers in preference to Auteuil, but what goes on in the case of Monsieur de Charlus and the violinist Morel is stranger and even more revealing.

These two fictions have as their physical foundations two real persons, Count Robert de Montesquiou and Leon Delafosse, both of whom were alive and in full possession of their faculties when Proust wrote and published his novel. His acquaintance with Montesquiou arose through the agency of Madeleine Lemaire in 1893, when he was still socially a nobody and only tolerated in the more easy-going drawing rooms because he could be counted on to write flattering things about those who received him in the gossip columns of *Le Figaro*.

Madeleine Lemaire was an atrocious flower painter (the one of whom the younger Dumas said, without a flattering intention, that only God had made more roses) and a wealthy woman, who had managed to make her little house, with its attached studio-ballroom, on the Rue de Monceaux a species of free port between the worlds of society and bohemia. Bohemians on the make frequented her five o'clocks, her Wednesdays, and her evenings of music and poetry readings to meet the very rich and the very well born, and those who were in society went to her house to meet the freaks who had produced the plays, novels, poems, and paintings that "everybody" was talking about. It was here, in this social no-man's land, that Proust was introduced to Montesquiou at his own request.

Proust attempted to play Montesquiou as he had already played Madame Strauss, the neurasthenic and temperamental widow of Bizet, and Madeleine Lemaire, by a process resembling that of courtship, which entailed the giving of endless "thoughtful" little gifts, the writing of mash notes, endless flattery, and the running of countless errands. If he could get Montesquiou, a member of one of the most unimpeachably aristocratic houses of France, to be his sponsor in society he would, truly, have arrived. He was disconcerted to find that Montesquiou was just as intelligent as he was, and quite able to see through him; but he did not make this discovery until Montesquiou wished him to.

The Count let him have all the rope he needed and then abruptly pulled him up short at one of Madame Lemaire's parties, following up a preliminary, public reprimand by sending for him to receive a further dressing-down at his home the following day. On that occasion Montesquiou told Proust how vulgar and foolish his conduct toward him had been, and how presumptuous it was of him to try to cut a figure in society when he was utterly unprepared to do so. Montesquiou then lectured him on his ignorance of society and of his chosen craft, and indeed of almost everything that he should know about life and art if he were to hope to substantiate his claim—the only one that would make an individual of his race and origins socially acceptable—to be an artist of distinction. He then undertook, if Proust would promise to behave himself and take his chosen profession seriously, to be his mentor.

Braced by this exhortation, which he was ultimately to travesty as one of Monsieur de Charlus's more grotesque performances, Proust experienced a species of aesthetic awakening and went off to reexamine much to which he was committed. *Sesame and Lilies* and Ruskin's moralism? *L'union pour l'Action morale* and the woozy uplift of Paul Desjardins? *Pastels* and the style and content of the works of Paul Bourget? The easy outpourings of Georges de Porto Riche? The aesthetics of William Morris and the Art Workers Guild as they came to one through the thrillingly progressive interior decorating department of the Paris branch of Maples? Were these enthusiasms quite what he had supposed? He realized that they might not be, and returned, with the air of being chastened, to sit at Montesquiou's feet as a pupil. He was unquestionably right to

do so. However absurdly and extravagantly he might behave when he was in one of his phases of frantic exhibi-
tionism, Montesquiou was nonetheless a man with a
highly developed literary intelligence and a refined sensi-
bility whose criticism was much admired by Bernard
Berenson. In the decade that followed this episode Montesquiou taught Proust almost all that he was ever to learn of
aesthetics and gave his whole approach to the arts and to
writing a new direction.

It may be said, incidentally, that what Montesquiou
had to teach Proust about life was as important as what
he had to tell him about the arts. When Proust criticizes
Balzac for the naïveté and credulity of his portraits of society women, he does so on the basis of a knowledge of this
field that he owes to Montesquiou, and when he, in due
course, came to write of such women, he could write of them
as Balzac could not because Montesquiou's experience had
been made available to him. There were, however, limits to
what Montesquiou could teach Proust about society, because he was effeminate and was not in the least interested
in masculine activities. Because Proust's identification was
with his mother, and he was, consequently, as effeminate as
Montesquiou, he was as ignorant as his mentor in this
quarter. He attempted to remedy this deficiency by pumping
male informants, but as he was not an interesting person
in the eyes of men with masculine interests he did not get
very far with this, and was compelled to rely on what he
could pick up from men such as Le Cuziat, and the head-
waiters, chauffeurs, mechanics, lift boys, and so on who
constituted the bulk of his male acquaintance. If Montesquiou had not told him what he knew about women,
Remembrance of Things Past would have been an even
stranger book than it is.

Though Proust was aware that he was learning all
through this period, and that what he was learning was
of vital importance to him, he was not satisfied with the
situation: Montesquiou kept him at arms' length physically
and showed no signs of becoming emotionally involved
with him. To break up this impasse—or for some other

reason of which there is no record (Phillipe Julian thinks
that it was done simply so that he could establish a claim
on his mentor's gratitude)—Proust introduced Montesquiou
to a young pianist of great beauty and genuine promise who
had been discovered by Conte Henri de Saussure, hoping
that they would become lovers. The pianist, Leon Delafosse,
had no money. He was the son of a widow who earned a
precarious living by giving piano lessons, and he was at
that stage in his career when a virtuoso needs all the social
and financial backing he can get if he is to establish himself
as a concert artist. It was Proust who told him how important to him Montesquiou's support could be. The Pianist
was tempted and fell; so did Montesquiou, even though he
understood the nature of Proust's maneuver and was at first
extremely unwilling to meet Delafosse. What followed had
elements in it that evidently took Proust by surprise. Delafosse fell in love with Montesquiou, and Montesquiou
with him. Montesquiou's love was, however, demanding
and possessive to an unusual degree, and he attempted to
take complete control of Delafosse's life and make him so
far as possible his own private property, much as Proust's
narrator was later to do with Albertine. It is evidence of the
genuineness of Delafosse's feelings for Montesquiou that
he was willing to submit to demands that were in the long
run fatal to his career. In the vital ten years in which he
should have been establishing himself as a public performer
he was in fact withdrawing into his lover's private world,
because his lover wished it to be that way. His mother
noticed his disappearance as a professional and his rebirth
as an object of scandal with growing dismay, and when the
liaison had persisted for more than five years began to do
all she could to break it up. At the same time Montesquiou
began to be more and more insistent on his exclusive rights
to the musician, to whom the position slowly became intolerable. Life was passing him by, and Montesquiou was,
as his mother was constantly telling him, treating him
like an old family servant with no right to an independent
existence.

A crisis came when Delafosse, who was capable of pro-

ducing compositions of his own which were not altogether
without distinction, was caught in the treacherous act of
dedicating one of his pieces for the piano to the Comtesse
Greffulhe, just as if he were still planning an independent
career. Montesquiou turned on him and delivered one of
those tirades for which he was famous, and which are one
of the distinguishing features of Proust's Monsieur de
Charlus. "Mediocre people never see the efforts one makes
to descend to their level," Delafosse was told, "and they
are incapable of climbing up to one's own.... You never
have been more than an instrument for expressing my
ideas—by yourself you will never be more than a musical
mechanic...."

The shattered pianist took himself off and was succored
by the Princesse Rachel de Brancovan, who attempted to
give him the support that Montesquiou had denied him
and to get his career going again. It was, however, too late;
he had missed the boat, and he was destined to dwindle
into obscurity without ever having enjoyed the pleasures
of a personal success.

It is interesting to see what Proust did with the material
that his involvement in the margin of this affair gave him:
he put on a mimetic performance, duplicating the main
features of the relationship with his friend, the mechanic
Agostinelli, and then made that, with Delafosse-Ago-
stinelli transformed into Albertine, one of the more important elements in his novel. There is nothing wrong with
that; all novelists appropriate other people's experience
and emotion in just this way. But Proust made use of the
material twice, once in describing the narrator's relationship with Albertine, and a second time in describing Monsieur de Charlus' relationship with Morel. When dealing
with the narrator's feelings for Albertine, Proust does
achieve a high level of objectivity in describing the games
an emotionally sterile person must play to try to invest his
relationships with some kind of meaning, but the treatment
of Monsieur de Charlus' relationship with Morel consists
quite simply of a systematic falsification of Proust's experience of Robert de Montesquiou and Henri Delafosse. On

his friend and intellectual creditor he unloaded all that is least creditable in himself, along with a great mound of garbage that he acquired from his partner, the charming Le Cuziat; and on Delafosse, whose career he did much to destroy, and who never did him any harm whatever, he discharged a stream of slanders of an almost unbelievable malignancy. The story of Morel's treatment of Jupien's niece is, even in this medium—which has so often been the means of settling old scores and accomplishing covert assassinations—an invention of almost unexampled ugliness. It would stand alone if it were not that Proust had also chosen to repay Madeleine Lemaire for the endless kindnesses she had shown him, and all the encouragement she had given him in the first stages of his social climbing, by caricaturing her, even more viciously than he had caricatured Montesquiou, as Madame Verdurin.

These are not by any means isolated examples of the falsifications which Proust resorted to in order to be treacherously cruel to his old friends and benefactors—only the outstanding ones. The Oriane he professed to have been in love with is a knife in the back for three women who were never anything but pleasant to him; Odette de Crecy is an act of treachery to Laure Haymann; and the story of Saint Loup is a desecration of what was then the freshly filled grave of Bertrand de Fenelon. In the light of the important part that these amiabilities play in the book I find it hard not to think of the *Remembrance of Things Past* as anything else but the last in the series of compulsive sadomasochistic exercises that begins with the "Confession of a Young Girl," particularly since the basic structure of the two works is the same. In both, a disguised confession of the author's homosexuality licenses a subsequent release of hostility.

When, toward the end of *Time Regained*, we encounter Monsieur de Charlus, broken by a stroke and reduced to a state of helpless dependence on Jupien, we recognize that we are assistants taking part in a magical exercise of the kind that showed us the young girl's mother lying stretched out on the terrace with her smashed head between the two stone balusters of the parapet, and which is related to the oper-

ations in which pins are pushed into wax dolls by simple
but malignant souls who wish to injure their enemies or,
to put it in another way, bring about a more satisfactory
ordering of reality. When one thinks of it in that way it is
to realize that something more important than the moral
and physical dissolution of Monsieur de Charlus has taken
place by the time we come to the end of *Time Regained*, and
that is that the narrator has been discovered to be the one
person who has learned anything from the set of experiences
that has made every other inhabitant of his universe stupid,
futile, hideous, or decrepit. He has not, as everyone has
supposed, been spending his days in bed, his evenings
camping at the Ritz or in fashionable drawing rooms, and
his nights cruising on the boulevards or haunting brothels:
he has been devoting himself to literature. With his wax
dolls, the notebooks piled on his bedroom mantlepiece, he
has reordered reality in his own interest, has made himself
a very important figure indeed, has strewn the ground with
the bodies of those who have ventured to despise him, and
has done what no one has ever done before: discarded the
false literature of the intellect and invented the literature
of intuition.

His self-dramatization is a very moving and almost per-
suasive affair—until you stop to ask yourself what his words
mean. For a start he writes off almost everything that has
ever been written by anyone else, with a deceptively easy
gesture:

> *How could the literature of description possibly have
> any value, when it is only beneath the surface of the
> little things which such a literature describes that
> reality has its hidden existence....*
> *The greatness, on the other hand, of fine art, of the
> art which Monsieur de Norpois would have called a
> dilettante's pastime, I had long come to see elsewhere:
> we have to rediscover, to reapprehend, to make our-
> selves fully aware of that reality remote from our daily
> preoccupations, from which we separate ourselves by
> an even greater gulf as the conventional knowledge
> which we substitute for it grows thicker and more*

*unpermeable, that reality which it is very easy for us
to die without ever having known, and which is quite
simply our life.*

A remarkable feat has been performed in this last sentence, which is to make a gramatically impeccable statement which has no meaning whatever. (I imagine that
thick and impermeable knowledge is what the things my
old nannie used to call sensible shoes would have to be
made of.) Proust goes on: "Real life, life at last laid bare and
illuminated—the only life in consequence which can be
said to be really lived—is literature, and life thus defined
is in a sense all the time immanent in ordinary men no less
than in the artist."

There is a major muddle here that is hard to straighten
out. Proust has told us that the intellect can't tell us anything useful about real life, so this laying bare and illuminating has to be an intuitive process. But what is laid
bare and illuminated is literature, if the grammar of the
sentence is to be relied upon. Literature, as I understand
it, is the general body of what has been written, or written
material, and I am not sure how to equate it with something described as "real life" or "time immanent in ordinary
men."

Proust is aware that there is a difficulty here and makes
a shooing gesture to try to persuade it to go away: "But most
men do not see it because they do not seek to shed light upon
it." I feel that I would run into mechanical difficulties if I
tried to shed light on the time immanent in my own life,
and I would be very surprised if I found myself seeing literature if I did.

Proust realizes that his shooing gesture has driven away
one difficulty and that another has now shown up of the
kind that occurs to me. He does his best to give the ordinary
man something to shed light on: "And therefore their past
is like a photographic darkroom encumbered with innumerable negatives which remain useless because the intellect has not developed them."

As soon as he has written this Proust realizes that it won't do, because he has previously told us that the intellect will destroy the value of these negatives as soon as it gets at them. Feeling trapped he boards a passing balloon and floats away: "But art," he goes on, "if it means awareness of our own life, means also awareness of the lives of other people—for style for the writer, no less than color for the painter is a question not of technique but of vision...."

It is hard to admire this evasive bit of slithering, and what follows suggests that for Proust "art" means something that he could say anything about that he happened to feel like saying:

> *Through art alone we are able to emerge from our-*
> *selves, to know what another person sees of a universe*
> *which is not the same as our own and of which, with-*
> *out art, the landscapes would remain as unknown to us*
> *as those that may exist on the moon. Thanks to art,*
> *instead of seeing one world only, our own, we see that*
> *world multiply itself and we have at our disposal as*
> *many worlds as there are original artists, worlds more*
> *different one from the other than those which revolve*
> *in infinite space, worlds which, centuries after the*
> *extinction of the fire from which their light first ema-*
> *nated, be that fire called Rembrandt or Vermeer, send*
> *us still each one its special radiance.*

One would not think this at all bad if it came from a provincial mayor who was doing his best to justify spending a little of the rate payers' money on pictures or a piece of sculpture, but can it be taken seriously? I don't feel that it can. Works of art appear to have meaning—for those who find meaning in them—for precisely the opposite reason to that proposed by Proust as the source of their value: they "mean" because they are expressions of a specific individual's experience of the common ground constituting the one, and only, universe of experience available to human beings. The examples given, of Rembrandt and Vermeer, are particularly ill chosen, since the secret of their enormous popularity rather plainly resides in the fact that most people have only to look at their works to recognize that they have originated in a familiar territory—acquaintance with the sort of visual array that is part of the common experience of everyday reality. It's interesting, in a way, that Proust hasn't noticed that Vermeer's pictures are largely concerned with giving one information about the things that were in front of the painter while he was painting them, and hence analogues of books belonging to the literature of description that he has been putting down as valueless. But then he wasn't very good at looking at pictures and thought that Helleu was the interesting painter of the day.

In all this, however, Proust has only been gathering speed for takeoff. He is now ready for a pronouncement:

> This work of the artist, this struggle to discern beneath matter, beneath experience, beneath words, something that is different from them, in a process exactly inverse to that which, in those everyday lives which we live with our gaze averted from ourself, is at every moment being accomplished by vanity and passion and the intellect, and habit too, when they smother our true impressions, so as entirely to conceal them from us, beneath a whole heap of verbal concepts and practical purposes which we falsely call life.

It is as difficult to think of any work of art which shows any sign of being the product of a struggle to discuss something different from matter that may be said to be beneath it, as it is to think of any way in which a struggle—which, to me at any rate, implies a prolonged and consciously directed effort—to find out what lies beneath experience and beneath words can be carried on without the use of the intellect. What these things are that are not matter, not experience, and not words, and *are* components of a reality that is more real than our everyday lives, I have no idea, and I do not think that Proust does either. The rest of the sentence is a confused reminiscence of Bergson. Proust goes on:

> In short, this art which is so complicated is the only living art. It alone expresses for others and renders

visible to ourselves that life of ours which cannot ef-
fectually observe itself and of which the observable
manifestations need to be translated and, often, to be
read backwards and laboriously deciphered.

The second sentence runs on with such authority that one almost lets the bogus entity it contains slip under one's guard: but just what is "that life of ours which cannot effectually observe itself," which produces "observable manifestations," and which is not the life we think we lead? That life of ours is, at least as far as I can make out, not a thing at all but a condition or a state of being. It would be very surprising if it could observe itself: if it is what it apparently has to be it cannot possibly have any of the necessary equipment for making observations. It would be just as surprising if it could produce any observable manifestations.

The question of the extent of Proust's borrowings from Bergson arises at this point, but is difficult to discuss since it is evident that Proust never quite understood what he took from that least rewarding of philosophers—and for the best of reasons: the ideas that he was lifting were not rational and are not, strictly speaking, comprehensible. The difficulty is greatest where the question is most crucial, in the matter of Bergson's idea of the past as a simultaneous continuity, all of which coexists with the present. It is not accessible to the intellect but can only be apprehended intuitively by the instinct, by a process of association that Proust called involuntary memory and claimed to have invented independently, although Bergson gives a clear enough account of the way it works in dogs and in people. Proust responded to suggestions that he was indebted in this quarter with rather graceless outbursts, but his more serious passages are very often parodies of parallel passages in Bergson's lectures. When borrowing from this source he often adopts the rather mawkish and affected tone that he brings to the repudiation of the intellect at the beginning of *Contre Sainte-Beuve:*

Our vanity, our passions, our spirit of imitation, our abstract intelligence, our habits have long been at work, and it is the task of art to undo this work of theirs, making us travel back in the direction from which we have come to the depths where what has really existed lies unknown within us. And surely this was a most tempting prospect, this task of recreating one's true life, of rejuvenating one's impressions. But it required courage of many kinds....

As always, it is astonishing to find how much plain bad writing there is in Proust's novel: here we travel back in the direction from which we have come and end up deep inside ourselves. But it is the word *courage* that is striking here. When Proust says that it required *courage* to embark upon the self-serving reordering of the reality of his experience which he describes as "this task of recreating his true life" one realizes just why the method of Sainte-Beuve was so objectionable to him. He has, by another route, reached precisely that point at which, at the start of *Le Père Goriot*, Balzac, in the characteristic style of the hard-selling salesman that Proust found so inartistic and so vulgar, made a similar commitment:

When you have read of the secret sorrows of Père Goriot, you will sit down to your dinner with a good appetite and charge your indifference to the author's account—accusing him of exaggerating or romanticizing. Ah, well! But let me tell you this—this drama is neither a fiction nor a romance. All is true, and so much so that everyone can see the makings of such a story in his own home, perhaps in his own heart.

So far as fiction is concerned what Proust calls "this work of the artist, this struggle to discern beneath matter, beneath experience, beneath words, something that is different from them" is simply this game called—Balzac put the phrase in English in his original text—"All is true." The writer gives the reader something that he has, in the

childish phrase, "made up" and offers him his fabrication
with his personal guarantee that this time his gift is something different. Balzac says it is not going to be one of your
ordinary fictions or romances; Proust promises that his
thing is not going to be one of those collages of untruths
belonging to the literature of description that people like
Balzac have been palming off on their readers as the real
thing. Balzac says that his thing is not only true in itself,
but also the container of truths that everyone will recognize
as true of their families and of what goes on inside themselves. Proust says that his book is to be made up of "a
whole host of truths concerning human passions and character and conduct" and this material is the substance of
his "true life."

I believe that Proust felt that the full horror of the threat
that was contained in the method of Sainte-Beuve was not
simply that it would reveal that this game is the basic reality of the craft of fiction, but that it might reveal the
motivations that led writers to devote a large part of their
lives to playing it. I think that his fear was well founded,
and that we already possess enough information about his
behavior and its compulsive patterns to be able to say that
his commitment to the reordering and reprocessing of his
past experience—which an outsider might call "writing
the *Remembrance of Things Past*" and which he called
"the task of recreating my true life"—was in fact a device
for structuring his time in such a way as to exempt him
from the necessity of entering into any meaningful human
relationships, paralleling in its function, and providing a
substitute for, the carefully maintained state of infantile
dependence on his mother which had served the same
purpose in the first part of his life. Writing the book was
the third aim, along with his invalidism and his homosexuality, that he had adopted for the execution of the behavioral policy to which he was committed by the impression
that he had gained of the relationship between his parents
in his very first years. It was a very similar policy to that
which committed Balzac to his compulsive pattern of debt-
building and incessant toil, and Baudelaire to his very

similar devices for ensuring that he would never escape from his primal situation and that he would end as one of the most miserable of losers. These two examples are relevant, because Proust was particularly keen to shield them from the threat that Sainte-Beuve stood for in his mind. It seems clear to me that his desperate anxiety to limit the critical function to enquiries into the meanings of works of art accepted as autonomous entities, existing independently of their creators, was motivated by the knowledge that the answers to the questions why did he write *that*, in *that* way, and not some *other* thing, in some *other* way, which are the fundamentals of behavioral criticism, would lead to the accomplishment of "the task of recreating my true life," which was the last thing that he wished to undertake or to have undertaken. Fiction is part of the general pattern of behavior of the person who writes it, and the more we know of that general pattern and the function of the given work of fiction within it the better our chances of understanding that work. The necessary corollary to this statement is, of course, that the aesthetic and sociological approaches to the novel as such are not likely to tell us very much about it: the essence of the form is a pathology, not an aesthetic, and if it can be said to be any one thing, that one thing is likely to be a mirror for the necessities which bear most urgently and pressingly upon its writer as an individual.

Bibliography

D. H. LAWRENCE

Emile Delavenay, *D. H. Lawrence: L'Homme et al genèse de son oeuvre.* Paris, 1969.
    This work is mentioned first, and out of alphabetical order, as the most searching and informative study of the relationship between Lawrence's life and work which has yet appeared.

Richard Aldington, *Portrait of a Genius, But....* London, 1950.

Dorothy Brett, *Lawrence and Brett, A Friendship.* London, 1933.

Witter Bynner, *Journey with Genius: Recollections and Reflections concerning D. H. Lawrence.* New York, 1951.

Catherine Carswell, *The Savage Pilgrimage.* London, 1932.

Jessie Chambers (E. T.), *D. H. Lawrence, A Personal Record.* London, 1935.

Helen Corke, *D. H. Lawrence: The Croyden Years.* Austin, 1965.

Ada Lawrence (Clarke) and Stuart Gelder, *Young Lorenzo.* London, 1932.

Frieda Lawrence, *Not I but the Wind....* London, 1935.
    Memoirs and Correspondence, edited by E. W. Tedlock. London, 1961.

Mabel Dodge Luhan, *Lorenzo in Taos.* New York, 1932.

Knud Merrild, *A Poet and Two Painters.* London, 1962.

Harry T. Moore, *The Intelligent Heart.* Farrar, Straus, and Young. New York, 1954.

John Middleton Murry, *Son of Woman.* London, 1931.
    Reminiscences of D. H. L. London, 1933.

Edward Nehls, *D. H. Lawrence: A Composite Biography,* 3 vols. New York, 1939.

MARCEL PROUST

George D. Painter, *Proust: The Early Years.*
    Proust: The Later Years. London, 1965.
    An exhaustive biography, with both the virtues and shortcomings of Harry T. Moore's biography of Lawrence, mentioned first, and out of alphabetical order, as the most complete study of the relationship between Proust's life and work which has so far appeared.

Charles Briand, *Le Secret de Marcel Proust.* Paris, 1950.

Marie Anne Cochet, *L'Ame proustienne*. Brussels, 1929.

Leon Dandel, *Salons et journaux*. Paris, 1932.

Robert Dreyfus, *Souvenirs sur Marcel Proust*. 1926.

E. de Gramont, Duchesse de Clermont-Tonnerre, *Robert de Montes-quiou et Marcel Proust*. Paris, 1925.
    Memoirs, 4 Vols. Paris, 1935.
    Marcel Proust. Paris, 1948.

Fernand Gregh, *L'Age d'or*. Paris, 1948.
    Mon amitié avec Marcel Proust. Paris, 1958.

Alec Hobson, *Hommage à Marcel Proust*. Paris, 1921.

Georges de Lauris, *A un ami*. Paris, 1948.
    Souvenirs d'une belle époque. Paris, 1948.

Robert Le Masle, *Le Professeur Adrien Proust*. Paris, 1935.

André Maurois, *A la recherche de Marcel Proust*. Paris, 1949.

Léon Pierre-Quint. *Marcel Proust, sa vie, son oeuvre*. Paris, 1935.

Maurice Sachs. *Le Sabbat*. Paris, 1946.

MADAME DE STAËL

Lucie Archard, *Rosalie de Constant*. Paris, 1902.

Dorette Berthoud, *La Seconde Madame Benjamin Constant*. Lausanne, 1943.

Lady Charlotte Blennerhassett, *Frau von Staël, ihre Freund und ihre Bedeutung in Politik und Literatur*, 2 vols. Berlin, 1887.

Charles Du Bos, *Grandeur et misère de Benjamin Constant*. Paris, 1948.

Jacques de Broglie, *Madame de Staël et sa cour au château de Chaumont*. Paris, 1936.

Edouard Chapusiot, *Madame de Staël et la police*. Paris, 1910.
    Necker. Paris 1938.

Benjamin Constant, *Journal intime* (definitive edition). Paris, 1952.
    Adolphe (definitive edition), edited by Jean Misker. Hachette Paris, 1957.
    Cécile, edited by Alfred Ronlin. Paris, 1951.

Emile Doud, *Un Confidant de Napoléon: le comte de Narbonne*. Paris, 1943.

André Firiot, *Madame de Staël, ou la gynandre*. Paris, 1939.

Paul Gautier, *Madame de Staël et Napoléon*. Paris, 1903.
    Mathieu de Montmorency et Madame de Staël. Paris, 1908.

Geneviève Gennari, *Le premier voyage de Madame de Staël en Italie*. Paris, 1947.

Henri Guillemin, *Benjamin Constant, Muscadin.*

Eduard Herriot, *Madame Récamier et ses amis*, 2 vols. Paris, 1904.

Beatrice Jasinski, *Madame de Staël: correspondence générale*, 3 vols. Paris, 1960.

Pierre Joly, *Necker.* Paris, 1931.

Pierre Kohler, *Madame de Staël et la Suisse.* Paris, 1916.
    Madame de Stael au château de Coppet. Paris, 1930.

Andre Lang, *Une vie d'orages.* Paris, 1958.

Pierre de Lacretelle, *Madame de Staël et les hommes.* Paris, 1939.

David Long, *Madame de Staël La vie dans l'oeuvre.* Paris, 1924.
    Madame de Staöl: La seconde vie. Paris, 1928.

Paul Léon, *Benjamin Constant.* Paris, 1930.

Maurice Le Vaillant, *Une amitié amoureuse: Madame de Staël et Madame Récamier.* Paris, 1956.
    Les amours de Benjamin Constant. Paris, 1958.

Roland de Margerie, *Le comte Louis de Narbonne.* Paris, 1944.

Jean Mistter, *Madame de Staël et Maurice O'Donnell.* Paris, 1926.

B. Munteano, *Les idées politiques de Madame de Staël.* Paris, 1931.

Madame Necker de Saussure, *Notice sur le caractère et les écrits de Madame de Staël.* Paris, 1820.
    Published as part of Auguste de Staël's seventeen-volume edition of his mother's works, *Les Oeuvres complètes de Madame la Baronne de Staël.*

Jean de Pange, *Madame de Staël et la découverte de l'Allemagne.* Paris, 1929.
    Monsieur de Staël. Paris, 1931.
    Auguste-Guillaume Schlegel et Madame de Staël. Paris, 1938.
    Le dernier amour de Madame de Staël. Geneva, 1944.

Gustave Rudler, *La jeunesse de Benjamin Constant.* Paris, 1908.

Jean de Salis, *Sismondi, la vie et l'oeuvre.* Paris, 1932.
    Harold Nicholson's *Benjamin Constant* (London, 1947) and Christopher Herold's *Mistress to an Age, a Life of Mme. de Staël.* (New York, 1958) are omitted from this list since they are both highly unreliable: they treat the era of the French Revolution and Napoleon in the light of the struggle against Hitler and the subsequent cold war with Russia.

MADAME DE CHARRIÈRE

Henri Bordeaux, *Vies intimes.* Paris, 1919.

Charlotte de Constant de Rebecque with Dorette Berthond, *Les Mariages Manqués de Belle de Zuylen.* Lausanne, 1940.

Rosalie de Constant, *Correspondence générale,* edited by Routin. Paris, 1955.

Philippe Godet, *Madame de Charrière et ses amis,* 2 vols. Geneva, 1906.
    Lettres de Belle de Zuylen à Constant d'Hermenches. Paris, 1905.

Dorothy Farnum, *The Dutch Divinity.* London, 1959.

Arnold Kerchoven, *Une Amie de Benjamin Constant.* Paris, 1913.

Frederick A. Pottle, *Boswell in Holland.* London, 1952.

Sainte-Beuve, *Benjamin Constant et Madame de Staël: derniers Portraits litteraires.* Paris, 1852.

Geoffrey Scott, *The Portrait of Zélide.* London, 1925.

GEORGE SAND

Henri Amic, *George Sand: mes souvenirs.* Paris, 1893.

Honoré de Balzac, *Lettres à l'étrangère.* Paris, 1952.

François Boury, *De quoi vivait George Sand.* Paris, 1952.

Casimir Carrère, *George Sand, amoureuse.* Geneva, 1968.

John Charpentier, *George Sand.* Paris, 1936.

Frédéric Chopin, *Souvenirs inédits.* Paris, 1904.

Louise Colet, *Lui.* Paris, 1860.

Eugène Delacroix, *Journal.* Paris, 1932.
    Correspondence générale. Paris, 1936–38.

Edouard Dolléans, *George Sand.* Paris, 1952.

Jeanne Galzy, *George Sand.* Paris, 1950.

Marcel Godeau, *Le Voyage à Majorque de George Sand et Frédéric Chopin.* Paris, 1959.

Robert Graves, *George Sand's A Winter in Majorca,* with commentary. London, 1962.

Henri Guillemin, *A vrai dire.* Paris, 1956.

Wladimir Karénine, *George Sand, sa vie et ses oeuvres.* Paris, 1926.

Jean Lounac, *George Sand, révolutionnaire.* Paris, 1948.

Charles, Vicomte de Spoelberch de Lovenjoul, *La Véritable histoire de "Elle et lui."* Paris, 1888.

Paul Marieton, *Les Amants de Venise.* Paris, 1903.

André Maurois, *Lélia, ou la vie de George Sand.* Paris, 1952.

Charles Maurras, *Les Amants de Venise.* Paris, 1903.

Alfred de Musset, *Confessions d'un enfant du siècle.* Paris, 1903.

Paul de Musset, *Lui et elle*. Paris, 1860.

Auguste Nicolas, *Aurélien de Sèze*. Paris, 1870.

Marie-Louise Pailleron, *George Sand*. Paris, 1942.
  George Sand et les hommes de '48. Paris, 1953.

Maurice Patunier, *Une expérience de Lélia, ou le fiasco du Comte Gazul*. Paris, 1934.

Samuel Rocheblave, *George Sand et sa fille*. Paris, 1905.

Aurore Sand, *Le Berry de George Sand*. Paris, 1927.

George Sand, *Lélia*. Paris, 1833.
  Lettres d'un voyageur. Paris, 1837.
  Un Hiver à Majorque. Paris, 1942.
  Lucrezia Floriani. Paris, 1847.
  Histoire de ma vie. Paris, 1854-1855.
  Elle et lui. Paris, 1859.
  Journal intime. Paris, 1926.

Mabel Silver, *Jules Sandeau, l'homme et la vie*. Paris, 1936.

"Daniel Stern" (Mme. d'Agoult), *Histoire de la révolution de 1848*. Paris, 1851
  Souvenirs. Paris, 1877.

Alexis de Tocqueville, *Souvenirs*. Paris, 1893.

Emile Vuillermoz, *Vie amoureuse de Fredéric Chopin*. Paris, 1886.

de Wodzinski, *Les trois romans de Frédéric Chopin*. Paris, 1886.